# C++ GUI Programming
# with Qt 3

# BRUCE PERENS' OPEN SOURCE SERIES

# C++ GUI Programming with Qt 3

Jasmin Blanchette

Mark Summerfield

Prentice Hall in association with Trolltech Press

**Library of Congress Cataloging-in-Publication Data**

A CIP catalog record for this book can be obtained from the Library of Congress

*Editorial/Production Supervision: Kathleen M. Caren*
*Cover Design Director: Jerry Votta*
*Art Director: Gail Cocker-Bogusz*
*Manufacturing Buyer: Maura Zaldivar*
*Acquisitions Editor: Jill Harry*
*Editorial Assistant: Brenda Mulligan*
*Marketing Manager: Dan Depasquale*

**Prentice Hall PTR offers excellent discounts on this book when ordered in quantity for bulk purchases or special sales. For more information, please contact: U.S. Corporate and Government Sales, 1-800-382-3419, corpsales@pearsontechgroup.com. For sales outside of the U.S., please contact: International Sales, 1-317-581-3793, international@pearsontechgroup.com.**

Printed in the United States of America

Second Printing

ISBN 0-13-124072-2

Pearson Education Ltd.
Pearson Education Australia Pty., Limited
Pearson Education Singapore, Pte. Ltd.
Pearson Education North Asia Ltd.
Pearson Education Canada, Ltd.
Pearson Educación de Mexico, S.A. de C.V.
Pearson Education-Japan
Pearson Education Malaysia, Pte. Ltd.

# Contents

## Part I:  Basic Qt

## Appendices

# Foreword

Why Qt? Why do programmers like us choose Qt? Sure, there are the obvious answers: Qt's single-source compatibility, its feature richness, its C++ performance, the availability of the source code, its documentation, the high-quality technical support, and all the other items mentioned in Trolltech's glossy marketing materials. This is all very well, but it misses the most important point: Qt is successful because programmers *like* it.

How come programmers like one technology, but dislike another? Personally, I believe software engineers enjoy technology that feels right, but dislike everything that doesn't. How else can we explain that some of the brightest programmers need help to program a VCR, or that most engineers seem to have trouble operating the company's phone system? I for one am perfectly capable of memorizing sequences of random numbers and commands, but if these are required to control my answering machine, I'd prefer not to have one. At Trolltech, our phone system forces us to hold the '*' key pressed down for two seconds before we are allowed to type in the other person's extension number. If you forget to do this but start typing the extension immediately, you have to dial the entire number again. Why '*'? Why not '#', or '1', or '5', or any of the other twenty keys on the phone? Why two seconds and not one, or three, or one and a half? Why anything at all? I find the phone so irritating that I avoid using it whenever I can. Nobody likes having to do random things, especially when those random things apparently depend on some equally random context you wish you didn't have to know about in the first place.

Programming can be a lot like using our phone system, only worse. And this is where Qt comes to the rescue. Qt is different. For one thing, Qt makes sense. And for another, Qt is fun. Qt lets you concentrate on your tasks. When Qt's original architects faced a problem, they didn't just look for a good solution, or a quick solution, or the simplest solution. They looked for the *right* solution, and then they documented it. Granted they made mistakes, and granted some of their design decisions didn't pass the test of time, but they still got a lot of things right, and what wasn't right could and can be corrected. You can see this by the fact that a system originally designed to bridge Windows 95 and Unix/Motif now unifies modern desktop systems as diverse as Windows XP, Mac OS X, and GNU/Linux with KDE.

Long before Qt became so popular and so widely used, the dedication of Qt's developers to finding the right solutions made Qt special. That dedication is just as strong today and affects everyone who maintains and develops Qt. For us, working on Qt is a responsibility and a privilege. We are proud of helping to make your professional and open source lives easier and more enjoyable.

One of the things that makes Qt a pleasure to use is its online documentation. But the documentation's focus is primarily on individual classes, with little said about how to build sophisticated real-world applications. This excellent book fills that gap. It shows you what Qt has to offer, how to program Qt the "Qt way", and how to get the best from Qt. The book will teach a C++ programmer how to program Qt, and provides enough advanced material to satisfy experienced Qt programmers. The book is packed with good examples, advice, and explanations, and will be the text that we use to induct all new programmers who join Trolltech.

Nowadays, there are a vast number of commercial and free Qt applications available for purchase or download. Some are specialized for particular vertical markets, while others are aimed at the mass-market. Seeing so many applications built with Qt fills us with pride and inspires us to make Qt even better. And with the help of this book, there will be more and higher quality Qt applications than ever before.

Matthias Ettrich
Oslo, Norway
November 2003

# Preface

The Qt toolkit is a C++ class library and a set of tools for building multiplat-form GUI programs using a "write once, compile anywhere" approach. Qt lets programmers use a single source tree for applications that will run on Windows 95 to XP, Mac OS X, Linux, Solaris, HP-UX, and many other versions of Unix with X11. A version of Qt is also available for Embedded Linux, with the same API.

The purpose of this book is to teach you how to write GUI programs using Qt 3. The book starts with "Hello Qt" and quickly moves on to more advanced topics, such as creating custom widgets and providing drag and drop. The text is complemented by a CD that contains the source code of the example programs. The CD also provides Qt and Borland C++ for Windows, Qt for Unix, and Qt for Mac OS X. Appendix A explains how to install the software.

The book focuses on explaining good idiomatic Qt 3 programming techniques rather than simply rehashing or summarizing Qt's extensive online documentation. And because we are involved in the development of Qt 4, we have tried to ensure that most of what we teach here will still be valid and sensible for Qt 4.

It is assumed that you have a basic knowledge of C++. The code examples use a subset of C++, avoiding many C++ features that are rarely needed when programming Qt. In the few places where a more advanced C++ construct is unavoidable, it is explained as it is used.

Qt made its reputation as a multiplatform toolkit, but because of its intuitive and powerful API, many organizations use Qt for single-platform development. Adobe Photoshop Album is just one example of a mass-market Windows application written in Qt. Many sophisticated software systems in vertical markets, such as 3D animation tools, digital film processing, electronic design automation (for chip design), oil and gas exploration, financial services, and medical imaging, are built with Qt. If you are making a living with a success-ful Windows product written in Qt, you can easily create new markets in the Mac OS X and Linux worlds simply by recompiling.

Qt is available under various licenses. If you want to build commercial applications, you must buy a commercial license; if you want to build open source programs, you can use a non-commercial Qt edition. (The editions of Qt on the CD are non-commercial.) Qt is the foundation on which the K Desktop Environment (KDE) and the many open source applications that go with it are built.

In addition to Qt's hundreds of classes, there are add-ons that extend Qt's scope and power. Some of these products, like the Qt/Motif integration module and Qt Script for Applications (QSA), are supplied by Trolltech, while others are provided by companies and by the open source community. See `http://www.trolltech.com/products/3rdparty/` for information on Qt add-ons. Qt also has a well-established and thriving user community that uses the `qt-interest` mailing list; see `http://lists.trolltech.com/` for details.

The book is divided into two parts. Part I covers all the concepts and practices necessary for programming GUI applications using Qt. Knowledge of this part alone is sufficient to write useful GUI applications. Part II covers central Qt topics in more depth and provides more specialized and advanced material. The chapters of Part II can be read in any order, but they assume familiarity with the contents of Part I.

If you spot errors in the book, have suggestions for the next edition, or want to give us feedback, we would be delighted to hear from you. You can reach us at `jasmin.blanchette@trolltech.com` and `mark.summerfield@trolltech.com`. The errata will be placed on `http://vig.prenhall.com/catalog/academic/product/0,4096,0131240722,00.html`.

# Acknowledgments

Our first acknowledgment goes to Eirik Chambe-Eng, Trolltech's president. Eirik not only enthusiastically encouraged us to write the book, he also allowed us to spend a considerable amount of our work time writing it. Eirik and Trolltech CEO Haavard Nord both read the manuscript and provided valuable feedback. Their generosity and foresight was aided and abetted by Matthias Ettrich, Trolltech's lead developer and our boss. Matthias cheerfully accepted our neglect of duty as we obsessed over the writing of this book and gave us a lot of advice on good Qt programming style.

We asked two Qt customers, Paul Curtis and Klaus Schmidinger, to be our external reviewers. Both are Qt experts with an amazing attention to technical detail, which they proved by spotting some very subtle errors in our manuscript and suggesting numerous improvements.

Within Trolltech, alongside Matthias, our most stalwart reviewer was Reginald Stadlbauer.* His technical insight was invaluable, and he taught us how to do some things in Qt that we didn't even know were possible.

Our other key reviewers within Trolltech were Trenton Schulz, Andy Shaw, and Andreas Aardal Hanssen. Trenton and Andy gave feedback on all aspects of the book and were especially helpful regarding Qt/Mac and Qt/Windows. Andreas gave us invaluable help refining Part I.

In addition to the reviewers mentioned above, we received expert help from Warwick Allison (2D graphics), Eirik Chambe-Eng (Qt's history), Matthias Ettrich (event processing and custom widgets), Harald Fernengel (databases), Volker Hilsheimer (ActiveX), Bradley Hughes (multithreading), Trond Kjernåsen (3D graphics and databases), Lars Knoll (2D graphics), Sam Magnuson (qmake), Dimitri Papadopoulos (Qt/X11), Paul Olav Tvete (custom widgets and Qt/Embedded), Rainer Schmid (networking and XML), and Gunnar Sletta (event processing).

Extra thanks are due to Trolltech's support team for helping to keep our support load under control while the book consumed so much of our time, and to Trolltech's system administrators for keeping our machines running and our networks communicating throughout the project.

We are also grateful to Troy Kitch from Borland for giving us permission to include Borland C++ compilers on the accompanying CD, and to the SQLite developers for putting their database into the public domain.

---

*Reginald has now moved to Germany, where he co-founded froglogic, a software consultancy.

On the production side, Rainer Schmid led the team that created the accompanying CD, ably supported by Harald Fernengel and Andy Shaw. Trolltech's Cathrine Bore handled the contracts and legalities on our behalf. Jeff Kingston, author of the Lout typesetting tool, gave us advice and enhanced the tool in the light of our feedback. Jill Harry of Prentice Hall had faith in the project from the start and ensured that all the practical matters were smoothly handled, leaving us free to concentrate on the writing. And Lisa Iarkowski turned our camera-ready manuscript into the beautiful volume you now hold in your hands.

# A Brief History of Qt

The Qt toolkit first became publicly available in May 1995. It was initially developed by Haavard Nord (Trolltech's CEO) and Eirik Chambe-Eng (Trolltech's president). Haavard and Eirik met each other at the Norwegian Institute of Technology in Trondheim, Norway, where they both graduated with master's degrees in computer science.

Haavard's interest in C++ GUI development began in 1988 when he was commissioned by a Swedish company to design and implement a C++ GUI toolkit. A couple of years later, in the summer of 1990, Haavard and Eirik were working together on a C++ database application for ultrasound images. The system needed to be able to run with a GUI on Unix, Macintosh, and Windows. One day that summer, Haavard and Eirik went outside to enjoy the sunshine, and as they sat on a park bench, Haavard said, "We need an object-oriented display system." The resulting discussion laid the intellectual foundation for the object-oriented multiplatform GUI toolkit they would soon go on to build.

In 1991, Haavard started writing the classes that eventually became Qt, collaborating with Eirik on the design. The following year, Eirik came up the idea for "signals and slots", a simple but powerful GUI programming paradigm. Haavard took the idea and produced a hand-coded implementation. By 1993, Haavard and Eirik had developed Qt's first graphics kernel and were able to implement their own widgets. At the end of the year, Haavard suggested that they go into business together to build "the world's best C++ GUI toolkit".

The year 1994 began inauspiciously with the two young programmers wanting to enter a well established market, with no customers, an unfinished product, and no money. Fortunately, both their wives had work and were willing to support their husbands for the two years Eirik and Haavard expected to need to develop the product and start earning an income.

They chose 'Q' as the class prefix because the letter looked beautiful in Haavard's Emacs font. The 't' was added to stand for "toolkit", inspired by "Xt", the X Toolkit. The company was incorporated on 4 March 1994, originally as "Quasar Technologies", then as "Troll Tech", and today as "Trolltech".

In April 1995, thanks to a contact made through one of Haavard's University professors, the Norwegian company Metis gave them a contract to develop software based on Qt. Around this time, Trolltech hired Arnt Gulbrandsen,* who devised and implemented an ingenious documentation system as well as contributing to Qt's code.

---

*Arnt left the company a few years ago to pursue his career in Germany.

On 20 May 1995, Qt 0.90 was uploaded to `sunsite.unc.edu`. Six days later, the release was announced on `comp.os.linux.announce`. This was Qt's first public release. Qt could be used for both Windows and Unix development, offering the same API on both platforms. Qt was available under two licenses from day one: A commercial license was required for commercial development and a free software edition was available for open source development. The Metis contract kept Trolltech afloat, while for ten long months no one bought a commercial Qt license.

In March 1996, the European Space Agency became the second Qt customer, with a purchase of ten commercial licenses. With unwavering faith, Eirik and Haavard hired another developer. Qt 0.97 was released at the end of May, and on 24 September 1996, Qt 1.0 came out. By the end of the year, Qt had reached version 1.1; eight customers, each in a different country, had bought 18 licenses between them. This year also saw the founding of the KDE project, led by Matthias Ettrich.

Qt 1.2 was released in April 1997. Matthias Ettrich's decision to use Qt to build KDE helped Qt become the de-facto standard for C++ GUI development on Linux. Qt 1.3 was released in September 1997.

Matthias joined Trolltech in 1998, and the last major Qt 1 release, 1.40, was made in September of that year. Qt 2.0 was released in June 1999. Qt 2 had many major architectural changes and was a much stronger and more mature product than its predecessor. It also featured forty new classes and Unicode support. Qt 2 had a new open source license, the Q Public License (QPL), which complied with the Open Source Definition. In August 1999, Qt won the LinuxWorld award for best library/tool. Around this time, Trolltech Pty Ltd (Australia) was established.

Trolltech released Qt/Embedded in 2000. It was designed to run on Embedded Linux devices and provided is own window system as a lightweight replacement for X11. Both Qt/Embedded and Qt/X11 were now offered under the widely used GNU General Public License (GPL) as well as under commercial licenses. By the end of 2000, Trolltech had established Trolltech Inc. (USA) and had released the first version of Qtopia, an environment for handheld devices. Qt/Embedded won the LinuxWorld "Best Embedded Linux Solution" award in both 2001 and 2002.

Qt 3.0 was released in 2001. Qt was now available on Windows, Unix, Linux, Embedded Linux, and Mac OS X. Qt 3.0 provided 42 new classes and the code surpassed 500,000 lines. Qt 3.0 won the Software Development Times "Jolt Productivity Award" in 2002.

Trolltech's sales have doubled year on year since the company's birth. This success is a reflection both of the quality of Qt and of how enjoyable it is to use. For most of the company's existence, sales and marketing were handled by just a couple of people. Yet, in less than a decade, Qt has gone from being a "secret" product, known only to a select group of professionals, to having thousands of customers and tens of thousands of open source developers all around the world.

# Part I

# Basic Qt

# Getting Started

This chapter shows how to combine basic C++ with the functionality provided by Qt to create a few small graphical user interface (GUI) applications. This chapter also introduces two key Qt ideas: "signals and slots" and layouts. In Chapter 2, we will go into more depth, and in Chapter 3, we will start building a realistic application.

## Hello Qt

Here's a very simple Qt program:

```
1  #include <qapplication.h>
2  #include <qlabel.h>

3  int main(int argc, char *argv[])
4  {
5      QApplication app(argc, argv);
6      QLabel *label - new QLabel("Hello Qt!", 0);
7      app.setMainWidget(label);
8      label->show();
9      return app.exec();
10 }
```

We will first study it line by line, then we will see how to compile and run it.

Lines 1 and 2 include the definitions of the `QApplication` and `QLabel` classes.

Line 5 creates a `QApplication` object to manage application-wide resources. The `QApplication` constructor requires `argc` and `argv` because Qt supports a few command-line arguments of its own.

Line 6 creates a `QLabel` widget that displays "Hello Qt!". In Qt terminology, a *widget* is a visual element in a user interface. Buttons, menus, scroll bars, and frames are all examples of widgets. Widgets can contain other widgets; for

3

example, an application window is usually a widget that contains a `QMenuBar`, a `QToolBar`, a `QStatusBar`, and some other widgets. The 0 argument to the `QLabel` constructor (a null pointer) means that the widget is a window in its own right, not a widget inside another window.

Line 7 makes the label the application's main widget. When the user closes the main widget (by clicking X in the window's title bar, for example), the program terminates. Without a main widget, the program would keep running in the background even after the user has closed the window.

Line 8 makes the label visible. Widgets are always created hidden, so that we can customize them before showing them, thereby avoiding flicker.

Line 9 passes control of the application on to Qt. At this point, the program enters a kind of stand-by mode, where it waits for user actions such as mouse clicks and key presses.

User actions generate *events* (also called "messages") to which the program can respond, usually by executing one or more functions. In this respect, GUI applications differ drastically from conventional batch programs, which typically process input, produce results, and terminate without human intervention.

**Figure 1.1.** Hello on Windows XP

It is now time to test the program on your machine. First, you will need to install Qt 3.2 (or a later Qt 3 release), a process that is explained in Appendix A. From now on, we will assume that you have a correctly installed copy of Qt 3.2 and that Qt's `bin` directory is in your `PATH` environment variable. (On Windows, this is done automatically by the Qt installation program, so you don't need to worry about it.)

You will also need the Hello program's source code in a file called `hello.cpp` in a directory called `hello`. You can type in `hello.cpp` yourself, or copy it from the CD provided with this book, where it is available as `\examples\chap01\hello\hello.cpp`.

From a command prompt, change directory to `hello`, then type

```
qmake -project
```

to create a platform-independent project file (`hello.pro`), then type

```
qmake hello.pro
```

to create a platform-specific makefile from the project file. Run `make` to build the program, and run the program by typing `hello` on Windows, `./hello` on Unix, and `open hello.app` on Mac OS X. If you are using Microsoft Visual C++, you will need to run `nmake` instead of `make`. Alternatively, you can create a Visual Studio project file from `hello.pro` by typing

```
qmake -tp vc hello.pro
```

and then build the program in Visual Studio.

**Figure 1.2.** A label with basic HTML formatting

Now let's have some fun: We will brighten up the label by using some simple HTML-style formatting. This can be done by replacing the line

```
QLabel *label = new QLabel("Hello Qt!", 0);
```

with

```
QLabel *label = new QLabel("<h2><i>Hello</i> "
                           "<font color=red>Qt!</font></h2>", 0);
```

and rebuilding the application.

## Making Connections

The next example illustrates how to respond to user actions. The application consists of a button that the user can click to quit. The source code is very similar to Hello, except that we are using a `QPushButton` instead of a `QLabel` as our main widget, and we are connecting a user action (clicking a button) to a piece of code.

This application's source code is on the CD in the file `\examples\chap01\quit\quit.cpp`.

**Figure 1.3.** The Quit application

```
1  #include <qapplication.h>
2  #include <qpushbutton.h>

3  int main(int argc, char *argv[])
4  {
5      QApplication app(argc, argv);
6      QPushButton *button = new QPushButton("Quit", 0);
```

```
 7        QObject::connect(button, SIGNAL(clicked()),
 8                              &app, SLOT(quit()));
 9        app.setMainWidget(button);
10        button->show();
11        return app.exec();
12 }
```

Qt's widgets emit *signals* to indicate that a user action or a change of state has occurred.* For instance, QPushButton emits a clicked() signal when the user clicks the button. A signal can be connected to a function (called a *slot* in that context), so that when the signal is emitted, the slot is automatically executed. In our example, we connect the button's clicked() signal to the QApplication object's quit() slot. The SIGNAL() and SLOT() macros are part of the syntax; they are explained in more detail in the next chapter.

We will now build the application. We assume that you have created a directory called quit containing quit.cpp. Run qmake in the quit directory to generate the project file, then run it again to generate a makefile:

```
qmake -project
qmake quit.pro
```

Now build the application, and run it. If you click Quit, or press Space (which presses the button), the application will terminate.

The next example demonstrates how to use signals and slots to synchronize two widgets. The application asks for the user's age, which the user can enter by manipulating either a spin box or a slider.

**Figure 1.4.** The Age application

The application consists of three widgets: a QSpinBox, a QSlider, and a QHBox (horizontal layout box). The QHBox is the application's main widget. The QSpinBox and the QSlider are rendered inside the QHBox; they are *children* of the QHBox.

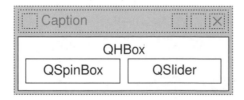

**Figure 1.5.** The Age application's widgets

---

*Qt signals are unrelated to Unix signals. In this book, we are only concerned with Qt signals.

```
1  #include <qapplication.h>
2  #include <qhbox.h>
3  #include <qslider.h>
4  #include <qspinbox.h>

5  int main(int argc, char *argv[])
6  {
7      QApplication app(argc, argv);

8      QHBox *hbox = new QHBox(0);
9      hbox->setCaption("Enter Your Age");
10     hbox->setMargin(6);
11     hbox->setSpacing(6);

12     QSpinBox *spinBox = new QSpinBox(hbox);
13     QSlider *slider = new QSlider(Qt::Horizontal, hbox);
14     spinBox->setRange(0, 130);
15     slider->setRange(0, 130);

16     QObject::connect(spinBox, SIGNAL(valueChanged(int)),
17                      slider, SLOT(setValue(int)));
18     QObject::connect(slider, SIGNAL(valueChanged(int)),
19                      spinBox, SLOT(setValue(int)));
20     spinBox->setValue(35);

21     app.setMainWidget(hbox);
22     hbox->show();

23     return app.exec();
24 }
```

Lines 8 to 11 set up the QHBox.* We call setCaption() to set the text displayed in the window's title bar. Then we put some space (6 pixels) around and in between the child widgets.

Lines 12 and 13 create a QSpinBox and a QSlider with the QHBox as the parent.

Even though we didn't set the position or size of any widget explicitly, the QSpinBox and QSlider appear nicely laid out side by side inside the QHBox. This is because QHBox automatically assigns reasonable positions and sizes to its children based on their needs. Qt provides many classes like QHBox to free us from the chore of hard-coding screen positions in our applications.

Lines 14 and 15 set the valid range for the spin box and the slider. (We can safely assume that the user is at most 130 years old.) The two connect() calls shown in lines 16 to 19 ensure that the spin box and the slider are synchronized so that they always show the same value. Whenever the value of one widget changes, its valueChanged(int) signal is emitted, and the setValue(int) slot of the other widget is called with the new value.

Line 20 sets the spin box value to 35. When this happens, the QSpinBox emits the valueChanged(int) signal with an int argument of 35. This argument is

---

*If you get a compiler error on the QHBox constructor, it means that you are using an older version of Qt. Make sure that you are using Qt 3.2.0 or a later Qt 3 release.

passed to the `QSlider`'s `setValue(int)` slot, which sets the slider value to 35. The slider then emits the `valueChanged(int)` signal, because its own value changed, triggering the spin box's `setValue(int)` slot. But at this point, `setValue(int)` doesn't emit any signal, since the spin box value is already 35. This prevents infinite recursion. Figure 1.6 summarizes the situation.

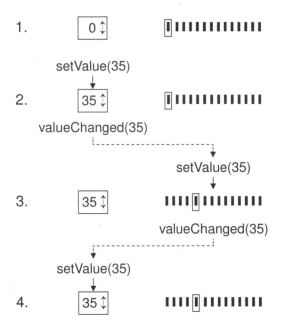

**Figure 1.6.** Changing one value changes both

Line 22 shows the `QHBox` and its two child widgets.

Qt's approach to building user interfaces is simple to understand and very flexible. The most common pattern that Qt programmers use is to instantiate the required widgets and then set their properties as necessary. Programmers add the widgets to layouts, which automatically take care of sizing and positioning. User interface behavior is managed by connecting widgets together using Qt's signals and slots mechanism.

## Using the Reference Documentation

Qt's reference documentation is an essential tool for any Qt developer, since it covers every class and function in Qt. (Qt 3.2 includes over 400 public classes and over 6000 functions.) This book makes use of many Qt classes and functions, but it doesn't mention them all, nor does it provide all the details of those it does mention. To get the most benefit from Qt, you should familiarize yourself with the Qt reference documentation.

## Widget Styles

The screenshots we have seen so far have been taken on Windows XP, but Qt applications look native on every supported platform. Qt achieves this by emulating the platform's look and feel, rather than wrapping a particular platform or toolkit's widget set.

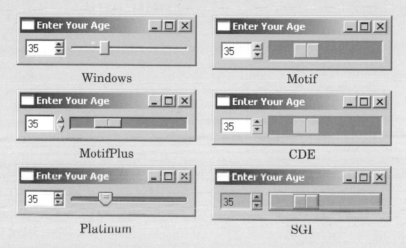

**Figure 1.7.** Styles available everywhere

Qt application users can override the default style by using the -style command-line option. For example, to launch the Age application with Platinum style on Unix, simply type

```
./age -style=Platinum
```

on the command line.

**Figure 1.8.** Platform-specific styles

Unlike the other styles, the Windows XP and Mac styles are only available on their native platforms, since they rely on the platforms' theme engines.

The documentation is available in HTML format in Qt's doc\html directory and can be read using any web browser. You can also use *Qt Assistant*, the Qt help browser, whose powerful search and indexing features make it quicker and easier to use than a web browser. To launch *Qt Assistant*, click Qt 3.2.x|Qt Assistant in the Start menu on Windows, type assistant on the command line on Unix, or double-click assistant in the Mac OS X Finder.

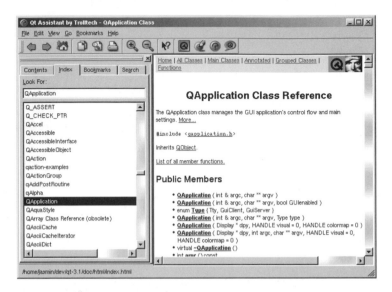

**Figure 1.9.** Qt's documentation in *Qt Assistant*

The links in the "API Reference" section on the home page provide different ways of navigating Qt's classes. The "All Classes" page lists every class in Qt's API. The "Main Classes" page lists only the most commonly used Qt classes. As an exercise, you might want to look up the classes and functions that we have used in this chapter. Note that inherited functions are documented in the base class; for example, QPushButton has no show() function of its own, but it inherits one from its ancestor QWidget. Figure 1.10 shows how the classes we have seen so far relate to each other.

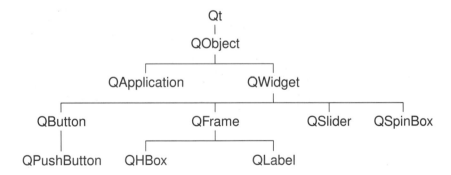

**Figure 1.10.** Inheritance tree for the Qt classes seen so far

The reference documentation for the current version of Qt and for some earlier versions is available online at http://doc.trolltech.com/. This site also hosts selected articles from *Qt Quarterly*, the Qt programmers' newsletter sent to all commercial licensees.

- Subclassing QDialog
- Signals and Slots in Depth
- Rapid Dialog Design
- Shape-Changing Dialogs
- Dynamic Dialogs
- Built-in Widget and Dialog Classes

# Creating Dialogs

This chapter will teach you how to create dialog boxes using Qt. They are called dialog boxes, or simply "dialogs", because they provide a means by which users and applications can "talk to" each other.

Dialogs present users with options and choices, and allow them to set the options to their preferred values and to make their choice. Most GUI applications consist of a main window with a menu bar and toolbar, along with dozens of dialogs that complement the main window. It is also possible to create dialog applications that respond directly to the user's choices by performing the appropriate actions (for example, a calculator application).

We will create our first dialog purely by writing code to show how it is done. Then we will see how to build dialogs using *Qt Designer*, Qt's visual design tool. Using *Qt Designer* is a lot faster than hand-coding and makes it simple to test different designs and to change designs later.

## Subclassing QDialog

Our first example is a Find dialog written entirely in C++. We will implement the dialog as a class in its own right. By doing so, we make it an independent, self-contained component, with its own signals and slots.

**Figure 2.1.** Find dialog on Linux (KDE)

11

The source code is spread across two files: `finddialog.h` and `finddialog.cpp`. We will start with `finddialog.h`.

```
1  #ifndef FINDDIALOG_H
2  #define FINDDIALOG_H

3  #include <qdialog.h>

4  class QCheckBox;
5  class QLabel;
6  class QLineEdit;
7  class QPushButton;
```

Lines 1 and 2 (and 27) prevent the header file from multiple inclusions.

Line 3 includes the definition of `QDialog`, the base class for dialogs in Qt. `QDialog` inherits `QWidget`.

Lines 4 to 7 are forward declarations of the Qt classes that we will use to implement the dialog. A *forward declaration* tells the C++ compiler that a class exists, without giving all the detail that a class definition (usually located in a header file of its own) provides. We will say more about this shortly.

We then define `FindDialog` as a subclass of `QDialog`:

```
8  class FindDialog : public QDialog
9  {
10     Q_OBJECT
11 public:
12     FindDialog(QWidget *parent = 0, const char *name = 0);
```

The `Q_OBJECT` macro at the beginning of the class definition is necessary for all classes that define signals or slots.

The `FindDialog` constructor is typical of Qt widget classes. The `parent` parameter specifies the parent widget, and the `name` parameter gives the widget a name. The name is optional; it is primarily used for debugging and testing.

```
13 signals:
14     void findNext(const QString &str, bool caseSensitive);
15     void findPrev(const QString &str, bool caseSensitive);
```

The `signals` section declares two signals that the dialog emits when the user clicks the Find button. If the Search backward option is enabled, the dialog emits `findPrev()`; otherwise, it emits `findNext()`.

The `signals` keyword is actually a macro. The C++ preprocessor converts it into standard C++ before the compiler sees it.

```
16 private slots:
17     void findClicked();
18     void enableFindButton(const QString &text);

19 private:
20     QLabel *label;
21     QLineEdit *lineEdit;
22     QCheckBox *caseCheckBox;
```

```
23        QCheckBox *backwardCheckBox;
24        QPushButton *findButton;
25        QPushButton *closeButton;
26   };

27   #endif
```

In the class's private section, we declare two slots. To implement the slots, we will need to access most of the dialog's child widgets, so we keep pointers to them as well. The `slots` keyword is, like `signals`, a macro that expands into a construct that the C++ compiler can digest.

Since all the variables are pointers and we don't use them in the header file, the compiler doesn't need the full class definitions; forward declarations are sufficient. We could have included the relevant header files (<qcheckbox.h>, <qlabel.h>, etc.) instead, but using forward declarations when it is possible makes compiling somewhat faster.

We will now look at `finddialog.cpp`, which contains the implementation of the FindDialog class:

```
1    #include <qcheckbox.h>
2    #include <qlabel.h>
3    #include <qlayout.h>
4    #include <qlineedit.h>
5    #include <qpushbutton.h>

6    #include "finddialog.h"
```

First, we include the header files for all the Qt classes we use, in addition to `finddialog.h`. For most Qt classes, the header file is a lower-case version of the class name with a `.h` extension.

```
7    FindDialog::FindDialog(QWidget *parent, const char *name)
8        : QDialog(parent, name)
9    {
10        setCaption(tr("Find"));

11        label = new QLabel(tr("Find &what:"), this);
12        lineEdit = new QLineEdit(this);
13        label->setBuddy(lineEdit);

14        caseCheckBox = new QCheckBox(tr("Match &case"), this);
15        backwardCheckBox = new QCheckBox(tr("Search &backward"), this);

16        findButton = new QPushButton(tr("&Find"), this);
17        findButton->setDefault(true);
18        findButton->setEnabled(false);

19        closeButton = new QPushButton(tr("Close"), this);
```

On line 8, we pass on the `parent` and `name` parameters to the base class constructor.

On line 10, we set the window's caption to "Find". The `tr()` function around the string marks it for translation to other languages. It is declared in `QObject` and every subclass that contains the `Q_OBJECT` macro. It's a good habit to surround every user-visible string with a `tr()`, even if you don't have immediate plans for translating your applications to other languages. Translating Qt applications is covered in Chapter 15.

Then we create the child widgets. We use ampersands ('&') to indicate accelerator keys. For example, line 16 creates a F̲ind button, which the user can activate by pressing Alt+F. Ampersands can also be used to control focus: On line 11 we create a label with an accelerator key (Alt+W), and on line 13 we set the label's buddy to be the line editor. A *buddy* is a widget that accepts the focus when the label's accelerator key is pressed. So when the user presses Alt+W (the label's accelerator), the focus goes to the line editor (the buddy).

On line 17, we make the Find button the dialog's default button by calling `setDefault(true)`.* The default button is the button that is pressed when the user hits Enter. On line 18, we disable the Find button. When a widget is disabled, it is usually shown grayed out and will not interact with the user.

```
20      connect(lineEdit, SIGNAL(textChanged(const QString &)),
21              this, SLOT(enableFindButton(const QString &)));
22      connect(findButton, SIGNAL(clicked()),
23              this, SLOT(findClicked()));
24      connect(closeButton, SIGNAL(clicked()),
25              this, SLOT(close()));
```

The private slot `enableFindButton(const QString &)` is called whenever the text in the line editor changes. The private slot `findClicked()` is called when the user clicks the Find button. The dialog closes itself when the user clicks Close. The `close()` slot is inherited from `QWidget`, and its default behavior is to hide the widget. We will look at the code for the `enableFindButton()` and `findClicked()` slots later on.

Since `QObject` is one of `FindDialog`'s ancestors, we can omit the `QObject::` prefix in front of the `connect()` calls.

```
26      QHBoxLayout *topLeftLayout = new QHBoxLayout;
27      topLeftLayout->addWidget(label);
28      topLeftLayout->addWidget(lineEdit);

29      QVBoxLayout *leftLayout = new QVBoxLayout;
30      leftLayout->addLayout(topLeftLayout);
31      leftLayout->addWidget(caseCheckBox);
32      leftLayout->addWidget(backwardCheckBox);

33      QVBoxLayout *rightLayout = new QVBoxLayout;
34      rightLayout->addWidget(findButton);
35      rightLayout->addWidget(closeButton);
36      rightLayout->addStretch(1);

37      QHBoxLayout *mainLayout = new QHBoxLayout(this);
38      mainLayout->setMargin(11);
```

---

* Qt provides TRUE and FALSE for all platforms and uses them throughout as synonyms for the standard `true` and `false`. Nevertheless, there is no reason to use the upper-case versions in your own code unless you need to use an old compiler that doesn't support `true` and `false`.

```
39        mainLayout->setSpacing(6);
40        mainLayout->addLayout(leftLayout);
41        mainLayout->addLayout(rightLayout);
42   }
```

Finally, we lay out the child widgets using *layout managers*. A layout manager is an object that manages the size and position of widgets. Qt provides three layout managers: QHBoxLayout lays out widgets horizontally from left to right (right to left for some cultures), QVBoxLayout lays out widgets vertically from top to bottom, and QGridLayout lays out widgets in a grid.

Layouts can contain both widgets and other layouts. By nesting QHBoxLayouts, QVBoxLayouts, and QGridLayouts in various combinations, it is possible to build very sophisticated dialogs.

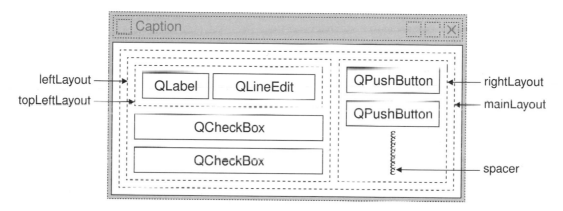

**Figure 2.2.** The Find dialog's layouts

For the Find dialog, we use two QHBoxLayouts and two QVBoxLayouts, as shown in Figure 2.2. The outer layout is the main layout; it is constructed with the FindDialog object (this) as its parent and is responsible for the dialog's entire area. The other three layouts are sub-layouts. The little "spring" at the bottom right of Figure 2.2 is a spacer item (or "stretch"). It uses up the empty space below the Find and Close buttons, ensuring that these buttons occupy the top of their layout.

One subtle aspect of the layout manager classes is that they are not widgets. Instead, they inherit QLayout, which in turn inherits QObject. In the figure, widgets are represented by solid outlines and layouts are represented by dashed outlines to highlight the difference between them. In a running application, layouts are invisible.

Although layout managers are not widgets, they can have a parent (and children). The meaning of "parent" is slightly different for layouts than for widgets. If a layout is constructed with a widget as its parent (as we did for main-Layout), the layout automatically installs itself on the widget. If a layout is constructed with no parent (as we did for topLeftLayout, leftLayout, and right-Layout), the layout must be inserted into another layout using addLayout().

Qt's parent–child mechanism is implemented in QObject, the base class of both QWidget and QLayout. When we create an object (a widget, layout, or other kind) with a parent, the parent adds the object to the list of its children. When the parent is deleted, it walks through its list of children and deletes each child. The children themselves then delete all of their children, and so on recursively until none remain.

The parent–child mechanism simplifies memory management a lot, reducing the risk of memory leaks. The only objects we must delete explicitly are the objects we create with new and that have no parent. And if we delete a child object before its parent, Qt will automatically remove that object from the parent's list of children.

For widgets, the parent has an additional meaning: Child widgets are shown within the parent's area. When we delete the parent widget, not only does the child vanish from memory, it also vanishes from the screen.

When we insert a layout into another using addLayout(), the inner layout is automatically made a child of the outer layout, to simplify memory management. In contrast, when we insert a widget into a layout using addWidget(), the widget doesn't change parent.

Figure 2.3 shows the parentage of the widgets and layouts. The parentage can easily be deduced from the FindDialog constructor code by looking at the lines that contain a new or an addLayout() call. The important thing to remember is that the layout managers are not parents of the widgets they manage.

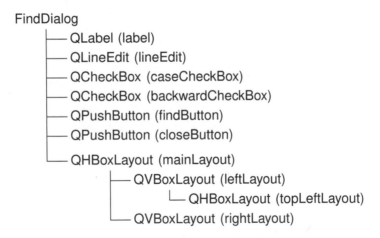

**Figure 2.3.** The Find dialog's parent–child relationships

In addition to the layout managers, Qt provides some *layout widgets*: QHBox (which we used in Chapter 1), QVBox, and QGrid. These classes serve both as parents and as layout managers for their child widgets. The layout widgets are more convenient to use than layout managers for small examples, but they are less flexible and require more resources.

This completes the review of FindDialog's constructor. Since we used new to create the dialog's widgets and layouts, it would seem that we need to write a destructor that calls delete on each of the widgets and layouts we created. But this isn't necessary, since Qt automatically deletes child objects when the parent is destroyed, and the objects we allocated with new are all descendants of the FindDialog.

Now we will look at the dialog's slots:

```
43  void FindDialog::findClicked()
44  {
45      QString text = lineEdit->text();
46      bool caseSensitive = caseCheckBox->isOn();

47      if (backwardCheckBox->isOn())
48          emit findPrev(text, caseSensitive);
49      else
50          emit findNext(text, caseSensitive);
51  }

52  void FindDialog::enableFindButton(const QString &text)
53  {
54      findButton->setEnabled(!text.isEmpty());
55  }
```

The findClicked() slot is called when the user clicks the Find button. It emits the findPrev() or the findNext() signal, depending on the Search backward option. The emit keyword is specific to Qt; like other Qt extensions, it is converted into standard C++ by the C++ preprocessor.

The enableFindButton() slot is called whenever the user changes the text in the line editor. It enables the button if there is some text in the editor, and disables it otherwise.

These two slots complete the dialog. We can now create a main.cpp file to test our FindDialog widget:

```
1   #include <qapplication.h>

2   #include "finddialog.h"

3   int main(int argc, char *argv[])
4   {
5       QApplication app(argc, argv);
6       FindDialog *dialog = new FindDialog;
7       app.setMainWidget(dialog);
8       dialog->show();
9       return app.exec();
10  }
```

To compile the program, run qmake as usual. Since the FindDialog class definition contains the Q_OBJECT macro, the makefile generated by qmake will include special rules to run moc, Qt's meta-object compiler.

For moc to work correctly, we must put the class definition in a header file, separate from the implementation file. The code generated by moc includes this header file and adds some magic of its own.

Classes that use the `Q_OBJECT` macro must have `moc` run on them. This isn't a problem because `qmake` automatically adds the necessary rules to the makefile. But if you forget to regenerate your makefile using `qmake` and `moc` isn't run, the linker will complain that some functions are declared but not implemented. The messages can be fairly obscure. GCC produces warnings like this one:

```
finddialog.o(.text+0x28): undefined reference to
'FindDialog::QPaintDevice virtual table'
```

Visual C++'s output starts like this:

```
finddialog.obj : error LNK2001: unresolved external symbol
"public:~virtual bool __thiscall FindDialog::qt_property(int,
int,class QVariant *)"
```

If this ever happens to you, run `qmake` again to update the makefile, then rebuild the application.

Now run the program. Verify that the accelerator keys Alt+W, Alt+C, Alt+B, and Alt+F trigger the correct behavior. Press Tab to navigate through the widgets with the keyboard. The default tab order is the order in which the widgets were created. This can be changed by calling `QWidget::setTabOrder()`.

Providing a sensible tab order and keyboard accelerators ensures that users who don't want to (or cannot) use a mouse are able to make full use of the application. Full keyboard control is also appreciated by fast typists.

In Chapter 3, we will use the Find dialog inside a real application, and we will connect the `findPrev()` and `findNext()` signals to some slots.

## Signals and Slots in Depth

The signals and slots mechanism is fundamental to Qt programming. It enables the application programmer to bind objects together without the objects knowing anything about each other. We have already connected some signals and slots together, declared our own signals and slots, implemented our own slots, and emitted our own signals. Let's take a moment to look at the mechanism more closely.

Slots are almost identical to ordinary C++ member functions. They can be virtual, they can be overloaded, they can be public, protected, or private, and they can be directly invoked like any other C++ member functions. The difference is that a slot can also be connected to a signal, in which case it is automatically called each time the signal is emitted.

The `connect()` statement looks like this:

```
connect(sender, SIGNAL(signal), receiver, SLOT(slot));
```

where *sender* and *receiver* are pointers to `QObject`s and where *signal* and *slot* are function signatures without parameter names. The SIGNAL() and SLOT() macros essentially convert their argument to a string.

In the examples we have seen so far, we have always connected different signals to different slots. There are more possibilities to explore:

- **One signal can be connected to many slots:**

```
connect(slider, SIGNAL(valueChanged(int)),
        spinBox, SLOT(setValue(int)));
connect(slider, SIGNAL(valueChanged(int)),
        this, SLOT(updateStatusBarIndicator(int)));
```

  When the signal is emitted, the slots are called one after the other, in an arbitrary order.

- **Many signals can be connected to the same slot:**

```
connect(lcd, SIGNAL(overflow()),
        this, SLOT(handleMathError()));
connect(calculator, SIGNAL(divisionByZero()),
        this, SLOT(handleMathError()));
```

  When either signal is emitted, the slot is called.

- **A signal can be connected to another signal:**

```
connect(lineEdit, SIGNAL(textChanged(const QString &)),
        this, SIGNAL(updateRecord(const QString &)));
```

  When the first signal is emitted, the second signal is emitted as well. Apart from that, signal–signal connections are indistinguishable from signal–slot connections.

- **Connections can be removed:**

```
disconnect(lcd, SIGNAL(overflow()),
           this, SLOT(handleMathError()));
```

  This is rarely needed, because Qt automatically removes all connections involving an object when that object is deleted.

When connecting a signal to a slot (or to another signal), they must both have the same parameter types in the same order:

```
connect(ftp, SIGNAL(rawCommandReply(int, const QString &)),
        this, SLOT(processReply(int, const QString &)));
```

Exceptionally, if a signal has more parameters than the slot it is connected to, the additional parameters are simply ignored:

```
connect(ftp, SIGNAL(rawCommandReply(int, const QString &)),
        this, SLOT(checkErrorCode(int)));
```

If the parameter types are incompatible, or if the signal or the slot doesn't exist, Qt will issue a warning at run-time. Similarly, Qt will give a warning if parameter names are included in the signal or slot signatures.

## Qt's Meta-Object System

One of Qt's major achievements has been the extension of C++ with a mechanism for creating independent software components that can be bound together without any component knowing anything about the other components it is connected to.

The mechanism is called the *meta-object system*, and it provides two key services: signals and slots, and introspection. The introspection functionality is necessary for implementing signals and slots, and allows application programmers to obtain "meta-information" about QObject subclasses at runtime, including the list of signals and slots supported by the object and its class name. The mechanism also supports properties (for *Qt Designer*) and text translation (for internationalization).

Standard C++ doesn't provide support for the dynamic meta-information needed by Qt's meta-object system. Qt solves this problem by providing a separate tool, moc, that parses Q_OBJECT class definitions and makes the information available through C++ functions. Since moc implements all its functionality using pure C++, Qt's meta-object system works with any C++ compiler.

The mechanism works as follows:

- The Q_OBJECT macro declares some introspection functions that must be implemented in every QObject subclass: metaObject(), className(), tr(), and a few more.

- Qt's moc tool generates implementations for the functions declared by Q_OBJECT and for all the signals.

- QObject member functions such as connect() and disconnect() use the introspection functions to do their work.

All of this is handled automatically by qmake, moc, and QObject, so you rarely need to think about it. But if you are curious, you can look at the C++ source files generated by moc to see how the implementation works.

So far, we have only used signals and slots with widgets. But the mechanism itself is implemented in QObject, and isn't limited to GUI programming. The mechanism can be used by any QObject subclass:

```
class Employee : public QObject
{
    Q_OBJECT
public:
    Employee() { mySalary = 0; }

    int salary() const { return mySalary; }

public slots:
    void setSalary(int newSalary);

signals:
```

```
        void salaryChanged(int newSalary);

private:
    int mySalary;
};

void Employee::setSalary(int newSalary)
{
    if (newSalary != mySalary) {
        mySalary = newSalary;
        emit salaryChanged(mySalary);
    }
}
```

Notice how the `setSalary()` slot is implemented. We only emit the `salary-Changed()` signal if `newSalary != mySalary`. This ensures that cyclic connections don't lead to infinite loops.

## Rapid Dialog Design

Qt is designed to be pleasant and intuitive to hand-code, and it is perfectly possible to develop Qt applications purely by writing C++ source code. *Qt Designer* expands the options available to programmers, allowing them to combine visually designed forms with their source code.

In this section, we will use *Qt Designer* to create the Go-to-Cell dialog shown in Figure 2.4. Whether we do it in code or in *Qt Designer*, creating a dialog always involves the same fundamental steps:

- Create and initialize the child widgets.
- Put the child widgets in layouts.
- Set the tab order.
- Establish signal–slot connections.
- Implement the dialog's custom slots.

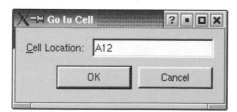

**Figure 2.4.** Go-to-Cell dialog

To launch *Qt Designer*, click Qt 3.2.x|Qt Designer in the Start menu on Windows, type `designer` on the command line on Unix, or double-click `designer` in the Mac OS X Finder. When *Qt Designer* starts, it will pop up a list of templates. Click the "Dialog" template, then click OK. You should now have a window called "Form1".

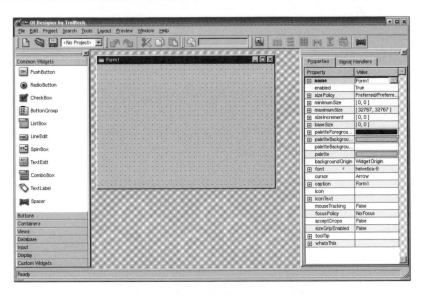

**Figure 2.5.** *Qt Designer* with an empty form

The first step is to create the child widgets and place them on the form. Create one text label, one line editor, one (horizontal) spacer, and two push buttons. For each item, click its name or icon in the "toolbox" at the left of *Qt Designer*'s main window and then click the form roughly where the item should go. Now drag the bottom of the form up to make it shorter. This should produce a form that is similar to Figure 2.6. Don't spend too much time positioning the items on the form; Qt's layout managers will lay them out precisely later on.

The spacer item is shown in *Qt Designer* as a blue spring. It is invisible in the final form.

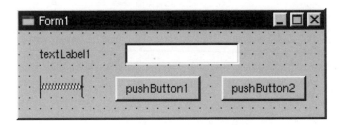

**Figure 2.6.** The form with some widgets

Set each widget's properties using the property editor on the right of *Qt Designer*'s main window:

1. Click the text label. Set its `name` property to "label" and its `text` property to "&Cell Location:".

2. Click the line editor. Set its `name` property to "lineEdit".

3. Click the spacer. Make sure that the spacer's `orientation` property is set to "Horizontal".

4. Click the first button. Set its name property to "okButton", its enabled property to "False", its default property to "True", and its text property to "OK".

5. Click the second button. Set its name property to "cancelButton" and its text property to "Cancel".

6. Click the background of the form to select the form itself. Set its name property to "GoToCellDialog" and its caption property to "Go to Cell".

All the widgets look fine now, except the text label, which shows &Cell Location. Click Tools|Set Buddy. Click the label and drag the rubber band to the line editor, then release. The label should now show Cell Location and have the line editor as its buddy. You can verify this by checking that the label's buddy property is set to "lineEdit".

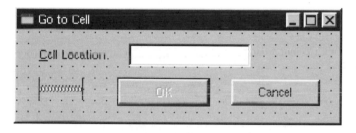

**Figure 2.7.** The form with properties set

The next step is to lay out the widgets on the form:

1. Click the Cell Location label and press Shift as you click the line editor next to it so that they are both selected. Click Layout|Lay Out Horizontally.

2. Click the spacer, then hold Shift as you click the form's OK and Cancel buttons. Click Layout|Lay Out Horizontally.

3. Click the background of the form to deselect any selected items, then click Layout|Lay Out Vertically.

4. Click Layout|Adjust Size to resize the form to its optimal size.

The red lines that appear on the form show the layouts that have been created. They never appear when the form is run.

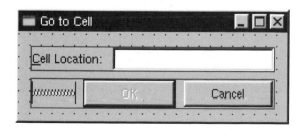

**Figure 2.8.** The form with the layouts

Now click Tools|Tab Order. A number in a blue circle will appear next to every widget that can accept focus. Click each widget in turn in the order you want them to accept focus, then press Esc.

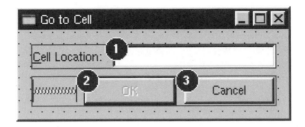

**Figure 2.9.** Setting the form's tab order

Now that the form has been designed, we are ready to make it functional by setting up some signal–slot connections and by implementing some custom slots. Click Edit|Connections to invoke the connection editor.

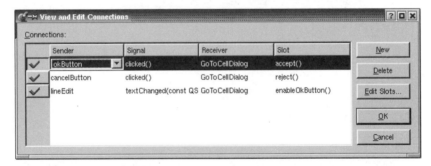

**Figure 2.10.** *Qt Designer*'s connection editor (after making the connections)

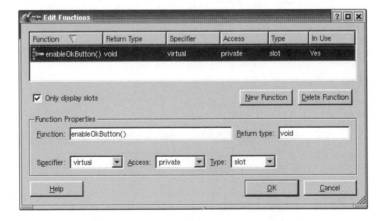

**Figure 2.11.** *Qt Designer*'s slot editor

We need to establish three connections. To create a connection, click New and set the Sender, Signal, Receiver, and Slot fields using the drop-down comboboxes.

Connect the okButton's clicked() signal to the GoToCellDialog's accept() slot. Connect the cancelButton's clicked() signal to the GoToCellDialog's reject() slot. Click Edit Slots to invoke *Qt Designer*'s slot editor (shown in Figure 2.11), and create an enableOkButton() private slot. Finally, connect the lineEdit's textChanged(const QString &) signal to the GoToCellDialog's new enableOkButton() slot.

To preview the dialog, click the Preview|Preview Form menu option. Check the tab order by pressing Tab repeatedly. Press Alt+C to move the focus to the line editor. Click Cancel to close the dialog.

Save the dialog as gotocelldialog.ui in a directory called gotocell, and create a main.cpp file in the same directory using a plain text editor:

```
#include <qapplication.h>

#include "gotocelldialog.h"

int main(int argc, char *argv[])
{
    QApplication app(argc, argv);
    GoToCellDialog *dialog = new GoToCellDialog;
    app.setMainWidget(dialog);
    dialog->show();
    return app.exec();
}
```

Now run qmake to create a .pro file and a makefile (qmake -project; qmake gotocell.pro). The qmake tool is smart enough to detect the user interface file gotocelldialog.ui and to generate the appropriate makefile rules to create gotocelldialog.h and gotocelldialog.cpp. The .ui file is converted to C++ by uic, Qt's user interface compiler.

One of the beauties of using *Qt Designer* is that it allows programmers great freedom to modify their form designs without disturbing their source code. When you develop a form purely by writing C++ code, changes to the design can be quite time-consuming. With *Qt Designer*, no time is lost since uic simply regenerates the source code for any forms that have changed.

If you run the program now, the dialog will work, but it doesn't function exactly as we want:

- The OK button is always disabled.
- The line editor accepts any text, instead of only accepting valid cell locations.

We must write some code to solve these problems.

Double-click the background of the form to invoke *Qt Designer*'s code editor. In the editor window, enter the following code:

```
#include <qvalidator.h>

void GoToCellDialog::init()
```

```
    {
        QRegExp regExp("[A-Za-z][1-9][0-9]{0,2}");
        lineEdit->setValidator(new QRegExpValidator(regExp, this));
    }

    void GoToCellDialog::enableOkButton()
    {
        okButton->setEnabled(lineEdit->hasAcceptableInput());
    }
```

The `init()` function is automatically called at the end of the form's constructor (generated by `uic`). We set up a validator to restrict the range of the input. Qt provides three built-in validator classes: `QIntValidator`, `QDoubleValidator`, and `QRegExpValidator`. Here we use a `QRegExpValidator` with the regular expression "[A-Za-z][1-9][0-9]{0,2}", which means: Allow one upper- or lower-case letter, followed by one digit in the range 1 to 9, followed by up to two digits each in the range 0 to 9. (For an introduction to regular expressions, see the `QRegExp` class documentation.)

By passing `this` to the `QRegExpValidator` constructor, we make it a child of the `GoToCellDialog` object. By doing so, we don't have to worry about deleting the `QRegExpValidator` later; it will be deleted automatically when its parent is deleted.

The `enableOkButton()` slot enables or disables the OK button, according to whether the line edit contains a valid cell location. `QLineEdit::hasAcceptable-Input()` uses the validator we set in the `init()` function.

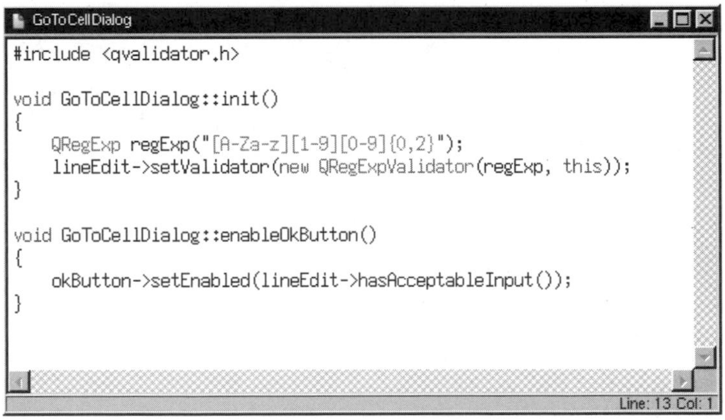

**Figure 2.12.** *Qt Designer*'s code editor

After typing the code, save the dialog again. This will effectively save two files: the user interface file `gotocelldialog.ui`, and the C++ source file `goto-celldialog.ui.h`. Make the application once more and run it again. Type "A12" in the line edit, and notice that the OK button becomes enabled. Try typing some random text to see how the validator does its job. Click Cancel to close the dialog.

In this example, we edited the dialog in *Qt Designer*, then we added some code using *Qt Designer*'s code editor. The dialog's user interface is saved in a .ui file (an XML-based file format), while the code is saved in a .ui.h file (a C++ source file). This split is very convenient for developers who want to edit the .ui.h file in their favorite text editor.

An alternative to the .ui.h approach is to create a .ui file with *Qt Designer* as usual, then create an additional class that inherits the uic-generated class and adds the extra functionality there. For example, for the Go-to-Cell dialog, this would mean creating a GoToCellDialogImpl class that inherits GoToCellDialog and that implements what's missing. It is straightforward to convert the .ui.h code to use this approach. The result is this header file:

```cpp
#ifndef GOTOCELLDIALOGIMPL_H
#define GOTOCELLDIALOGIMPL_H

#include "gotocelldialog.h"

class GoToCellDialogImpl : public GoToCellDialog
{
    Q_OBJECT
public:
    GoToCellDialogImpl(QWidget *parent = 0, const char *name = 0);

private slots:
    void enableOkButton();
};

#endif
```

And this source file:

```cpp
#include <qlineedit.h>
#include <qpushbutton.h>
#include <qvalidator.h>

#include "gotocelldialogimpl.h"

GoToCellDialogImpl::GoToCellDialogImpl(QWidget *parent,
                                       const char *name)
    : GoToCellDialog(parent, name)
{
    QRegExp regExp("[A-Za-z][1-9][0-9]{0,2}");
    lineEdit->setValidator(new QRegExpValidator(regExp, this));
}

void GoToCellDialogImpl::enableOkButton()
{
    okButton->setEnabled(lineEdit->hasAcceptableInput());
}
```

Developers who prefer the subclassing approach would probably call the base class GoToCellDialogBase and the derived class GoToCellDialog, keeping the better name for the class that contains all the functionality.

The `uic` tool provides command-line options to simplify the creation of sub-classes based on forms created with *Qt Designer*. Use `-subdecl` to generate a skeleton header file, and use `-subimpl` to generate the matching implementation file.

In this book, we use the `.ui.h` approach since this is the most common practice, and since it is easy to convert `.ui.h` files into subclasses. You might want to read the "Designer Approach" chapter in *Qt Designer*'s manual for a technical appreciation of the differences between subclassing and using `.ui.h` files. Another chapter in the manual, "Creating Dialogs", demonstrates how to use *Qt Designer*'s Members tab to declare member variables in `uic`-generated classes.

## Shape-Changing Dialogs

We have seen how to create dialogs that always show the same widgets whenever they are used. In some cases, it is desirable to provide dialogs that can change shape. The two most common kinds of shape-changing dialogs are *extension dialogs* and *multi-page dialogs*. Both types of dialog can be implemented in Qt, either purely in code or using *Qt Designer*.

Extension dialogs usually present a simple appearance but have a toggle button that allows the user to switch between the dialog's simple and extended appearances. Extension dialogs are commonly used for applications that are trying to cater for both casual and power users, hiding the advanced options unless the user explicitly asks to see them. In this section, we will use *Qt Designer* to create the extension dialog shown in Figure 2.13.

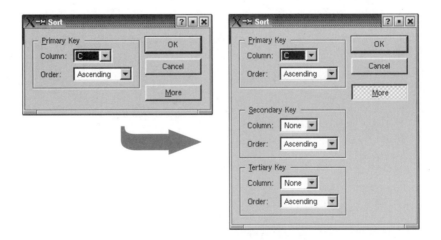

**Figure 2.13.** Sort dialog with simple and extended appearances

The dialog is a Sort dialog in a spreadsheet application, where the user can select one or several columns to sort on. The dialog's simple appearance allows the user to enter a single sort key, and its extended appearance provides for two extra sort keys. A More button lets the user switch between the simple and extended appearances.

We will create the widget with its extended appearance in *Qt Designer*, and hide the secondary and tertiary keys at run-time as needed. The widget looks complicated, but it's fairly easy to do in *Qt Designer*. The trick is to do the primary key part first, then copy and paste it twice to obtain the secondary and tertiary keys:

1. Create a group box, two text labels, two comboboxes, and one horizontal spacer.

2. Drag the bottom-right corner of the group box to make it larger.

3. Move the other widgets into the group box and position them approximately as shown in Figure 2.14 (a).

4. Drag the right edge of the second combobox to make it about twice as wide as the first combobox.

5. Set the group box's `title` property to "&Primary Key", the first label's `text` property to "Column:", and the second label's `text` property to "Order:".

6. Double-click the first combobox to pop up *Qt Designer*'s list box editor, and create one item with the text "None".

7. Double-click the second combobox and create an "Ascending" item and a "Descending" item.

8. Click the group box, then click Layout|Lay Out in a Grid. This will produce the layout shown in Figure 2.14 (b).

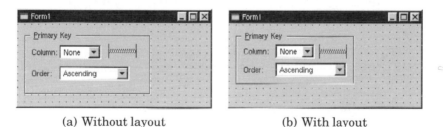

      (a) Without layout            (b) With layout

**Figure 2.14.** Laying out the group box's children in a grid

If a layout doesn't turn out quite right or if you make a mistake, you can always click Edit|Undo, then roughly reposition the widgets being laid out and try again.

We will now add the Secondary Key and Tertiary Key group boxes:

1. Make the dialog window tall enough for the extra parts. Select the group box, click Edit|Copy, then click Edit|Paste twice to obtain two additional group boxes. Drag the two new group boxes to the approximate positions that they should occupy. Change their `title` property to "&Secondary Key" and "&Tertiary Key".

2. Create the OK, Cancel, and More buttons.

3. Set the OK button's `default` property to "True" and the More button's `toggle` property to "True".

4. Create two vertical spacers.

5. Arrange the OK, Cancel, and More buttons vertically, with a vertical spacer between the Cancel and More buttons. Then select all four items and click Layout|Lay Out Vertically.

6. Place the second vertical spacer between the primary key group box and the secondary key group box.

7. Set the two vertical spacer items' `sizeHint` property to (20, 10).

8. Arrange the widgets in the grid-like pattern shown in Figure 2.15 (a).

9. Click Layout|Lay Out in a Grid. The form should now match Figure 2.15 (b).

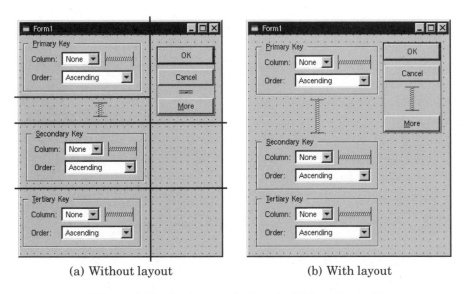

(a) Without layout                     (b) With layout

**Figure 2.15.** Laying out the form's children in a grid

The resulting grid layout has two columns and four rows, giving a total of eight cells. The Primary Key group box, the leftmost vertical spacer item, the Secondary Key group box, and the Tertiary Key group box each occupy a single cell. The vertical layout that contains the OK, Cancel, and More buttons occupies two cells. That leaves two empty cells in the bottom-right of the dialog. If this isn't what you have, undo the layout, reposition the widgets, and try again.

Change the form's `resizeMode` property from "Auto" to "Fixed", making the dialog non-resizable by the user. The layout then takes over the responsibility for resizing, and resizes the dialog automatically when child widgets are shown or hidden, ensuring that the dialog is always displayed at its optimal size.

Rename the form "SortDialog" and change its caption to "Sort". Set the names of the child widgets to those shown in Figure 2.16.

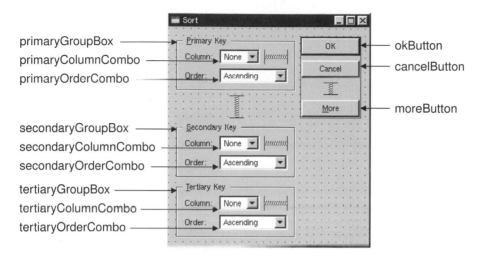

**Figure 2.16.** Naming the form's widgets

Finally, set up the connections:

1. Connect the okButton's clicked() signal to the form's accept() slot.

2. Connect the cancelButton's clicked() signal to the form's reject() slot.

3. Connect the moreButton's toggled(bool) signal to the secondaryGroupBox's setShown(bool) slot.

4. Connect the moreButton's toggled(bool) signal to the tertiaryGroupBox's setShown(bool) slot.

Double-click the form to launch *Qt Designer*'s C++ code editor and type in the following code:

```
1  void SortDialog::init()
2  {
3      secondaryGroupBox->hide();
4      tertiaryGroupBox->hide();
5      setColumnRange('A', 'Z');
6  }

7  void SortDialog::setColumnRange(QChar first, QChar last)
8  {
9      primaryColumnCombo->clear();
10     secondaryColumnCombo->clear();
11     tertiaryColumnCombo->clear();

12     secondaryColumnCombo->insertItem(tr("None"));
13     tertiaryColumnCombo->insertItem(tr("None"));

14     primaryColumnCombo->setMinimumSize(
15             secondaryColumnCombo->sizeHint());
```

```
16      QChar ch = first;
17      while (ch <= last) {
18          primaryColumnCombo->insertItem(ch);
19          secondaryColumnCombo->insertItem(ch);
20          tertiaryColumnCombo->insertItem(ch);
21          ch = ch.unicode() + 1;
22      }
23  }
```

The init() function hides the secondary and tertiary key parts of the dialog.

The setColumnRange() slot initializes the contents of the comboboxes based on the selected columns in the spreadsheet. We insert a "None" item in the comboboxes for the (optional) secondary and tertiary keys. Although we have not created this slot using *Qt Designer*'s slot editor, *Qt Designer* will detect that we have created a new slot in code, and uic will automatically generate the correct function declaration in the SortDialog class definition.

Lines 14 and 15 present a subtle layout idiom. The QWidget::sizeHint() function returns a widget's "ideal" size, which the layout system tries to honor. This explains why different kinds of widgets, or similar widgets with different contents, may be assigned different sizes by the layout system. For comboboxes, this means that the secondary and tertiary comboboxes, which contain "None", end up larger than the primary combobox, which contains only single-letter entries. To avoid this inconsistency, we set the primary combobox's minimum size to the *secondary* combobox's ideal size.

Here is a main() test function that sets the range to include columns 'C' to 'F' and then shows the dialog:

```
#include <qapplication.h>

#include "sortdialog.h"

int main(int argc, char *argv[])
{
    QApplication app(argc, argv);
    SortDialog *dialog = new SortDialog;
    app.setMainWidget(dialog);
    dialog->setColumnRange('C', 'F');
    dialog->show();
    return app.exec();
}
```

That completes the extension dialog. As the example illustrates, an extension dialog isn't much more difficult to design than a plain dialog: All we need is a toggle button, a few extra signal–slot connections, and a non-resizable layout.

The other common type of shape-changing dialogs, multi-page dialogs, are even easier to create in Qt, either in code or using *Qt Designer*. These dialogs can be built in many different ways.

- A `QTabWidget` can be used in its own right. It provides a tab bar along the top that controls a built-in `QWidgetStack`.

- A `QListBox` and a `QWidgetStack` can be used together, with the `QListBox`'s current item determining which page the `QWidgetStack` shows.

- A `QListView` or a `QIconView` can be used with a `QWidgetStack` in a similar way to a `QListBox`.

The `QWidgetStack` class is covered in Chapter 6 (Layout Management).

# Dynamic Dialogs

Dynamic dialogs are dialogs that are created from a *Qt Designer* `.ui` file at runtime. Dynamic dialogs are not converted into C++ code by uic. Instead, the `.ui` file is loaded at run-time using the `QWidgetFactory` class, in the following way:

```
QDialog *sortDialog = (QDialog *)
                    QWidgetFactory::create("sortdialog.ui");
```

We can access the form's child widgets using `QObject::child()`:

```
QComboBox *primaryColumnCombo = (QComboBox *)
        sortDialog->child("primaryColumnCombo", "QComboBox");
```

The `child()` function returns a null pointer if the dialog has no child that matches the given name and type.

The `QWidgetFactory` class is located in a separate library. To use `QWidgetFactory` from a Qt application, we must add this line to the application's `.pro` file:

```
LIBS            += -lqui
```

This syntax works on all platforms, even though it has a definite Unix flavor.

Dynamic dialogs make it possible to change the layout of the form without recompiling the application. For a complete example of an application that uses a dynamic dialog, see the "Subclassing and Dynamic Dialogs" chapter in the *Qt Designer* manual.

# Built-in Widget and Dialog Classes

Qt provides a complete set of built-in widgets and common dialogs that cater for most situations. In this section, we present screenshots of almost all of them. A few specialized widgets are deferred until later: Main window widgets such as `QMenuBar`, `QPopupMenu`, and `QToolBar` are covered in Chapter 3, and database widgets such as `QDataView` and `QDataTable` are covered in Chapter 12. Most of the built-in widgets and dialogs are used in the examples presented in this book. In the screenshots below, the widgets are shown using the classic Windows style.

| QPushButton | QCheckBox | QRadioButton |

**Figure 2.17.** Qt's button widgets

Qt provides three kinds of "buttons": QPushButton, QCheckBox, and QRadioButton. QPushButton is most commonly used to initiate an action when it is clicked, but it can also behave like a toggle button (click to press down, click to release). QRadioButtons are usually used inside a QButtonGroup and are mutually exclusive within their group, whereas QCheckBox can be used for independent on/off options.

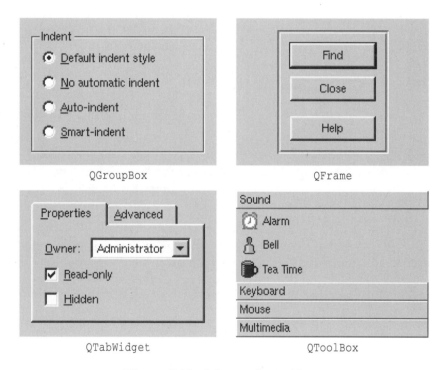

**Figure 2.18.** Qt's container widgets

Qt's container widgets are widgets that contain other widgets. QFrame can also be used on its own to simply to draw lines and is inherited by many other widget classes, notably QLabel and QLineEdit. QButtonGroup is not shown; it is visually identical to QGroupBox.

QTabWidget and QToolBox are multi-page widgets. Each page is a child widget, and the pages are numbered from 0.

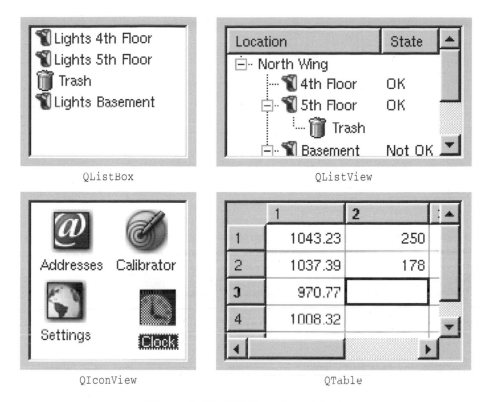

**Figure 2.19.** Qt's item view widgets

The item views are optimized for handling large amounts of data, and often use scroll bars. The scroll bar mechanism is implemented in QScrollView, a base class for item views and other kinds of views.

**Figure 2.20.** Qt's display widgets

Qt provides a few widgets that are used purely for displaying information. QLabel is the most important of these, and it can be used for showing rich text (using a simple HTML-like syntax) and images.

QTextBrowser (not shown) is a read-only QTextEdit subclass that has basic HTML support including lists, tables, images, and hypertext links; *Qt Assistant* uses QTextBrowser to present documentation to the user.

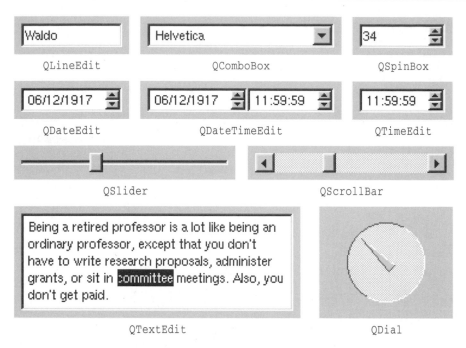

**Figure 2.21.** Qt's input widgets

Qt provides many widgets for data entry. QLineEdit can restrict its input using an input mask or a validator. QTextEdit is a QScrollView subclass capable of editing large amounts of text.

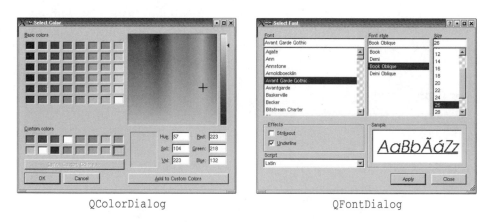

**Figure 2.22.** Qt's color dialog and font dialog

Qt provides the standard set of common dialogs that make it easy to ask the user to select a color, font, or file, or to print a document.

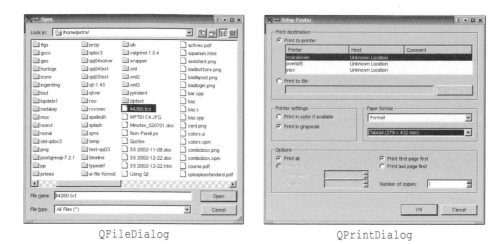

QFileDialog                    QPrintDialog

**Figure 2.23.** Qt's file dialog and print dialog

On Windows and Mac OS X, Qt uses the native dialogs rather than its own common dialogs when possible.

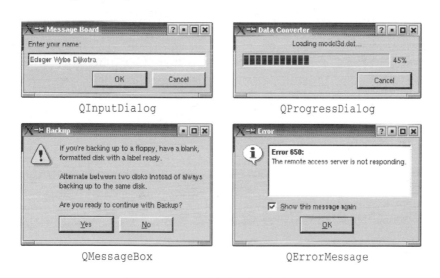

QInputDialog                    QProgressDialog

QMessageBox                    QErrorMessage

**Figure 2.24.** Qt's feedback dialogs

Qt provides a versatile message box and an error dialog that remembers which messages it has shown. The progress of time-consuming operations can be indicated using QProgressDialog or using the QProgressBar shown earlier. QInputDialog is very convenient when a single line of text or a single number is required from the user.

Finally, QWizard provides a framework for creating wizards. *Qt Designer* provides a "Wizard" template for creating wizards visually.

**Figure 2.25.** Qt's QWizard dialog

A lot of ready-to-use functionality is provided by the built-in widgets and common dialogs. More specialized requirements can often be satisfied by connecting signals to slots and implementing custom behavior in the slots.

In some situations, it may be desirable to create a custom widget from scratch. Qt makes this straightforward, and custom widgets can access all the same platform-independent drawing functionality as Qt's built-in widgets. Custom widgets can even be integrated with *Qt Designer* so that they can be used in the same way as Qt's built-in widgets. Chapter 5 explains how to create custom widgets.

# Creating Main Windows

This chapter will teach you how to create main windows using Qt. By the end, you will be able to build an application's entire user interface, complete with menus, toolbars, status bar, and as many dialogs as the application requires.

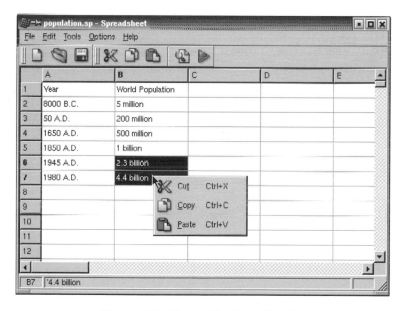

**Figure 3.1.** Spreadsheet application

An application's main window provides the framework upon which the application's user interface is built. The main window for the Spreadsheet application shown in Figure 3.1 will form the basis of this chapter. The Spreadsheet application makes use of the Find, Go-to-Cell, and Sort dialogs that we created in Chapter 2.

Behind most GUI applications lies a body of code that provides the underlying functionality—for example, code to read and write files or to process the data presented in the user interface. In Chapter 4, we will see how to implement such functionality, again using the Spreadsheet application as our example.

## Subclassing QMainWindow

An application's main window is created by subclassing QMainWindow. Many of the techniques we saw in Chapter 2 for creating dialogs are also relevant for creating main windows, since both QDialog and QMainWindow inherit from QWidget.

Main windows can be created using *Qt Designer*, but in this chapter we will use code to demonstrate how it's done. If you prefer the more visual approach, see the "Creating a Main Window Application" chapter in *Qt Designer*'s manual.

The source code for the Spreadsheet application's main window is spread across mainwindow.h and mainwindow.cpp. Let's start with the header file:

```
#ifndef MAINWINDOW_H
#define MAINWINDOW_H

#include <qmainwindow.h>
#include <qstringlist.h>

class QAction;
class QLabel;
class FindDialog;
class Spreadsheet;

class MainWindow : public QMainWindow
{
    Q_OBJECT
public:
    MainWindow(QWidget *parent = 0, const char *name = 0);

protected:
    void closeEvent(QCloseEvent *event);
    void contextMenuEvent(QContextMenuEvent *event);
```

We define the class MainWindow as a subclass of QMainWindow. It contains the Q_OBJECT macro because it provides its own signals and slots.

The closeEvent() function is a virtual function in QWidget that is automatically called when the user closes the window. It is reimplemented in MainWindow so that we can ask the user the standard question "Do you want to save your changes?" and to save user preferences to disk.

Similarly, the contextMenuEvent() function is called when the user right-clicks a widget or presses a platform-specific Menu key. It is reimplemented in MainWindow to pop up a context menu.

```
private slots:
    void newFile();
```

```
    void open();
    bool save();
    bool saveAs();
    void find();
    void goToCell();
    void sort();
    void about();
```

Some menu options, like File|New and Help|About, are implemented as private slots in `MainWindow`. Most slots have `void` as their return value, but `save()` and `saveAs()` return a `bool`. The return value is ignored when a slot is executed in response to a signal, but when we call a slot as a function the return value is available to us just as it is when we call any ordinary C++ function.

```
    void updateCellIndicators();
    void spreadsheetModified();
    void openRecentFile(int param);

private:
    void createActions();
    void createMenus();
    void createToolBars();
    void createStatusBar();
    void readSettings();
    void writeSettings();
    bool maybeSave();
    void loadFile(const QString &fileName);
    void saveFile(const QString &fileName);
    void setCurrentFile(const QString &fileName);
    void updateRecentFileItems();
    QString strippedName(const QString &fullFileName);
```

The main window needs some more private slots and several private functions to support the user interface.

```
    Spreadsheet *spreadsheet;
    FindDialog *findDialog;
    QLabel *locationLabel;
    QLabel *formulaLabel;
    QLabel *modLabel;
    QStringList recentFiles;
    QString curFile;
    QString fileFilters;
    bool modified;

    enum { MaxRecentFiles = 5 };
    int recentFileIds[MaxRecentFiles];

    QPopupMenu *fileMenu;
    QPopupMenu *editMenu;
    QPopupMenu *selectSubMenu;
    QPopupMenu *toolsMenu;
    QPopupMenu *optionsMenu;
    QPopupMenu *helpMenu;
    QToolBar *fileToolBar;
    QToolBar *editToolBar;
```

```
        QAction *newAct;
        QAction *openAct;
        QAction *saveAct;
        ...
        QAction *aboutAct;
        QAction *aboutQtAct;
    };

    #endif
```

In addition to its private slots and private functions, `MainWindow` also has lots of private variables. All of these will be explained as we use them.

We will now review the implementation:

```
    #include <qaction.h>
    #include <qapplication.h>
    #include <qcombobox.h>
    #include <qfiledialog.h>
    #include <qlabel.h>
    #include <qlineedit.h>
    #include <qmenubar.h>
    #include <qmessagebox.h>
    #include <qpopupmenu.h>
    #include <qsettings.h>
    #include <qstatusbar.h>

    #include "cell.h"
    #include "finddialog.h"
    #include "gotocelldialog.h"
    #include "mainwindow.h"
    #include "sortdialog.h"
    #include "spreadsheet.h"
```

We include the header files for the Qt classes used in our subclass, and also some custom header files, notably `finddialog.h`, `gotocelldialog.h`, and `sortdialog.h` from Chapter 2.

```
    MainWindow::MainWindow(QWidget *parent, const char *name)
        : QMainWindow(parent, name)
    {
        spreadsheet = new Spreadsheet(this);
        setCentralWidget(spreadsheet);

        createActions();
        createMenus();
        createToolBars();
        createStatusBar();

        readSettings();

        setCaption(tr("Spreadsheet"));
        setIcon(QPixmap::fromMimeSource("icon.png"));

        findDialog = 0;
        fileFilters = tr("Spreadsheet files (*.sp)");
        modified = false;
    }
```

In the constructor, we begin by creating a `Spreadsheet` widget and setting it to be the main window's central widget. The central widget occupies the area between the toolbars and the status bar. The `Spreadsheet` class is a `QTable` subclass with some spreadsheet capabilities, such as support for spreadsheet formulas. We will implement it in Chapter 4.

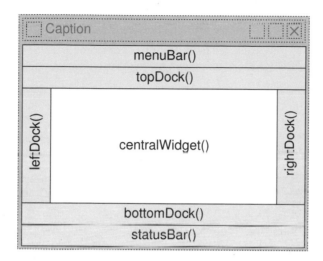

**Figure 3.2.** `QMainWindow`'s constituent widgets

Then we call the private functions `createActions()`, `createMenus()`, `create-ToolBars()`, and `createStatusBar()` to create the rest of the main window. We also call the private function `readSettings()` to read the application's stored settings.

We set the window's icon to `icon.png`, a PNG file. Qt supports many image formats, including BMP, GIF,* JPEG, MNG, PNG, PNM, XBM, and XPM. Calling `QWidget::setIcon()` sets the icon shown in the top-left corner of the window. Unfortunately, there is no platform-independent way of setting the application icon that appears on the desktop. The procedure is explained at `http://doc.trolltech.com/3.2/appicon.html`.

GUI applications generally use many images, with some images being used in several different contexts. Qt has a variety of methods for providing images to the application. The most common are:

- Storing images in files and loading them at run-time.

- Including XPM files in the source code. (This works because XPM files are also valid C++ files.)

- Using Qt's "image collection" mechanism.

---

*If you are in a country that recognizes software patents and where Unisys holds a patent on LZW decompression, Unisys may require you to license the technology to use GIF. Because of this, GIF support is disabled in Qt by default. We believe that this patent will have expired worldwide by the end of 2004.

Here we use the "image collection" approach because it is easier and more efficient than loading files at run-time, and it works with any supported file format. The images are stored in the source tree in a subdirectory called images. By adding the entry

```
IMAGES        = images/icon.png \
                images/new.png \
                images/open.png \
                ...
                images/find.png \
                images/gotocell.png
```

to the application's .pro file, we tell uic to generate a C++ source code file that contains the data for all the specified images. The data is then compiled into the application's executable and can be retrieved using QPixmap::fromMime-Source(). This has the advantage that icons and other images cannot get lost; they are always in the executable.

If you use *Qt Designer* to create your main windows as well as your dialogs, you can also use it to handle your .pro file and to visually add images to the image collection.

## Creating Menus and Toolbars

Most modern GUI applications provide both menus and toolbars, and typically they contain more or less the same commands. The menus enable users to explore the application and learn how to do new things, while the toolbars provide quick access to frequently used functionality.

Qt simplifies the programming of menus and toolbars through its "action" concept. An *action* is an item that can be added to a menu, a toolbar, or both. Creating menus and toolbars in Qt involves these steps:

• Create the actions.

• Add the actions to menus.

• Add the actions to toolbars.

In the Spreadsheet application, actions are created in createActions():

```
void MainWindow::createActions()
{
    newAct = new QAction(tr("&New"), tr("Ctrl+N"), this);
    newAct->setIconSet(QPixmap::fromMimeSource("new.png"));
    newAct->setStatusTip(tr("Create a new spreadsheet file"));
    connect(newAct, SIGNAL(activated()), this, SLOT(newFile()));
```

The New action has a shortcut key (New), an accelerator (Ctrl+N), a parent (the main window), an icon (new.png), and a status tip. We connect the action's activated() signal to the main window's private newFile() slot, which we'll implement in the next section. Without the connection, nothing would happen when the user chooses the File|New menu item or clicks the New toolbar button.

The other actions for the File, Edit, and Tools menus are very similar to the New action.

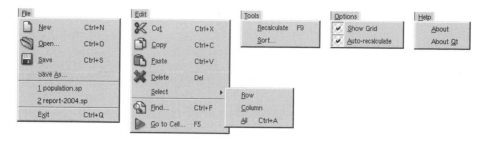

**Figure 3.3.** The Spreadsheet application's menus

The Show Grid action in the Options menu is different:

```
showGridAct = new QAction(tr("&Show Grid"), 0, this);
showGridAct->setToggleAction(true);
showGridAct->setOn(spreadsheet->showGrid());
showGridAct->setStatusTip(tr("Show or hide the spreadsheet's "
                             "grid"));
connect(showGridAct, SIGNAL(toggled(bool)),
        spreadsheet, SLOT(setShowGrid(bool)));
```

Show Grid is a toggle action. It is rendered with a checkmark in the menu and implemented as a toggle button in the toolbar. When the action is turned on, the Spreadsheet component displays a grid. We initialize the action with the default for the Spreadsheet component, so that they are synchronized at start up. Then we connect the Show Grid action's `toggled(bool)` signal to the Spreadsheet component's `setShowGrid(bool)` slot, which it inherits from QTable. Once this action is added to a menu or toolbar, the user can toggle the grid on and off.

The Show Grid and Auto-recalculate actions are independent toggle actions. QAction also provides for mutually exclusive actions through its QActionGroup subclass.

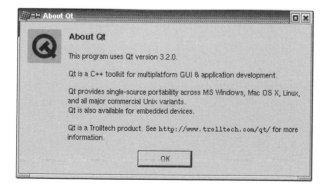

**Figure 3.4.** About Qt

```
        aboutQtAct = new QAction(tr("About &Qt"), 0, this);
        aboutQtAct->setStatusTip(tr("Show the Qt library's About box"));
        connect(aboutQtAct, SIGNAL(activated()), qApp, SLOT(aboutQt()));
    }
```

For About Qt, we use the `QApplication` object's `aboutQt()` slot, accessible through the `qApp` global variable.

Now that we have created the actions, we can move on to building a menu system through which the actions can be invoked:

```
    void MainWindow::createMenus()
    {
        fileMenu = new QPopupMenu(this);
        newAct->addTo(fileMenu);
        openAct->addTo(fileMenu);
        saveAct->addTo(fileMenu);
        saveAsAct->addTo(fileMenu);
        fileMenu->insertSeparator();
        exitAct->addTo(fileMenu);

        for (int i = 0; i < MaxRecentFiles; ++i)
            recentFileIds[i] = -1;
```

In Qt, all menus are instances of `QPopupMenu`. We create the File menu and then add the New, Open, Save, Save As, and Exit actions to it. We insert a separator to visually group closely related items together. The `for` loop takes care of initializing the `recentFilesIds` array. We will use `recentFilesIds` in the next section when implementing the File menu slots.

```
        editMenu = new QPopupMenu(this);
        cutAct->addTo(editMenu);
        copyAct->addTo(editMenu);
        pasteAct->addTo(editMenu);
        deleteAct->addTo(editMenu);

        selectSubMenu = new QPopupMenu(this);
        selectRowAct->addTo(selectSubMenu);
        selectColumnAct->addTo(selectSubMenu);
        selectAllAct->addTo(selectSubMenu);
        editMenu->insertItem(tr("&Select"), selectSubMenu);

        editMenu->insertSeparator();
        findAct->addTo(editMenu);
        goToCellAct->addTo(editMenu);
```

The Edit menu includes a submenu. The submenu, like the menu it belongs to, is a `QPopupMenu`. We simply create the submenu with `this` as parent and insert it into the Edit menu where we want it to appear.

```
        toolsMenu = new QPopupMenu(this);
        recalculateAct->addTo(toolsMenu);
        sortAct->addTo(toolsMenu);

        optionsMenu = new QPopupMenu(this);
        showGridAct->addTo(optionsMenu);
```

```
    autoRecalcAct->addTo(optionsMenu);

    helpMenu = new QPopupMenu(this);
    aboutAct->addTo(helpMenu);
    aboutQtAct->addTo(helpMenu);

    menuBar()->insertItem(tr("&File"), fileMenu);
    menuBar()->insertItem(tr("&Edit"), editMenu);
    menuBar()->insertItem(tr("&Tools"), toolsMenu);
    menuBar()->insertItem(tr("&Options"), optionsMenu);
    menuBar()->insertSeparator();
    menuBar()->insertItem(tr("&Help"), helpMenu);
}
```

We create the Tools, Options, and Help menus in a similar fashion, and we insert all the menus into the menu bar. The QMainWindow::menuBar() function returns a pointer to a QMenuBar. (The menu bar is created the first time menuBar() is called.) We insert a separator between the Options and Help menu. In Motif and similar styles, the separator pushes the Help menu to the right; in other styles, the separator is ignored.

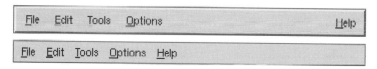

**Figure 3.5.** Menu bar in Motif and Windows styles

Creating toolbars is very similar to creating menus:

```
void MainWindow::createToolBars()
{
    fileToolBar = new QToolBar(tr("File"), this);
    newAct->addTo(fileToolBar);
    openAct->addTo(fileToolBar);
    saveAct->addTo(fileToolBar);

    editToolBar = new QToolBar(tr("Edit"), this);
    cutAct->addTo(editToolBar);
    copyAct->addTo(editToolBar);
    pasteAct->addTo(editToolBar);
    editToolBar->addSeparator();
    findAct->addTo(editToolBar);
    goToCellAct->addTo(editToolBar);
}
```

We create a File toolbar and an Edit toolbar. Just like a popup menu, a toolbar can have separators.

**Figure 3.6.** The Spreadsheet application's toolbars

Now that we have finished the menus and toolbars, we will add a context menu to complete the interface:

```
void MainWindow::contextMenuEvent(QContextMenuEvent *event)
{
    QPopupMenu contextMenu(this);
    cutAct->addTo(&contextMenu);
    copyAct->addTo(&contextMenu);
    pasteAct->addTo(&contextMenu);
    contextMenu.exec(event->globalPos());
}
```

When the user clicks the right mouse button (or presses the Menu key on some keyboards), a "context menu" event is sent to the widget. By reimplementing the `QWidget::contextMenuEvent()` function, we can respond to this event and pop up a context menu at the current mouse pointer position.

**Figure 3.7.** The Spreadsheet application's context menu

Just like signals and slots, *events* are a fundamental aspect of Qt programming. Events are generated by Qt's kernel to report mouse clicks, key presses, resize requests, and similar occurrences. They can be handled by reimplementing virtual functions, as we are doing here.

We have chosen to implement the context menu in `MainWindow` because that's where we store the actions, but it would also have been possible to implement it in `Spreadsheet`. When the user right-clicks the `Spreadsheet` widget, Qt sends a context menu event to that widget first. If `Spreadsheet` reimplements `contextMenuEvent()` and handles the event, the event stops there; otherwise, it is sent to the parent (the `MainWindow`). Events are fully explained in Chapter 7.

The context menu event handler differs from all the code seen so far because it creates a widget (a `QPopupMenu`) as a variable on the stack. We could just as easily have used `new` and `delete`:

```
QPopupMenu *contextMenu = new QPopupMenu(this);
cutAct->addTo(contextMenu);
copyAct->addTo(contextMenu);
pasteAct->addTo(contextMenu);
contextMenu->exec(event->globalPos());
delete contextMenu;
```

Another noteworthy aspect of the code is the `exec()` call. `QPopupMenu::exec()` shows the popup menu at a given screen position and waits until the user chooses an option (or dismisses the popup menu) before it returns. At this point, the `QPopupMenu` object has achieved its purpose, so we can destroy it. If

the QPopupMenu object is located on the stack, it is destroyed automatically at
the end of the function; otherwise, we must call delete.

We have now completed the user interface part of the menus and toolbars. We
still have not implemented all of the slots or written code to handle the File
menu's recently opened files. The next two sections will address these issues.

## Implementing the File Menu

In this section, we will implement the slots and private functions necessary to
make the File menu options work.

```
void MainWindow::newFile()
{
    if (maybeSave()) {
        spreadsheet->clear();
        setCurrentFile("");
    }
}
```

The newFile() slot is called when the user clicks the File|New menu option or
clicks the New toolbar button. The maybeSave() private function asks the user
"Do you want to save your changes?" if there are unsaved changes. It returns
true if the user chooses either Yes or No (saving the document on Yes), and it
returns false if the user chooses Cancel. The setCurrentFile() private function
updates the window's caption to indicate that an untitled document is being
edited.

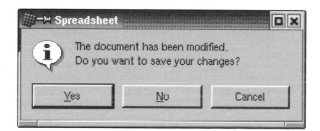

**Figure 3.8.** "Do you want to save your changes?"

```
bool MainWindow::maybeSave()
{
    if (modified) {
        int ret = QMessageBox::warning(this, tr("Spreadsheet"),
                tr("The document has been modified.\n"
                    "Do you want to save your changes?"),
                QMessageBox::Yes | QMessageBox::Default,
                QMessageBox::No,
                QMessageBox::Cancel | QMessageBox::Escape);
        if (ret == QMessageBox::Yes)
            return save();
        else if (ret == QMessageBox::Cancel)
            return false;
```

```
        }
        return true;
    }
```

In `maybeSave()`, we display the message box shown in Figure 3.8. The message box has a Yes, a No, and a Cancel button. The `QMessageBox::Default` modifier makes Yes the default button. The `QMessageBox::Escape` modifier makes the Esc key a synonym for No.

The call to `warning()` may look a bit complicated at first sight, but the general syntax is straightforward:

```
QMessageBox::warning(parent, caption, messageText,
                     button0, button1, ...);
```

`QMessageBox` also provides `information()`, `question()`, and `critical()`, which behave like `warning()` but display a different icon.

Information      Question      Warning      Critical

**Figure 3.9.** Message box icons

```
void MainWindow::open()
{
    if (maybeSave()) {
        QString fileName =
                QFileDialog::getOpenFileName(".", fileFilters, this);
        if (!fileName.isEmpty())
            loadFile(fileName);
    }
}
```

The `open()` slot corresponds to File|Open. Like `newFile()`, it first calls `maybe-Save()` to handle any unsaved changes. Then it uses the static convenience function `QFileDialog::getOpenFileName()` to obtain a file name. The function pops up a file dialog, lets the user choose a file, and returns the file name—or an empty string if the user clicked Cancel.

We give the `getOpenFileName()` function three arguments. The first argument tells it which directory it should start from, in our case the current directory. The second argument, `fileFilters`, specifies the file filters. A file filter consists of a descriptive text and a wildcard pattern. In the `MainWindow` constructor, `fileFilters` was initialized as follows:

```
fileFilters = tr("Spreadsheet files (*.sp)");
```

Had we supported comma-separated values files and Lotus 1-2-3 files in addition to Spreadsheet's native file format, we would have initialized the variable as follows:

```
fileFilters = tr("Spreadsheet files (*.sp)\n"
                 "Comma-separated values files (*.csv)\n"
                 "Lotus 1-2-3 files (*.wk?)");
```

Finally, the third argument to `getOpenFileName()` specifies that the `QFileDialog` that pops up should be a child of the main window.

The parent–child relationship doesn't mean the same thing for dialogs as for other widgets. A dialog is always a top-level widget (a window in its own right), but if it has a parent, it is centered on top of the parent by default. A child dialog also shares the parent's taskbar entry.

```
void MainWindow::loadFile(const QString &fileName)
{
    if (spreadsheet->readFile(fileName)) {
        setCurrentFile(fileName);
        statusBar()->message(tr("File loaded"), 2000);
    } else {
        statusBar()->message(tr("Loading canceled"), 2000);
    }
}
```

The `loadFile()` private function was called in `open()` to load the file. We make it an independent function because we will need the same functionality to load recently opened files.

We use `Spreadsheet::readFile()` to read the file from the disk. If loading is successful, we call `setCurrentFile()` to update the window's caption. Otherwise, `Spreadsheet::loadFile()` will have already notified the user of the problem through a message box. In general, it is good practice to let the lower-level components issue error messages, since they can provide the precise details of what went wrong.

In both cases, we display a message in the status bar for 2000 milliseconds (2 seconds) to keep the user informed about what the application is doing.

```
bool MainWindow::save()
{
    if (curFile.isEmpty()) {
        return saveAs();
    } else {
        saveFile(curFile);
        return true;
    }
}

void MainWindow::saveFile(const QString &fileName)
{
    if (spreadsheet->writeFile(fileName)) {
        setCurrentFile(fileName);
        statusBar()->message(tr("File saved"), 2000);
    } else {
        statusBar()->message(tr("Saving canceled"), 2000);
    }
}
```

The save() slot corresponds to File|Save. If the file already has a name because it was opened before or has already been saved, save() calls saveFile() with that name; otherwise, it simply calls saveAs().

```
bool MainWindow::saveAs()
{
    QString fileName =
            QFileDialog::getSaveFileName(".", fileFilters, this);
    if (fileName.isEmpty())
        return false;

    if (QFile::exists(fileName)) {
        int ret = QMessageBox::warning(this, tr("Spreadsheet"),
                        tr("File %1 already exists.\n"
                            "Do you want to overwrite it?")
                        .arg(QDir::convertSeparators(fileName)),
                        QMessageBox::Yes | QMessageBox::Default,
                        QMessageBox::No | QMessageBox::Escape);
        if (ret == QMessageBox::No)
            return true;
    }
    if (!fileName.isEmpty())
        saveFile(fileName);
    return true;
}
```

The saveAs() slot corresponds to File|Save As. We call QFileDialog::getSave-FileName() to obtain a file name from the user. If the user clicks Cancel, we return false, which is propagated up to maybeSave(). Otherwise, the returned file name may be a new name or the name of an existing file. In the case of an existing file, we call QMessageBox::warning() to display the message box shown in Figure 3.10.

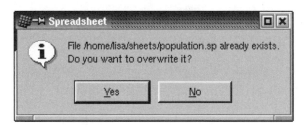

**Figure 3.10.** "Do you want to overwrite it?"

The text we passed to the message box is

```
tr("File %1 already exists\n"
    "Do you want to override it?")
.arg(QDir::convertSeparators(fileName))
```

The QString::arg() function replaces the lowest-numbered "*%n*" parameter with its argument and returns the resulting string. For example, if the file name is A:\tab04.sp, the code above is equivalent to

```
"File A:\\tab04.sp already exists.\n"
"Do you want to override it?"
```

assuming that the application isn't translated into another language. The `QDir::convertSeparators()` call converts forward slashes, which Qt uses as a portable directory separator, into the platform-specific separator ('/' on Unix and Mac OS X, '\' on Windows).

```
void MainWindow::closeEvent(QCloseEvent *event)
{
    if (maybeSave()) {
        writeSettings();
        event->accept();
    } else {
        event->ignore();
    }
}
```

When the user clicks File|Exit, or clicks X in the window's title bar, the `QWidget::close()` slot is called. This sends a "close" event to the widget. By reimplementing `QWidget::closeEvent()`, we can intercept attempts to close the main window and decide whether we want the window to close or not.

If there are unsaved changes and the user chooses Cancel, we "ignore" the event and leave the window unaffected by it. Otherwise, we accept the event, resulting in Qt closing the window and the application terminating.

```
void MainWindow::setCurrentFile(const QString &fileName)
{
    curFile = fileName;
    modLabel->clear();
    modified = false;

    if (curFile.isEmpty()) {
        setCaption(tr("Spreadsheet"));
    } else {
        setCaption(tr("%1 - %2").arg(strippedName(curFile))
                                .arg(tr("Spreadsheet")));
        recentFiles.remove(curFile);
        recentFiles.push_front(curFile);
        updateRecentFileItems();
    }
}

QString MainWindow::strippedName(const QString &fullFileName)
{
    return QFileInfo(fullFileName).fileName();
}
```

In `setCurrentFile()`, we set the `curFile` private variable that stores the name of the file being edited, clear the MOD status indicator, and update the caption. Notice how `arg()` is used with two "%*n*" parameters. The first call to `arg()` replaces "%1"; the second call replaces "%2". It would have been easier to write

```
    setCaption(strippedName(curFile) + tr(" - Spreadsheet"));
```

but using `arg()` gives more flexibility to translators. We remove the file's path with `strippedName()` to make the file name more user-friendly.

If there is a file name, we update `recentFiles`, the application's recently opened files list. We call `remove()` to remove any occurrence of the file name in the list; then we call `push_front()` to add the file name as the first item. Calling `remove()` first is necessary to avoid duplicates. After updating the list, we call the private function `updateRecentFileItems()` to update the entries in the File menu.

The `recentFiles` variable is of type `QStringList` (list of `QString`s). Chapter 11 explains container classes such as `QStringList` in detail and how they relate to the C++ Standard Template Library (STL).

This almost completes the implementation of the File menu. There is one function and one supporting slot that we have not implemented yet. Both are concerned with managing the recently opened files list.

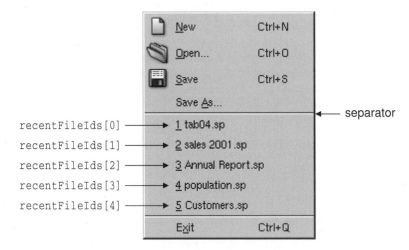

**Figure 3.11.** File menu with recently opened files

```
void MainWindow::updateRecentFileItems()
{
    while ((int)recentFiles.size() > MaxRecentFiles)
        recentFiles.pop_back();

    for (int i = 0; i < (int)recentFiles.size(); ++i) {
        QString text = tr("&%1 %2")
                          .arg(i + 1)
                          .arg(strippedName(recentFiles[i]));
        if (recentFileIds[i] == -1) {
            if (i == 0)
                fileMenu->insertSeparator(fileMenu->count() - 2);
            recentFileIds[i] =
                    fileMenu->insertItem(text, this,
```

```
                                            SLOT(openRecentFile(int)),
                                            0, -1,
                                            fileMenu->count() - 2);
                fileMenu->setItemParameter(recentFileIds[i], i);
            } else {
                fileMenu->changeItem(recentFileIds[i], text);
            }
        }
    }
```

The updateRecentFileItems() private function is called to update the recently opened files menu items. We begin by making sure that there are no more items in the recentFiles list than are allowed (MaxRecentFiles, defined as 5 in mainwindow.h), removing any extra items from the end of the list.

Then, for each entry, we either create a new menu item or reuse an existing item if one exists. The very first time we create a menu item, we also insert a separator. We do this here and not in createMenus() to ensure that we never display two separators in a row. The setItemParameter() call will be explained in a moment.

It may seem strange that we create items in updateRecentFileItems() but never delete items. This is because we can assume that the recently opened files list never shrinks during a session.

The QPopupMenu::insertItem() function we called has the following syntax:

```
    fileMenu->insertItem(text, receiver, slot, accelerator, id, index);
```

The *text* is the text displayed in the menu. We use strippedName() to remove the path from the file names. We could keep the full file names, but that would make the File menu very wide. If full file names are preferred, the best solution is to put the recently opened files in a submenu.

The *receiver* and *slot* parameters specify the slot that should be called when the user chooses the item. In our example, we connect to MainWindow's open-RecentFile(int) slot.

For *accelerator* and *id*, we pass default values, meaning that the menu item has no accelerator and an automatically generated ID. We store the generated ID in the recentFileIds array so that we can access the items later.

The *index* is the position where we want to insert the item. By passing the value fileMenu->count() − 2, we insert it above the Exit item's separator.

```
    void MainWindow::openRecentFile(int param)
    {
        if (maybeSave())
            loadFile(recentFiles[param]);
    }
```

The openRecentFile() slot is where everything falls into place. The slot is called when a recently opened file is chosen from the File menu. The int parameter is the value that we set earlier with setItemParameter(). We chose the values in such a way that we can use them magically as indexes into the `recentFiles` list.

| | Menu items | | | | Recently opened files | |
|---|---|---|---|---|---|---|
| ID | text | param | | index | value |
| −32 | 1 tab04.sp | 0 | → | 0 | A:\tab04.sp |
| −33 | 2 sales 2001.sp | 1 | → | 1 | C:\sales 2001.sp |
| −34 | 3 Annual Report.sp | 2 | → | 2 | D:\Annual Report.sp |
| −35 | 4 population.sp | 3 | → | 3 | C:\population.sp |
| −36 | 5 Customers.sp | 4 | → | 4 | C:\Customers.sp |

**Figure 3.12.** Managing recently opened files

This is one way to solve the problem. A less elegant solution would have been to create five actions and connect them to five separate slots.

## Setting Up the Status Bar

With the menus and toolbars complete, we are ready to tackle the Spreadsheet application's status bar. In its normal state, the status bar contains three indicators: the current cell's location, the current cell's formula, and MOD. The status bar is also used to display status tips and other temporary messages.

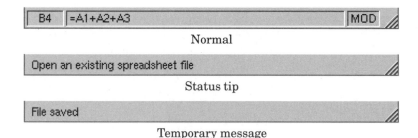

Figure 3.13. The Spreadsheet application's status bar

The `MainWindow` constructor calls `createStatusBar()` to set up the status bar:

```
void MainWindow::createStatusBar()
{
    locationLabel = new QLabel(" W999 ", this);
    locationLabel->setAlignment(AlignHCenter);
    locationLabel->setMinimumSize(locationLabel->sizeHint());

    formulaLabel = new QLabel(this);

    modLabel = new QLabel(tr(" MOD "), this);
    modLabel->setAlignment(AlignHCenter);
    modLabel->setMinimumSize(modLabel->sizeHint());
```

```
        modLabel->clear();

        statusBar()->addWidget(locationLabel);
        statusBar()->addWidget(formulaLabel, 1);
        statusBar()->addWidget(modLabel);

        connect(spreadsheet, SIGNAL(currentChanged(int, int)),
                this, SLOT(updateCellIndicators()));
        connect(spreadsheet, SIGNAL(modified()),
                this, SLOT(spreadsheetModified()));

        updateCellIndicators();
    }
```

The `QMainWindow::statusBar()` function returns a pointer to the status bar. (The status bar is created the first time `statusBar()` is called.) The status indicators are simply `QLabel`s whose text we change whenever necessary. When constructing the `QLabel`s, we pass `this` as the parent, but it doesn't really matter since `QStatusBar::addWidget()` automatically "reparents" them to make them children of the status bar.

Figure 3.13 shows that the three labels have different space requirements. The cell location and MOD indicators require very little space, and when the window is resized, any extra space should go to the cell formula indicator in the middle. This is achieved by specifying a stretch factor of 1 in its `QStatus-Bar::addWidget()` call. The other two indicators have the default stretch factor of 0, meaning that they prefer not to be stretched.

When `QStatusBar` lays out indicator widgets, it tries to respect each widget's ideal size as given by `QWidget::sizeHint()` and then stretches any stretchable widgets to fill the available space. A widget's ideal size is itself dependent on the widget's content and varies as we change the content. To avoid constant resizing of the location and MOD indicators, we set their minimum sizes to be wide enough to contain the largest possible text on each of the indicators ("W999" and "MOD"), with a little extra space. We also set their alignment to `AlignHCenter` to horizontally center their text.

Near the end of the function, we connect two of `Spreadsheet`'s signals to two of `MainWindow`'s slots: `updateCellIndicators()` and `spreadsheetModified()`.

```
    void MainWindow::updateCellIndicators()
    {
        locationLabel->setText(spreadsheet->currentLocation());
        formulaLabel->setText(" " + spreadsheet->currentFormula());
    }
```

The `updateCellIndicator()` slot updates the cell location and the cell formula indicators. It is called whenever the user moves the cell cursor to a new cell. The slot is also used as an ordinary function at the end of `createStatusBar()` to initialize the indicators. This is necessary because `Spreadsheet` doesn't emit a `currentChanged()` signal at startup.

```
    void MainWindow::spreadsheetModified()
    {
```

```
        modLabel->setText(tr("MOD"));
        modified = true;
        updateCellIndicators();
    }
```

The `spreadsheetModified()` slot updates all three indicators so that they reflect the current state of affairs, and sets the `modified` variable to `true`. (We used the `modified` variable when implementing the File menu to determine whether or not there were unsaved changes.)

## Using Dialogs

In this section, we will explain how to use dialogs in Qt—how to create and initialize them, run them, and respond to choices made by the user interacting with them. We will make use of the Find, Go-to-Cell, and Sort dialogs that we created in Chapter 2. We will also create a simple About box.

We will begin with the Find dialog. Since we want the user to be able to switch between the main Spreadsheet window and the Find dialog at will, the Find dialog must be modeless. A *modeless* window is one that runs independently of any other windows in the application.

When modeless dialogs are created, they normally have their signals connected to slots that respond to the user's interactions.

```
    void MainWindow::find()
    {
        if (!findDialog) {
            findDialog = new FindDialog(this);
            connect(findDialog, SIGNAL(findNext(const QString &, bool)),
                    spreadsheet, SLOT(findNext(const QString &, bool)));
            connect(findDialog, SIGNAL(findPrev(const QString &, bool)),
                    spreadsheet, SLOT(findPrev(const QString &, bool)));
        }

        findDialog->show();
        findDialog->raise();
        findDialog->setActiveWindow();
    }
```

The Find dialog is a window that enables the user to search for text in the spreadsheet. The `find()` slot is called when the user clicks Edit|Find to pop up the Find dialog. At that point, several scenarios are possible:

- This is the first time the user has invoked the Find dialog.

- The Find dialog was invoked before, but the user closed it.

- The Find dialog was invoked before and is still visible.

If the Find dialog doesn't already exist, we create it and connect its `findNext()` and `findPrev()` signals to `Spreadsheet`'s matching slots. We could also have created the dialog in the `MainWindow` constructor, but delaying its creation makes startup faster. Also, if the dialog is never used, it is never created, saving both time and memory.

Then we call `show()`, `raise()`, and `setActiveWindow()` to ensure that the window is visible, on top of the others, and active. A call to `show()` alone is sufficient to make a hidden window visible, but the Find dialog may be invoked when its window is already visible, in which case `show()` does nothing. Since we must make the dialog's window visible, active, and on top regardless of its previous state, we must use the `raise()` and `setActiveWindow()` calls. An alternative would have been to write

```
if (findDialog->isHidden()) {
    findDialog->show();
} else {
    findDialog->raise();
    findDialog->setActiveWindow();
}
```

the programming equivalent of driving along at 90 in a 100 km/h zone.

We will now look at the Go-to-Cell dialog. We want the user to pop it up, use it, and close it without being able to switch from the Go-to-Cell dialog to any other window in the application. This means that the Go-to-Cell dialog must be modal. A *modal* window is a window that pops up when invoked and blocks the application, preventing any other processing or interactions from taking place until the window is closed. With the exception of the Find dialog, all the dialogs we have used so far have been modal.

A dialog is modeless if it's invoked using `show()` (unless we call `setModal()` beforehand to make it modal); it is modal if it's invoked using `exec()`. When we invoke modal dialogs using `exec()`, we typically don't need to set up any signal–slot connections.

```
void MainWindow::goToCell()
{
    GoToCellDialog dialog(this);
    if (dialog.exec()) {
        QString str = dialog.lineEdit->text();
        spreadsheet->setCurrentCell(str.mid(1).toInt() - 1,
                                    str[0].upper().unicode() - 'A');
    }
}
```

The `QDialog::exec()` function returns `true` if the dialog is accepted, `false` otherwise. (Recall that when we created the Go-to-Cell dialog using *Qt Designer* in Chapter 2, we connected OK to `accept()` and Cancel to `reject()`.) If the user chooses OK, we set the current cell to the value in the line editor; if the user chooses Cancel, `exec()` returns `false` and we do nothing.

The `QTable::setCurrentCell()` function expects two arguments: a row index and a column index. In the Spreadsheet application, cell A1 is cell (0, 0) and cell B27 is cell (26, 1). To obtain the row index from the QString returned by `QLabel::text()`, we extract the row number using `QString::mid()` (which returns a substring from the start position to the end of the string), convert it to an `int` using `QString::toInt()`, and subtract 1 to make it 0-based. For the column number, we subtract the numeric value of 'A' from the numeric value of the string's upper-cased first character.

Unlike Find, the Go-to-Cell dialog is created on the stack. This is a common programming pattern for modal dialogs, just as it is for context menus, since we don't need the dialog after we have used it.

We will now turn to the Sort dialog. The Sort dialog is a modal dialog that allows the user to sort the currently selected area by the columns they specify. Figure 3.14 shows an example of sorting, with column B as the primary sort key and column A as the secondary sort key (both ascending).

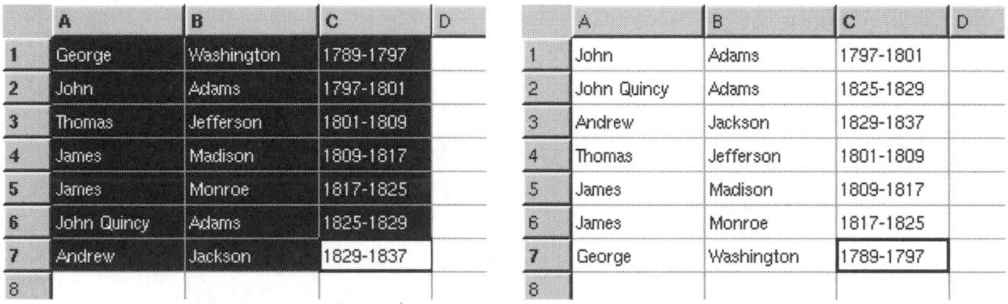

| | A | B | C | D |
|---|---|---|---|---|
| 1 | George | Washington | 1789-1797 | |
| 2 | John | Adams | 1797-1801 | |
| 3 | Thomas | Jefferson | 1801-1809 | |
| 4 | James | Madison | 1809-1817 | |
| 5 | James | Monroe | 1817-1825 | |
| 6 | John Quincy | Adams | 1825-1829 | |
| 7 | Andrew | Jackson | 1829-1837 | |
| 8 | | | | |

| | A | B | C | D |
|---|---|---|---|---|
| 1 | John | Adams | 1797-1801 | |
| 2 | John Quincy | Adams | 1825-1829 | |
| 3 | Andrew | Jackson | 1829-1837 | |
| 4 | Thomas | Jefferson | 1801-1809 | |
| 5 | James | Madison | 1809-1817 | |
| 6 | James | Monroe | 1817-1825 | |
| 7 | George | Washington | 1789-1797 | |
| 8 | | | | |

(a) Before sort                                    (b) After sort

**Figure 3.14.** Sorting the spreadsheet's selected area

```
void MainWindow::sort()
{
    SortDialog dialog(this);
    QTableSelection sel = spreadsheet->selection();
    dialog.setColumnRange('A' + sel.leftCol(), 'A' + sel.rightCol());

    if (dialog.exec()) {
        SpreadsheetCompare compare;
        compare.keys[0] =
            dialog.primaryColumnCombo->currentItem();
        compare.keys[1] =
            dialog.secondaryColumnCombo->currentItem() - 1;
        compare.keys[2] =
            dialog.tertiaryColumnCombo->currentItem() - 1;
        compare.ascending[0] =
            (dialog.primaryOrderCombo->currentItem() == 0);
        compare.ascending[1] =
            (dialog.secondaryOrderCombo->currentItem() == 0);
        compare.ascending[2] =
            (dialog.tertiaryOrderCombo->currentItem() == 0);
        spreadsheet->sort(compare);
    }
}
```

The code in `sort()` follows a similar pattern to that used for `goToCell()`:

- We create the dialog on the stack and initialize it.

- We pop up the dialog using `exec()`.

- If the user clicks OK, we extract the values entered by the user from the dialog's widgets and make use of them.

The `compare` object stores the primary, secondary, and tertiary sort keys and sort orders. (We will see the definition of the `SpreadsheetCompare` class in the next chapter.) The object is used by `Spreadsheet::sort()` to compare two rows. The `keys` array stores the column numbers of the keys. For example, if the selection extends from C2 to E5, column C has position 0. The `ascending` array stores the order associated with each key as a `bool`. `QComboBox::currentItem()` returns the index of the currently selected item, starting at 0. For the secondary and tertiary keys, we subtract one from the current item to account for the "None" item.

The `sort()` dialog does the job, but it is very fragile. It takes for granted that the Sort dialog is implemented in a certain way, with comboboxes and "None" items. This means that if we redesign the Sort dialog, we may also need to rewrite this code. While this approach is adequate for a dialog that is only called from one place, it opens the door to maintenance nightmares if the dialog is used in several places.

A more robust approach is to make the `SortDialog` class smarter by having it create a `SpreadsheetCompare` object itself, which can then be accessed by its caller. This simplifies `MainWindow::sort()` significantly:

```
void MainWindow::sort()
{
    SortDialog dialog(this);
    QTableSelection sel = spreadsheet->selection();
    dialog.setColumnRange('A' + sel.leftCol(), 'A' + sel.rightCol());
    if (dialog.exec())
        spreadsheet->performSort(dialog.comparisonObject());
}
```

This approach leads to loosely coupled components and is almost always the right choice for dialogs that will be called from more than one place.

A more radical approach is to pass a pointer to the `Spreadsheet` object when initializing the `SortDialog` object and to allow the dialog to operate directly on the `Spreadsheet`. This makes the `SortDialog` much less general, since it will only work on a certain type of widget, but it simplifies the code ever further by eliminating the `SortDialog::setColumnRange()` function. The `MainWindow::sort()` function then becomes

```
void MainWindow::sort()
{
    SortDialog dialog(this);
    dialog.setSpreadsheet(spreadsheet);
```

```
        dialog.exec();
    }
```

This approach mirrors the first: Instead of the caller needing intimate knowledge of the dialog, the dialog needs intimate knowledge of the data structures supplied by the caller. This approach may be useful where the dialog needs to apply changes live. But just as the caller code is fragile using the first approach, this third approach breaks if the data structures change.

Some developers choose just one approach to using dialogs and stick with that. This has the benefit of familiarity and simplicity since all their dialog usages follow the same pattern, but it also misses the benefits of the approaches that are not used. The decision on which approach to use should be made on a per-dialog basis.

We will round off this section with a simple About box. We could create a custom dialog like the Find or Go-to-Cell dialogs to present the "about" information, but since most About boxes are highly stylized, Qt provides a simpler solution.

```
void MainWindow::about()
{
    QMessageBox::about(this, tr("About Spreadsheet"),
            tr("<h2>Spreadsheet 1.0</h2>"
               "<p>Copyright &copy; 2003 Software Inc."
               "<p>Spreadsheet is a small application that "
               "demonstrates <b>QAction</b>, <b>QMainWindow</b>, "
               "<b>QMenuBar</b>, <b>QStatusBar</b>, "
               "<b>QToolBar</b>, and many other Qt classes."));
}
```

The About box is obtained by calling `QMessageBox::about()`, a static convenience function. The function is very similar to `QMessageBox::warning()`, except that it uses the parent window's icon instead of the standard "warning" icon.

**Figure 3.15.** About Spreadsheet

So far we have used several convenience static functions from both `QMessageBox` and `QFileDialog`. These functions create a dialog, initialize it, and call `exec()` on it. It is also possible, although less convenient, to create a `QMessageBox` or a `QFileDialog` widget like any other widget and explicitly call `exec()`, or even `show()`, on it.

# Storing Settings

In the `MainWindow` constructor, we called `readSettings()` to load the application's stored settings. Similarly, in `closeEvent()`, we called `writeSettings()` to save the settings. These two functions are the last `MainWindow` member functions that need to be implemented.

The arrangement we opted for in `MainWindow`, with all the `QSettings`-related code in `readSettings()` and `writeSettings()`, is just one of many possible approaches. A `QSettings` object can be created to query or modify some setting at any time during the execution of the application and from anywhere in the code.

```
void MainWindow::writeSettings()
{
    QSettings settings;
    settings.setPath("software-inc.com", "Spreadsheet");
    settings.beginGroup("/Spreadsheet");
    settings.writeEntry("/geometry/x", x());
    settings.writeEntry("/geometry/y", y());
    settings.writeEntry("/geometry/width", width());
    settings.writeEntry("/geometry/height", height());
    settings.writeEntry("/recentFiles", recentFiles);
    settings.writeEntry("/showGrid", showGridAct->isOn());
    settings.writeEntry("/autoRecalc", showGridAct->isOn());
    settings.endGroup();
}
```

The `writeSettings()` function saves the main window's geometry (position and size), the list of recently opened files, and the Show Grid and Auto-recalculate options.

`QSettings` stores the application's settings in platform-specific locations. On Windows, it uses the system registry; on Unix, it stores the data in text files; on Mac OS X, it uses the Carbon preferences API. The `setPath()` call provides `QSettings` with the organization's name (as an Internet domain name) and the product's name. This information is used in a platform specific way to find a location for the settings.

`QSettings` stores settings as *key–value* pairs. The *key* is similar to a file system path and should always start with the name of the application. For example, `/Spreadsheet/geometry/x` and `/Spreadsheet/showGrid` are valid keys. (The `beginGroup()` call saves us from writing `/Spreadsheet` in front of every key.) The *value* can be an `int`, a `bool`, a `double`, a `QString`, or a `QStringList`.

```
void MainWindow::readSettings()
{
    QSettings settings;
    settings.setPath("software-inc.com", "Spreadsheet");
    settings.beginGroup("/Spreadsheet");

    int x = settings.readNumEntry("/geometry/x", 200);
    int y = settings.readNumEntry("/geometry/y", 200);
```

```
    int w = settings.readNumEntry("/geometry/width", 400);
    int h = settings.readNumEntry("/geometry/height", 400);
    move(x, y);
    resize(w, h);

    recentFiles = settings.readListEntry("/recentFiles");
    updateRecentFileItems();

    showGridAct->setOn(
            settings.readBoolEntry("/showGrid", true));
    autoRecalcAct->setOn(
            settings.readBoolEntry("/autoRecalc", true));

    settings.endGroup();
}
```

The `readSettings()` function loads the settings that were saved by `writeSettings()`. The second argument to the "read" functions specifies a default value, in case there are no settings available. The default values are used the first time the application is run.

We have now completed the Spreadsheet's `MainWindow` implementation. In the following sections, we will discuss how the Spreadsheet application can be modified to handle multiple documents and how to implement a splash screen. We will complete its functionality in the next chapter.

## Multiple Documents

We are now ready to code the Spreadsheet application's `main()` function:

```
    #include <qapplication.h>

    #include "mainwindow.h"

    int main(int argc, char *argv[])
    {
        QApplication app(argc, argv);
        MainWindow mainWin;
        app.setMainWidget(&mainWin);
        mainWin.show();
        return app.exec();
    }
```

This `main()` function is a little bit different from those we have written so far: We have created the `MainWindow` instance as a variable on the stack instead of using `new`. The `MainWindow` instance is then automatically destroyed when the function terminates.

With the `main()` function shown above, the Spreadsheet application provides a single main window and can only handle one document at a time. If we want to edit multiple documents at the same time, we could start multiple instances of the Spreadsheet application. But this isn't as convenient for users as having a single instance of the application providing multiple main windows, just as one instance of a web browser can provide multiple browser windows simultaneously.

We will modify the Spreadsheet application so that it can handle multiple documents. First, we need a slightly different File menu:

- File|New creates a new main window with an empty document, instead of recycling the current main window.
- File|Close closes the current main window.
- File|Exit closes all windows.

**Figure 3.16.** The new File menu

In the original version of the File menu, there was no Close option because that would have been the same as Exit.

This is the new `main()` function:

```
#include <qapplication.h>

#include "mainwindow.h"

int main(int argc, char *argv[])
{
    QApplication app(argc, argv);
    MainWindow *mainWin = new MainWindow;
    mainWin->show();
    QObject::connect(&app, SIGNAL(lastWindowClosed()),
                     &app, SLOT(quit()));
    return app.exec();
}
```

We connect QApplication's `lastWindowClosed()` slot to QApplication's `quit()` slot, which will terminate the application.

With multiple windows, it now makes sense to create MainWindow with new, because then we can use `delete` on a main window when we have finished with it to save memory. This issue doesn't arise if the application uses just one main window.

This is the new `MainWindow::newFile()` slot:

```
void MainWindow::newFile()
{
    MainWindow *mainWin = new MainWindow;
    mainWin->show();
}
```

We simply create a new MainWindow instance. It may seem odd that we don't keep any pointer to the new window, but that isn't a problem since Qt keeps track of all the windows for us.

These are the actions for Close and Exit:

```
closeAct = new QAction(tr("&Close"), tr("Ctrl+W"), this);
connect(closeAct, SIGNAL(activated()), this, SLOT(close()));

exitAct = new QAction(tr("E&xit"), tr("Ctrl+Q"), this);
connect(exitAct, SIGNAL(activated()),
        qApp, SLOT(closeAllWindows()));
```

QApplication's closeAllWindows() slot closes all of the application's windows, unless one of them rejects the close event. This is exactly the behavior we need here. We don't have to worry about unsaved changes because that's handled in MainWindow::closeEvent() whenever a window is closed.

It looks as if we have finished making the application capable of handling multiple windows. Unfortunately, there is a hidden problem lurking: If the user keeps creating and closing main windows, the machine might run out of memory! This is because we keep creating MainWindow widgets in newFile() but we never delete them. When the user closes a main window, the default behavior is to hide it, so it still remains in memory. With many main windows, this can be a problem.

The solution is to add the WDestructiveClose flag to the constructor:

```
MainWindow::MainWindow(QWidget *parent, const char *name)
    : QMainWindow(parent, name, WDestructiveClose)
{
    ...
}
```

This tells Qt to delete the window when it is closed. The WDestructiveClose flag is one of many flags that can be passed to the QWidget constructor to influence a widget's behavior. Most of the other flags are rarely needed in Qt applications.

Memory leaking isn't the only problem that we must deal with. Our original application design included an implied assumption that we would only have one main window. With multiple windows, each main window has its own recently opened files list and its own options. Clearly, the recently opened files list should be global to the whole application. We can achieve this quite easily by declaring the recentFiles variable static, so that only one instance of it exists for the whole application. But then we must ensure that wherever we called updateRecentFileItems() to update the File menu, we must call it on all main windows. Here's the code to achieve this:

```
QWidgetList *list = QApplication::topLevelWidgets();
QWidgetListIt it(*list);
QWidget *widget;
while ((widget = it.current())) {
    if (widget->inherits("MainWindow"))
        ((MainWindow *)widget)->updateRecentFileItems();
    ++it;
}
delete list;
```

The code iterates over all the application's top-level widgets and calls `update-RecentFileItems()` on all widgets of type `MainWindow`. Similar code can be used for synchronizing the Show Grid and Auto-recalculate options, or to make sure that the same file isn't loaded twice. The `QWidgetList` type is a typedef for `QPtrList<QWidget>`, which is presented in Chapter 11 (Container Classes).

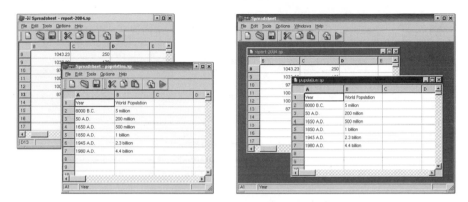

**Figure 3.17.** SDI vs. MDI

Applications that provide one document per main window are said to be SDI (single document interface) applications. A popular alternative is MDI (multiple document interface), where the application has a single main window that manages multiple document windows within its central area. Qt can be used to create both SDI and MDI applications on all its supported platforms. Figure 3.17 shows the Spreadsheet application using both approaches. MDI is explained in Chapter 6 (Layout Management).

## Splash Screens

Many applications present a splash screen at startup. Some developers use a splash screen to disguise a slow startup, while others do it to satisfy their marketing departments. Adding a splash screen to Qt applications is very easy using the `QSplashScreen` class.

The `QSplashScreen` class shows an image before the application proper has started. It can also draw a message on the image, to inform the user about the progress of the application's initialization process. Typically, the splash screen code is located in `main()`, before the call to `QApplication::exec()`.

Below is an example `main()` function that uses `QSplashScreen` to present a splash screen in an application that loads modules and establishes network connections at startup.

```
int main(int argc, char *argv[])
{
    QApplication app(argc, argv);
```

```
QSplashScreen *splash =
        new QSplashScreen(QPixmap::fromMimeSource("splash.png"));
splash->show();

splash->message(QObject::tr("Setting up the main window..."),
            Qt::AlignRight | Qt::AlignTop, Qt::white);
MainWindow mainWin;
app.setMainWidget(&mainWin);

splash->message(QObject::tr("Loading modules..."),
            Qt::AlignRight | Qt::AlignTop, Qt::white);
loadModules();

splash->message(QObject::tr("Establishing connections..."),
            Qt::AlignRight | Qt::AlignTop, Qt::white);
establishConnections();

mainWin.show();
splash->finish(&mainWin);
delete splash;

return app.exec();
}
```

**Figure 3.18.** A `QSplashScreen` widget

We have now completed the Spreadsheet application's user interface. In the next chapter, we will complete the application by implementing the core spreadsheet functionality.

# Implementing Application Functionality

In the previous two chapters, we explained how to create the Spreadsheet application's user interface. In this chapter, we will complete the program by coding its underlying functionality. Among other things, we will see how to load and save files, how to store data in memory, how to implement clipboard operations, and how to add support for spreadsheet formulas to QTable.

## The Central Widget

The central area of a QMainWindow can be occupied by any kind of widget. Here's an overview of the possibilities:

**1. Use a standard Qt widget.**

A standard widget like QTable or QTextEdit can be used as a central widget. In this case, the application's functionality, such as loading and saving files, must be implemented elsewhere (for example, in a QMainWindow subclass).

**2. Use a custom widget.**

Specialized applications often need to show data in a custom widget. For example, an icon editor program would have an IconEditor widget as its central widget. Chapter 5 explains how to write custom widgets in Qt.

**3. Use a plain QWidget with a layout manager.**

Sometimes the application's central area is occupied by many widgets. This can be done by using a QWidget as the parent of all the other widgets, and using layout managers to size and position the child widgets.

69

**4. Use a splitter.**

Another way of using multiple widgets together is to use a QSplitter. The QSplitter arranges its child widgets side by side like a QHBox, or in a column like a QVBox, with splitter handles to give some sizing control to the user. Splitters can contain all kinds of widgets, including other splitters.

**5. Use an MDI workspace.**

If the application uses MDI, the central area is occupied by a QWorkspace widget, and each of the MDI windows is a child of that widget.

Layouts, splitters, and MDI workspaces can be used in combination with standard Qt widgets or with custom widgets. Chapter 6 covers these classes in depth.

For the Spreadsheet application, a QTable subclass is used as the central widget. The QTable class already provides most of the spreadsheet capability we need, but it doesn't understand spreadsheet formulas like "=A1+A2+A3", and it doesn't support clipboard operations. We will implement this missing functionality in the Spreadsheet class, which inherits from QTable.

## Subclassing QTable

We will now start implementing the Spreadsheet widget, beginning with the header file:

```
#ifndef SPREADSHEET_H
#define SPREADSHEET_H

#include <qstringlist.h>
#include <qtable.h>

class Cell;
class SpreadsheetCompare;
```

The header starts with forward declarations for the Cell and SpreadsheetCompare classes.

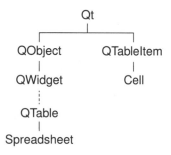

**Figure 4.1.** Inheritance tree for Spreadsheet and Cell

The attributes of a `QTable` cell, such as its text and its alignment, are stored in a `QTableItem`. Unlike `QTable`, `QTableItem` isn't a widget class; it is a pure data class. The `Cell` class is a `QTableItem` subclass. In addition to the standard `QTableItem` attributes, `Cell` stores a cell's formula.

We will explain the `Cell` class when we present its implementation in the last section of this chapter.

```cpp
class Spreadsheet : public QTable
{
    Q_OBJECT
public:
    Spreadsheet(QWidget *parent = 0, const char *name = 0);

    void clear();
    QString currentLocation() const;
    QString currentFormula() const;
    bool autoRecalculate() const { return autoRecalc; }
    bool readFile(const QString &fileName);
    bool writeFile(const QString &fileName);
    QTableSelection selection();
    void sort(const SpreadsheetCompare &compare);
```

The `Spreadsheet` class inherits from `QTable`. Subclassing `QTable` is very similar to subclassing `QDialog` or `QMainWindow`.

In Chapter 3, we relied on many public functions in `Spreadsheet` when we implemented `MainWindow`. For example, we called `clear()` from `MainWindow::newFile()` to reset the spreadsheet. We also used some functions inherited from `QTable`, notably `setCurrentCell()` and `setShowGrid()`.

```cpp
public slots:
    void cut();
    void copy();
    void paste();
    void del();
    void selectRow();
    void selectColumn();
    void selectAll();
    void recalculate();
    void setAutoRecalculate(bool on);
    void findNext(const QString &str, bool caseSensitive);
    void findPrev(const QString &str, bool caseSensitive);

signals:
    void modified();
```

`Spreadsheet` provides many slots that implement actions from the Edit, Tools, and Options menus.

```cpp
protected:
    QWidget *createEditor(int row, int col, bool initFromCell) const;
    void endEdit(int row, int col, bool accepted, bool wasReplacing);
```

Spreadsheet reimplements two virtual functions from QTable. These functions are called by QTable itself when the user starts editing the value of a cell. We need to reimplement them to support spreadsheet formulas.

```
private:
    enum { MagicNumber = 0x7F51C882, NumRows = 999, NumCols = 26 };

    Cell *cell(int row, int col) const;
    void setFormula(int row, int col, const QString &formula);
    QString formula(int row, int col) const;
    void somethingChanged();

    bool autoRecalc;
};
```

In the class's private section, we define three constants, four functions, and one variable.

```
class SpreadsheetCompare
{
public:
    bool operator()(const QStringList &row1,
                    const QStringList &row2) const;

    enum { NumKeys = 3 };
    int keys[NumKeys];
    bool ascending[NumKeys];
};

#endif
```

The header file ends with the SpreadsheetCompare class declaration. We will explain this when we review Spreadsheet::sort().

We will now look at the implementation, explaining each function in turn:

```
#include <qapplication.h>
#include <qclipboard.h>
#include <qdatastream.h>
#include <qfile.h>
#include <qlineedit.h>
#include <qmessagebox.h>
#include <qregexp.h>
#include <qvariant.h>

#include <algorithm>
#include <vector>
using namespace std;

#include "cell.h"
#include "spreadsheet.h"
```

We include the header files for the Qt classes the application will use. We also include the standard C++ <algorithm> and <vector> header files. The using namespace directive imports all the symbols from the std namespace into the global namespace, allowing us to write stable_sort() and vector<T> instead of std::stable_sort() and std::vector<T>.

```
Spreadsheet::Spreadsheet(QWidget *parent, const char *name)
    : QTable(parent, name)
{
    autoRecalc = true;
    setSelectionMode(Single);
    clear();
}
```

In the constructor, we set the QTable selection mode to Single. This ensures that only one rectangular area in the spreadsheet can be selected at a time.

```
void Spreadsheet::clear()
{
    setNumRows(0);
    setNumCols(0);
    setNumRows(NumRows);
    setNumCols(NumCols);
    for (int i = 0; i < NumCols; i++)
        horizontalHeader()->setLabel(i, QChar('A' + i));
    setCurrentCell(0, 0);
}
```

The clear() function is called from the Spreadsheet constructor to initialize the spreadsheet. It is also called from MainWindow::newFile().

We resize the spreadsheet down to 0 × 0, effectively clearing the whole spreadsheet, and resize it again to NumCols × NumRows (26 × 999). We change the column labels to "A", "B", ..., "Z" (the default is "1", "2", ..., "26") and move the cell cursor to cell A1.

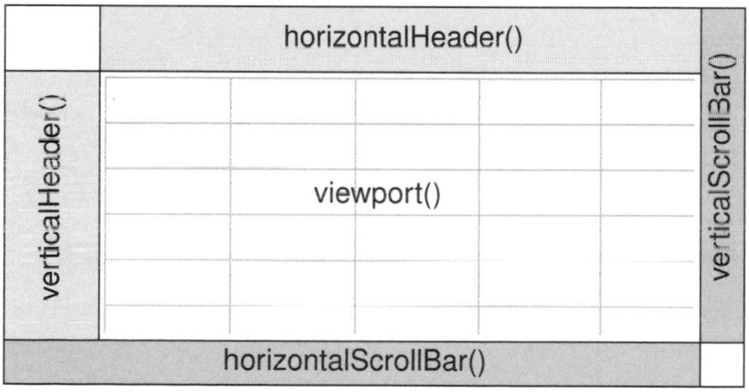

**Figure 4.2.** QTable's constituent widgets

A QTable is composed of many child widgets. It has a horizontal QHeader at the top, a vertical QHeader on the left, a QScrollBar on the right, and a QScrollBar at the bottom. The area in the middle is occupied by a special widget called the *viewport*, on which QTable draws the cells. The different child widgets are accessible through functions in QTable and its base class, QScrollView. For example, in clear(), we access the table's top QHeader through QTable:: horizontalHeader().

## Storing Data as Items

In the Spreadsheet application, every non-empty cell is stored in memory as an individual `QTableItem` object. This pattern of storing data as items is not specific to `QTable`; Qt's `QIconView`, `QListBox`, and `QListView` classes also operate on items (`QIconViewItems`, `QListBoxItems`, and `QListViewItems`).

Qt's item classes can be used out of the box as data holders. For example, a `QTableItem` already stores a few attributes, including a string, a pixmap, and a pointer back to the `QTable`. By subclassing the item class, we can store additional data and reimplement virtual functions to use that data.

Many toolkits provide a `void` pointer in their item classes to store custom data. Qt doesn't burden every item with a pointer that may not be used; instead, it gives programmers the freedom to subclass the item classes and to store the data there, possibly as a pointer to another data structure. If a `void` pointer is required, it can be trivially achieved by subclassing an item class and adding a `void` pointer member variable.

With `QTable`, it is possible to bypass the item mechanism by reimplementing low-level functions such as `paintCell()` and `clearCell()`. If the data to display in a `QTable` is already available in memory in another data structure, this approach can be used to avoid data duplication. For details, see the *Qt Quarterly* article "A Model/View Table for Large Datasets", available online at `http://doc.trolltech.com/qq/qq07-big-tables.html`.

Qt 4 is expected to be more flexible than Qt 3 for storing data. In addition to supporting items, Qt 4 will probably offer a single unified item type usable by all item views, and the item views will not take ownership of the items they display, making it possible to display the same items in multiple views simultaneously.

`QScrollView` is the natural base class for widgets that can present lots of data. It provides a scrollable viewport and two scroll bars, which can be turned on and off. It is covered in Chapter 6.

```
Cell *Spreadsheet::cell(int row, int col) const
{
    return (Cell *)item(row, col);
}
```

The `cell()` private function returns the `Cell` object for a given row and column. It is almost the same as `QTable::item()`, except that it returns a `Cell` pointer instead of a `QTableItem` pointer.

```
QString Spreadsheet::formula(int row, int col) const
{
    Cell *c = cell(row, col);
    if (c)
        return c->formula();
    else
```

```
        return "";
}
```

The `formula()` private function returns the formula for a given cell. If `cell()` returns a null pointer, the cell is empty, so we return an empty string.

```
void Spreadsheet::setFormula(int row, int col,
                             const QString &formula)
{
    Cell *c = cell(row, col);
    if (c) {
        c->setFormula(formula);
        updateCell(row, col);
    } else {
        setItem(row, col, new Cell(this, formula));
    }
}
```

The `setFormula()` private function sets the formula for a given cell. If the cell already has a `Cell` object, we reuse it and call `updateCell()` to tell `QTable` to repaint the cell if it's shown on screen. Otherwise, we create a new `Cell` object and call `QTable::setItem()` to insert it into the table and repaint the cell. We don't need to worry about deleting the `Cell` object later on; `QTable` takes ownership of the cell and will delete it automatically at the right time.

```
QString Spreadsheet::currentLocation() const
{
    return QChar('A' + currentColumn())
           + QString::number(currentRow() + 1);
}
```

The `currentLocation()` function returns the current cell's location in the usual spreadsheet format of column letter followed by row number. `MainWindow::updateCellIndicators()` uses it to show the location in the status bar.

```
QString Spreadsheet::currentFormula() const
{
    return formula(currentRow(), currentColumn());
}
```

The `currentFormula()` function returns the current cell's formula. It is called from `MainWindow::updateCellIndicators()`.

```
QWidget *Spreadsheet::createEditor(int row, int col,
                                   bool initFromCell) const
{
    QLineEdit *lineEdit = new QLineEdit(viewport());
    lineEdit->setFrame(false);
    if (initFromCell)
        lineEdit->setText(formula(row, col));
    return lineEdit;
}
```

The `createEditor()` function is reimplemented from `QTable`. It is called when the user starts editing a cell—either by clicking the cell, pressing F2, or simply starting to type. Its role is to create an editor widget to be shown on top of the cell. If the user clicked the cell or pressed F2 to edit the cell, initFromCell is true and the editor must start with the current cell's content. If the user simply started typing, the cell's previous content is ignored.

The default behavior of this function is to create a QLineEdit and initialize it with the cell's text if initFromCell is true. We reimplement the function to show the cell's formula instead of the cell's text.

We create the QLineEdit as a child of the QTable's viewport. QTable takes care of resizing the QLineEdit to match the cell's size and of positioning it over the cell that is to be edited. QTable also takes care of deleting the QLineEdit when it is no longer needed.

Cell                        QLineEdit

**Figure 4.3.** Editing a cell by superimposing a QLineEdit

In many cases, the formula and the text are the same; for example, the formula "Hello" evaluates to the string "Hello", so if the user types "Hello" into a cell and presses Enter, that cell will show the text "Hello". But there are some exceptions:

- If the formula is a number, it is interpreted as such. For example, the formula "1.50" evaluates to the double value 1.5, which is rendered as a right-aligned "1.5" in the spreadsheet.

- If the formula starts with a single quote, the rest of the formula is interpreted as text. For example, the formula "'12345" evaluates to the string "12345".

- If the formula starts with an equals sign ('='), the formula is interpreted as an arithmetic formula. For example, if cell A1 contains "12" and cell A2 contains "6", the formula "=A1+A2" evaluates to 18.

The task of converting a formula into a value is performed by the Cell class. For the moment, the important thing to bear in mind is that the text shown in the cell is the result of evaluating the formula, not the formula itself.

```
void Spreadsheet::endEdit(int row, int col, bool accepted,
                          bool wasReplacing)
{
    QLineEdit *lineEdit = (QLineEdit *)cellWidget(row, col);
    if (!lineEdit)
        return;
    QString oldFormula = formula(row, col);
    QString newFormula = lineEdit->text();

    QTable::endEdit(row, col, false, wasReplacing);

    if (accepted && newFormula != oldFormula) {
        setFormula(row, col, newFormula);
```

```
            somethingChanged();
        }
    }
```

The `endEdit()` function is reimplemented from `QTable`. It is called when the user has finished editing a cell, either by clicking elsewhere in the spreadsheet (which confirms the edit), by pressing Enter (which also confirms the edit), or by pressing Esc (which rejects the edit). The function's purpose is to transfer the editor's content back into the `Cell` object if the edit is confirmed.

The editor is available from `QTable::cellWidget()`. We can safely cast it to a `QLineEdit` since the widget we create in `createEditor()` is always a `QLineEdit`.

QLineEdit        Cell

**Figure 4.4.** Returning a `QLineEdit`'s content to a cell

In the middle of the function, we call `QTable`'s implementation of `endEdit()`, because `QTable` needs to know when editing has finished. We pass `false` as third argument to `endEdit()` to prevent it from modifying the table item, since we want to create or modify it ourselves. If the new formula is different from the old one, we call `setFormula()` to modify the `Cell` object and call `something-Changed()`.

```
void Spreadsheet::somethingChanged()
{
    if (autoRecalc)
        recalculate();
    emit modified();
}
```

The `somethingChanged()` private function recalculates the whole spreadsheet if Auto-recalculate is enabled and emits the `modified()` signal.

## Loading and Saving

We will now implement the loading and saving of Spreadsheet files using a custom binary format. We will do this using `QFile` and `QDataStream`, which together provide platform-independent binary I/O.

We will start with writing a Spreadsheet file:

```
bool Spreadsheet::writeFile(const QString &fileName)
{
    QFile file(fileName);
    if (!file.open(IO_WriteOnly)) {
        QMessageBox::warning(this, tr("Spreadsheet"),
                             tr("Cannot write file %1:\n%2.")
                             .arg(file.name())
                             .arg(file.errorString())));
        return false;
```

```
    }

    QDataStream out(&file);
    out.setVersion(5);

    out << (Q_UINT32)MagicNumber;

    QApplication::setOverrideCursor(waitCursor);
    for (int row = 0; row < NumRows; ++row) {
        for (int col = 0; col < NumCols; ++col) {
            QString str = formula(row, col);
            if (!str.isEmpty())
                out << (Q_UINT16)row << (Q_UINT16)col << str;
        }
    }
    QApplication::restoreOverrideCursor();
    return true;
}
```

The `writeFile()` function is called from `MainWindow::saveFile()` to write the file to disk. It returns `true` on success, `false` on error.

We create a `QFile` object with the given file name and call `open()` to open the file for writing. We also create a `QDataStream` object that operates on the `QFile` and use it to write out the data. Just before we write the data, we change the application's cursor to the standard wait cursor (usually an hourglass) and restore the normal cursor once all the data is written. At the end of the function, the file is automatically closed by `QFile`'s destructor.

`QDataStream` supports basic C++ types as well as many of Qt's types. The syntax is modeled after the standard `<iostream>` classes. For example,

```
    out << x << y << z;
```

writes the variables `x`, `y`, and `z` to a stream, and

```
    in >> x >> y >> z;
```

reads them from a stream.

Because the C++ basic types `char`, `short`, `int`, `long`, and `long long` may have different sizes on different platforms, it is safest to cast these values to one of `Q_INT8`, `Q_UINT8`, `Q_INT16`, `Q_UINT16`, `Q_INT32`, `Q_UINT32`, `Q_INT64`, and `Q_UINT64`, which are guaranteed to be of the size they advertise (in bits).

`QDataStream` is very versatile. It can be used on a `QFile`, but also on a `QBuffer`, a `QSocket`, or a `QSocketDevice`. Similarly, `QFile` can be used with a `QTextStream` instead of `QDataStream`, or even raw. Chapter 10 explains these classes in depth.

The Spreadsheet application's file format is fairly simple. A Spreadsheet file starts with a 32-bit number that identifies the file format (`MagicNumber`, defined as 0x7F51C882 in `spreadsheet.h`). Then come a series of blocks, each of which contains a single cell's row, column, and formula. To save space, we don't write out empty cells.

**Figure 4.5.** The Spreadsheet file format

The precise binary representation of the data types is determined by QData-Stream. For example, a Q_UINT16 is represented as two bytes in big-endian order, and a QString as the string's length followed by the Unicode characters.

The binary representation of Qt types has evolved quite a lot since Qt 1.0. It is likely to continue evolving in future Qt releases to keep pace with the evolution of existing types and to allow for new Qt types. By default, QDataStream uses the most recent version of the binary format (version 5 in Qt 3.2), but it can be set to read older versions. To avoid any compatibility problems if the application is recompiled later using a newer Qt release, we tell QDataStream to use version 5 irrespective of the version of Qt we are compiling against.

```cpp
bool Spreadsheet::readFile(const QString &fileName)
{
    QFile file(fileName);
    if (!file.open(IO_ReadOnly)) {
        QMessageBox::warning(this, tr("Spreadsheet"),
                             tr("Cannot read file %1:\n%2.")
                             .arg(file.name())
                             .arg(file.errorString()));
        return false;
    }

    QDataStream in(&file);
    in.setVersion(5);

    Q_UINT32 magic;
    in >> magic;
    if (magic != MagicNumber) {
        QMessageBox::warning(this, tr("Spreadsheet"),
                             tr("The file is not a "
                                "Spreadsheet file."));
        return false;
    }

    clear();

    Q_UINT16 row;
    Q_UINT16 col;
    QString str;

    QApplication::setOverrideCursor(waitCursor);
    while (!in.atEnd()) {
        in >> row >> col >> str;
        setFormula(row, col, str);
    }
    QApplication::restoreOverrideCursor();
    return true;
}
```

The `readFile()` function is very similar to `writeFile()`. We use `QFile` to read in the file, but this time using the `IO_ReadOnly` flag rather than `IO_WriteOnly`. Then we set the `QDataStream` version to 5. The format for reading must always be the same as for writing.

If the file has the correct magic number at the beginning, we call `clear()` to blank out all the cells in the spreadsheet and we read in the cell data. The call to `clear()` is necessary to blank out the cells that are not specified in the file.

## Implementing the Edit Menu

We are now ready to implement the slots that correspond to the application's Edit menu.

```
void Spreadsheet::cut()
{
    copy();
    del();
}
```

The `cut()` slot corresponds to Edit|Cut. The implementation is simple since Cut is the same as Copy followed by Delete.

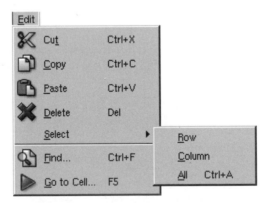

**Figure 4.6.** The Spreadsheet application's Edit menu

```
void Spreadsheet::copy()
{
    QTableSelection sel = selection();
    QString str;

    for (int i = 0; i < sel.numRows(); ++i) {
        if (i > 0)
            str += "\n";
        for (int j = 0; j < sel.numCols(); ++j) {
            if (j > 0)
                str += "\t";
            str += formula(sel.topRow() + i, sel.leftCol() + j);
        }
    }
```

```
    QApplication::clipboard()->setText(str);
}
```

The `copy()` slot corresponds to Edit|Copy. It iterates over the current selection. Each selected cell's formula is added to a `QString`, with rows separated by newline characters and columns separated by tab characters.

"Red\t Green\t Blue\n Cyan\t Magenta\t Yellow"

**Figure 4.7.** Copying a selection onto the clipboard

The system clipboard is available in Qt through the `QApplication::clipboard()` static function. By calling `QClipboard::setText()`, we make the text available on the clipboard, both to this application and to other applications that support plain text. Our format with tab and newline characters as separator is understood by a variety of applications, including Microsoft Excel.

```
QTableSelection Spreadsheet::selection()
{
    if (QTable::selection(0).isEmpty())
        return QTableSelection(currentRow(), currentColumn(),
                               currentRow(), currentColumn());
    return QTable::selection(0);
}
```

The `selection()` private function returns the current selection. It depends on `QTable::selection()`, which returns a selection by number. Since we set the selection mode to `Single`, there is only one selection, numbered 0. But it's also possible that there is no selection at all. This is because `QTable` doesn't treat the current cell as a selection in its own right. This behavior is reasonable, but slightly inconvenient here, so we implement a `selection()` function that either returns the current selection or, if there isn't one, the current cell.

```
void Spreadsheet::paste()
{
    QTableSelection sel = selection();
    QString str = QApplication::clipboard()->text();
    QStringList rows = QStringList::split("\n", str, true);
    int numRows = rows.size();
    int numCols = rows.first().contains("\t") + 1;

    if (sel.numRows() * sel.numCols() != 1
        && (sel.numRows() != numRows
            || sel.numCols() != numCols)) {
        QMessageBox::information(this, tr("Spreadsheet"),
            tr("The information cannot be pasted because the "
```

```
                             "copy and paste areas aren't the same size."));
            return;
        }

        for (int i = 0; i < numRows; ++i) {
            QStringList cols = QStringList::split("\t", rows[i], true);
            for (int j = 0; j < numCols; ++j) {
                int row = sel.topRow() + i;
                int col = sel.leftCol() + j;
                if (row < NumRows && col < NumCols)
                    setFormula(row, col, cols[j]);
            }
        }
        somethingChanged();
    }
```

The `paste()` slot corresponds to Edit|Paste. We fetch the text on the clipboard and call the static function `QStringList::split()` to break the string into a `QStringList`. Each row becomes one string in the `QStringList`.

Next, we determine the dimension of the copy area. The number of rows is the number of strings in the `QStringList`; the number of columns is the number of tab characters in the first row, plus 1.

If only one cell is selected, we use that cell as the top-left corner of the paste area. Otherwise, we use the current selection as the paste area.

To perform the paste, we iterate over the rows and split each of them into cells by using `QStringList::split()` again, but this time using tab as the separator. Figure 4.8 illustrates the steps.

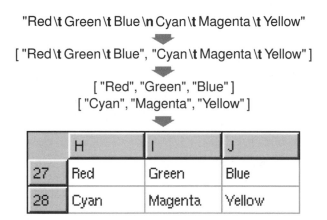

**Figure 4.8.** Pasting clipboard text into the spreadsheet

```
void Spreadsheet::del()
{
    QTableSelection sel = selection();
    for (int i = 0; i < sel.numRows(); ++i) {
        for (int j = 0; j < sel.numCols(); ++j)
            delete cell(sel.topRow() + i, sel.leftCol() + j);
```

```
    }
    clearSelection();
}
```

The `del()` slot corresponds to Edit|Delete. It is sufficient to use `delete` on each of the `Cell` objects in the selection to clear the cells. The `QTable` notices when its `QTableItem`s are deleted and automatically repaints itself. If we call `cell()` with the location of a deleted cell, it will return a null pointer.

```
void Spreadsheet::selectRow()
{
    clearSelection();
    QTable::selectRow(currentRow());
}

void Spreadsheet::selectColumn()
{
    clearSelection();
    QTable::selectColumn(currentColumn());
}

void Spreadsheet::selectAll()
{
    clearSelection();
    selectCells(0, 0, NumRows - 1, NumCols - 1);
}
```

The `selectRow()`, `selectColumn()`, and `selectAll()` functions correspond to the Edit|Select|Row, Edit|Select|Column, and Edit|Select|All menu options. The implementation relies on `QTable`'s `selectRow()`, `selectColumn()`, and `selectCells()` functions.

```
void Spreadsheet::findNext(const QString &str, bool caseSensitive)
{
    int row = currentRow();
    int col = currentColumn() + 1;

    while (row < NumRows) {
        while (col < NumCols) {
            if (text(row, col).contains(str, caseSensitive)) {
                clearSelection();
                setCurrentCell(row, col);
                setActiveWindow();
                return;
            }
            ++col;
        }
        col = 0;
        ++row;
    }
    qApp->beep();
}
```

The `findNext()` slot iterates through the cells starting from the cell to the right of the cursor and moving right until the last column is reached, then continues from the first column in the row below, and so on until the text is found or until the very last cell is reached. For example, if the current cell is cell C27, we search D27, E27, ..., Z27, then A28, B28, C28, ..., Z28, and so on until Z999. If we find a match, we clear the current selection, we move the cell cursor to the cell that matched, and we make the window that contains the `Spreadsheet` active. If no match is found, we make the application beep to indicate that the search finished unsuccessfully.

```
void Spreadsheet::findPrev(const QString &str, bool caseSensitive)
{
    int row = currentRow();
    int col = currentColumn() - 1;

    while (row >= 0) {
        while (col >= 0) {
            if (text(row, col).contains(str, caseSensitive)) {
                clearSelection();
                setCurrentCell(row, col);
                setActiveWindow();
                return;
            }
            --col;
        }
        col = NumCols - 1;
        --row;
    }
    qApp->beep();
}
```

The `findPrev()` slot is similar to `findNext()`, except that it iterates backward and stops at cell A1.

## Implementing the Other Menus

We will now implement the slots for the Tools and Options menus.

**Figure 4.9.** The Spreadsheet application's Tools and Options menus

```
void Spreadsheet::recalculate()
{
    int row;

    for (row = 0; row < NumRows; ++row) {
        for (int col = 0; col < NumCols; ++col) {
            if (cell(row, col))
                cell(row, col)->setDirty();
        }
    }
    for (row = 0; row < NumRows; ++row) {
```

```
            for (int col = 0; col < NumCols; ++col) {
                if (cell(row, col))
                    updateCell(row, col);
            }
        }
    }
```

The `recalculate()` slot corresponds to Tools|Recalculate. It is also called auto-matically by `Spreadsheet` when necessary.

We iterate over all the cells and call `setDirty()` on every cell to mark each one as requiring recalculation. The next time `QTable` calls `text()` on a `Cell` to obtain the value to show in the spreadsheet, the value will be recalculated.

Then we call `updateCell()` on all the cells to repaint the whole spreadsheet. The repaint code in `QTable` then calls `text()` on each visible cell to obtain the value to display. Because we called `setDirty()` on every cell, the calls to `text()` will use a freshly calculated value. The calculation is performed by the `Cell` class.

```
void Spreadsheet::setAutoRecalculate(bool on)
{
    autoRecalc = on;
    if (autoRecalc)
        recalculate();
}
```

The `setAutoRecalculate()` slot corresponds to Options|Auto-recalculate. If the fea-ture is turned on, we recalculate the whole spreadsheet immediately to make sure that it's up to date. Afterward, `recalculate()` is called automatically from `somethingChanged()`.

We don't need to implement anything for Options|Show Grid because `QTable` already provides a `setShowGrid(bool)` slot. All that remains is `Spreadsheet::sort()`, which we called from `MainWindow::sort()`:

```
void Spreadsheet::sort(const SpreadsheetCompare &compare)
{
    vector<QStringList> rows;
    QTableSelection sel = selection();
    int i;

    for (i = 0; i < sel.numRows(); ++i) {
        QStringList row;
        for (int j = 0; j < sel.numCols(); ++j)
            row.push_back(formula(sel.topRow() + i,
                                  sel.leftCol() + j));
        rows.push_back(row);
    }

    stable_sort(rows.begin(), rows.end(), compare);

    for (i = 0; i < sel.numRows(); ++i) {
        for (int j = 0; j < sel.numCols(); ++j)
            setFormula(sel.topRow() + i, sel.leftCol() + j,
                       rows[i][j]);
```

```
    }

    clearSelection();
    somethingChanged();
}
```

Sorting operates on the current selection and reorders the rows according to the sort keys and sort orders stored in the `compare` object. We represent each row of data with a `QStringList` and store the selection as a vector of rows. The `vector<T>` class is a standard C++ class; it is explained in Chapter 11 (Container Classes). For simplicity, we sort by formula rather than by value.

|   | C | D | E |
|---|---|---|---|
| 2 | Edsger | Dijkstra | 1930-05-11 |
| 3 | Tony | Hoare | 1934-01-11 |
| 4 | Niklaus | Wirth | 1934-02-15 |
| 5 | Donald | Knuth | 1938-01-10 |

| index | value |
|-------|-------|
| 0 | [ "Edsger", "Dijkstra", "1930-05-11" ] |
| 1 | [ "Tony", "Hoare", "1934-01-11" ] |
| 2 | [ "Niklaus", "Wirth", "1934-02-15" ] |
| 3 | [ "Donald", "Knuth", "1938-01-10" ] |

**Figure 4.10.** Storing the selection as a vector of rows

We call the standard C++ `stable_sort()` function on the rows to perform the actual sorting. The `stable_sort()` function accepts a begin iterator, an end iterator, and a comparison function. The comparison function is a function that takes two arguments (two `QStringList`s) and that returns `true` if the first argument is "less than" the second argument, `false` otherwise. The `compare` object we pass as the comparison function isn't really a function, but it can be used as one, as we will see shortly.

| index | value |
|-------|-------|
| 0 | [ "Donald", "Knuth", "1938-01-10" ] |
| 1 | [ "Edsger", "Dijkstra", "1930-05-11" ] |
| 2 | [ "Niklaus", "Wirth", "1934-02-15" ] |
| 3 | [ "Tony", "Hoare", "1934-01-11" ] |

|   | C | D | E |
|---|---|---|---|
| 2 | Donald | Knuth | 1938-01-10 |
| 3 | Edsger | Dijkstra | 1930-05-11 |
| 4 | Niklaus | Wirth | 1934-02-15 |
| 5 | Tony | Hoare | 1934-01-11 |

**Figure 4.11.** Putting the data back into the table after sorting

After performing the `stable_sort()`, we move the data back into the table, clear the selection, and call `somethingChanged()`.

In `spreadsheet.h`, the `SpreadsheetCompare` class was defined like this:

```cpp
class SpreadsheetCompare
{
public:
    bool operator()(const QStringList &row1,
                    const QStringList &row2) const;

    enum { NumKeys = 3 };
    int keys[NumKeys];
```

```
        bool ascending[NumKeys];
};
```

The `SpreadsheetCompare` class is special because it implements a `()` operator. This allows us to use the class as if it were a function. Such classes are called *functors*. To understand how functors work, we will start with a simple example:

```
class Square
{
public:
    int operator()(int x) const { return x * x; }
};
```

The `Square` class provides one function, `operator()(int)`, that returns the square of its parameter. By naming the function `operator()(int)` rather than, say, `compute(int)`, we gain the capability of using an object of type `Square` as if it were a function:

```
Square square;
int y = square(5);
```

Now let's see an example involving `SpreadsheetCompare`:

```
QStringList row1, row2;
SpreadsheetCompare compare;
...
if (compare(row1, row2)) {
    // row1 is less than row2
}
```

The `compare` object can be used just as if it had been a plain `compare()` function. Additionally, it can access all the sort keys and sort orders, which it stores as member variables.

An alternative to this scheme would have been to store the sort keys and sort orders in global variables and use a plain `compare()` function. However, communicating through global variables is inelegant and can lead to subtle bugs. Functors are a more powerful idiom for interfacing with template functions such as `stable_sort()`.

Here is the implementation of the function that is used to compare two spreadsheet rows:

```
bool SpreadsheetCompare::operator()(const QStringList &row1,
                                    const QStringList &row2) const
{
    for (int i = 0; i < NumKeys; ++i) {
        int column = keys[i];
        if (column != -1) {
            if (row1[column] != row2[column]) {
                if (ascending[i])
                    return row1[column] < row2[column];
                else
                    return row1[column] > row2[column];
            }
```

```
        }
    }
    return false;
}
```

It returns `true` if the first row is less than the second row; otherwise, it returns `false`. The standard `stable_sort()` function uses the result of this function to perform the sort.

The `SpreadsheetCompare` object's `keys` and `ascending` arrays are populated in the `MainWindow::sort()` function (shown in Chapter 2). Each key holds a column index, or −1 ("None").

We compare the corresponding cell entries in the two rows for each key in order. As soon as we find a difference, we return an appropriate `true` or `false` value. If all the comparisons turn out to be equal, we return `false`. The `stable_sort()` function uses the order before the sort to resolve tie situations; if `row1` preceded `row2` originally and neither compares as "less than" the other, `row1` will still precede `row2` in the result. This is what distinguishes `std::stable_sort()` from its more famous (but less stable) cousin `std::sort()`.

We have now completed the `Spreadsheet` class. In the next section, we will review the `Cell` class. This class is used to hold cell formulas and provides a reimplementation of the `text()` function that `Spreadsheet` calls to display the result of calculating a cell's formula.

## Subclassing QTableItem

The `Cell` class inherits from `QTableItem`. The class is designed to work well with `Spreadsheet`, but it has no specific dependencies on that class and could in theory be used in any `QTable`.

Here's the header file:

```
#ifndef CELL_H
#define CELL_H

#include <qtable.h>
#include <qvariant.h>

class Cell : public QTableItem
{
public:
    Cell(QTable *table, const QString &formula);

    void setFormula(const QString &formula);
    QString formula() const;
    void setDirty();
    QString text() const;
    int alignment() const;

private:
    QVariant value() const;
```

```
    QVariant evalExpression(const QString &str, int &pos) const;
    QVariant evalTerm(const QString &str, int &pos) const;
    QVariant evalFactor(const QString &str, int &pos) const;

    QString formulaStr;
    mutable QVariant cachedValue;
    mutable bool cacheIsDirty;
};

#endif
```

The `Cell` class extends `QTableItem` by adding three private variables:

- `formulaStr` stores the cell's formula as a `QString`.

- `cachedValue` caches the cell's value as a `QVariant`.

- `cacheIsDirty` is `true` if the cached value isn't up to date.

The `QVariant` type can hold values of many C++ and Qt types. We use it because some cells have a `double` value, while others have a `QString` value.

The `cachedValue` and `cacheIsDirty` variables are declared with the C++ `mutable` keyword. This allows us to modify these variables in const functions. Alternatively, we could recalculate the value each time `text()` is called, but that would be needlessly inefficient.

Notice that there is no `Q_OBJECT` macro in the class definition. `Cell` is a plain C++ class, with no signals or slots. In fact, because `QTableItem` doesn't inherit from `QObject`, we cannot have signals and slots in `Cell` as it stands. Qt's item classes don't inherit from `QObject` to keep their overhead to the barest minimum. If signals and slots are needed, they can be implemented in the widget that contains the items or, exceptionally, using multiple inheritance with `QObject`.

Here's the start of `cell.cpp`:

```
#include <qlineedit.h>
#include <qregexp.h>

#include "cell.h"

Cell::Cell(QTable *table, const QString &formula)
    : QTableItem(table, OnTyping)
{
    setFormula(formula);
}
```

The constructor accepts a pointer to a `QTable` and a formula. The pointer is passed on to the `QTableItem` constructor and is accessible afterward as `QTableItem::table()`. The second argument to the base class constructor, `OnTyping`, means that an editor pops up when the user starts typing in the current cell.

```
void Cell::setFormula(const QString &formula)
{
    formulaStr = formula;
```

```
        cacheIsDirty = true;
    }
```

The setFormula() function sets the cell's formula. It also sets the cacheIsDirty flag to true, meaning that cachedValue must be recalculated before a valid value can be returned. It is called from the Cell constructor and from Spreadsheet::setFormula().

```
    QString Cell::formula() const
    {
        return formulaStr;
    }
```

The formula() function is called from Spreadsheet::formula().

```
    void Cell::setDirty()
    {
        cacheIsDirty = true;
    }
```

The setDirty() function is called to force a recalculation of the cell's value. It simply sets cacheIsDirty to true. The recalculation isn't performed until it is really necessary.

```
    QString Cell::text() const
    {
        if (value().isValid())
            return value().toString();
        else
            return "####";
    }
```

The text() function is reimplemented from QTableItem. It returns the text that should be shown in the spreadsheet. It relies on value() to compute the cell's value. If the value is invalid (presumably because the formula is wrong), we return "####".

The value() function used by text() returns a QVariant. A QVariant can store values of different types, such as double and QString, and provides functions to convert the variant to other types. For example, calling toString() on a variant that holds a double value produces a string representation of the double. A QVariant constructed using the default constructor is an "invalid" variant.

```
    int Cell::alignment() const
    {
        if (value().type() == QVariant::String)
            return AlignLeft | AlignVCenter;
        else
            return AlignRight | AlignVCenter;
    }
```

The alignment() function is reimplemented from QTableItem. It returns the alignment for the cell's text. We have chosen to left-align string values and to right-align numeric values. We vertically center all values.

```
    const QVariant Invalid;
    QVariant Cell::value() const
    {
        if (cacheIsDirty) {
            cacheIsDirty = false;

            if (formulaStr.startsWith("'")) {
                cachedValue = formulaStr.mid(1);
            } else if (formulaStr.startsWith("=")) {
                cachedValue = Invalid;
                QString expr = formulaStr.mid(1);
                expr.replace(" ", "");
                int pos = 0;
                cachedValue = evalExpression(expr, pos);
                if (pos < (int)expr.length())
                    cachedValue = Invalid;
            } else {
                bool ok;
                double d = formulaStr.toDouble(&ok);
                if (ok)
                    cachedValue = d;
                else
                    cachedValue = formulaStr;
            }
        }
        return cachedValue;
    }
```

The `value()` private function returns the cell's value. If `cacheIsDirty` is `true`, we need to recalculate the value.

If the formula starts with a single quote (for example, "'12345"), the value is the string from position 1 to the end. (The single quote occupies position 0.)

If the formula starts with '=', we take the string from position 1 and delete any spaces it may contain. Then we call `evalExpression()` to compute the value of the expression. The `pos` argument is passed by reference; it indicates the position of the character where parsing should begin. After the call to `evalExpression()`, `pos` is equal to the length of the expression that was successfully parsed. If the parse failed before the end, we set `cachedValue` to be `Invalid`.

If the formula doesn't begin with a single quote or an equals sign ('='), we attempt to convert it to a floating point value using `toDouble()`. If the conversion works, we set `cachedValue` to be the resulting number; otherwise, we set `cachedValue` to be the formula string. For example, a formula of "1.50" causes `toDouble()` to set `ok` to `true` and return 1.5, while a formula of "World Population" causes `toDouble()` to set `ok` to `false` and return 0.0.

The `value()` function is a const function. We had to declare `cachedValue` and `cacheIsValid` as mutable variables so that the compiler will allow us to modify them in const functions. It might be tempting to make `value()` non-const and remove the `mutable` keywords, but that would not compile because we call `value()` from `text()`, a const function. In C++, caching and `mutable` usually go hand in hand.

We have now completed the Spreadsheet application, apart from parsing formulas. The rest of this section covers `evalExpression()` and the two helper functions `evalTerm()` and `evalFactor()`. The code is a bit complicated, but it is included here to make the application complete. Since the code is not related to GUI programming, you can safely skip it and continue reading from Chapter 5.

The `evalExpression()` function returns the value of a spreadsheet expression. An expression is defined as one or more terms separated by '+' or '–' operators; for example, "2∗C5+D6" is an expression with "2∗C5" as its first term and "D6" as its second term. The terms themselves are defined as one or more factors separated by '∗' or '/' operators; for example, "2∗C5" is a term with "2" as its first factor and "C5" as its second factor. Finally, a factor can be a number ("2"), a cell location ("C5"), or an expression in parentheses, optionally preceded by a unary minus. By breaking down expressions into terms and terms into factors, we ensure that the operators are applied with the correct precedence.

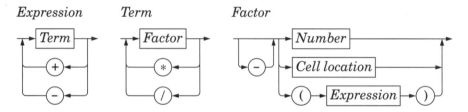

**Figure 4.12.** Syntax diagram for spreadsheet expressions

The syntax of spreadsheet expressions is defined in Figure 4.12. For each symbol in the grammar (*Expression*, *Term*, and *Factor*), there is a corresponding `Cell` member function that parses it and whose structure closely follows the grammar. Parsers written this way are called recursive-descent parsers.

Let's start with `evalExpression()`, the function that parses an *Expression*:

```
QVariant Cell::evalExpression(const QString &str, int &pos) const
{
    QVariant result = evalTerm(str, pos);
    while (pos < (int)str.length()) {
        QChar op = str[pos];
        if (op != '+' && op != '-')
            return result;
        ++pos;

        QVariant term = evalTerm(str, pos);
        if (result.type() == QVariant::Double
                && term.type() == QVariant::Double) {
            if (op == '+')
                result = result.toDouble() + term.toDouble();
            else
                result = result.toDouble() - term.toDouble();
        } else {
            result = Invalid;
```

```
        }
    }
    return result;
}
```

First, we call `evalTerm()` to get the value of the first term. If the following character is '+' or '–', we continue by calling `evalTerm()` a second time; otherwise, the expression consists of a single term, and we return its value as the value of the whole expression. After we have the value of the first two terms, we compute the result of the operation, depending on the operator. If both terms evaluated to a `double`, we compute the result as a `double`; otherwise, we set the result to be `Invalid`.

We continue like this until there are no more terms. This works correctly because addition and subtraction are left-associative; that is, "1–2–3" means "(1–2)–3", not "1–(2–3)".

```
QVariant Cell::evalTerm(const QString &str, int &pos) const
{
    QVariant result = evalFactor(str, pos);
    while (pos < (int)str.length()) {
        QChar op = str[pos];
        if (op != '*' && op != '/')
            return result;
        ++pos;

        QVariant factor = evalFactor(str, pos);
        if (result.type() == QVariant::Double
                && factor.type() == QVariant::Double) {
            if (op == '*') {
                result = result.toDouble() * factor.toDouble();
            } else {
                if (factor.toDouble() == 0.0)
                    result = Invalid;
                else
                    result = result.toDouble() / factor.toDouble();
            }
        } else {
            result = Invalid;
        }
    }
    return result;
}
```

The `evalTerm()` function is very similar to `evalExpression()`, except that it deals with multiplication and division. The only subtlety in `evalTerm()` is that we must avoid division by zero. While it is generally inadvisable to test floating point values for equality because of rounding errors, it is safe to do so to prevent division by zero.

```
QVariant Cell::evalFactor(const QString &str, int &pos) const
{
    QVariant result;
    bool negative = false;
```

```
    if (str[pos] == '-') {
        negative = true;
        ++pos;
    }

    if (str[pos] == '(') {
        ++pos;
        result = evalExpression(str, pos);
        if (str[pos] != ')')
            result = Invalid;
        ++pos;
    } else {
        QRegExp regExp("[A-Za-z][1-9][0-9]{0,2}");
        QString token;

        while (str[pos].isLetterOrNumber() || str[pos] == '.') {
            token += str[pos];
            ++pos;
        }

        if (regExp.exactMatch(token)) {
            int col = token[0].upper().unicode() - 'A';
            int row = token.mid(1).toInt() - 1;

            Cell *c = (Cell *)table()->item(row, col);
            if (c)
                result = c->value();
            else
                result = 0.0;
        } else {
            bool ok;
            result = token.toDouble(&ok);
            if (!ok)
                result = Invalid;
        }
    }

    if (negative) {
        if (result.type() == QVariant::Double)
            result = -result.toDouble();
        else
            result = Invalid;
    }
    return result;
}
```

The evalFactor() function is a bit more complicated than evalExpression()
and evalTerm(). We start by noting whether the factor is negated. We then see
if it begins with an open parenthesis. If it does, we evaluate the contents of
the parentheses as an expression by calling evalExpression(). This is where
recursion occurs in the parser; evalExpression() calls evalTerm(), which calls
evalFactor(), which calls evalExpression() again.

If the factor isn't a nested expression, we extract the next token, which may
be a cell location or a number. If the token matches the QRegExp, we take it to
be a cell reference and we call value() on the cell at the given location. The

cell could be anywhere in the spreadsheet, and it could have dependencies on other cells. The dependencies are not a problem; they will simply trigger more `value()` calls and (for "dirty" cells) more parsing until all the dependent cell values are calculated. If the token isn't a cell location, we take it to be a number.

What happens if cell A1 contains the formula "=A1"? Or if cell A1 contains "=A2" and cell A2 contains "=A1"? Although we have not written any special code to detect circular dependencies, the parser handles these cases gracefully by returning an invalid `QVariant`. This works because we set `cacheIsDirty` to `false` and `cachedValue` to `Invalid` in `value()` before we call `evalExpression()`. If `evalExpression()` recursively calls `value()` on the same cell, it returns `Invalid` immediately, and the whole expression then evaluates to `Invalid`.

We have now completed the formula parser. It would be straightforward to extend it to handle predefined spreadsheet functions, like "sum()" and "avg()", by extending the grammatical definition of *Factor*. Another easy extension is to implement the '+' operator with string operands (as concatenation); this requires no changes to the grammar.

# Creating Custom Widgets

This chapter explains how to create custom widgets using Qt. Custom widgets can be created by subclassing an existing Qt widget or by subclassing `QWidget` directly. We will demonstrate both approaches, and we will also see how to integrate a custom widget with *Qt Designer* so that it can be used just like a built-in Qt widget. We will round off the chapter by presenting a custom widget that uses a powerful technique for eliminating flicker: double buffering.

## Customizing Qt Widgets

In some cases, we find that a Qt widget requires more customization than is possible by setting its properties in *Qt Designer* or by calling its functions. A simple and direct solution is to subclass the relevant widget class and adapt it to suit our needs.

**Figure 5.1.** The `HexSpinBox` widget

In this section, we will develop a hexadecimal spin box to show how this works. `QSpinBox` only supports decimal integers, but by subclassing it's quite easy to make it accept and display hexadecimal values.

```
#ifndef HEXSPINBOX_H
#define HEXSPINBOX_H

#include <qspinbox.h>

class HexSpinBox : public QSpinBox
{
```

```
public:
    HexSpinBox(QWidget *parent, const char *name = 0);

protected:
    QString mapValueToText(int value);
    int mapTextToValue(bool *ok);
};

#endif
```

The HexSpinBox inherits most of its functionality from QSpinBox. It provides a typical constructor and reimplements two virtual functions from QSpinBox. Since the class doesn't define its own signals and slots, it doesn't need the Q_OBJECT macro.

```
#include <qvalidator.h>

#include "hexspinbox.h"

HexSpinBox::HexSpinBox(QWidget *parent, const char *name)
    : QSpinBox(parent, name)
{
    QRegExp regExp("[0-9A-Fa-f]+");
    setValidator(new QRegExpValidator(regExp, this));
    setRange(0, 255);
}
```

The user can modify a spin box's current value either by clicking its up and down arrows or by typing a value into the spin box's line editor. In the latter case, we want to restrict the user's input to legitimate hexadecimal numbers. To achieve this, we use a QRegExpValidator that accepts one or more characters from the ranges '0' to '9', 'A' to 'F', and 'a' to 'f'. We also set the default range to be 0 to 255 (0x00 to 0xFF), which is more appropriate for a hexadecimal spin box than QSpinBox's default of 0 to 99.

```
QString HexSpinBox::mapValueToText(int value)
{
    return QString::number(value, 16).upper();
}
```

The mapValueToText() function converts an integer value to a string. QSpinBox calls it to update the editor part of the spin box when the user presses the spin box's up or down arrows. We use the static function QString::number() with a second argument of 16 to convert the value to lower-case hexadecimal, and call QString::upper() on the result to make it upper-case.

```
int HexSpinBox::mapTextToValue(bool *ok)
{
    return text().toInt(ok, 16);
}
```

The mapTextToValue() function performs the reverse conversion, from a string to an integer value. It is called by QSpinBox when the user types a value into the editor part of the spin box and presses Enter. We use the QString::toInt()

function to attempt to convert the current text (returned by `QSpinBox::text()`) to an integer value, again using base 16.

If the conversion is successful, `toInt()` sets `*ok` to `true`; otherwise, it sets it to `false`. This behavior happens to be exactly what `QSpinBox` expects.

We have now finished the hexadecimal spin box. Customizing other Qt widgets follows the same pattern: Pick a suitable Qt widget, subclass it, and reimplement some virtual functions to change its behavior. This technique is common in Qt programming; in fact, we have already used it in Chapter 4 when we subclassed `QTable` and reimplemented `createEditor()` and `endEdit()`.

## Subclassing QWidget

Most custom widgets are simply a combination of existing widgets, whether they are built-in Qt widgets or other custom widgets such as `HexSpinBox`. Custom widgets that are built by composing existing widgets can usually be developed in *Qt Designer*:

- Create a new form using the "Widget" template.
- Add the necessary widgets to the form, then lay them out.
- Set up the signals and slots connections and add any necessary code (either in a `.ui.h` file or in a subclass) to provide the desired behavior.

Naturally, this can also be done entirely in code. Whichever approach is taken, the resulting class inherits directly from `QWidget`.

If the widget has no signals and slots of its own and doesn't reimplement any virtual functions, it is even possible to simply assemble the widget by aggregating existing widgets without a subclass. That's the approach we used in Chapter 1 to create the Age application, with a `QHBox`, a `QSpinBox`, and a `QSlider`. Even so, we could just as easily have subclassed `QHBox` and created the `QSpinBox` and `QSlider` in the subclass's constructor.

When none of Qt's widgets are suitable for the task at hand, and when there's no way to combine or adapt existing widgets to obtain the desired result, we can still create the widget we want. This is achieved by subclassing `QWidget` and reimplementing a few event handlers to paint the widget and to respond to mouse clicks. This approach gives us complete freedom to define and control both the appearance and the behavior of our widget. Qt's built-in widgets, like `QLabel`, `QPushButton`, and `QTable`, are implemented this way. If they didn't exist in Qt, it would still be possible to create them ourselves using the public functions provided by `QWidget` in a totally platform-independent manner.

To demonstrate how to write a custom widget using this approach, we will create the `IconEditor` widget shown in Figure 5.2. The `IconEditor` is a widget that could be used in an icon editing program.

Let's begin by reviewing the header file.

```
#ifndef ICONEDITOR_H
#define ICONEDITOR_H

#include <qimage.h>
#include <qwidget.h>

class IconEditor : public QWidget
{
    Q_OBJECT
    Q_PROPERTY(QColor penColor READ penColor WRITE setPenColor)
    Q_PROPERTY(QImage iconImage READ iconImage WRITE setIconImage)
    Q_PROPERTY(int zoomFactor READ zoomFactor WRITE setZoomFactor)
public:
    IconEditor(QWidget *parent = 0, const char *name = 0);

    void setPenColor(const QColor &newColor);
    QColor penColor() const { return curColor; }
    void setZoomFactor(int newZoom);
    int zoomFactor() const { return zoom; }
    void setIconImage(const QImage &newImage);
    const QImage &iconImage() const { return image; }
    QSize sizeHint() const;
```

The `IconEditor` class uses the `Q_PROPERTY()` macro to declare three custom properties: `penColor`, `iconImage`, and `zoomFactor`. Each property has a type, a "read" function, and a "write" function. For example, the `penColor` property is of type `QColor` and can be read and written using the `penColor()` and `setPenColor()` functions.

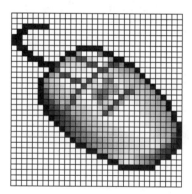

**Figure 5.2.** The `IconEditor` widget

When we make use of the widget in *Qt Designer*, custom properties appear in *Qt Designer*'s property editor below the properties inherited from `QWidget`. Properties may be of any type supported by `QVariant`. The `Q_OBJECT` macro is necessary for classes that define properties.

```
protected:
    void mousePressEvent(QMouseEvent *event);
    void mouseMoveEvent(QMouseEvent *event);
    void paintEvent(QPaintEvent *event);
```

```
private:
    void drawImagePixel(QPainter *painter, int i, int j);
    void setImagePixel(const QPoint &pos, bool opaque);

    QColor curColor;
    QImage image;
    int zoom;
};

#endif
```

`IconEditor` reimplements three protected functions from `QWidget` and has a few private functions and variables. The three private variables hold the values of the three properties.

The implementation file begins with `#include` directives and the `IconEditor`'s constructor:

```
#include <qpainter.h>

#include "iconeditor.h"

IconEditor::IconEditor(QWidget *parent, const char *name)
    : QWidget(parent, name, WStaticContents)
{
    setSizePolicy(QSizePolicy::Minimum, QSizePolicy::Minimum);
    curColor = black;
    zoom = 8;
    image.create(16, 16, 32);
    image.fill(qRgba(0, 0, 0, 0));
    image.setAlphaBuffer(true);
}
```

The constructor has some subtle aspects such as the `setSizePolicy()` call and the `WStaticContents` flag. We will discuss them shortly.

The zoom factor is set to 8, meaning that each pixel in the icon will be rendered as an $8 \times 8$ square. The pen color is set to black; the `black` symbol is a predefined value in the `Qt` class (`QObject`'s base class).

The icon data is stored in the `image` member variable and can be accessed through the `setIconImage()` and `iconImage()` functions. An icon editor program would typically call `setIconImage()` when the user opens an icon file and `iconImage()` to retrieve the icon when the user wants to save it.

The `image` variable is of type `QImage`. We initialize it to $16 \times 16$ pixels and 32-bit depth, clear the image data, and enable the alpha buffer.

The `QImage` class stores an image in a hardware-independent fashion. It can be set to use a 1-bit, 8-bit, or 32-bit depth. An image with 32-bit depth uses 8 bits for each of the red, green, and blue components of a pixel. The remaining 8 bits store the pixel's alpha component—that is, its opacity. For example, a pure red color's red, green, blue, and alpha components have the values 255, 0, 0, and 255. In Qt, this color can be specified as

```
QRgb red = qRgba(255, 0, 0, 255);
```

or as

```
QRgb red = qRgb(255, 0, 0);
```

QRgb is simply a typedef for unsigned int, and qRgb() and qRgba() are inline functions that combine their arguments into one 32-bit integer value. It is also possible to write

```
QRgb red = 0xFFFF0000;
```

where the first FF corresponds to the alpha component and the second FF to the red component. In the IconEditor constructor, we fill the QImage with a transparent color by using 0 as the alpha component.

Qt provides two types for storing colors: QRgb and QColor. While QRgb is only a typedef used in QImage to store 32-bit pixel data, QColor is a class with many useful functions and is widely used in Qt to store colors. In the IconEditor widget, we only use QRgb when dealing with the QImage; we use QColor for everything else, including the penColor property.

```
QSize IconEditor::sizeHint() const
{
    QSize size = zoom * image.size();
    if (zoom >= 3)
        size += QSize(1, 1);
    return size;
}
```

The sizeHint() function is reimplemented from QWidget and returns the ideal size of a widget. Here, we take the image size multiplied by the zoom factor, with one extra pixel in each direction to accommodate a grid if the zoom factor is 3 or more. (We don't show a grid if the zoom factor is 2 or 1, because the grid would hardly leave any room for the icon's pixels.)

A widget's size hint is mostly useful in conjunction with layouts. Qt's layout managers try as much as possible to respect a widget's size hint when they lay out a form's child widgets. For IconEditor to be a good layout citizen, it must report a credible size hint.

In addition to the size hint, widgets have a size policy that tells the layout system whether they like to be stretched and shrunk. By calling setSizePolicy() in the constructor with QSizePolicy::Minimum as horizontal and vertical policies, we tell any layout manager that is responsible for this widget that the widget's size hint is really its minimum size. In other words, the widget can be stretched if required, but it should never shrink below the size hint. This can be overridden in *Qt Designer* by setting the widget's sizePolicy property. The meaning of the various size policies is explained in Chapter 6 (Layout Management).

```
void IconEditor::setPenColor(const QColor &newColor)
{
    curColor = newColor;
}
```

The `setPenColor()` function sets the current pen color. The color will be used for newly drawn pixels.

```
void IconEditor::setIconImage(const QImage &newImage)
{
    if (newImage != image) {
        image = newImage.convertDepth(32);
        image.detach();
        update();
        updateGeometry();
    }
}
```

The `setIconImage()` function sets the image to edit. We call `convertDepth()` to make the image 32-bit if it isn't already. Elsewhere in the code, we will assume that the image data is stored as 32-bit `QRgb` values.

We also call `detach()` to take a deep copy of the data stored in the image. This is necessary because the image data might be stored in ROM. `QImage` tries to save time and memory by copying the image data only when explicitly requested to do so. This optimization is called *explicit sharing* and is discussed with `QMemArray<T>` in the "Pointer-Based Containers" section of Chapter 11.

After setting the `image` variable, we call `QWidget::update()` to force a repainting of the widget using the new image. Next, we call `QWidget::updateGeometry()` to tell any layout that contains the widget that the widget's size hint has changed. The layout will then automatically adapt to the new size hint.

```
void IconEditor::setZoomFactor(int newZoom)
{
    if (newZoom < 1)
        newZoom = 1;

    if (newZoom != zoom) {
        zoom = newZoom;
        update();
        updateGeometry();
    }
}
```

The `setZoomFactor()` function sets the zoom factor for the image. To prevent division by zero later, we correct any value below 1. Again, we call `update()` and `updateGeometry()` to repaint the widget and to notify any managing layout about the size hint change.

The `penColor()`, `iconImage()`, and `zoomFactor()` functions are implemented as inline functions in the header file.

We will now review the code for the `paintEvent()` function. This function is `IconEditor`'s most important function. It is called whenever the widget needs repainting. The default implementation in `QWidget` does nothing, leaving the widget blank.

Just like contextMenuEvent() and closeEvent(), which we met in Chapter 3, paintEvent() is an event handler. Qt has many other event handlers, each of which corresponds to a different type of event. Chapter 7 covers event processing in depth.

There are many situations when a paint event is generated and paintEvent() is called:

- When a widget is shown for the first time, the system automatically generates a paint event to force the widget to paint itself.

- When a widget is resized, the system automatically generates a paint event.

- If the widget is obscured by another window and then revealed again, a paint event is generated for the area that was hidden (unless the window system stored the area).

We can also force a paint event by calling QWidget::update() or QWidget::repaint(). The difference between these two functions is that repaint() forces an immediate repaint, whereas update() simply schedules a paint event for when Qt next processes events. (Both functions do nothing if the widget isn't visible on screen.) If update() is called multiple times, Qt compresses the consecutive paint events into a single paint event to avoid flicker. In IconEditor, we always use update().

Here's the code:

```
void IconEditor::paintEvent(QPaintEvent *)
{
    QPainter painter(this);

    if (zoom >= 3) {
        painter.setPen(colorGroup().foreground());
        for (int i = 0; i <= image.width(); ++i)
            painter.drawLine(zoom * i, 0,
                             zoom * i, zoom * image.height());
        for (int j = 0; j <= image.height(); ++j)
            painter.drawLine(0, zoom * j,
                             zoom * image.width(), zoom * j);
    }

    for (int i = 0; i < image.width(); ++i) {
        for (int j = 0; j < image.height(); ++j)
            drawImagePixel(&painter, i, j);
    }
}
```

We start by constructing a QPainter object on the widget. If the zoom factor is 3 or more, we draw the horizontal and vertical lines that form the grid using the QPainter::drawLine() function.

A call to QPainter::drawLine() has the following syntax:

```
painter.drawLine(x1, y1, x2, y2);
```

where (*x1*, *y1*) is the position of one end of the line and (*x2*, *y2*) is the position of the other end. There is also an overloaded version of the function that takes two `QPoint`s instead of four `int`s.

The top-left pixel of a Qt widget is located at position (0, 0), and the bottom-right pixel is located at (`width()` – 1, `height()` – 1). This is similar to the conventional Cartesian coordinate system, but upside down, and makes a lot of sense in GUI programming. It is perfectly possible to change `QPainter`'s coordinate system by using transformations, such as translation, scaling, rotation, and shearing. This is covered in Chapter 8 (2D and 3D Graphics).

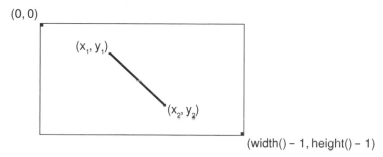

**Figure 5.3.** Drawing a line using `QPainter`

Before we call `drawLine()` on the `QPainter`, we set the line's color using `setPen()`. We could hard-code a color, like black or gray, but a better approach is to use the widget's palette.

Every widget is equipped with a palette that specifies which colors should be used for what. For example, there is a palette entry for the background color of widgets (usually light gray) and one for the color of text on that background (usually black). By default, a widget's palette adopts the window system's color scheme. By using colors from the palette, we ensure that `IconEditor` respects the user's preferences.

A widget's palette consists of three color groups: active, inactive, and disabled. Which color group should be used depends on the widget's current state:

- The active color group is used for widgets in the currently active window.

- The inactive color group is used for widgets in the other windows.

- The disabled color group is used for disabled widgets in any window.

The `QWidget::palette()` function returns the widget's palette as a `QPalette` object. The color groups are available through `QPalette`'s `active()`, `inactive()`, and `disabled()` functions, and are of type `QColorGroup`. For convenience, `QWidget::colorGroup()` returns the correct color group for the current state of the widget, so we rarely need to access the palette directly.

The `paintEvent()` function finishes by drawing the image itself, using the `IconEditor::drawImagePixel()` function to draw each of the icon's pixels as filled squares.

```
void IconEditor::drawImagePixel(QPainter *painter, int i, int j)
{
    QColor color;
    QRgb rgb = image.pixel(i, j);

    if (qAlpha(rgb) == 0)
        color = colorGroup().base();
    else
        color.setRgb(rgb);

    if (zoom >= 3) {
        painter->fillRect(zoom * i + 1, zoom * j + 1,
                          zoom - 1, zoom - 1, color);
    } else {
        painter->fillRect(zoom * i, zoom * j,
                          zoom, zoom, color);
    }
}
```

The `drawImagePixel()` function draws a zoomed pixel using a `QPainter`. The `i` and `j` parameters are pixel coordinates in the `QImage`—not in the widget. (If the zoom factor is 1, the two coordinate systems coincide exactly.) If the pixel is transparent (its alpha component is 0), we use the current color group's "base" color (typically white) to draw the pixel; otherwise, we use the pixel's color in the image. Then we call `QPainter::fillRect()` to draw a filled square. If the grid is shown, the square is reduced by one pixel in both directions to avoid painting over the grid.

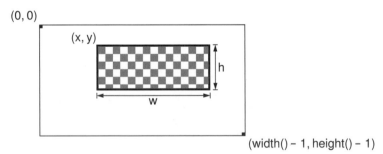

**Figure 5.4.** Drawing a rectangle using `QPainter`

The call to `QPainter::fillRect()` has the following syntax:

```
painter->fillRect(x, y, w, h, brush);
```

where $(x, y)$ is the position of the top-left corner of the rectangle, $w \times h$ is the size of the rectangle, and *brush* specifies the color to fill with and the fill pattern to use. By passing a `QColor` as the brush, we obtain a solid fill pattern.

```
void IconEditor::mousePressEvent(QMouseEvent *event)
{
    if (event->button() == LeftButton)
        setImagePixel(event->pos(), true);
    else if (event->button() == RightButton)
```

```
            setImagePixel(event->pos(), false);
    }
```

When the user presses a mouse button, the system generates a "mouse press" event. By reimplementing QWidget::mousePressEvent(), we can respond to this event and set or clear the image pixel under the mouse cursor.

If the user pressed the left mouse button, we call the private function setImagePixel() with true as the second argument, telling it to set the pixel to the current pen color. If the user pressed the right mouse button, we also call setImagePixel(), but pass false to clear the pixel.

```
    void IconEditor::mouseMoveEvent(QMouseEvent *event)
    {
        if (event->state() & LeftButton)
            setImagePixel(event->pos(), true);
        else if (event->state() & RightButton)
            setImagePixel(event->pos(), false);
    }
```

The mouseMoveEvent() handles "mouse move" events. By default, these events are only generated when the user is holding down a button. It is possible to change this behavior by calling QWidget::setMouseTracking(), but we don't need to do so for this example.

Just as pressing the left or right mouse button sets or clears a pixel, keeping it pressed and hovering over a pixel is also enough to set or clear a pixel. Since it's possible to hold more than one button pressed down at a time, the value returned by QMouseEvent::state() is a bitwise OR of the mouse buttons (and of modifier keys like Shift and Ctrl). We test whether a certain button is pressed down using the & operator, and if it is, we call setImagePixel().

```
    void IconEditor::setImagePixel(const QPoint &pos, bool opaque)
    {
        int i = pos.x() / zoom;
        int j = pos.y() / zoom;

        if (image.rect().contains(i, j)) {
            if (opaque)
                image.setPixel(i, j, penColor().rgb());
            else
                image.setPixel(i, j, qRgba(0, 0, 0, 0));

            QPainter painter(this);
            drawImagePixel(&painter, i, j);
        }
    }
```

The setImagePixel() function is called from mousePressEvent() and mouseMoveEvent() to set or clear a pixel. The pos parameter is the position of the mouse on the widget.

The first step is to convert the mouse position from widget coordinates to image coordinates. This is done by dividing the x and y components of the mouse position by the zoom factor. Next, we check whether the point is within

the correct range. The check is easily made using `QImage::rect()` and `QRect::`
`contains()`; this effectively checks that i is between 0 and `image.width() - 1`
and that j is between 0 and `image.height() - 1`.

Depending on the `opaque` parameter, we set or clear the pixel in the image.
Clearing a pixel is really setting it to be transparent. At the end, we call
`drawImagePixel()` to repaint the individual pixel that changed.

Now that we have reviewed the member functions, we will return to the
`WStaticContents` flag that we used in the constructor. This flag tells Qt that
the widget's content doesn't change when the widget is resized and that the
content stays rooted to the widget's top-left corner. Qt uses this information
to avoid needlessly repainting areas that are already shown when resizing
the widget.

Normally, when a widget is resized, Qt generates a paint event for the widget's
entire visible area. But if the widget is created with the `WStaticContents` flag,
the paint event's region is restricted to the pixels that were not previously
shown. If the widget is resized to a smaller size, no paint event is generated
at all.

**Figure 5.5.** Resizing a `WStaticContents` widget

The `IconEditor` widget is now complete. Using the information and examples
from earlier chapters, we could write code that uses the `IconEditor` as a
window in its own right, as a central widget in a `QMainWindow`, as a child widget
inside a layout, or as a child widget inside a `QScrollView` (p. 145). In the next
section, we will see how to integrate it with *Qt Designer*.

## Integrating Custom Widgets with Qt Designer

Before we can use custom widgets in *Qt Designer*, we must make *Qt Designer*
aware of them. There are two techniques for doing this: the "simple custom
widget" approach and the plugin approach.

The "simple custom widget" approach consists of filling in a dialog box in *Qt
Designer* with some information about the custom widget. The widget can
then be used in forms developed using *Qt Designer*, but the widget is only represented by an icon and a dark gray rectangle while the form is edited or previewed. Here's how to integrate the `HexSpinBox` widget using this approach:

1. Click Tools|Custom|Edit Custom Widget. This will launch *Qt Designer*'s custom widget editor.

2. Click New Widget.

3. Change the class name from `MyCustomWidget` to `HexSpinBox` and the header file from `mycustomwidget.h` to `hexspinbox.h`.

4. Change the size hint to (60, 20).

5. Change the size policy to (Minimum, Fixed).

The widget will then be available in the "Custom Widgets" section of *Qt Designer*'s toolbox.

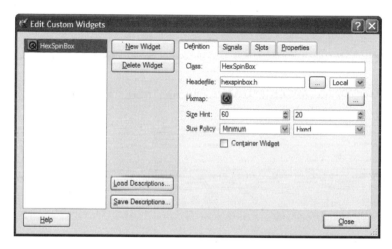

**Figure 5.6.** *Qt Designer*'s custom widget editor

The plugin approach requires the creation of a plugin library that *Qt Designer* can load at run-time and use to create instances of the widget. The real widget is then used by *Qt Designer* when editing the form and for previewing. We will integrate the `IconEditor` as a plugin to demonstrate how to do it.

First, we must subclass `QWidgetPlugin` and reimplement some virtual functions. We can do everything in the same source file. We will assume that the plugin source code is located in a directory called `iconeditorplugin` and that the `IconEditor` source code is located in a parallel directory called `iconeditor`.

Here's the header file:

```
#include <qwidgetplugin.h>

#include "../iconeditor/iconeditor.h"

class IconEditorPlugin : public QWidgetPlugin
{
public:
    QStringList keys() const;
    QWidget *create(const QString &key, QWidget *parent,
                    const char *name);
```

```
        QString includeFile(const QString &key) const;
        QString group(const QString &key) const;
        QIconSet iconSet(const QString &key) const;
        QString toolTip(const QString &key) const;
        QString whatsThis(const QString &key) const;
        bool isContainer(const QString &key) const;
    };
```

The `IconEditorPlugin` subclass is a factory class that encapsulates the `IconEditor` widget. The functions are used by *Qt Designer* to create instances of the class and to obtain information about it.

```
    QStringList IconEditorPlugin::keys() const
    {
        return QStringList() << "IconEditor";
    }
```

The `keys()` function returns a list of widgets provided by the plugin. The example plugin only provides the `IconEditor` widget.

```
    QWidget *IconEditorPlugin::create(const QString &, QWidget *parent,
                                      const char *name)
    {
        return new IconEditor(parent, name);
    }
```

The `create()` function is called by *Qt Designer* to create an instance of a widget class. The first argument is the widget's class name. We can ignore it in this example, because we only provide one class. All the other functions also take a class name as their first argument.

```
    QString IconEditorPlugin::includeFile(const QString &) const
    {
        return "iconeditor.h";
    }
```

The `includeFile()` function returns the name of the header file for the specified widget encapsulated by the plugin. The header file is included in the code generated by the `uic` tool.

```
    bool IconEditorPlugin::isContainer(const QString &) const
    {
        return false;
    }
```

The `isContainer()` function returns `true` if the widget can contain other widgets; otherwise, it returns `false`. For example, `QFrame` is a widget that can contain other widgets. We return `false` for the `IconEditor`, since it doesn't make sense for it to contain other widgets. Strictly speaking, any widget can contain other widgets, but *Qt Designer* disallows this when `isContainer()` returns `false`.

```
    QString IconEditorPlugin::group(const QString &) const
    {
        return "Plugin Widgets";
    }
```

The group() function returns the name of the toolbox group this custom widget should belong to. If the name isn't already in use, *Qt Designer* automatically creates a new group for the widget.

```
QIconSet IconEditorPlugin::iconSet(const QString &) const
{
    return QIconSet(QPixmap::fromMimeSource("iconeditor.png"));
}
```

The iconSet() function returns the icon to use to represent the custom widget in *Qt Designer*'s toolbox.

```
QString IconEditorPlugin::toolTip(const QString &) const
{
    return "Icon Editor";
}
```

The toolTip() function returns the tooltip to show when the mouse hovers over the custom widget in *Qt Designer*'s toolbox.

```
QString IconEditorPlugin::whatsThis(const QString &) const
{
    return "Widget for creating and editing icons";
}
```

The whatsThis() function returns the "What's This?" text for *Qt Designer* to display.

```
Q_EXPORT_PLUGIN(IconEditorPlugin)
```

At the end of the source file that implements the plugin class, we must use the Q_EXPORT_PLUGIN() macro to make the plugin available to *Qt Designer*.

The .pro file for building the plugin looks like this:

```
TEMPLATE       = lib
CONFIG        += plugin
HEADERS        = ../iconeditor/iconeditor.h
SOURCES        = iconeditorplugin.cpp \
                 ../iconeditor/iconeditor.cpp
IMAGES         = images/iconeditor.png
DESTDIR        = $(QTDIR)/plugins/designer
```

The .pro file assumes that the QTDIR environment variable is set to the directory where Qt is installed. When you type make or nmake to build the plugin, it will automatically install itself in *Qt Designer*'s plugins directory.

Once the plugin is built, the IconEditor widget can be used in *Qt Designer* in the same way as any of Qt's built-in widgets.

## Double Buffering

Double buffering is a technique that can be used to provide a snappier user interface and to eliminate flicker. Flicker occurs when the same pixel is painted multiple times with different colors in a very short period of time. If this occurs for only one pixel, it isn't a problem, but if it occurs for lots of pixels at the same time, it can be distracting for the user.

When Qt generates a paint event, it first erases the widget using the palette's background color. Then, in `paintEvent()`, the widget only needs to paint the pixels that are not the same color as the background. This two-step approach is very convenient, because it means we can simply paint what we need on the widget without worrying about the other pixels.

Unfortunately, the two-step approach is also a major source of flicker. For example, if the user resizes the widget, the widget is first cleared in its entirety, and then the pixels are painted. The flicker is even worse if the window system shows the contents of the window as it is resized, because then the widget is repeatedly erased and painted.

**Figure 5.7.** Resizing a widget that has no provision against flicker

The `WStaticContents` flag used to implement the `IconEditor` widget is one solution to this problem, but it can only be used for widgets whose content is independent of the size of the widget. Such widgets are rare. Most widgets tend to stretch their contents to consume all the available space. They need to be completely repainted when they are resized. We can still avoid flicker, but the solution is slightly more complicated.

The first rule to avoid flicker is to construct the widget with the `WNoAutoErase` flag. This flag tells Qt *not* to erase the widget before a paint event. The old pixels are then left unchanged, and any newly revealed pixels are undefined.

**Figure 5.8.** Resizing a `WNoAutoErase` widget

When using `WNoAutoErase`, it is important that the paint handler sets all the pixels explicitly. Any pixel that is not set in the paint event will keep its previous value, which isn't necessarily the background color.

The second rule to avoid flicker is to paint every pixel just once. The easiest way to implement this requirement is to draw the whole widget in an off-screen pixmap and to copy the pixmap onto the widget in one go. Using this approach, it doesn't matter if some pixels are painted multiple times because the painting takes place off-screen. This is double buffering.

Adding double buffering to a custom widget to eliminate flicker is straightforward. Suppose the original paint event handler looks like this:

```
void MyWidget::paintEvent(QPaintEvent *)
{
    QPainter painter(this);
    drawMyStuff(&painter);
}
```

The double-buffered version looks like this:

```
void MyWidget::paintEvent(QPaintEvent *event)
{
    static QPixmap pixmap;
    QRect rect = event->rect();

    QSize newSize = rect.size().expandedTo(pixmap.size());
    pixmap.resize(newSize);
    pixmap.fill(this, rect.topLeft());

    QPainter painter(&pixmap, this);
    painter.translate(-rect.x(), -rect.y());
    drawMyStuff(&painter);
    bitBlt(this, rect.x(), rect.y(), &pixmap, 0, 0,
           rect.width(), rect.height());
}
```

First, we resize a `QPixmap` to be at least as large as the bounding rectangle of the region to repaint. (A "region" is very often either a rectangle or an L-shaped area, but it can be arbitrarily complex.) We make the `QPixmap` a static variable to avoid repeatedly allocating and deallocating it. For the same reason, we never shrink the `QPixmap`; the calls to `QSize::expandedTo()` and `QPixmap::resize()` ensure that it is always large enough. After resizing, we fill the `QPixmap` with the widget's erase color or background pixmap using `QPixmap::fill()`. The second argument to `fill()` specifies which point in the widget the `QPixmap`'s top-left pixel corresponds to. (This makes a difference if the widget is to be erased using a pixmap instead of a uniform color.)

The `QPixmap` class is similar to both `QImage` and `QWidget`. Like a `QImage`, it stores an image, but the color depth and possibly the colormap are aligned with the display, rather like a hidden `QWidget`. If the window system is running in 8-bit mode, all widgets and pixmaps are restricted to 256 colors, and Qt automatically maps 24-bit color specifications onto 8-bit colors. (Qt's color allocation strategy is controlled by calling `QApplication::setColorSpec()`.)

Next, we create a `QPainter` to operate on the pixmap. By passing the `this` pointer to the constructor, we tell `QPainter` to adopt some of the widget's settings, such as its font. We translate the painter to paint the correct rectangle into the pixmap, before we perform the drawing using the `QPainter` as usual.

Finally, we copy the pixmap to the widget using the `bitBlt()` global function, whose name stands for "bit-block transfer".

Double buffering is not only useful for avoiding flicker. It is beneficial if the widget's rendering is complex and needed repeatedly. We can then store a pixmap permanently with the widget, always ready for the next paint event, and copy the pixmap to the widget whenever we receive a paint event. It is especially helpful when we want to do small modifications, such as drawing a rubber band, without recomputing the whole widget's rendering over and over.

We will round off this chapter by reviewing the `Plotter` custom widget. This widget uses double buffering, and also demonstrates some other aspects of Qt programming, including keyboard event handling, manual layout, and coordinate systems.

The `Plotter` widget displays one or more curves specified as vectors of coordinates. The user can draw a rubber band on the image, and the `Plotter` will zoom in on the area enclosed by the rubber band. The user draws the rubber band by clicking a point on the graph, dragging the mouse to another position with the left mouse button held down, and releasing the mouse button.

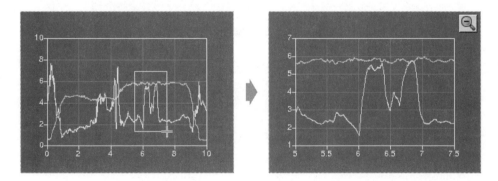

**Figure 5.9.** Zooming in on the `Plotter` widget

The user can zoom in repeatedly by drawing a rubber band multiple times, zooming out using the Zoom Out button, and then zooming back in using the Zoom In button. The Zoom In and Zoom Out buttons appear the first time they become available, so that they don't clutter the display if the user doesn't zoom the graph.

The `Plotter` widget can hold the data for any number of curves. It also maintains a stack of `PlotSettings`, each of which corresponds to a particular zoom level.

Let's review the class, starting with `plotter.h`:

```
#ifndef PLOTTER_H
#define PLOTTER_H

#include <qpixmap.h>
#include <qwidget.h>

#include <map>
#include <vector>

class QToolButton;
class PlotSettings;

typedef std::vector<double> CurveData;
```

We include the standard `<map>` and `<vector>` header files. We don't import all the std namespace's symbols into the global namespace, because it's bad style to do this in a header file.

We define `CurveData` as a synonym for `std::vector<double>`. We will store a curve's points as successive pairs of *x* and *y* values in the vector. For example, the curve defined by the points (0, 24), (1, 44), (2, 89) is represented by the vector |0, 24, 1, 44, 2, 89|.

```
class Plotter : public QWidget
{
    Q_OBJECT
public:
    Plotter(QWidget *parent = 0, const char *name = 0,
            WFlags flags = 0);

    void setPlotSettings(const PlotSettings &settings);
    void setCurveData(int id, const CurveData &data);
    void clearCurve(int id);
    QSize minimumSizeHint() const;
    QSize sizeHint() const;

public slots:
    void zoomIn();
    void zoomOut();
```

We provide three public functions for setting up the plot, and two public slots for zooming in and out. We also reimplement `minimumSizeHint()` and `sizeHint()` from `QWidget`.

```
protected:
    void paintEvent(QPaintEvent *event);
    void resizeEvent(QResizeEvent *event);
    void mousePressEvent(QMouseEvent *event);
    void mouseMoveEvent(QMouseEvent *event);
    void mouseReleaseEvent(QMouseEvent *event);
    void keyPressEvent(QKeyEvent *event);
    void wheelEvent(QWheelEvent *event);
```

In the protected section of the class, we declare all the `QWidget` event handlers that we need to reimplement.

```
private:
    void updateRubberBandRegion();
    void refreshPixmap();
    void drawGrid(QPainter *painter);
    void drawCurves(QPainter *painter);

    enum { Margin = 40 };

    QToolButton *zoomInButton;
    QToolButton *zoomOutButton;
    std::map<int, CurveData> curveMap;
    std::vector<PlotSettings> zoomStack;
    int curZoom;
    bool rubberBandIsShown;
    QRect rubberBandRect;
    QPixmap pixmap;
};
```

In the private section of the class, we declare a constant, a few functions for painting the widget, and several member variables. The `Margin` constant is used to provide some spacing around the graph.

Among the member variables is `pixmap` of type `QPixmap`. This variable holds a copy of the whole widget's rendering, identical to what is shown on screen. The plot is always drawn onto this off-screen pixmap first; then the pixmap is copied onto the widget.

```
class PlotSettings
{
public:
    PlotSettings();

    void scroll(int dx, int dy);
    void adjust();
    double spanX() const { return maxX - minX; }
    double spanY() const { return maxY - minY; }

    double minX;
    double maxX;
    int numXTicks;
    double minY;
    double maxY;
    int numYTicks;

private:
    void adjustAxis(double &min, double &max, int &numTicks);
};

#endif
```

The `PlotSettings` class specifies the range of the *x* and *y* axes and the number of ticks for these axes. Figure 5.10 shows the correspondence between a `PlotSettings` object and the scales on a `Plotter` widget.

By convention, `numXTicks` and `numYTicks` are off by one; if `numXTicks` is 5, `Plotter` will actually draw 6 tick marks on the *x* axis. This simplifies the calculations later on.

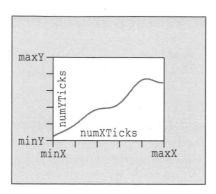

**Figure 5.10.** `PlotSettings`'s member variables

Now let's review the implementation file:

```cpp
#include <qpainter.h>
#include <qstyle.h>
#include <qtoolbutton.h>

#include <cmath>
using namespace std;

#include "plotter.h"
```

We include the expected header files and import all the std namespace's symbols into the global namespace.

```cpp
Plotter::Plotter(QWidget *parent, const char *name, WFlags flags)
    : QWidget(parent, name, flags | WNoAutoErase)
{
    setBackgroundMode(PaletteDark);
    setSizePolicy(QSizePolicy::Expanding, QSizePolicy::Expanding);
    setFocusPolicy(StrongFocus);
    rubberBandIsShown = false;

    zoomInButton = new QToolButton(this);
    zoomInButton->setIconSet(QPixmap::fromMimeSource("zoomin.png"));
    zoomInButton->adjustSize();
    connect(zoomInButton, SIGNAL(clicked()), this, SLOT(zoomIn()));

    zoomOutButton = new QToolButton(this);
    zoomOutButton->setIconSet(
            QPixmap::fromMimeSource("zoomout.png"));
    zoomOutButton->adjustSize();
    connect(zoomOutButton, SIGNAL(clicked()), this, SLOT(zoomOut()));

    setPlotSettings(PlotSettings());
}
```

The `Plotter` has a `flags` parameter in addition to `parent` and `name`. This parameter is simply passed on to the base class constructor, along with `WNoAutoErase`. The parameter is especially useful for widgets that are likely to be used as stand-alone windows, because it allows the user of the class to configure the window frame and title bar.

The setBackgroundMode() call tells QWidget to use the "dark" component of the palette as the color for erasing the widget, instead of the "background" component. Although we pass the WNoAutoErase flag to the base class constructor, Qt still needs a default color that it may use to fill any newly revealed pixels when the widget is resized to a larger size, before paintEvent() even has the chance to paint the new pixels. Since the background of the Plotter widget will be dark, it makes sense to paint these pixels dark.

The setSizePolicy() call sets the widget's size policy to QSizePolicy::Expanding in both directions. This tells any layout manager that is responsible for the widget that the widget is especially willing to grow, but can also shrink. This setting is typical for widgets that can take up a lot of screen space. The default is QSizePolicy::Preferred in both directions, which means that the widget prefers to be the size of its size hint, but it can be shrunk down to its minimum size hint or expanded indefinitely if necessary.

The setFocusPolicy() call makes the widget accept focus by clicking or by pressing Tab. When the Plotter has focus, it will receive events for key presses. The Plotter widget understands a few keys: + to zoom in, - to zoom out, and the arrow keys to scroll up, down, left, and right.

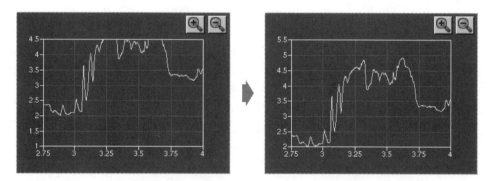

**Figure 5.11.** Scrolling the Plotter widget

Still in the constructor, we create two QToolButtons, each with an icon. These buttons allow the user to navigate through the zoom stack. The button's icons are stored in an image collection. Any application that uses the Plotter widget will need this entry in its .pro file:

```
IMAGES          += images/zoomin.png \
                   images/zoomout.png
```

The calls to adjustSize() on the buttons sets their sizes to be that of their size hints.

The call to setPlotSettings() at the end does the rest of the initialization.

```
void Plotter::setPlotSettings(const PlotSettings &settings)
{
    zoomStack.resize(1);
    zoomStack[0] = settings;
```

```
        curZoom = 0;
        zoomInButton->hide();
        zoomOutButton->hide();
        refreshPixmap();
    }
```

The `setPlotSettings()` function is used to specify the `PlotSettings` to use for displaying the plot. It is called by the `Plotter` constructor, and can be called by users of the class. The plotter starts out at its default zoom level. Each time the user zooms in, a new `PlotSettings` instance is created and put onto the zoom stack.

The zoom stack is represented by two member variables:

- `zoomStack` holds the different zoom settings as a `vector<PlotSettings>`.
- `curZoom` holds the current `PlotSettings`'s index in the `zoomStack`.

After a call to `setPlotSettings()`, the zoom stack contains only one entry, and the Zoom In and Zoom Out buttons are hidden. These buttons will not be shown until we call `show()` on them in the `zoomIn()` and `zoomOut()` slots. (Normally, it is sufficient to call `show()` on the top-level widget to show all the children. But when we explicitly call `hide()` on a child widget, it is hidden until we call `show()` on it.)

The call to `refreshPixmap()` is necessary to update the display. Usually, we would call `update()`, but here we do things slightly differently because we want to keep a `QPixmap` up to date at all times. After regenerating the pixmap, `refreshPixmap()` calls `update()` to copy the pixmap onto the widget.

```
    void Plotter::zoomOut()
    {
        if (curZoom > 0) {
            --curZoom;
            zoomOutButton->setEnabled(curZoom > 0);
            zoomInButton->setEnabled(true);
            zoomInButton->show();
            refreshPixmap();
        }
    }
```

The `zoomOut()` slot zooms out if the graph is zoomed in. It decrements the current zoom level and enables the Zoom Out button depending on whether the graph can be zoomed out any more or not. The Zoom In button is enabled and shown, and the display is updated with a call to `refreshPixmap()`.

```
    void Plotter::zoomIn()
    {
        if (curZoom < (int)zoomStack.size() - 1) {
            ++curZoom;
            zoomInButton->setEnabled(
                    curZoom < (int)zoomStack.size() - 1);
            zoomOutButton->setEnabled(true);
            zoomOutButton->show();
            refreshPixmap();
```

```
    }
}
```

If the user has previously zoomed in and then out again, the PlotSettings for the next zoom level will be in the zoom stack, and we can zoom in. (Otherwise, it is still possible to zoom in using a rubber band.)

The slot increments curZoom to move one level deeper into the zoom stack, sets the Zoom In button enabled or disabled depending on whether it's possible to zoom in any further, and enables and shows the Zoom Out button. Again, we call refreshPixmap() to make the plotter use the latest zoom settings.

```
void Plotter::setCurveData(int id, const CurveData &data)
{
    curveMap[id] = data;
    refreshPixmap();
}
```

The setCurveData() function sets the curve data for a given curve ID. If a curve with the same ID already exists in the plotter, it is replaced with the new curve data; otherwise, the new curve is simply inserted. The curves are stored in the curveMap member variable of type map<int, CurveData>.

Again, we call our own refreshPixmap() function, rather than update(), to update the display.

```
void Plotter::clearCurve(int id)
{
    curveMap.erase(id);
    refreshPixmap();
}
```

The clearCurve() function removes a curve from curveMap.

```
QSize Plotter::minimumSizeHint() const
{
    return QSize(4 * Margin, 4 * Margin);
}
```

The minimumSizeHint() function is similar to sizeHint(); just as sizeHint() specifies a widget's ideal size, minimumSizeHint() specifies a widget's ideal minimum size. A layout never resizes a widget below its minimum size hint.

The value we return is 160 × 160 to allow for the margin on all four sides and some space for the plot itself. Below that size, the plot would be too small to be useful.

```
QSize Plotter::sizeHint() const
{
    return QSize(8 * Margin, 6 * Margin);
}
```

In sizeHint(), we return an "ideal" size in proportion to the margin and with a pleasing 4:3 aspect ratio.

This finishes the review of the `Plotter`'s public functions and slots. Now let's review the protected event handlers.

```
void Plotter::paintEvent(QPaintEvent *event)
{
    QMemArray<QRect> rects = event->region().rects();
    for (int i = 0; i < (int)rects.size(); ++i)
        bitBlt(this, rects[i].topLeft(), &pixmap, rects[i]);

    QPainter painter(this);

    if (rubberBandIsShown) {
        painter.setPen(colorGroup().light());
        painter.drawRect(rubberBandRect.normalize());
    }
    if (hasFocus()) {
        style().drawPrimitive(QStyle::PE_FocusRect, &painter,
                              rect(), colorGroup(),
                              QStyle::Style_FocusAtBorder,
                              colorGroup().dark());
    }
}
```

Normally, `paintEvent()` is the place where we perform all the drawing. But here all the plot drawing is done beforehand in `refreshPixmap()`, so we can render the entire plot simply by copying the pixmap onto the widget.

The call to `QRegion::rect()` returns an array of `QRect`s that define the region to repaint. We use `bitBlt()` to copy each rectangular area from the pixmap to the widget. The `bitBlt()` global function has the following syntax:

```
bitBlt(dest, destPos, source, sourceRect);
```

where *source* is the source widget or pixmap, *sourceRect* is the rectangle in the source that should be copied, *dest* is the destination widget or pixmap, and *destPos* is the top-left position in the destination.

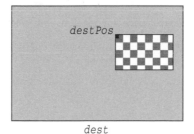

**Figure 5.12.** Copying arbitrary rectangles to and from pixmaps and widgets

It would have been equally correct to call `bitBlt()` just once on the region's bounding rectangle, as we did in a previous code snippet (p. 113). However, because we call `update()` to erase and redraw the rubber band repeatedly in the mouse event handlers (as we will see shortly), and the rubber band outline is basically four tiny rectangles (two 1-pixel-wide rectangles and two

1-pixel-high rectangles), we gain some speed by breaking the region down into its constituent rectangles and calling `bitBlt()` for each rectangle.

Once the plot is shown on screen, we draw the rubber band and the focus rectangle on top of it. For the rubber band, we use the "light" component from the widget's current color group as the pen color to ensure good contrast with the "dark" background. Notice that we draw directly on the widget, leaving the off-screen pixmap untouched. The focus rectangle is drawn using the widget style's `drawPrimitive()` function with `PE_FocusRect` as its first argument.

The `QWidget::style()` function returns the widget style to use to draw the widget. In Qt, a widget style is a subclass of `QStyle`. The built-in styles include `QWindowsStyle`, `QWindowsXPStyle`, `QMotifStyle`, and `QMacStyle`. Each of these styles reimplements the virtual functions in `QStyle` to perform the drawing in the correct way for the platform the style is emulating. The `drawPrimitive()` function is one of these functions; it draws "primitive elements" like panels, buttons, and focus rectangles. The widget style is usually the same for all widgets in an application (`QApplication::style()`), but it can be overridden on a per-widget basis using `QWidget::setStyle()`.

By subclassing `QStyle`, it is possible to define a custom style. This can be done to give a distinctive look to an application or a suite of applications. While it is generally advisable to use the target platform's native look and feel, Qt offers a lot of flexibility if you want to be adventurous.

Qt's built-in widgets rely almost exclusively on `QStyle` to paint themselves. This is why they look like native widgets on all platforms supported by Qt. Custom widgets can be made style-aware either by using `QStyle` to paint themselves or by using built-in Qt widgets as child widgets. For `Plotter`, we use both approaches: The focus rectangle is drawn using `QStyle`, and the Zoom In and Zoom Out buttons are built-in Qt widgets.

```
void Plotter::resizeEvent(QResizeEvent *)
{
    int x = width() - (zoomInButton->width()
                          + zoomOutButton->width() + 10);
    zoomInButton->move(x, 5);
    zoomOutButton->move(x + zoomInButton->width() + 5, 5);
    refreshPixmap();
}
```

Whenever the `Plotter` widget is resized, Qt generates a "resize" event. Here, we reimplement `resizeEvent()` to place the Zoom In and Zoom Out buttons at the top right of the `Plotter` widget.

We move the Zoom In button and the Zoom Out button to be side by side, separated by a 5-pixel gap and with a 5-pixel offset from the top and right edges of the parent widget.

If we wanted the buttons to stay rooted to the top-left corner, whose coordinates are (0, 0), we would simply have moved them there in the `Plotter` constructor. But we want to track the top-right corner, whose coordinates depend on the size of the widget. Because of this, it's necessary to reimplement re-sizeEvent() and to set the position there.

We didn't set any positions for the buttons in the Plotter constructor. This isn't an issue, since Qt always generates a resize event before a widget is shown for the first time.

An alternative to reimplementing resizeEvent() and laying out the child widgets manually would have been to use a layout manager (for example, QGrid-Layout). However, it would have been a little more complicated and would have consumed more resources. When we write widgets from scratch as we are doing here, laying out our child widgets manually is usually the right approach.

At the end, we call refreshPixmap() to redraw the pixmap at the new size.

```cpp
void Plotter::mousePressEvent(QMouseEvent *event)
{
    if (event->button() == LeftButton) {
        rubberBandIsShown = true;
        rubberBandRect.setTopLeft(event->pos());
        rubberBandRect.setBottomRight(event->pos());
        updateRubberBandRegion();
        setCursor(crossCursor);
    }
}
```

When the user presses the left mouse button, we start displaying a rubber band. This involves setting rubberBandIsShown to true, initializing the rubber-BandRect member variable with the current mouse pointer position, scheduling a paint event to paint the rubber band, and changing the mouse cursor to have a crosshair shape.

Qt provides two mechanisms for controlling the mouse cursor's shape:

- QWidget::setCursor() sets the cursor shape to use when the mouse hovers over a particular widget. If no cursor is set for a widget, the parent widget's cursor is used. The default for top-level widgets is an arrow cursor.

- QApplication::setOverrideCursor() sets the cursor shape for the entire application, overriding the cursors set by individual widgets until restore-OverrideCursor() is called.

In Chapter 4, we called QApplication::setOverrideCursor() with waitCursor to change the application's cursor to the standard wait cursor.

```cpp
void Plotter::mouseMoveEvent(QMouseEvent *event)
{
    if (event->state() & LeftButton) {
        updateRubberBandRegion();
        rubberBandRect.setBottomRight(event->pos());
        updateRubberBandRegion();
    }
}
```

When the user moves the mouse cursor while holding the left button, we call updateRubberBandRegion() to schedule a paint event to repaint the area where the rubber band was, we update rubberBandRect to account for the mouse move, and we call updateRubberBandRegion() a second time to repaint the area where the rubber band has moved to. This effectively erases the rubber band and redraws it at the new coordinates.

The rubberBandRect variable is of type QRect. A QRect can be defined either as an $(x, y, w, h)$ quadruple—where $(x, y)$ is the position of the top-left corner and $w \times h$ is the size of the rectangle—or as a top-left and a bottom-right coordinate pair. Here, we have used the coordinate pair representation. We set the point where the user clicked the first time as the top-left corner and the current mouse position as the bottom-right corner.

If the user moves the mouse upward or leftward, it's likely that rubberBand-Rect's nominal bottom-right corner will end up above or to the left of its top-left corner. If this occurs, the QRect will have a negative width or height. QRect has a normalize() function that adjusts the top-left and bottom-right coordinates to obtain a nonnegative width and height.

```
void Plotter::mouseReleaseEvent(QMouseEvent *event)
{
    if (event->button() == LeftButton) {
        rubberBandIsShown = false;
        updateRubberBandRegion();
        unsetCursor();

        QRect rect = rubberBandRect.normalize();
        if (rect.width() < 4 || rect.height() < 4)
            return;
        rect.moveBy(-Margin, -Margin);

        PlotSettings prevSettings = zoomStack[curZoom];
        PlotSettings settings;
        double dx = prevSettings.spanX() / (width() - 2 * Margin);
        double dy = prevSettings.spanY() / (height() - 2 * Margin);
        settings.minX = prevSettings.minX + dx * rect.left();
        settings.maxX = prevSettings.minX + dx * rect.right();
        settings.minY = prevSettings.maxY - dy * rect.bottom();
        settings.maxY = prevSettings.maxY - dy * rect.top();
        settings.adjust();

        zoomStack.resize(curZoom + 1);
        zoomStack.push_back(settings);
        zoomIn();
    }
}
```

When the user releases the left mouse button, we erase the rubber band and restore the standard arrow cursor. If the rubber band is at least 4 × 4, we perform the zoom. If the rubber band is smaller than that, it's likely that the user clicked the widget by mistake or to give it focus, so we do nothing.

The code to perform the zoom is a bit complicated. This is because we deal with two coordinate systems at the same time: widget coordinates and plotter coordinates. Most of the work we perform here is to convert the `rubberBandRect` from widget coordinates to plotter coordinates.

Once we have done the conversion, we call `PlotSettings::adjust()` to round the numbers and find a sensible number of ticks for each axis.

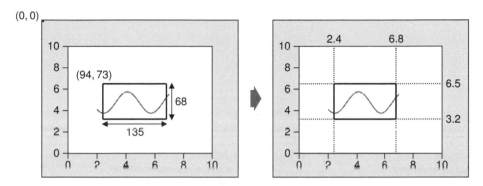

**Figure 5.13.** Converting the rubber band from widget to plotter coordinates

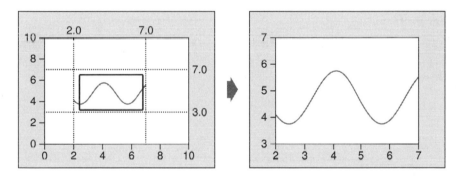

**Figure 5.14.** Adjusting plotter coordinates and zooming in on the rubber band

Then we perform the zoom. The zoom is achieved by pushing the new `PlotSettings` that we have just calculated on top of the zoom stack and calling `zoomIn()` to do the job.

```
void Plotter::keyPressEvent(QKeyEvent *event)
{
    switch (event->key()) {
    case Key_Plus:
        zoomIn();
        break;
    case Key_Minus:
        zoomOut();
        break;
    case Key_Left:
        zoomStack[curZoom].scroll(-1, 0);
        refreshPixmap();
```

```
        break;
    case Key_Right:
        zoomStack[curZoom].scroll(+1, 0);
        refreshPixmap();
        break;
    case Key_Down:
        zoomStack[curZoom].scroll(0, -1);
        refreshPixmap();
        break;
    case Key_Up:
        zoomStack[curZoom].scroll(0, +1);
        refreshPixmap();
        break;
    default:
        QWidget::keyPressEvent(event);
    }
}
```

When the user presses a key and the `Plotter` widget has focus, the `keyPress-Event()` function is called. We reimplement it here to respond to six keys: +, -, Up, Down, Left, and Right. If the user pressed a key that we are not handling, we call the base class implementation. For simplicity, we ignore the Shift, Ctrl, and Alt modifier keys, which are available through `QKeyEvent::state()`.

```
void Plotter::wheelEvent(QWheelEvent *event)
{
    int numDegrees = event->delta() / 8;
    int numTicks = numDegrees / 15;

    if (event->orientation() == Horizontal)
        zoomStack[curZoom].scroll(numTicks, 0);
    else
        zoomStack[curZoom].scroll(0, numTicks);
    refreshPixmap();
}
```

Wheel events occur when a mouse wheel is turned. Most mice only provide a vertical wheel, but some also have a horizontal wheel. Qt supports both kinds of wheels. Wheel events go to the widget that has the focus. The `delta()` function returns the distance the wheel was rotated in eighths of a degree. Mice typically work in steps of 15 degrees.

The most common use of the wheel mouse is to scroll a scroll bar. When we subclass `QScrollView` (covered in Chapter 6) to provide scroll bars, `QScrollView` handles the wheel mouse events automatically, so we don't need to reimplement `wheelEvent()` ourselves. Qt classes like `QListView`, `QTable`, and `QTextEdit` that inherit `QScrollView` also support wheel events without needing additional code.

This finishes the implementation of the event handlers. Now let's review the private functions.

```
void Plotter::updateRubberBandRegion()
{
    QRect rect = rubberBandRect.normalize();
```

```
        update(rect.left(), rect.top(), rect.width(), 1);
        update(rect.left(), rect.top(), 1, rect.height());
        update(rect.left(), rect.bottom(), rect.width(), 1);
        update(rect.right(), rect.top(), 1, rect.height());
    }
```

The `updateRubberBand()` function is called from `mousePressEvent()`, `mouseMove-Event()`, and `mouseReleaseEvent()` to erase or redraw the rubber band. It consists of four calls to `update()` that schedule a paint event for the four small rectangular areas that are covered by the rubber band.

## Using NOT to Draw the Rubber Band

A common way to draw a rubber band is to use the NOT (or the XOR) mathematical operator, which replaces each pixel value on the rubber band rectangle with the opposite bit pattern. Here's a new version of `updateRubber-BandRegion()` that does this:

```
void Plotter::updateRubberBandRegion()
{
    QPainter painter(this);
    painter.setRasterOp(NotROP);
    painter.drawRect(rubberBandRect.normalize());
}
```

The `setRasterOp()` call sets the painter's raster operation to be `NotROP`. In the original version, we kept the default value, `CopyROP`, which told `QPainter` to simply copy the new value over the original.

When we call `updateRubberBandRegion()` a second time with the same coordinates, the original pixels are restored, since two NOTs cancel each other out.

The advantage of using NOT is that it's easy to implement and it eliminates the need to keep a copy of the covered areas. But it isn't generally applicable. For example, if we draw text instead of a rubber band, the text could become very hard to read. Also, NOT doesn't always produce good contrast; for example, medium gray stays medium gray. Finally, NOT isn't supported on Mac OS X.

Another approach is to render the rubber band as an animated dotted line. This is often used in image manipulation programs, because it provides good contrast no matter what colors are found in the image. To do this in Qt, the trick is to reimplement `QObject::timerEvent()` to erase the rubber band and then repaint it but starting drawing the dots at a slightly different offset each time, producing the illusion of movement.

```
void Plotter::refreshPixmap()
{
    pixmap.resize(size());
    pixmap.fill(this, 0, 0);
    QPainter painter(&pixmap, this);
    drawGrid(&painter);
```

```
        drawCurves(&painter);
        update();
    }
```

The `refreshPixmap()` function redraws the plot onto the off-screen pixmap and updates the display.

We resize the pixmap to have the same size as the widget and fill it with the widget's erase color. This color is the "dark" component of the palette, because of the call to `setBackgroundMode()` in the `Plotter` constructor.

Then we create a `QPainter` to draw on the pixmap and call `drawGrid()` and `drawCurves()` to perform the drawing. At the end, we call `update()` to schedule a paint event for the whole widget. The pixmap is copied to the widget in the `paintEvent()` function (p. 121).

```
    void Plotter::drawGrid(QPainter *painter)
    {
        QRect rect(Margin, Margin,
                   width() - 2 * Margin, height() - 2 * Margin);
        PlotSettings settings = zoomStack[curZoom];
        QPen quiteDark = colorGroup().dark().light();
        QPen light = colorGroup().light();

        for (int i = 0; i <= settings.numXTicks; ++i) {
            int x = rect.left() + (i * (rect.width() - 1)
                                   / settings.numXTicks);
            double label = settings.minX + (i * settings.spanX()
                                            / settings.numXTicks);
            painter->setPen(quiteDark);
            painter->drawLine(x, rect.top(), x, rect.bottom());
            painter->setPen(light);
            painter->drawLine(x, rect.bottom(), x, rect.bottom() + 5);
            painter->drawText(x - 50, rect.bottom() + 5, 100, 15,
                              AlignHCenter | AlignTop,
                              QString::number(label));
        }
        for (int j = 0; j <= settings.numYTicks; ++j) {
            int y = rect.bottom() - (j * (rect.height() - 1)
                                     / settings.numYTicks);
            double label = settings.minY + (j * settings.spanY()
                                            / settings.numYTicks);
            painter->setPen(quiteDark);
            painter->drawLine(rect.left(), y, rect.right(), y);
            painter->setPen(light);
            painter->drawLine(rect.left() - 5, y, rect.left(), y);
            painter->drawText(rect.left() - Margin, y - 10,
                              Margin - 5, 20,
                              AlignRight | AlignVCenter,
                              QString::number(label));
        }
        painter->drawRect(rect);
    }
```

The `drawGrid()` function draws the grid behind the curves and the axes.

The first `for` loop draws the grid's vertical lines and the ticks along the *x* axis. The second `for` loop draws the grid's horizontal lines and the ticks along the *y* axis. The `drawText()` function is used to draw the numbers corresponding to the tick mark on both axes.

The calls to `drawText()` have the following syntax:

```
painter.drawText(x, y, w, h, alignment, text);
```

where (*x*, *y*, *w*, *h*) define a rectangle, `alignment` the position of the text within that rectangle, and `text` the text to draw.

```
void Plotter::drawCurves(QPainter *painter)
{
    static const QColor colorForIds[6] = {
        red, green, blue, cyan, magenta, yellow
    };
    PlotSettings settings = zoomStack[curZoom];
    QRect rect(Margin, Margin,
               width() - 2 * Margin, height() - 2 * Margin);

    painter->setClipRect(rect.x() + 1, rect.y() + 1,
                         rect.width() - 2, rect.height() - 2);

    map<int, CurveData>::const_iterator it = curveMap.begin();
    while (it != curveMap.end()) {
        int id = (*it).first;
        const CurveData &data = (*it).second;
        int numPoints = 0;
        int maxPoints = data.size() / 2;
        QPointArray points(maxPoints);

        for (int i = 0; i < maxPoints; ++i) {
            double dx = data[2 * i] - settings.minX;
            double dy = data[2 * i + 1] - settings.minY;
            double x = rect.left() + (dx * (rect.width() - 1)
                                        / settings.spanX());
            double y = rect.bottom() - (dy * (rect.height() - 1)
                                        / settings.spanY());
            if (fabs(x) < 32768 && fabs(y) < 32768) {
                points[numPoints] = QPoint((int)x, (int)y);
                ++numPoints;
            }
        }
        points.truncate(numPoints);
        painter->setPen(colorForIds[(uint)id % 6]);
        painter->drawPolyline(points);
        ++it;
    }
}
```

The `drawCurves()` function draws the curves on top of the grid. We start by calling `setClipRect()` to set the `QPainter`'s clip region to the rectangle that contains the curves (excluding the margins). `QPainter` will then ignore drawing operations on pixels outside the area.

Next, we iterate over all the curves, and for each curve, we iterate over the $(x, y)$ coordinate pairs that constitute it. The `first` member of the iterator's value gives us the ID of the curve and the `second` member gives us the curve data.

The inner part of the `for` loop converts a coordinate pair from plotter coordinates to widget coordinates and stores it in the `points` variable, provided that it lies within reasonable bounds. If the user zooms in a lot, we could easily end up with numbers that cannot be represented as 16-bit signed integers, leading to incorrect rendering by some window systems.

Once we have converted all the points of a curve to widget coordinates, we set the pen color for the curve (using one of a set of predefined colors) and call `drawPolyline()` to draw a line that goes through all the curve's points.

This is the complete `Plotter` class. All that remains are a few functions in `PlotSettings`.

```
PlotSettings::PlotSettings()
{
    minX = 0.0;
    maxX = 10.0;
    numXTicks = 5;

    minY = 0.0;
    maxY = 10.0;
    numYTicks = 5;
}
```

The `PlotSettings` constructor initializes both axes to the range 0 to 10 with 5 tick marks.

```
void PlotSettings::scroll(int dx, int dy)
{
    double stepX = spanX() / numXTicks;
    minX += dx * stepX;
    maxX += dx * stepX;

    double stepY = spanY() / numYTicks;
    minY += dy * stepY;
    maxY += dy * stepY;
}
```

The `scroll()` function increments (or decrements) `minX`, `maxX`, `minY`, and `maxY` by the interval between two ticks times a given number. This function is used to implement scrolling in `Plotter::keyPressEvent()`.

```
void PlotSettings::adjust()
{
    adjustAxis(minX, maxX, numXTicks);
    adjustAxis(minY, maxY, numYTicks);
}
```

The `adjust()` function is called from `mouseReleaseEvent()` to round the `minX`, `maxX`, `minY`, and `maxY` values to "nice" values and to determine the number of ticks appropriate for each axis. The private function `adjustAxis()` does its work one axis at a time.

```
    void PlotSettings::adjustAxis(double &min, double &max,
                                  int &numTicks)
{
    const int MinTicks = 4;
    double grossStep = (max - min) / MinTicks;
    double step = pow(10, floor(log10(grossStep)));

    if (5 * step < grossStep)
        step *= 5;
    else if (2 * step < grossStep)
        step *= 2;

    numTicks = (int)(ceil(max / step) - floor(min / step));
    min = floor(min / step) * step;
    max = ceil(max / step) * step;
}
```

The `adjustAxis()` function converts its `min` and `max` parameters into "nice" numbers and sets its `numTicks` parameter to the number of ticks it calculates to be appropriate for the given [`min`, `max`] range. Because `adjustAxis()` needs to modify the actual variables (`minX`, `maxX`, `numXTicks`, etc.) and not just copies, its parameters are non-const references.

Most of the code in `adjustAxis()` simply attempts to determine an appropriate value for the interval between two ticks (the "step"). To obtain nice numbers along the axis, we must select the step with care. For example, a step value of 3.8 would lead to an axis with multiples of 3.8, which is difficult for people to relate to. For axes labelled in decimal notation, "nice" step values are numbers of the form $10^n$, $2 \cdot 10^n$, or $5 \cdot 10^n$.

We start by computing the "gross step", a kind of maximum for the step value. Then we find the corresponding number of the form $10^n$ that is smaller than or equal to the gross step. We do this by taking the decimal logarithm of the gross step, then rounding that value down to a whole number, then raising 10 to the power of this rounded number. For example, if the gross step is 236, we compute $\log 236 = 2.37291\ldots$; then we round it down to 2 and obtain $10^2 = 100$ as the candidate step value of the form $10^n$.

Once we have the first candidate step value, we can use it to calculate the other two candidates: $2 \cdot 10^n$ and $5 \cdot 10^n$. For the example above, the two other candidates are 200 and 500. The 500 candidate is larger than the gross step, so we can't use it. But 200 is smaller than 236, so we use 200 for the step size in this example.

It's fairly easy to derive `numTicks`, `min`, and `max` from the step value. The new `min` value is obtained by rounding the original `min` down to the nearest multiple of the step, and the new `max` value is obtained by rounding up to the nearest multiple of the step. The new `numTicks` is the number of intervals between the the rounded `min` and `max` values. For example, if `min` is 240 and `max` is 1184 upon entering the function, the new range becomes [200, 1200], with 5 tick marks.

This algorithm will give suboptimal results in some cases. A more sophisticated algorithm is described in Paul S. Heckbert's article "Nice Numbers for

Graph Labels" published in *Graphics Gems* (ISBN 0-12-286166-3). Also of interest is the *Qt Quarterly* article "Fast and Flicker-Free", available online at `http://doc.trolltech.com/qq/qq06-flicker-free.html`, which presents some more ideas for eliminating flicker.

This chapter has brought us to the end of Part I. It has explained how to customize an existing Qt widget and how to build a widget from the ground up using `QWidget` as the base class. We have already seen how to compose a widget from existing widgets in Chapter 2, and we will explore the theme further in Chapter 6.

At this point, we know enough to write complete GUI applications using Qt. In Part II, we will explore Qt in greater depth, so that we can make full use of Qt's power.

# Part II

# Intermediate Qt

# Layout Management

Every widget that is placed on a form must be given an appropriate size and position. Some large widgets may also need scroll bars to give the user access to all their contents. In this chapter, we will review the different ways of laying out widgets on a form, and also see how to implement dockable windows and MDI windows.

## Basic Layouts

Qt provides three basic ways of managing the layout of child widgets on a form: absolute positioning, manual layout, and layout managers. We will look at each of these approaches in turn, using the Find File dialog shown in Figure 6.1 as our example.

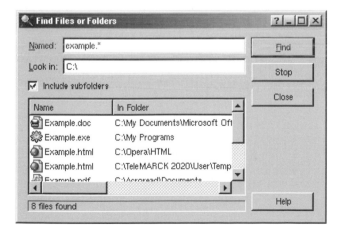

**Figure 6.1.** The Find File dialog

Absolute positioning is the crudest way of laying out widgets. It is achieved by assigning hard-coded sizes and positions (geometries) to the form's child widgets and a fixed size to the form. Here's what the `FindFileDialog` constructor looks like using absolute positioning:

```
FindFileDialog::FindFileDialog(QWidget *parent, const char *name)
    : QDialog(parent, name)
{
    ...
    namedLabel->setGeometry(10, 10, 50, 20);
    namedLineEdit->setGeometry(70, 10, 200, 20);
    lookInLabel->setGeometry(10, 35, 50, 20);
    lookInLineEdit->setGeometry(70, 35, 200, 20);
    subfoldersCheckBox->setGeometry(10, 60, 260, 20);
    listView->setGeometry(10, 85, 260, 100);
    messageLabel->setGeometry(10, 190, 260, 20);
    findButton->setGeometry(275, 10, 80, 25);
    stopButton->setGeometry(275, 40, 80, 25);
    closeButton->setGeometry(275, 70, 80, 25);
    helpButton->setGeometry(275, 185, 80, 25);

    setFixedSize(365, 220);
}
```

Absolute positioning has many disadvantages. The foremost problem is that the user cannot resize the window. Another problem is that some text may be truncated if the user chooses an unusually large font or if the application is translated into another language. And this approach also requires us to perform tedious position and size calculations.

An alternative to absolute positioning is manual layout. With manual layout, the widgets are still given absolute positions, but their sizes are made proportional to the size of the window rather than being entirely hard-coded. This can be achieved by reimplementing the form's `resizeEvent()` function to set its child widgets' geometries:

```
FindFileDialog::FindFileDialog(QWidget *parent, const char *name)
    : QDialog(parent, name)
{
    ...
    setMinimumSize(215, 170);
    resize(365, 220);
}

void FindFileDialog::resizeEvent(QResizeEvent *)
{
    int extraWidth = width() - minimumWidth();
    int extraHeight = height() - minimumHeight();

    namedLabel->setGeometry(10, 10, 50, 20);
    namedLineEdit->setGeometry(70, 10, 50 + extraWidth, 20);
    lookInLabel->setGeometry(10, 35, 50, 20);
    lookInLineEdit->setGeometry(70, 35, 50 + extraWidth, 20);
    subfoldersCheckBox->setGeometry(10, 60, 110 + extraWidth, 20);
```

```
    listView->setGeometry(10, 85,
                          110 + extraWidth, 50 + extraHeight);
    messageLabel->setGeometry(10, 140 + extraHeight,
                              110 + extraWidth, 20);
    findButton->setGeometry(125 + extraWidth, 10, 80, 25);
    stopButton->setGeometry(125 + extraWidth, 40, 80, 25);
    closeButton->setGeometry(125 + extraWidth, 70, 80, 25);
    helpButton->setGeometry(125 + extraWidth, 135 + extraHeight,
                            80, 25);
}
```

We set the form's minimum size to 215 × 170 in the FindFileDialog constructor and its initial size to 365 × 220. In the resizeEvent() function, we give any extra space to the widgets that we want to grow.

Just like absolute positioning, manual layout requires a lot of hard-coded constants to be calculated by the programmer. Writing code like this is tiresome, especially if the design changes. And there is still the risk of text truncation. The risk can be avoided by taking account of the child widgets' size hints, but that would complicate the code even further.

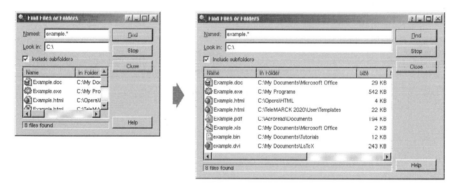

**Figure 6.2.** Resizing a resizable dialog

The best solution for laying out widgets on a form is to use Qt's layout managers. The layout managers provide sensible defaults for every type of widget and take into account each widget's size hint, which in turn typically depends on the widget's font, style, and contents. Layout managers also respect minimum and maximum sizes, and automatically adjust the layout in response to font changes, text changes, and window resizing.

Qt provides three layout managers: QHBoxLayout, QVBoxLayout, and QGridLayout. These classes inherit QLayout, which provides the basic framework for layouts. All three classes are fully supported by *Qt Designer* and can also be used in code. Chapter 2 presented examples of both approaches.

Here's the FindFileDialog code using layout managers:

```
FindFileDialog::FindFileDialog(QWidget *parent, const char *name)
    : QDialog(parent, name)
{
    ...
```

```
QGridLayout *leftLayout = new QGridLayout;
leftLayout->addWidget(namedLabel, 0, 0);
leftLayout->addWidget(namedLineEdit, 0, 1);
leftLayout->addWidget(lookInLabel, 1, 0);
leftLayout->addWidget(lookInLineEdit, 1, 1);
leftLayout->addMultiCellWidget(subfoldersCheckBox, 2, 2, 0, 1);
leftLayout->addMultiCellWidget(listView, 3, 3, 0, 1);
leftLayout->addMultiCellWidget(messageLabel, 4, 4, 0, 1);

QVBoxLayout *rightLayout = new QVBoxLayout;
rightLayout->addWidget(findButton);
rightLayout->addWidget(stopButton);
rightLayout->addWidget(closeButton);
rightLayout->addStretch(1);
rightLayout->addWidget(helpButton);

QHBoxLayout *mainLayout = new QHBoxLayout(this);
mainLayout->setMargin(11);
mainLayout->setSpacing(6);
mainLayout->addLayout(leftLayout);
mainLayout->addLayout(rightLayout);
}
```

The layout is handled by one QHBoxLayout, one QGridLayout, and one QVBoxLayout. The QGridLayout on the left and the QVBoxLayout on the right are placed side by side by the outer QHBoxLayout. The margin around the dialog is 11 pixels and the spacing between the child widgets is 6 pixels.

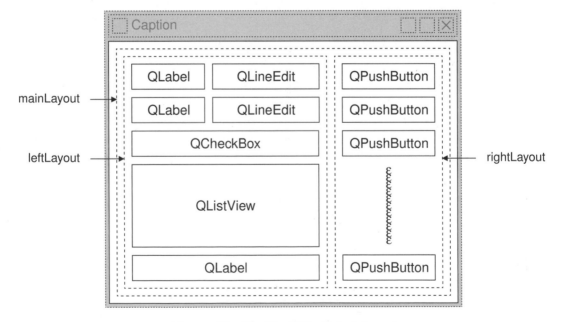

**Figure 6.3.** The Find File dialog's layout

QGridLayout works on a two-dimensional grid of cells. The QLabel at the top-left corner of the layout is at position (0, 0), and the corresponding QLineEdit is at position (0, 1). The QCheckBox spans two columns; it occupies the cells in positions (2, 0) and (2, 1). The QListView and the QLabel beneath it also span two columns. The calls to addMultiCellWidget() have the following syntax:

```
leftLayout->addMultiCellWidget(widget, row1, row2, col1, col2);
```

where *widget* is the child widget to insert into the layout, (*row1*, *col1*) is the top-left cell occupied by the widget, and (*row2*, *col2*) is the bottom-right cell occupied by the widget.

The same dialog could be created visually in *Qt Designer* by placing the child widgets in their approximate positions, selecting those that need to be laid out together, and clicking Layout|Lay Out Horizontally, Layout|Lay Out Vertically, or Layout|Lay Out in a Grid. We used this approach in Chapter 2 for creating the Spreadsheet application's Go-to-Cell and Sort dialogs.

Using layout managers provides additional benefits to those we have discussed so far. If we add a widget to a layout or remove a widget from a layout, the layout will automatically adapt to the new situation. The same applies if we call hide() or show() on a child widget. If a child widget's size hint changes, the layout will be automatically redone, taking into account the new size hint. Also, layout managers automatically set a minimum size for the form as a whole, based on the form's child widgets' minimum sizes and size hints.

In every example presented so far, we have simply put the widgets in layouts, with spacer items to consume any excess space. Sometimes this isn't sufficient to make the layout look exactly the way we want. In such situations, we can adjust the layout by changing the size policies and size hints of the widgets being laid out.

A widget's size policy tells the layout system how it should stretch or shrink. Qt provides sensible default size policy values for all its built-in widgets, but since no single default can account for every possible layout, it is still common for developers to change the size policies for one or two widgets on a form. A size policy has both a horizontal and a vertical component. The most useful values for each component are Fixed, Minimum, Maximum, Preferred, and Expanding:

- Fixed means that the widget cannot grow or shrink. The widget always stays at the size of its size hint.

- Minimum means that the widget's size hint is its minimum size. The widget cannot shrink below the size hint, but it can grow to fill available space if necessary.

- Maximum means that the widget's size hint is its maximum size. The widget can be shrunk down to its minimum size hint.

- Preferred means that the widget's size hint is its preferred size, but that the widget can still shrink or grow if necessary.

- Expanding means that the widget can shrink or grow and that it is especially willing to grow.

Figure 6.4 summarizes the meaning of the different size policies, using a
`QLabel` showing the text "Some Text" as an example.

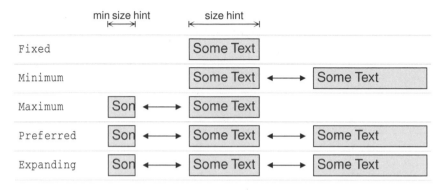

**Figure 6.4.** The meaning of the different size policies

When a form that contains both `Preferred` and `Expanding` widgets is resized,
extra space is given to the `Expanding` widgets, while the `Preferred` widgets stay
at their size hint.

There are two other size policies: `MinimumExpanding` and `Ignored`. The former
was necessary in a few rare cases in older versions of Qt, but it isn't useful
any more; a better approach is to use `Expanding` and reimplement `minimumSize-
Hint()` appropriately. The latter is similar to `Expanding`, except that it ignores
the widget's size hint.

In addition to the size policy's horizontal and vertical components, the `QSize-
Policy` class stores both a horizontal and a vertical stretch factor. These stretch
factors can be used to indicate that different child widgets should grow at
different rates when the form expands. For example, if we have a `QListView`
above a `QTextEdit` and we want the `QTextEdit` to be twice as tall as the `QList-
View`, we can set the `QTextEdit`'s vertical stretch factor to 2 and the `QListView`'s
vertical stretch factor to 1.

Another way of influencing a layout is to set a minimum size, a maximum
size, or a fixed size on the child widgets. The layout manager will respect
these constraints when laying out the widgets. And if this isn't sufficient, we
can always derive from the child widget's class and reimplement `sizeHint()` to
obtain the size hint we need.

## Splitters

A splitter is a widget that contains other widgets and that separates them
with splitter handles. Users can change the sizes of a splitter's child widgets
by dragging the handles. Splitters can often be used as an alternative to layout
managers, to give more control to the user.

Qt supports splitters with the `QSplitter` widget. The child widgets of a
`QSplitter` are automatically placed side by side (or one below the other) in the

order in which they are created, with splitter bars between adjacent widgets. Here's the code for creating the window depicted in Figure 6.5:

```cpp
#include <qapplication.h>
#include <qsplitter.h>
#include <qtextedit.h>

int main(int argc, char *argv[])
{
    QApplication app(argc, argv);

    QSplitter splitter(Qt::Horizontal);
    splitter.setCaption(QObject::tr("Splitter"));
    app.setMainWidget(&splitter);

    QTextEdit *firstEditor = new QTextEdit(&splitter);
    QTextEdit *secondEditor = new QTextEdit(&splitter);
    QTextEdit *thirdEditor = new QTextEdit(&splitter);

    splitter.show();
    return app.exec();
}
```

The example consists of three `QTextEdits` laid out horizontally by a `QSplitter` widget. Unlike layout managers, which simply lay out a form's child widgets, `QSplitter` inherits from `QWidget` and can be used like any other widget.

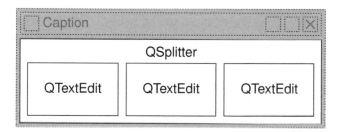

**Figure 6.5.** The Splitter application's widgets

A `QSplitter` can lay out its child widgets either horizontally or vertically. Complex layouts can be achieved by nesting horizontal and vertical `QSplitters`. For example, the Mail Client application shown in Figure 6.6 consists of a horizontal `QSplitter` that contains a vertical `QSplitter` on its right side.

Here's the code in the constructor of the Mail Client application's `QMainWindow` subclass:

```cpp
MailClient::MailClient(QWidget *parent, const char *name)
    : QMainWindow(parent, name)
{
    horizontalSplitter = new QSplitter(Horizontal, this);
    setCentralWidget(horizontalSplitter);

    foldersListView = new QListView(horizontalSplitter);
    foldersListView->addColumn(tr("Folders"));
    foldersListView->setResizeMode(QListView::AllColumns);
```

```
verticalSplitter = new QSplitter(Vertical, horizontalSplitter);

messagesListView = new QListView(verticalSplitter);
messagesListView->addColumn(tr("Subject"));
messagesListView->addColumn(tr("Sender"));
messagesListView->addColumn(tr("Date"));
messagesListView->setAllColumnsShowFocus(true);
messagesListView->setShowSortIndicator(true);
messagesListView->setResizeMode(QListView::AllColumns);

textEdit = new QTextEdit(verticalSplitter);
textEdit->setReadOnly(true);

horizontalSplitter->setResizeMode(foldersListView,
                                  QSplitter::KeepSize);
verticalSplitter->setResizeMode(messagesListView,
                                QSplitter::KeepSize);
...
readSettings();
}
```

We create the horizontal QSplitter first and set it to be the QMainWindow's central widget. Then we create the child widgets and their child widgets.

**Figure 6.6.** The Mail Client application on Mac OS X

When the user resizes a window, QSplitter normally distributes the space so that the relative sizes of the child widgets stay the same. In the Mail Client example, we don't want this behavior; instead we want the two QListViews to maintain their size and we want to give any extra space to the QTextEdit. This is achieved by the two setResizeMode() calls near the end.

When the application is started, QSplitter gives the child widgets appropriate sizes based on their initial sizes. We can move the splitter handles programmatically by calling QSplitter::setSizes(). The QSplitter class also provides a means of saving and restoring its state the next time the application is run. Here's the writeSettings() function that saves the Mail Client's settings:

```
void MailClient::writeSettings()
{
    QSettings settings;
    settings.setPath("software-inc.com", "MailClient");
    settings.beginGroup("/MailClient");

    QString str;
    QTextOStream out1(&str);
    out1 << *horizontalSplitter;
    settings.writeEntry("/horizontalSplitter", str);
    QTextOStream out2(&str);
    out2 << *verticalSplitter;
    settings.writeEntry("/verticalSplitter", str);

    settings.endGroup();
}
```

Here's the corresponding readSettings() function:

```
void MailClient::readSettings()
{
    QSettings settings;
    settings.setPath("software-inc.com", "MailClient");
    settings.beginGroup("/MailClient");

    QString str1 = settings.readEntry("/horizontalSplitter");
    QTextIStream in1(&str1);
    in1 >> *horizontalSplitter;
    QString str2 = settings.readEntry("/verticalSplitter");
    QTextIStream in2(&str2);
    in2 >> *verticalSplitter;

    settings.endGroup();
}
```

These functions rely on QTextIStream and QTextOStream, two QTextStream convenience subclasses.

By default, a splitter handle is shown as a rubber band while the user is dragging it, and the widgets on either side of the splitter handle are resized only when the user releases the mouse button. To make QSplitter resize the child widgets in real time, we would call setOpaqueResize(true).

QSplitter is fully supported by *Qt Designer*. To put widgets into a splitter, place the child widgets approximately in their desired positions, select them, and click Layout|Lay Out Horizontally (in Splitter) or Layout|Lay Out Vertically (in Splitter).

# Widget Stacks

Another useful widget for managing layouts is QWidgetStack. This widget contains a set of child widgets, or "pages", and shows only one at a time, hiding the others from the user. The pages are numbered from 0. If we want to make a specific child widget visible, we can call raiseWidget() with either a page number or a pointer to the child widget.

**Figure 6.7.** QWidgetStack

The QWidgetStack itself is invisible and provides no intrinsic means for the user to change page. The small arrows and the dark gray frame in Figure 6.7 are provided by *Qt Designer* to make the QWidgetStack easier to design with.

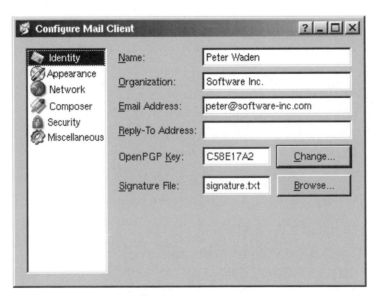

**Figure 6.8.** The Configure dialog

The Configure dialog shown in Figure 6.8 is an example that uses QWidget-Stack. The dialog consists of a QListBox on the left and a QWidgetStack on the right. Each item in the QListBox corresponds to a different page in the QWid-getStack. Forms like this are very easy to create using *Qt Designer*:

1. Create a new form based on the "Dialog" or the "Widget" template.

2. Add a list box and a widget stack to the form.

3. Fill each widget stack page with child widgets and layouts.
(To create a new page, right-click and choose Add Page; to switch pages, click the tiny left or right arrow located at the top-right of the widget stack.)

4. Lay the widgets out side by side using a horizontal layout.

5. Connect the list box's `highlighted(int)` signal to the widget stack's `raiseWidget(int)` slot.

6. Set the value of the list box's `currentItem` property to 0.

Since we have implemented page-switching using predefined signals and slots, the dialog will exhibit the correct page-switching behavior when previewed in *Qt Designer*.

## Scroll Views

The `QScrollView` class provides a scrollable viewport, two scroll bars, and a "corner" widget (usually an empty `QWidget`). If we want to add scroll bars to a widget, it is much simpler to use a `QScrollView` than to instantiate our own `QScrollBars` and implement the scrolling functionality ourselves.

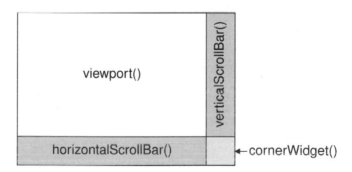

**Figure 6.9.** `QScrollView`'s constituent widgets

The easiest way to use `QScrollView` is to call `addChild()` with the widget we want to add scroll bars to. `QScrollView` automatically reparents the widget to make it a child of the viewport (accessible through `QScrollView::viewport()`) if it isn't already. For example, if we want scroll bars around the `IconEditor` widget we developed in Chapter 5, we can write this:

```
#include <qapplication.h>
#include <qscrollview.h>

#include "iconeditor.h"

int main(int argc, char *argv[])
{
```

```
        QApplication app(argc, argv);

        QScrollView scrollView;
        scrollView.setCaption(QObject::tr("Icon Editor"));
        app.setMainWidget(&scrollView);

        IconEditor *iconEditor = new IconEditor;
        scrollView.addChild(iconEditor);

        scrollView.show();
        return app.exec();
    }
```

By default, the scroll bars are only displayed when the viewport is smaller than the child widget. We can force the scroll bars to always be shown by writing this code:

```
        scrollView.setHScrollBarMode(QScrollView::AlwaysOn);
        scrollView.setVScrollBarMode(QScrollView::AlwaysOn);
```

When the child widget's size hint changes, `QScrollView` automatically adapts to the new size hint.

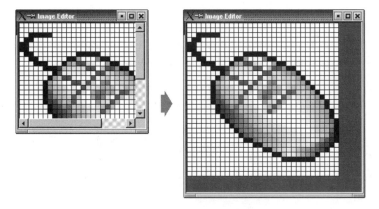

**Figure 6.10.** Resizing a `QScrollView`

An alternative way of using a `QScrollView` with a widget is to make the widget inherit `QScrollView` and to reimplement `drawContents()` to draw the contents. This is the approach used by Qt classes like `QIconView`, `QListBox`, `QListView`, `QTable`, and `QTextEdit`. If a widget is likely to require scroll bars, it's usually a good idea to implement it as a subclass of `QScrollView`.

To show how this works, we will implement a new version of the `IconEditor` class as a `QScrollView` subclass. We will call the new class `ImageEditor`, since its scroll bars make it capable of handling large images.

```
        #ifndef IMAGEEDITOR_H
        #define IMAGEEDITOR_H

        #include <qimage.h>
        #include <qscrollview.h>
```

```
class ImageEditor : public QScrollView
{
    Q_OBJECT
    Q_PROPERTY(QColor penColor READ penColor WRITE setPenColor)
    Q_PROPERTY(QImage image READ image WRITE setImage)
    Q_PROPERTY(int zoomFactor READ zoomFactor WRITE setZoomFactor)

public:
    ImageEditor(QWidget *parent = 0, const char *name = 0);

    void setPenColor(const QColor &newColor);
    QColor penColor() const { return curColor; }
    void setZoomFactor(int newZoom);
    int zoomFactor() const { return zoom; }
    void setImage(const QImage &newImage);
    const QImage &image() const { return curImage; }

protected:
    void contentsMousePressEvent(QMouseEvent *event);
    void contentsMouseMoveEvent(QMouseEvent *event);
    void drawContents(QPainter *painter, int x, int y,
                      int width, int height);

private:
    void drawImagePixel(QPainter *painter, int i, int j);
    void setImagePixel(const QPoint &pos, bool opaque);
    void resizeContents();

    QColor curColor;
    QImage curImage;
    int zoom;
};

#endif
```

The header file is very similar to the original (p. 100). The main difference is
that we inherit from QScrollView instead of QWidget. We will run into the other
differences as we review the class's implementation.

```
ImageEditor::ImageEditor(QWidget *parent, const char *name)
    : QScrollView(parent, name, WStaticContents | WNoAutoErase)
{
    curColor = black;
    zoom = 8;
    curImage.create(16, 16, 32);
    curImage.fill(qRgba(0, 0, 0, 0));
    curImage.setAlphaBuffer(true);
    resizeContents();
}
```

The constructor passes the WStaticContents and WNoAutoErase flags to the
QScrollView. These flags are actually set on the viewport. We don't set a size
policy, because QScrollView's default of (Expanding, Expanding) is appropriate.

In the original version, we didn't call updateGeometry() in the constructor
because we could depend on Qt's layout managers picking up the initial widget

size by themselves. But here we must give the QScrollView base class an initial size to work with, and we do this with the resizeContents() call.

```
void ImageEditor::resizeContents()
{
    QSize size = zoom * curImage.size();
    if (zoom >= 3)
        size += QSize(1, 1);
    QScrollView::resizeContents(size.width(), size.height());
}
```

The resizeContents() **private function calls** QScrollView::resizeContents() with the size of the content part of the QScrollView. The QScrollView displays scroll bars depending on the content's size in relation to the viewport's size.

We don't need to reimplement sizeHint(); QScrollView's version uses the content's size to provide a reasonable size hint.

```
void ImageEditor::setImage(const QImage &newImage)
{
    if (newImage != curImage) {
        curImage = newImage.convertDepth(32);
        curImage.detach();
        resizeContents();
        updateContents();
    }
}
```

In many of the original IconEditor functions, we called update() to schedule a repaint and updateGeometry() to propagate a size hint change. In the QScrollView versions, these calls are replaced by resizeContents() to inform the QScrollView about a change of the content's size and updateContents() to force a repaint.

```
void ImageEditor::drawContents(QPainter *painter, int, int, int, int)
{
    if (zoom >= 3) {
        painter->setPen(colorGroup().foreground());
        for (int i = 0; i <= curImage.width(); ++i)
            painter->drawLine(zoom * i, 0,
                              zoom * i, zoom * curImage.height());
        for (int j = 0; j <= curImage.height(); ++j)
            painter->drawLine(0, zoom * j,
                              zoom * curImage.width(), zoom * j);
    }

    for (int i = 0; i < curImage.width(); ++i) {
        for (int j = 0; j < curImage.height(); ++j)
            drawImagePixel(painter, i, j);
    }
}
```

The drawContents() function is called by QScrollView to repaint the content's area. The QPainter object is already initialized to account for the scrolling offset. We just need to perform the drawing as we normally do in a paint-Event().

The second, third, fourth, and fifth parameters specify the rectangle that must be redrawn. We could use this information to only draw the rectangle that needs repainting, but for the sake of simplicity we redraw everything.

The drawImagePixel() function that is called near the end of drawContents() is essentially the same as in the original IconEditor class (p. 106), so it is not reproduced here.

```
void ImageEditor::contentsMousePressEvent(QMouseEvent *event)
{
    if (event->button() == LeftButton)
        setImagePixel(event->pos(), true);
    else if (event->button() == RightButton)
        setImagePixel(event->pos(), false);
}

void ImageEditor::contentsMouseMoveEvent(QMouseEvent *event)
{
    if (event->state() & LeftButton)
        setImagePixel(event->pos(), true);
    else if (event->state() & RightButton)
        setImagePixel(event->pos(), false);
}
```

Mouse events for the content part of the scroll view can be handled by reimplementing special event handlers in QScrollView, whose names all start with contents. Behind the scenes, QScrollView automatically converts the viewport coordinates to content coordinates, so we don't need to convert them ourselves.

```
void ImageEditor::setImagePixel(const QPoint &pos, bool opaque)
{
    int i = pos.x() / zoom;
    int j = pos.y() / zoom;

    if (curImage.rect().contains(i, j)) {
        if (opaque)
            curImage.setPixel(i, j, penColor().rgb());
        else
            curImage.setPixel(i, j, qRgba(0, 0, 0, 0));

        QPainter painter(viewport());
        painter.translate(-contentsX(), -contentsY());
        drawImagePixel(&painter, i, j);
    }
}
```

The setImagePixel() function is called from contentsMousePressEvent() and contentsMouseMoveEvent() to set or clear a pixel. The code is almost the same as the original version, except for the way the QPainter object is initialized. We pass viewport() as the parent because the painting is performed on the viewport, and we translate the QPainter's coordinate system to account for the scrolling offset.

We could replace the three lines that deal with the QPainter with this line:

```
updateContents(i * zoom, j * zoom, zoom, zoom);
```

This would tell QScrollView to update only the small rectangular area occupied by the (zoomed) image pixel. But since we didn't optimize drawContents() to draw only the necessary area, this would be inefficient, so it's better to construct a QPainter and do the painting ourselves.

If we use ImageEditor now, it is practically indistinguishable from the original, QWidget-based IconEditor used inside a QScrollView widget. However, for certain more sophisticated widgets, subclassing QScrollView is the more natural approach. For example, a class such as QTextEdit that implements word-wrapping needs tight integration between the document that is shown and the QScrollView.

Also note that you should subclass QScrollView if the contents are likely to be very tall or wide, because some window systems don't support widgets that are larger than 32,767 pixels.

One thing that the ImageEditor example doesn't demonstrate is that we can put child widgets in the viewport area. The child widgets simply need to be added using addWidget(), and can be moved using moveWidget(). Whenever the user scrolls the content area, QScrollView automatically moves the child widgets on screen. (If the QScrollView contains many child widgets, this can slow down scrolling. We can call enableClipper(true) to optimize this case.) One example where this approach would make sense is for a web browser. Most of the contents would be drawn directly on the viewport, but buttons and other form-entry elements would be represented by child widgets.

## Dock Windows

Dock windows are windows that can be docked in dock areas. Toolbars are the primary example of dock windows, but there can be other types.

QMainWindow provides four dock areas: one above, one below, one to the left, and one to the right of the window's central widget. When we create QToolBars, they automatically put themselves in their parent's top dock area.

**Figure 6.11.** Floating dock windows

Every dock window has a handle. This appears as two gray lines at the left or top of each dock window shown in Figure 6.12. Users can move dock windows from one dock area to another by dragging the handle. They can also detach a dock window from an area and let the dock window float as a top-level window by dragging the dock window outside of any dock area. Free floating dock windows have their own caption, and can have a close button. They are always "on top" of their main window.

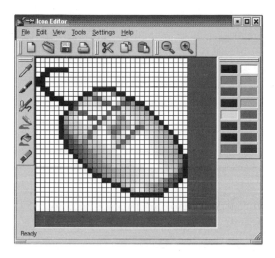

**Figure 6.12.** A `QMainWindow` with five dock windows

To turn on the close button when the dock window is floating, call `setClose Mode()` as follows:

```
dockWindow->setCloseMode(QDockWindow::Undocked);
```

`QDockArea` provides a context menu with the list of all dock windows and toolbars. Once a dock window is closed, the user can restore it using the context menu.

**Figure 6.13.** A `QDockArea` context menu

Dock windows must be subclasses of `QDockWindow`. If we just need a toolbar with buttons and some other widgets, we can use `QToolBar`, which inherits `QDockWindow`. Here's how to create a `QToolBar` containing a `QComboBox`, a `QSpinBox`, and some toolbar buttons, and how to put it in the bottom dock area:

```
QToolBar *toolBar = new QToolBar(tr("Font"), this);
QComboBox *fontComboBox = new QComboBox(true, toolBar);
```

```
QSpinBox *fontSize = new QSpinBox(toolBar);
boldAct->addTo(toolBar);
italicAct->addTo(toolBar);
underlineAct->addTo(toolBar);
moveDockWindow(toolBar, DockBottom);
```

This toolbar would look ugly if the user moves it to a QMainWindow's left or right dock areas because the QComboBox and the QSpinBox require too much horizontal space. To prevent this from happening, we can call QMainWindow::setDockEnabled() as follows:

```
setDockEnabled(toolBar, DockLeft, false);
setDockEnabled(toolBar, DockRight, false);
```

If what we need is something more like a floating widget or tool palette, we can use QDockWindow directly, by calling setWidget() to set the widget to be shown inside the QDockWindow. The widget can be as complicated as we like. If we want the user to be able to resize the dock window even when it's in a dock area, we can call setResizeEnabled() on the dock window. The dock window will then be rendered with a splitter-like handle on the side.

If we want the widget to change itself depending on whether it is put in a horizontal or in a vertical dock area, we can reimplement QDockWindow::setOrientation() and change it there.

If we want to save the position of all the toolbars and other dock windows so that we can restore them the next time the application is run, we can write code that is similar to the code we used to save a QSplitter's state (p. 143), using QMainWindow's << operator to write out the state and QMainWindow's >> operator to read it back in.

Applications like Microsoft Visual Studio and *Qt Designer* make extensive use of dock windows to provide a very flexible user interface. In Qt, this kind of user interface is usually achieved by using a QMainWindow with many custom QDockWindows and a QWorkspace in the middle to control MDI child windows.

## Multiple Document Interface

Applications that provide multiple documents within the main window's central area are called MDI (multiple document interface) applications. In Qt, an MDI application is created by using the QWorkspace class as the central widget and by making each document window a child of the QWorkspace.

It is conventional for MDI applications to provide a Windows menu that includes some commands for managing the windows and the list of windows. The active window is identified with a checkmark. The user can make any window active by clicking its entry in the Windows menu.

In this section, we will develop the Editor application shown in Figure 6.14 to demonstrate how to create an MDI application and how to implement its Windows menu.

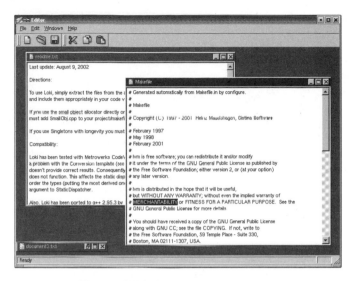

**Figure 6.14.** The Editor application

The application consists of two classes: `MainWindow` and `Editor`. Its code is on the CD, and since most of it is the same or similar to the Spreadsheet application from Part I, we will only present the new code.

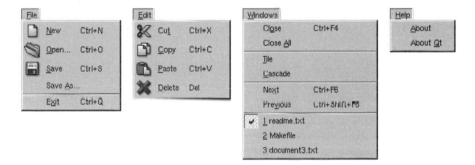

**Figure 6.15.** The Editor application's menus

Let's start with the `MainWindow` class.

```
MainWindow::MainWindow(QWidget *parent, const char *name)
    : QMainWindow(parent, name)
{
    workspace = new QWorkspace(this);
    setCentralWidget(workspace);
    connect(workspace, SIGNAL(windowActivated(QWidget *)),
            this, SLOT(updateMenus()));
    connect(workspace, SIGNAL(windowActivated(QWidget *)),
            this, SLOT(updateModIndicator()));

    createActions();
    createMenus();
    createToolBars();
```

```
    createStatusBar();

    setCaption(tr("Editor"));
    setIcon(QPixmap::fromMimeSource("icon.png"));
}
```

In the `MainWindow` constructor, we create a `QWorkspace` widget and make it the central widget. We connect the `QWorkspace`'s `windowActivated()` signal to two private slots. These slots ensure that the menus and the status bar always reflect the state of the currently active child window.

```
void MainWindow::newFile()
{
    Editor *editor = createEditor();
    editor->newFile();
    editor->show();
}
```

The `newFile()` slot corresponds to the File|New menu option. It depends on the `createEditor()` private function to create a child `Editor` window.

```
Editor *MainWindow::createEditor()
{
    Editor *editor = new Editor(workspace);
    connect(editor, SIGNAL(copyAvailable(bool)),
            this, SLOT(copyAvailable(bool)));
    connect(editor, SIGNAL(modificationChanged(bool)),
            this, SLOT(updateModIndicator()));
    return editor;
}
```

The `createEditor()` function creates an `Editor` widget and sets up two signal–slot connections. The first connection ensures that Edit|Cut and Edit| Copy are enabled or disabled depending on whether there is any selected text. The second connection ensures that the MOD indicator in the status bar is always up to date.

Because we are using MDI, it is possible that there will be multiple `Editor` widgets in use. This is a concern since we are only interested in responding to the `copyAvailable(bool)` and `modificationChanged()` signals from the active `Editor` window, not from the others. But these signals can only ever be emitted by the active window, so this isn't really a problem.

```
void MainWindow::open()
{
    Editor *editor = createEditor();
    if (editor->open())
        editor->show();
    else
        editor->close();
}
```

The `open()` function corresponds to File|Open. It creates a new `Editor` for the new document and calls `open()` on the `Editor`. It makes more sense to implement the file operations in the `Editor` class than in the `MainWindow` class, because each `Editor` needs to maintain its own independent state. If the `open()` fails, we simply close the editor since the user will have already been notified of the error.

```
void MainWindow::save()
{
    if (activeEditor()) {
        activeEditor()->save();
        updateModIndicator();
    }
}
```

The `save()` slot calls `save()` on the active editor, if there is one. Again, the code that performs the real work is located in the `Editor` class.

```
Editor *MainWindow::activeEditor()
{
    return (Editor *)workspace->activeWindow();
}
```

The `activeEditor()` private function returns the active child window as an `Editor` pointer.

```
void MainWindow::cut()
{
    if (activeEditor())
        activeEditor()->cut();
}
```

The `cut()` slot calls `cut()` on the active editor. The `copy()`, `paste()`, and `del()` slots follow the same pattern.

```
void MainWindow::updateMenus()
{
    bool hasEditor = (activeEditor() != 0);
    saveAct->setEnabled(hasEditor);
    saveAsAct->setEnabled(hasEditor);
    pasteAct->setEnabled(hasEditor);
    deleteAct->setEnabled(hasEditor);
    copyAvailable(activeEditor()
                    && activeEditor()->hasSelectedText());
    closeAct->setEnabled(hasEditor);
    closeAllAct->setEnabled(hasEditor);
    tileAct->setEnabled(hasEditor);
    cascadeAct->setEnabled(hasEditor);
    nextAct->setEnabled(hasEditor);
    previousAct->setEnabled(hasEditor);

    windowsMenu->clear();
    createWindowsMenu();
}
```

The `updateMenus()` slot is called whenever a window is activated (or when the last window is closed) to update the menu system, thanks to the signal–slot connection we put in the `MainWindow` constructor.

Most menu options only make sense if there is an active window, so we disable them if there isn't one. Then we clear the Windows menu and call createWindowsMenu() to reinitialize it with a fresh list of child windows.

```
void MainWindow::createWindowsMenu()
{
    closeAct->addTo(windowsMenu);
    closeAllAct->addTo(windowsMenu);
    windowsMenu->insertSeparator();
    tileAct->addTo(windowsMenu);
    cascadeAct->addTo(windowsMenu);
    windowsMenu->insertSeparator();
    nextAct->addTo(windowsMenu);
    previousAct->addTo(windowsMenu);

    if (activeEditor()) {
        windowsMenu->insertSeparator();
        windows = workspace->windowList();
        int numVisibleEditors = 0;

        for (int i = 0; i < (int)windows.count(); ++i) {
            QWidget *win = windows.at(i);
            if (!win->isHidden()) {
                QString text = tr("%1 %2")
                                   .arg(numVisibleEditors + 1)
                                   .arg(win->caption());
                if (numVisibleEditors < 9)
                    text.prepend("&");
                int id = windowsMenu->insertItem(
                            text, this, SLOT(activateWindow(int)));
                bool isActive = (activeEditor() == win);
                windowsMenu->setItemChecked(id, isActive);
                windowsMenu->setItemParameter(id, i);
                ++numVisibleEditors;
            }
        }
    }
}
```

The createWindowsMenu() private function fills the Windows menu with actions and a list of visible windows. The actions are all typical of such menus and are easily implemented using QWorkspace's closeActiveWindow(), closeAllWindows(), tile(), and cascade() slots.

The entry for the active window is shown with a checkmark next to its name. When the user chooses a window entry, the activateWindow() slot is called with the index in the windows list as the parameter, because of the call to setItemParameter(). This is very similar to what we did in Chapter 3 when we implemented the Spreadsheet application's recently opened files list (p. 54).

For the first nine entries, we put an ampersand in front of the number to make that number's single digit into a shortcut key. We don't provide a shortcut key for the other entries.

```
void MainWindow::activateWindow(int param)
{
    QWidget *win = windows.at(param);
    win->show();
    win->setFocus();
}
```

The `activateWindow()` function is called when a window is chosen from the Windows menu. The `int` parameter is the value that we set with `setItemParameter()`. The `windows` data member holds the list of windows and was set in `createWindowsMenu()`.

```
void MainWindow::copyAvailable(bool available)
{
    cutAct->setEnabled(available);
    copyAct->setEnabled(available);
}
```

The `copyAvailable()` slot is called whenever text is selected or deselected in an editor. It is also called from `updateMenus()`. It enables or disables the Cut and Copy actions.

```
void MainWindow::updateModIndicator()
{
    if (activeEditor() && activeEditor()->isModified())
        modLabel->setText(tr("MOD"));
    else
        modLabel->clear();
}
```

The `updateModIndicator()` updates the MOD indicator in the status bar. It is called whenever text is modified in an editor. It is also called when a new window is activated.

```
void MainWindow::closeEvent(QCloseEvent *event)
{
    workspace->closeAllWindows();
    if (activeEditor())
        event->ignore();
    else
        event->accept();
}
```

The `closeEvent()` function is reimplemented to close all child windows. If one of the child widgets "ignores" its close event (presumably because the user canceled an "unsaved changes" message box), we ignore the close event for the `MainWindow`; otherwise we accept it, resulting in Qt closing the window. If we didn't reimplement `closeEvent()` in `MainWindow`, the user would not be given the opportunity to save any unsaved changes.

We have now finished our review of `MainWindow`, so we can move on to the `Editor` implementation. The `Editor` class represents one child window. It inherits from `QTextEdit`, which provides the text editing functionality. Just as any Qt widget can be used as a stand-alone window, any Qt widget can be used as a child window in an MDI workspace.

Here's the class definition:

```
class Editor : public QTextEdit
{
    Q_OBJECT
public:
    Editor(QWidget *parent = 0, const char *name = 0);

    void newFile();
    bool open();
    bool openFile(const QString &fileName);
    bool save();
    bool saveAs();
    QSize sizeHint() const;

signals:
    void message(const QString &fileName, int delay);

protected:
    void closeEvent(QCloseEvent *event);

private:
    bool maybeSave();
    void saveFile(const QString &fileName);
    void setCurrentFile(const QString &fileName);
    QString strippedName(const QString &fullFileName);
    bool readFile(const QString &fileName);
    bool writeFile(const QString &fileName);

    QString curFile;
    bool isUntitled;
    QString fileFilters;
};
```

Four of the private functions that were in the Spreadsheet application's Main-
Window class (p. 51) are also present in the Editor class: maybeSave(), saveFile(),
setCurrentFile(), and strippedName().

```
Editor::Editor(QWidget *parent, const char *name)
    : QTextEdit(parent, name)
{
    setWFlags(WDestructiveClose);
    setIcon(QPixmap::fromMimeSource("document.png"));

    isUntitled = true;
    fileFilters = tr("Text files (*.txt)\n"
                     "All files (*)");
}
```

The Editor constructor sets the WDestructiveClose flag using setWFlags().
When a class constructor doesn't provide a flags parameter (as is the case
with QTextEdit), we can still set most flags using setWFlags().

Since we allow users to create any number of editor windows, we must make
some provision for naming them so that they can be distinguished before they
have been saved for the first time. One common way of handling this is to
allocate names that include a number (for example, document1.txt). We use the

isUntitled variable to distinguish between names supplied by the user and names we have created programmatically.

After the constructor, we expect either newFile() or open() to be called.

```
void Editor::newFile()
{
    static int documentNumber = 1;

    curFile = tr("document%1.txt").arg(documentNumber);
    setCaption(curFile);
    isUntitled = true;
    ++documentNumber;
}
```

The newFile() function generates a name like document2.txt for the new document. The code belongs in newFile(), rather than the constructor, because we don't want to consume numbers when we call open() to open an existing document in a newly created Editor. Since documentNumber is declared static, it is shared across all Editor instances.

```
bool Editor::open()
{
    QString fileName =
            QFileDialog::getOpenFileName(".", fileFilters, this);
    if (fileName.isEmpty())
        return false;

    return openFile(fileName);
}
```

The open() function tries to open an existing file using openFile().

```
bool Editor::save()
{
    if (isUntitled) {
        return saveAs();
    } else {
        saveFile(curFile);
        return true;
    }
}
```

The save() function uses the isUntitled variable to determine whether it should call saveFile() or saveAs().

```
void Editor::closeEvent(QCloseEvent *event)
{
    if (maybeSave())
        event->accept();
    else
        event->ignore();
}
```

The closeEvent() function is reimplemented to allow the user to save unsaved changes. The logic is coded in the maybeSave() function, which pops up a message box that asks, "Do you want to save your changes?" If maybeSave()

returns true, we accept the close event; otherwise, we "ignore" it and leave the
window unaffected by it.

```cpp
void Editor::setCurrentFile(const QString &fileName)
{
    curFile = fileName;
    setCaption(strippedName(curFile));
    isUntitled = false;
    setModified(false);
}
```

The setCurrentFile() function is called from openFile() and saveFile() to update the curFile and isUntitled variables, to set the window caption, and to
set the editor's "modified" flag to false. The Editor class inherits setModified()
and isModified() from QTextEdit, so it doesn't need to maintain its own modified flag. Whenever the user modifies the text in the editor, QTextEdit emits the
modificationChanged() signal and sets its internal modified flag to true.

```cpp
QSize Editor::sizeHint() const
{
    return QSize(72 * fontMetrics().width('x'),
                 25 * fontMetrics().lineSpacing());
}
```

The sizeHint() function returns a size based on the width of the letter 'x' and
the height of a text line. QWorkspace uses the size hint to give an initial size to
the window.

Finally, here's the Editor application's main.cpp file:

```cpp
#include <qapplication.h>

#include "mainwindow.h"

int main(int argc, char *argv[])
{
    QApplication app(argc, argv);
    MainWindow mainWin;
    app.setMainWidget(&mainWin);

    if (argc > 1) {
        for (int i = 1; i < argc; ++i)
            mainWin.openFile(argv[i]);
    } else {
        mainWin.newFile();
    }

    mainWin.show();
    return app.exec();
}
```

If the user specifies any files on the command line, we attempt to load them.
Otherwise, we start with an empty document. Qt-specific command-line options, such as -style and -font, are automatically removed from the argument
list by the QApplication constructor. So if we write

```
editor -style=motif readme.txt
```

on the command line, the Editor application starts up with one document, readme.txt.

MDI is one way of handling multiple documents simultaneously. Another approach is to use multiple top-level windows. This approach is covered in the "Multiple Documents" section of Chapter 3.

# Event Processing

GUI applications are event-driven: Everything that happens once the application has started is the result of an event. When we program with Qt, we seldom need to think about events, because Qt widgets emit signals when something significant occurs. Events become useful when we write our own custom widgets or when we want to modify the behavior of existing Qt widgets.

In this chapter, we will explore Qt's event model. We will see how to handle the different types of events in Qt. We will also look at how to use event filters to monitor events before they reach their destinations. Finally, we will examine Qt's event loop, reviewing how to keep the user interface responsive during intensive processing.

## Reimplementing Event Handlers

Events are generated by the window system or by Qt in response to various occurrences. When the user presses or releases a key or mouse button, a key or mouse event is generated. When a window is moved to reveal a window that was underneath, a paint event is generated to tell the newly visible window that it needs to repaint itself. An event is also generated whenever a widget gains or loses keyboard focus. Most events are generated in response to user actions, but some, like timer events, are generated independently by the system.

Events should not be confused with signals. Signals are useful when *using* a widget, whereas events are useful when *implementing* a widget. For example, when we are using QPushButton, we are more interested in its clicked() signal than in the low-level mouse or key events that caused the signal to be emitted. But if we are implementing a class like QPushButton, we need to write code to handle mouse and key events and emit the clicked() signal when necessary.

Events are notified to objects through their `event()` function, inherited from `QObject`. The `event()` implementation in `QWidget` forwards the most common types of events to specific event handlers, such as `mousePressEvent()`, `keyPress-Event()`, and `paintEvent()`, and ignores other kinds of events.

We have already seen many event handlers when implementing `MainWindow`, `IconEditor`, `Plotter`, `ImageEditor`, and `Editor` in the previous chapters. There are many other types of events, listed in the `QEvent` reference documentation, and it is also possible to create custom event types and dispatch custom events ourselves. Custom events are particularly useful in multithreaded applications, so they are discussed in Chapter 17 (Multithreading). Here, we will review two event types that deserve more explanation: key events and timer events.

Key events are handled by reimplementing `keyPressEvent()` and `keyRelease-Event()`. The `Plotter` widget reimplements `keyPressEvent()`. Normally, we only need to reimplement `keyPressEvent()` since the only keys for which release is important are the modifier keys Ctrl, Shift, and Alt, and these can be checked for in a `keyPressEvent()` using `state()`. For example, if we were implementing a `CodeEditor` widget, its stripped-down `keyPressEvent()` that distinguishes between Home and Ctrl+Home would look like this:

```
void CodeEditor::keyPressEvent(QKeyEvent *event)
{
    switch (event->key()) {
    case Key_Home:
        if (event->state() & ControlButton)
            goToBeginningOfDocument();
        else
            goToBeginningOfLine();
        break;
    case Key_End:
        ...
    default:
        QWidget::keyPressEvent(event);
    }
}
```

The Tab and Backtab (Shift+Tab) keys are special cases. They are handled by `QWidget::event()` before it calls `keyPressEvent()`, with the semantic of passing the focus to the next or previous widget in the focus chain. This behavior is usually what we want, but in a `CodeEditor` widget, we might prefer to make Tab indent a line. The `event()` reimplementation would then look like this:

```
bool CodeEditor::event(QEvent *event)
{
    if (event->type() == QEvent::KeyPress) {
        QKeyEvent *keyEvent = (QKeyEvent *)event;
        if (keyEvent->key() == Key_Tab) {
            insertAtCurrentPosition('\t');
            return true;
        }
    }
```

```
        return QWidget::event(event);
    }
```

If the event is a key press, we cast the QEvent object to a QKeyEvent and check which key was pressed. If the key is Tab, we do some processing and return true to tell Qt that we have handled the event. If we returned false, Qt would propagate the event to the parent widget.

A higher-level approach for implementing key bindings is to use a QAction. For example, if goToBeginningOfLine() and goToBeginningOfDocument() are public slots in the CodeEditor widget, and the CodeEditor is used as the central widget in a MainWindow class, we could add the key bindings with the following code:

```
MainWindow::MainWindow(QWidget *parent, const char *name)
    : QMainWindow(parent, name)
{
    editor = new CodeEditor(this);
    setCentralWidget(editor);

    goToBeginningOfLineAct =
            new QAction(tr("Go to Beginning of Line"),
                        tr("Home"), this);
    connect(goToBeginningOfLineAct, SIGNAL(activated()),
            editor, SLOT(goToBeginningOfLine()));

    goToBeginningOfDocumentAct =
            new QAction(tr("Go to Beginning of Document"),
                        tr("Ctrl+Home"), this);
    connect(goToBeginningOfDocumentAct, SIGNAL(activated()),
            editor, SLOT(goToBeginningOfDocument()));
    ...
}
```

This makes it easy to add the commands to a menu or a toolbar, as we saw in Chapter 3. If the commands don't appear in the user interface, the QAction objects could be replaced with a QAccel object, the class used by QAction internally to support key bindings.

The choice between reimplementing keyPressEvent() and using QAction (or QAccel) is similar to that between reimplementing resizeEvent() and using a QLayout subclass. If we are implementing a custom widget by subclassing QWidget, it's straightforward to reimplement a few more event handlers and hard-code the behavior there. But if we are merely using a widget, the higher-level interfaces provided by QAction and QLayout are more convenient.

Another common type of event is the timer event. While most types of events occur as a result of a user action, timer events allow applications to perform processing at regular time intervals. Timer events can be used to implement blinking cursors and other animations, or simply to refresh the display.

To demonstrate timer events, we will implement a Ticker widget. This widget shows a text banner that scrolls left by one pixel every 30 milliseconds. If the widget is wider than the text, the text is repeated as often as necessary to fill the entire width of the widget.

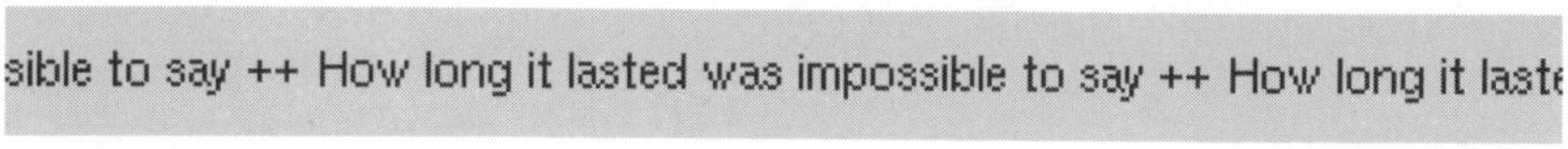

sible to say ++ How long it lasted was impossible to say ++ How long it laste

**Figure 7.1.** The Ticker widget

Here's the header file:

```
#ifndef TICKER_H
#define TICKER_H

#include <qwidget.h>

class Ticker : public QWidget
{
    Q_OBJECT
    Q_PROPERTY(QString text READ text WRITE setText)
public:
    Ticker(QWidget *parent = 0, const char *name = 0);

    void setText(const QString &newText);
    QString text() const { return myText; }
    QSize sizeHint() const;

protected:
    void paintEvent(QPaintEvent *event);
    void timerEvent(QTimerEvent *event);
    void showEvent(QShowEvent *event);
    void hideEvent(QHideEvent *event);

private:
    QString myText;
    int offset;
    int myTimerId;
};

#endif
```

We reimplement four event handlers in Ticker, three of which we have not seen before: timerEvent(), showEvent(), and hideEvent().

Now let's review the implementation:

```
#include <qpainter.h>

#include "ticker.h"

Ticker::Ticker(QWidget *parent, const char *name)
    : QWidget(parent, name)
{
    offset = 0;
    myTimerId = 0;
}
```

The constructor initializes the offset variable to 0. The $x$ coordinate at which the text is drawn is derived from the offset value.

```
void Ticker::setText(const QString &newText)
{
    myText = newText;
    update();
    updateGeometry();
}
```

The setText() function sets the text to display. It calls update() to force a repaint and updateGeometry() to notify any layout manager responsible for the Ticker widget about a size hint change.

```
QSize Ticker::sizeHint() const
{
    return fontMetrics().size(0, text());
}
```

The sizeHint() function returns the space needed by the text as the widget's ideal size. The QWidget::fontMetrics() function returns a QFontMetrics object that can be queried to obtain information relating to the widget's font. In this case, we ask for the size required by the given text.

```
void Ticker::paintEvent(QPaintEvent *)
{
    QPainter painter(this);

    int textWidth = fontMetrics().width(text());
    if (textWidth < 1)
        return;
    int x = -offset;
    while (x < width()) {
        painter.drawText(x, 0, textWidth, height(),
                         AlignLeft | AlignVCenter, text());
        x += textWidth;
    }
}
```

The paintEvent() function draws the text using QPainter::drawText(). It uses fontMetrics() to ascertain how much horizontal space the text requires, and then draws the text as many times as necessary to fill the entire width of the widget, taking offset into account.

```
void Ticker::showEvent(QShowEvent *)
{
    myTimerId = startTimer(30);
}
```

The showEvent() function starts a timer. The call to QObject::startTimer() returns an ID number, which we can use later to identify the timer. QObject supports multiple independent timers, each with its own time interval. After the call to startTimer(), Qt will generate a timer event approximately every 30 milliseconds; the accuracy depends on the underlying operating system.

We could have called startTimer() in the Ticker constructor, but we save some resources by having Qt generate timer events only when the widget is actually visible.

```
void Ticker::timerEvent(QTimerEvent *event)
{
    if (event->timerId() == myTimerId) {
        ++offset;
        if (offset >= fontMetrics().width(text()))
            offset = 0;
        scroll(-1, 0);
    } else {
        QWidget::timerEvent(event);
    }
}
```

The `timerEvent()` function is called at intervals by the system. It increments `offset` by 1 to simulate movement, wrapping at the width of the text. Then it scrolls the contents of the widget one pixel to the left using `QWidget::scroll()`. It would have been sufficient to call `update()` instead of `scroll()`, but `scroll()` is more efficient and prevents flicker, because it simply moves the existing pixels on screen and only generates a paint event for the widget's newly revealed area (a 1-pixel-wide strip in this case).

If the timer event isn't for the timer we are interested in, we pass it on to our base class.

```
void Ticker::hideEvent(QHideEvent *)
{
    killTimer(myTimerId);
}
```

The `hideEvent()` function calls `QObject::killTimer()` to stop the timer.

Timer events are low-level, and if we need multiple timers, it can become cumbersome to keep track of all the timer IDs. In such situations, it is usually easier to create a `QTimer` object for each timer. `QTimer` emits the `timeout()` signal at each time interval. `QTimer` also provides a convenient interface for single-shot timers (timers that time out just once).

## Installing Event Filters

One really powerful feature of Qt's event model is that a `QObject` instance can be set to monitor the events of another `QObject` instance before the latter object even sees them.

Let's suppose that we have a `CustomerInfoDialog` widget composed of several `QLineEdit`s and that we want to use the Space key to move the focus to the next `QLineEdit`. This non-standard behavior might be appropriate for an in-house application whose users are trained in its use. A straightforward solution is to subclass `QLineEdit` and reimplement `keyPressEvent()` to call `focusNextPrev-Child()`, like this:

```
void MyLineEdit::keyPressEvent(QKeyEvent *event)
{
    if (event->key() == Key_Space)
        focusNextPrevChild(true);
```

```
        else
            QLineEdit::keyPressEvent(event);
    }
```

This approach has many disadvantages. Because `MyLineEdit` isn't a standard Qt class, it must be integrated with *Qt Designer* if we want to design forms that make use of it. Also, if we use several different kinds of widgets in the form (for example, `QComboBoxes` and `QSpinBoxes`), we must also subclass them to make them exhibit the same behavior and integrate them with *Qt Designer* as well.

A better solution is to make `CustomerInfoDialog` monitor its child widgets' key press events and implement the required behavior in the monitoring code. This can be achieved using event filters. Setting up an event filter involves two steps:

1. Register the monitoring object with the target object by calling `install-EventFilter()` on the target.

2. Handle the target object's events in the monitor's `eventFilter()` function.

A good place to register the monitoring object is in the `CustomerInfoDialog` constructor:

```
CustomerInfoDialog::CustomerInfoDialog(QWidget *parent,
                                             const char *name)
    : QDialog(parent, name)
{
    ...
    firstNameEdit->installEventFilter(this);
    lastNameEdit->installEventFilter(this);
    cityEdit->installEventFilter(this);
    phoneNumberEdit->installEventFilter(this);
}
```

Once the event filter is registered, the events that are sent to the `firstName-Edit`, `lastNameEdit`, `cityEdit`, and `phoneNumberEdit` widgets are first sent to the `CustomerInfoDialog`'s `eventFilter()` function before they are sent on to their intended destination. (If multiple event filters are installed on the same object, the filters are activated in turn, from the most recently installed back to the first installed.)

Here's the `eventFilter()` function that receives the events:

```
bool CustomerInfoDialog::eventFilter(QObject *target, QEvent *event)
{
    if (target == firstNameEdit || target == lastNameEdit
            || target == cityEdit || target == phoneNumberEdit) {
        if (event->type() == QEvent::KeyPress) {
            QKeyEvent *keyEvent = (QKeyEvent *)event;
            if (keyEvent->key() == Key_Space) {
                focusNextPrevChild(true);
                return true;
            }
        }
    }
```

```
        }
        return QDialog::eventFilter(target, event);
    }
```

First, we check to see if the target widget is one of the QLineEdits. It's easy to forget that the base class, QDialog, might monitor some widgets of its own. (In Qt 3.2, this is not the case for QDialog. However, other Qt widget classes, such as QMainWindow, do monitor some of their child widgets for various reasons.)

If the event is a key press, we cast it to QKeyEvent and check which key is pressed. If the pressed key is Space, we call focusNextPrevChild() to pass focus on to the next widget in the focus chain, and we return true to tell Qt that we have handled the event. If we returned false, Qt would send the event to its intended target, resulting in a spurious space being inserted into the QLineEdit.

If the event isn't a Space key press, we pass control to the base class's implementation of eventFilter().

Qt offers five levels at which events can be processed and filtered:

### 1. We can reimplement a specific event handler.

Reimplementing event handlers such as mousePressEvent(), keyPressEvent(), and paintEvent() is by far the most common way to process events. We have already seen many examples of this.

### 2. We can reimplement QObject::event().

By reimplementing the event() function, we can process events before they reach the specific event handlers. This approach is mostly needed to override the default meaning of the Tab key, as shown earlier (p. 164). This is also used to handle rare types of events for which no specific event handler exists (for example, LayoutDirectionChange). When we reimplement event(), we need to call the base class's event() function for handling the cases we don't explicitly handle.

### 3. We can install an event filter on a single QObject.

Once an object has been registered using installEventFilter(), all the events for the target object are first sent to the monitoring object's eventFilter() function. We have used this approach to handle Space key presses in the CustomerInfoDialog example above.

### 4. We can install an event filter on the QApplication object.

Once an event filter has been registered for qApp (the unique QApplication object), every event for every object in the application is sent to the eventFilter() function before it is sent to any other event filter. This approach is mostly useful for debugging and for hiding Easter eggs. It can also be used to handle mouse events sent to disabled widgets, which QApplication normally discards.

### 5. We can subclass QApplication and reimplement notify().

Qt calls `QApplication::notify()` to send out an event. Reimplementing this function is the only way to get all the events, before any event filters get the opportunity to look at them. Event filters are generally more useful, because there can be any number of concurrent event filters, but only one `notify()` function.

Many event types, including mouse and key events, can be propagated. If the event has not been handled on the way to its target object or by the target object itself, the whole event processing process is repeated, but this time with the target object's parent as the new target. This continues, going from parent to parent, until either the event is handled or the top-level object is reached.

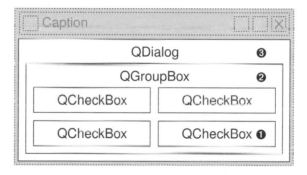

**Figure 7.2.** Event propagation in a dialog

Figure 7.2 shows how a key press event is propagated from child to parent in a dialog. When the user presses a key, the event is first sent to the widget that has focus, in this case the bottom-right `QCheckBox`. If the `QCheckBox` doesn't handle the event, Qt sends it to the `QGroupBox`, and finally to the `QDialog` object.

## Staying Responsive During Intensive Processing

When we call `QApplication::exec()`, we start Qt's event loop. Qt issues a few events on startup to show and paint the widgets. After that, the event loop is running, constantly checking to see if any events have occurred and dispatching these events to `QObjects` in the application.

While one event is being processed, additional events may be generated and appended to Qt's event queue. If we spend too much time processing a particular event, the user interface will become unresponsive. For example, any events generated by the window system while the application is saving a file to disk will not be processed until the file is saved. During the save, the application will not respond to requests from the window system to repaint itself.

One solution is to use multiple threads: one thread for the application's user interface and another thread to perform file saving (or any other time-consuming operation). This way, the application's user interface will stay responsive while the file is being saved. We will see how to achieve this in Chapter 17.

A simpler solution is to make frequent calls to `QApplication::processEvents()` in the file saving code. This function tells Qt to process any pending events, and then returns control to the caller. In fact, `QApplication::exec()` is little more than a `while` loop around a `processEvents()` function call.

Here's an example of how we can keep the user interface responsive using `processEvents()`, based on the file saving code for `Spreadsheet` (p. 77):

```
bool Spreadsheet::writeFile(const QString &fileName)
{
    QFile file(fileName);
    ...
    for (int row = 0; row < NumRows; ++row) {
        for (int col = 0; col < NumCols; ++col) {
            QString str = formula(row, col);
            if (!str.isEmpty())
                out << (Q_UINT16)row << (Q_UINT16)col << str;
        }
        qApp->processEvents();
    }
    return true;
}
```

One danger with this approach is that the user might close the main window while the application is still saving, or even click File|Save a second time, resulting in undefined behavior. The easiest solution to this problem is to replace the

```
qApp->processEvents();
```

call with a

```
qApp->eventLoop()->processEvents(QEventLoop::ExcludeUserInput);
```

call, which tells Qt to ignore mouse and key events.

Often, we want to show a `QProgressDialog` while a long running operation is taking place. `QProgressDialog` has a progress bar that keeps the user informed about the progress being made by the application. `QProgressDialog` also provides a Cancel button that allows the user to abort the operation. Here's the code for saving a Spreadsheet file using this approach:

```
bool Spreadsheet::writeFile(const QString &fileName)
{
    QFile file(fileName);
    ...
    QProgressDialog progress(tr("Saving file..."), tr("Cancel"),
                             NumRows);
    progress.setModal(true);
    for (int row = 0; row < NumRows; ++row) {
        progress.setProgress(row);
        qApp->processEvents();
```

```
        if (progress.wasCanceled()) {
            file.remove();
            return false;
        }

        for (int col = 0; col < NumCols; ++col) {
            QString str = formula(row, col);
            if (!str.isEmpty())
                out << (Q_UINT16)row << (Q_UINT16)col << str;
        }
    }
    return true;
}
```

We create a QProgressDialog with NumRows as the total number of steps. Then, for each row, we call setProgress() to update the progress bar. QProgressDialog automatically computes a percentage by dividing the current progress value by the total number of steps. We call QApplication::processEvents() to process any repaint events or any user clicks or key presses (for example, to allow the user to click Cancel). If the user clicks Cancel, we abort the save and remove the file.

We don't call show() on the QProgressDialog because progress dialogs do that for themselves. If the operation turns out to be short, presumably because the file to save is small or because the machine is fast, QProgressDialog will detect this and will not show itself at all.

There is a completely different way of dealing with long running operations. Instead of performing the processing when the user requests, we can defer the processing until the application is idle. This can work if the processing can be safely interrupted and resumed, since we cannot predict how long the application will be idle.

In Qt, this approach can be implemented by using a special kind of timer: a 0-millisecond timer. These timers time out whenever there are no pending events. Here's an example timerEvent() implementation that shows the idle processing approach:

```
    void Spreadsheet::timerEvent(QTimerEvent *event)
    {
        if (event->timerId() == myTimerId) {
            while (step < MaxStep && !qApp->hasPendingEvents()) {
                performStep(step);
                ++step;
            }
        } else {
            QTable::timerEvent(event);
        }
    }
```

If hasPendingEvents() returns true, we stop processing and give control back to Qt. The processing will resume when Qt has handled all its pending events.

# 2D and 3D Graphics

In this chapter, we will explore Qt's graphics capabilities. The cornerstone of Qt's 2D drawing engine is QPainter, which can be used to draw on a widget on the screen, on an off-screen pixmap, or on a physical printer. Qt also includes a QCanvas class that provides a higher-level way of doing graphics, using an item-based approach that can efficiently handle thousands and thousands of items of various shapes. Many predefined items are provided, and it is easy to create custom canvas items.

An alternative to QPainter and QCanvas is to use the OpenGL library. OpenGL is a standard library for drawing 3D graphics, but it can also be used for drawing 2D graphics. It is very easy to integrate OpenGL code into Qt applications, as we will demonstrate.

## Painting with QPainter

A QPainter can be used to draw on a "paint device", such as a widget or a pixmap. QPainter is useful when we write custom widgets or custom item classes with their own look and feel. QPainter is also the class to use for printing; this will be explained in detail later in the chapter.

QPainter can draw geometric shapes: points, lines, rectangles, ellipses, arcs, chords, pie segments, polygons, and cubic Bézier curves. It can also draw pixmaps, images, and text.

When we pass a paint device to the QPainter constructor, QPainter adopts some settings from the device and initializes other settings to default values. These settings influence the way drawing is performed. The three most important are the painter's pen, brush, and font:

- The *pen* is used for drawing lines and geometric shape boundaries. It consists of a color, a width, a line style, a cap style, and a join style.

175

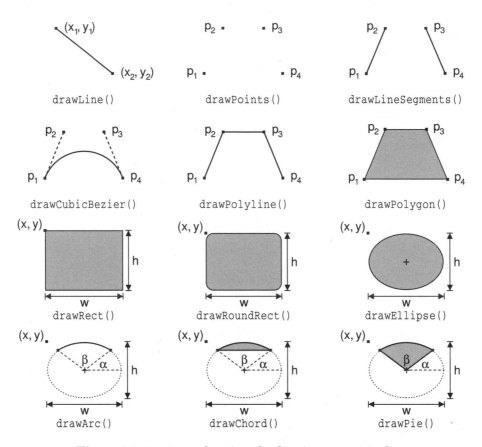

**Figure 8.1.** QPainter functions for drawing geometric shapes

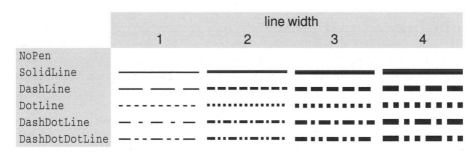

**Figure 8.2.** Pen styles

- The *brush* is the pattern used for filling geometric shapes. It consists of a color and a style.

- The *font* is used for drawing text. A font has many attributes, including a family and a point size.

These settings can be modified by calling one of setPen(), setBrush(), and setFont() with a QPen, QBrush, or QFont object.

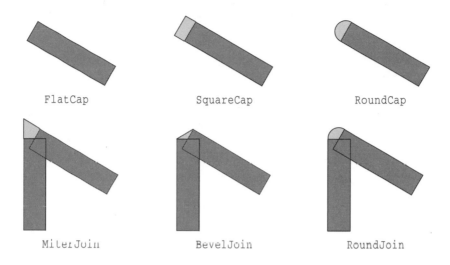

**Figure 8.3.** Cap and join styles

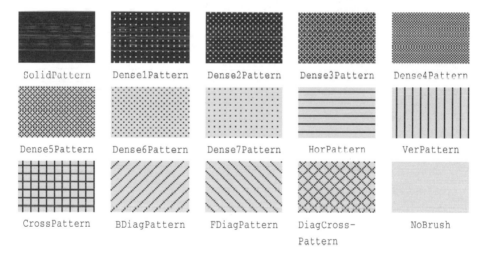

**Figure 8.4.** Brush styles

Here's the code to draw the ellipse shown in Figure 8.5 (a):

```
QPainter painter(this);
painter.setPen(QPen(black, 3, DashDotLine));
painter.setBrush(QBrush(red, SolidPattern));
painter.drawEllipse(20, 20, 100, 60);
```

Here's the code to draw the pie segment shown in Figure 8.5 (b):

```
QPainter painter(this);
painter.setPen(QPen(black, 5, SolidLine));
painter.setBrush(QBrush(red, DiagCrossPattern));
painter.drawPie(20, 20, 100, 60, 60 * 16, 270 * 16);
```

The last two arguments to `drawPie()` are expressed in sixteenths of a degree.

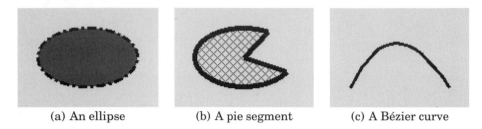

| (a) An ellipse | (b) A pie segment | (c) A Bézier curve |

**Figure 8.5.** Geometric shape examples

Here's the code to draw the cubic Bézier curve shown in Figure 8.5 (c):

```
QPainter painter(this);
QPointArray points(4);
points[0] = QPoint(20, 80);
points[1] = QPoint(50, 20);
points[2] = QPoint(80, 20);
points[3] = QPoint(120, 80);
painter.setPen(QPen(black, 3, SolidLine));
painter.drawCubicBezier(points);
```

The current state of a painter can be saved on a stack by calling save() and restored later on by calling restore(). This can be useful if we want to temporarily change some painter settings and then reset them to their previous values.

The other settings that control a painter, in addition to the pen, brush, and font, are:

- The *background color* is used to fill the background of geometric shapes (beneath the brush pattern), text, or bitmaps when the *background mode* is OpaqueMode (the default is TransparentMode).

- The *raster operation* specifies how the newly drawn pixels should interact with the pixels already present on the paint device. The default is Copy-ROP, which means that the new pixels are simply copied onto the device, ignoring the previous pixel value. Other raster operations include XorROP, NotROP, AndROP, and NotAndROP.

- The *brush origin* is the starting point for brush patterns, normally the top-left corner of the widget.

- The *clip region* is the area of the device that can be painted. Drawing operations performed outside the clip region are ignored.

- The *viewport*, *window*, and *world matrix* determine how logical QPainter coordinates map to physical paint device coordinates. By default, these are set up so that the logical and physical coordinate systems coincide.

Let's take a closer look at the coordinate system defined by the viewport, window, and world matrix. (In this context, the term "window" does not refer to a window in the sense of a top-level widget, and the "viewport" has nothing to do with QScrollView's viewport.)

The viewport and the window are tightly bound. The viewport is an arbitrary rectangle specified in physical coordinates. The window specifies the same rectangle, but in logical coordinates. When we do the painting, we specify points in logical coordinates, and those coordinates are converted into physical coordinates in a linear algebraic manner, based on the current window–viewport settings.

By default, the viewport and the window are set to the device's rectangle. For example, if the device is a 320 × 200 widget, both the viewport and the window are the same 320 × 200 rectangle with its top-left corner at position (0, 0). In this case, the logical and physical coordinate systems are the same.

The window–viewport mechanism is useful to make the drawing code independent of the size or resolution of the paint device. We can always do the arithmetic to map logical coordinates to physical coordinates ourselves, but it's usually simpler to let QPainter do the work. For example, if we want the logical coordinates to extend from (–50, –50) to (+50, +50), with (0, 0) in the middle, we can set the window as follows:

```
painter.setWindow(QRect(-50, -50, 100, 100));
```

The (–50, –50) pair specifies the origin, and the (100, 100) pair specifies the width and height. This means that the logical coordinates (–50, –50) now correspond to the physical coordinates (0, 0), and the logical coordinates (+50, +50) correspond to the physical coordinates (320, 200). In this example, as is often the case, we don't need to change the viewport.

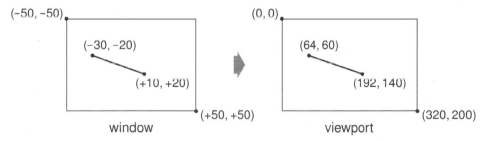

**Figure 8.6.** Converting logical coordinates into physical coordinates

Now comes the world matrix. The world matrix is a transformation matrix that is applied in addition to the window–viewport conversion. It allows us to translate, scale, rotate, or shear the items we are drawing. For example, if we wanted to draw text at a 45° angle, we would use this code:

```
QWMatrix matrix;
matrix.rotate(45.0);
painter.setWorldMatrix(matrix);
painter.drawText(rect, AlignCenter, tr("Revenue"));
```

The logical coordinates we pass to drawText() are transformed by the world matrix, then mapped to physical coordinates using the window–viewport settings.

If we specify multiple transformations, they are applied in the order in which they are given. For example, if we want to use the point (10, 20) as the rotation's pivot point, we can do so by translating the window, performing the rotation, and then translating the window back to its original position:

```
QWMatrix matrix;
matrix.translate(-10.0, -20.0);
matrix.rotate(45.0);
matrix.translate(+10.0, +20.0);
painter.setWorldMatrix(matrix);
painter.drawText(rect, AlignCenter, tr("Revenue"));
```

A simpler way to specify transformations is to use `QPainter`'s `translate()`, `scale()`, `rotate()`, and `shear()` convenience functions:

```
painter.translate(-10.0, -20.0);
painter.rotate(45.0);
painter.translate(+10.0, +20.0);
painter.drawText(rect, AlignCenter, tr("Revenue"));
```

But if we want to use the same transformations repeatedly, it's faster to store them in a `QWMatrix` object and set the world matrix on the painter whenever the transformations are needed.

If we want to just save the world matrix and restore it later, we can use `saveWorldMatrix()` and `restoreWorldMatrix()`.

**Figure 8.7.** The `OvenTimer` widget

To illustrate painter transformations, we will review the code of the `OvenTimer` widget shown in Figure 8.7. The `OvenTimer` widget is modeled after the physical oven timers that were used before it was common to have ovens with clocks built-in. The user can click a notch to set the duration. The wheel automatically turns counterclockwise until 0 is reached, at which point `OvenTimer` emits the `timeout()` signal.

```
class OvenTimer : public QWidget
{
    Q_OBJECT
public:
    OvenTimer(QWidget *parent, const char *name = 0);

    void setDuration(int secs);
```

```
    int duration() const;
    void draw(QPainter *painter);

signals:
    void timeout();

protected:
    void paintEvent(QPaintEvent *event);
    void mousePressEvent(QMouseEvent *event);

private:
    QDateTime finishTime;
    QTimer *updateTimer;
    QTimer *finishTimer;
};
```

The OvenTimer class inherits QWidget and reimplements two virtual functions:
paintEvent() and mousePressEvent().

```
#include <qpainter.h>
#include <qpixmap.h>
#include <qtimer.h>

#include <cmath>
using namespace std;

#include "oventimer.h"

const double DegreesPerMinute = 7.0;
const double DegreesPerSecond = DegreesPerMinute / 60;
const int MaxMinutes = 45;
const int MaxSeconds = MaxMinutes * 60;
const int UpdateInterval = 10;

OvenTimer::OvenTimer(QWidget *parent, const char *name)
    : QWidget(parent, name)
{
    finishTime = QDateTime::currentDateTime();
    updateTimer = new QTimer(this);
    finishTimer = new QTimer(this);
    connect(updateTimer, SIGNAL(timeout()), this, SLOT(update()));
    connect(finishTimer, SIGNAL(timeout()), this, SIGNAL(timeout()));
}
```

In the constructor, we create two QTimer objects: updateTimer is used to refresh
the appearance of the widget at regular intervals, and finishTimer emits the
widget's timeout() signal when the timer reaches 0.

```
void OvenTimer::setDuration(int secs)
{
    if (secs > MaxSeconds)
        secs = MaxSeconds;
    finishTime = QDateTime::currentDateTime().addSecs(secs);
    updateTimer->start(UpdateInterval * 1000, false);
    finishTimer->start(secs * 1000, true);
    update();
}
```

The setDuration() function sets the duration of the oven timer to the given number of seconds. The false argument passed in the updateTimer's start() call tells Qt that this a repeating timer that will time out every 10 seconds. The finishTimer only needs to timeout once, so we use a true argument to indicate that it is a single-shot timer. We compute the finish time by adding the duration in seconds to the current time, obtained from QDateTime::current-DateTime(), and store it in the finishTime private variable.

The finishTime variable is of type QDateTime, the **Qt** data type for storing a date and a time. The date component of the QDateTime is important in situations where the current time is before midnight and the finish time is after midnight.

```
int OvenTimer::duration() const
{
    int secs = QDateTime::currentDateTime().secsTo(finishTime);
    if (secs < 0)
        secs = 0;
    return secs;
}
```

The duration() function returns the number of seconds left before the timer is due to finish.

```
void OvenTimer::mousePressEvent(QMouseEvent *event)
{
    QPoint point = event->pos() - rect().center();
    double theta = atan2(-(double)point.x(), -(double)point.y())
                   * 180 / 3.14159265359;
    setDuration((int)(duration() + theta / DegreesPerSecond));
    update();
}
```

If the user clicks the widget, we find the closest notch using a subtle but effective mathematical formula, and we use the result to set the new duration. Then we schedule a repaint. The notch that the user clicked will now be at the top and will move counterclockwise as time passes until 0 is reached.

```
void OvenTimer::paintEvent(QPaintEvent *)
{
    QPainter painter(this);
    int side = QMIN(width(), height());
    painter.setViewport((width() - side) / 2, (height() - side) / 2,
                        side, side);
    painter.setWindow(-50, -50, 100, 100);
    draw(&painter);
}
```

In paintEvent(), we set the viewport to be the largest square area that fits inside the widget, and we set the window to be the rectangle (–50, –50, 100, 100), that is, the 100 × 100 rectangle extending from (–50, –50) to (+50, +50). The QMIN() macro returns the lowest of its two arguments.

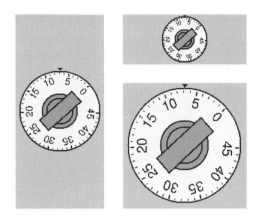

**Figure 8.8.** The `OvenTimer` widget at three different sizes

If we had not set the viewport to be a square, the oven timer would be an ellipse when the widget is resized to a non-square rectangle. In general, if we want to avoid such deformations, we must set the viewport and the window to rectangles with the same aspect ratio.

The window setting of ( 50, 50, 100, 100) was also chosen bearing these issues in mind:

- `QPainter`'s draw functions take `int` coordinate values. If we choose a window that is too small, we might not be able to specify all the points we need as integers.

- If we use a large window and use `drawText()` to draw some text, we will need a larger font to compensate.

This makes (–50, –50, 100, 100) a better choice than, say, (–5, –5, 10, 10) or (–2000, –2000, 4000, 4000).

Now let's look at the drawing code:

```
void OvenTimer::draw(QPainter *painter)
{
    static const QCOORD triangle[3][2] = {
        { -2, -49 }, { +2, -49 }, { 0, -47 }
    };
    QPen thickPen(colorGroup().foreground(), 2);
    QPen thinPen(colorGroup().foreground(), 1);

    painter->setPen(thinPen);
    painter->setBrush(colorGroup().foreground());
    painter->drawConvexPolygon(QPointArray(3, &triangle[0][0]));
```

We start by drawing the tiny triangle that marks the 0 position at the top of the widget. The triangle is specified by three hard-coded coordinates, and we use `drawConvexPolygon()` to render it. We could have used `drawPolygon()`, but when we know the polygon we are drawing is convex, we can save some microseconds by calling `drawConvexPolygon()`.

What is so convenient about the window–viewport mechanism is that we can hard-code the coordinates we use in the draw commands and still get good resizing behavior. Nor do we have to worry about non-square widgets; this is handled by setting the viewport appropriately.

```
painter->setPen(thickPen);
painter->setBrush(colorGroup().light());
painter->drawEllipse(-46, -46, 92, 92);
painter->setBrush(colorGroup().mid());
painter->drawEllipse(-20, -20, 40, 40);
painter->drawEllipse(-15, -15, 30, 30);
```

We draw the outer circle and the two inner circles. The outer circle is filled with the palette's "light" component (typically white), while the two inner circles are filled with the "mid" component (typically medium gray).

```
int secs = duration();
painter->rotate(secs * DegreesPerSecond);
painter->drawRect(-8, -25, 16, 50);

for (int i = 0; i <= MaxMinutes; ++i) {
    if (i % 5 == 0) {
        painter->setPen(thickPen);
        painter->drawLine(0, -41, 0, -44);
        painter->drawText(-15, -41, 30, 25,
                        AlignHCenter | AlignTop,
                        QString::number(i));
    } else {
        painter->setPen(thinPen);
        painter->drawLine(0, -42, 0, -44);
    }
    painter->rotate(-DegreesPerMinute);
}
}
```

We draw the knob, the notches, and at every fifth notch we draw the number of minutes. We call `rotate()` to rotate the painter's coordinate system. In the old coordinate system, the 0-minute mark was on top; now, the 0-minute mark is moved to the place that's appropriate for the time left. We draw the rectangular knob handle after the rotation, since its orientation depends on the rotation angle.

In the `for` loop, we draw the tick marks along the outer circle's edge and the numbers for each multiple of 5 minutes. The text is put in an invisible rectangle underneath the tick mark. At the end of one iteration, we rotate the painter clockwise by 7°, the amount corresponding to one minute. The next time we draw a tick mark, it will be at a different position around the circle, although the coordinates we pass to the `drawLine()` and `drawText()` calls are always the same.

Another way of implementing an oven timer would have been to compute the $(x, y)$ positions ourselves, using `sin()` and `cos()` to find the positions along the circle. But then we would still need to use a translation and a rotation to draw the text at an angle.

There is one issue left: flicker. Every ten seconds, we repaint the widget entirely, causing it to flicker each time. The solution is to add double buffering. This can be done by passing the `WNoAutoErase` to the base class constructor and by replacing the `paintEvent()` function shown earlier with this one:

```
void OvenTimer::paintEvent(QPaintEvent *event)
{
    static QPixmap pixmap;
    QRect rect = event->rect();

    QSize newSize = rect.size().expandedTo(pixmap.size());
    pixmap.resize(newSize);
    pixmap.fill(this, rect.topLeft());

    QPainter painter(&pixmap, this);
    int side = QMIN(width(), height());
    painter.setViewport((width() - side) / 2 - event->rect().x(),
                        (height() - side) / 2 - event->rect().y(),
                        side, side);
    painter.setWindow(-50, -50, 100, 100);
    draw(&painter);
    bitBlt(this, event->rect().topLeft(), &pixmap);
}
```

This time, we paint on a pixmap instead of on the widget directly. The pixmap is given the size of the area to repaint, and the window–viewport pair is initialized in such a way that the painting is performed the same as if it was done directly on the widget. The `draw()` function is also unchanged. At the end, we copy the pixmap onto the widget using `bitBlt()`.

This is similar to what we explained in the "Double Buffering" section of Chapter 5 (p. 113), but there's one important difference: In Chapter 5, we used `translate()` to translate the painter, while here we subtract the paint event's $x$ and $y$ coordinates when setting up the viewport. Using translation here would not be as convenient, because the translation would have to be expressed in logical window coordinates, whereas the event's rectangle is in physical coordinates.

# Graphics with QCanvas

`QCanvas` offers a higher-level interface for doing graphics than `QPainter` provides. A `QCanvas` can contain items of any shape and uses double buffering internally to avoid flicker. For applications that need to present many user-manipulable items, like data visualization programs and 2D games, using `QCanvas` is often a better approach than reimplementing `QWidget::paintEvent()` or `QScrollView::drawContents()` and painting everything manually.

The items shown on a `QCanvas` are instances of `QCanvasItem` or of one of its subclasses. Qt provides a useful set of predefined subclasses: `QCanvasLine`, `QCan-`

vasRectangle, QCanvasPolygon, QCanvasPolygonalItem, QCanvasEllipse, QCanvas-Spline, QCanvasSprite, and QCanvasText. These classes can themselves be subclassed to provide custom canvas items.

A QCanvas and its QCanvasItems are purely data and have no visual representation. To render the canvas and its items, we must use a QCanvasView widget. This separation of the data from its visual representation makes it possible to have multiple QCanvasView widgets visualizing the same canvas. Each of these QCanvasViews can present its own portion of the canvas, possibly with different transformation matrices.

QCanvas is highly optimized to handle a large number of items. When an item changes, QCanvas only redraws the "chunks" that have changed. It also provides an efficient collision-detection algorithm. For these reasons alone, it's worth considering QCanvas as an alternative to reimplementing QWidget::paintEvent() or QScrollView::drawContents().

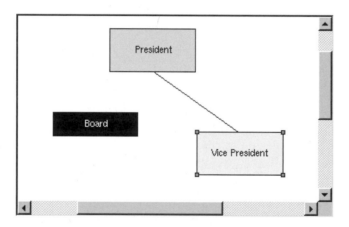

**Figure 8.9.** The DiagramView widget

To demonstrate QCanvas usage, we present the code for the DiagramView widget, a minimalist diagram editor. The widget supports two kinds of shapes (boxes and lines) and provides a context menu that lets the user add new boxes and lines, copy and paste them, delete them, and edit their properties.

```
class DiagramView : public QCanvasView
{
    Q_OBJECT
public:
    DiagramView(QCanvas *canvas, QWidget *parent = 0,
                const char *name = 0);

public slots:
    void cut();
    void copy();
    void paste();
    void del();
    void properties();
    void addBox();
```

```
    void addLine();
    void bringToFront();
    void sendToBack();
```

The `DiagramView` class inherits `QCanvasView`, which itself inherits `QScrollView`. It provides many public slots that an application could connect to. The slots are also used by the widget itself to implement its context menu.

```
protected:
    void contentsContextMenuEvent(QContextMenuEvent *event);
    void contentsMousePressEvent(QMouseEvent *event);
    void contentsMouseMoveEvent(QMouseEvent *event);
    void contentsMouseDoubleClickEvent(QMouseEvent *event);

private:
    void createActions();
    void addItem(QCanvasItem *item);
    void setActiveItem(QCanvasItem *item);
    void showNewItem(QCanvasItem *item);

    QCanvasItem *pendingItem;
    QCanvasItem *activeItem;
    QPoint lastPos;
    int minZ;
    int maxZ;

    QAction *cutAct;
    QAction *copyAct;
    ...
    QAction *sendToBackAct;
};
```

The protected and private members of the class will be explained shortly.

**Figure 8.10.** The `DiagramBox` and `DiagramLine` canvas items

Along with the `DiagramView` class, we also need to define two custom canvas item classes to represent the shapes we want to draw. We will call these classes `DiagramBox` and `DiagramLine`.

```
class DiagramBox : public QCanvasRectangle
{
public:
    enum { RTTI = 1001 };

    DiagramBox(QCanvas *canvas);
    ~DiagramBox();

    void setText(const QString &newText);
    QString text() const { return str; }
    void drawShape(QPainter &painter);
```

```
    QRect boundingRect() const;
    int rtti() const { return RTTI; }

private:
    QString str;
};
```

The DiagramBox class is a type of canvas item that displays a box and a piece of text. It inherits some of its functionality from QCanvasRectangle, a QCanvas-Item subclass that displays a rectangle. To QCanvasRectangle we add the ability to show some text in the middle of the rectangle and the ability to show tiny squares ("handles") at each corner to indicate that an item is active. In a real-world application, we would make it possible to click and drag the handles to resize the box, but to keep the code short we will not do so here.

The rtti() function is reimplemented from QCanvasItem. Its name stands for "run-time type identification", and by comparing its return value with the RTTI constant, we can determine whether an arbitrary item in the canvas is a DiagramBox or not. We could perform the same check using C++'s dynamic_cast<T>() mechanism, but that would restrict us to C++ compilers that support this feature.

The value of 1001 is arbitrary. Any value above 1000 is acceptable, as long as it doesn't collide with other item types used in the same application.

```
class DiagramLine : public QCanvasLine
{
public:
    enum { RTTI = 1002 };

    DiagramLine(QCanvas *canvas);
    ~DiagramLine();

    QPoint offset() const { return QPoint((int)x(), (int)y()); }
    void drawShape(QPainter &painter);
    QPointArray areaPoints() const;
    int rtti() const { return RTTI; }
};
```

The DiagramLine class is a canvas item that displays a line. It inherits some of its functionality from QCanvasLine, and adds the ability to show handles at each end to indicate that the line is active.

Now we will review the implementations of these three classes.

```
DiagramView::DiagramView(QCanvas *canvas, QWidget *parent,
                         const char *name)
    : QCanvasView(canvas, parent, name)
{
    pendingItem = 0;
    activeItem = 0;
    minZ = 0;
    maxZ = 0;
    createActions();
}
```

The `DiagramView` constructor takes a canvas as its first argument and passes it on to the base class constructor. The `DiagramView` will show this canvas.

The `QActions` are created in the `createActions()` private function. We have implemented several versions of this function in earlier chapters, and this one follows the same pattern, so we will not reproduce it here.

```cpp
void DiagramView::contentsContextMenuEvent(QContextMenuEvent *event)
{
    QPopupMenu contextMenu(this);
    if (activeItem) {
        cutAct->addTo(&contextMenu);
        copyAct->addTo(&contextMenu);
        deleteAct->addTo(&contextMenu);
        contextMenu.insertSeparator();
        bringToFrontAct->addTo(&contextMenu);
        sendToBackAct->addTo(&contextMenu);
        contextMenu.insertSeparator();
        propertiesAct->addTo(&contextMenu);
    } else {
        pasteAct->addTo(&contextMenu);
        contextMenu.insertSeparator();
        addBoxAct->addTo(&contextMenu);
        addLineAct->addTo(&contextMenu);
    }
    contextMenu.exec(event->globalPos());
}
```

The `contentsContextMenuEvent()` function is reimplemented from `QScrollView` to create a context menu.

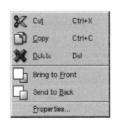

**Figure 8.11.** The `DiagramView` widget's context menus

If an item is active, the menu is populated with the actions that make sense on an item: Cut, Copy, Delete, Bring to Front, Send to Back, and Properties. Otherwise, the menu is populated with Paste, Add Box, and Add Line.

```cpp
void DiagramView::addBox()
{
    addItem(new DiagramBox(canvas()));
}

void DiagramView::addLine()
{
    addItem(new DiagramLine(canvas()));
}
```

The addBox() and addLine() slots create a DiagramBox or a DiagramLine item on the canvas and then call addItem() to perform the rest of the work.

```
void DiagramView::addItem(QCanvasItem *item)
{
    delete pendingItem;
    pendingItem = item;
    setActiveItem(0);
    setCursor(crossCursor);
}
```

The addItem() private function changes the cursor to a crosshair and sets pendingItem to be the newly created item. The item is not visible in the canvas until we call show() on it.

When the user chooses Add Box or Add Line from the context menu, the cursor changes to a crosshair. The item is not actually added until the user clicks on the canvas.

```
void DiagramView::contentsMousePressEvent(QMouseEvent *event)
{
    if (event->button() == LeftButton && pendingItem) {
        pendingItem->move(event->pos().x(), event->pos().y());
        showNewItem(pendingItem);
        pendingItem = 0;
        unsetCursor();
    } else {
        QCanvasItemList items = canvas()->collisions(event->pos());
        if (items.empty())
            setActiveItem(0);
        else
            setActiveItem(*items.begin());
    }
    lastPos = event->pos();
}
```

If users press the left mouse button while the cursor is a crosshair, they have already asked to create a box or line, and have now clicked the canvas at the position where they want the new item to appear. We move the "pending" item to the position of the click, show it, and reset the cursor to the normal arrow cursor.

Any other mouse press event on the canvas is interpreted as an attempt to select or deselect an item. We call collisions() on the canvas to obtain a list of all the items under the cursor and make the first item the current item. If the list contains many items, the first one is always the one that is rendered on top of the others.

```
void DiagramView::contentsMouseMoveEvent(QMouseEvent *event)
{
    if (event->state() & LeftButton) {
        if (activeItem) {
            activeItem->moveBy(event->pos().x() - lastPos.x(),
                               event->pos().y() - lastPos.y());
            lastPos = event->pos();
```

```
                    canvas()->update();
            }
        }
    }
```

The user can move an item on the canvas by pressing the left mouse button on an item and dragging. Each time we get a mouse move event, we move the item by the horizontal and vertical distance by which the mouse moved and call `update()` on the canvas. Whenever we modify a canvas item, we must call `update()` to notify the canvas that it needs to redraw itself.

```
void DiagramView::contentsMouseDoubleClickEvent(QMouseEvent *event)
{
    if (event->button() == LeftButton && activeItem
            && activeItem->rtti() == DiagramBox::RTTI) {
        DiagramBox *box = (DiagramBox *)activeItem;
        bool ok;

        QString newText = QInputDialog::getText(
                tr("Diagram"), tr("Enter new text:"),
                QLineEdit::Normal, box->text(), &ok, this);
        if (ok) {
            box->setText(newText);
            canvas()->update();
        }
    }
}
```

If the user double-clicks an item, we call the item's `rtti()` function and compare its return value with `DiagramBox::RTTI` (defined as 1001).

**Figure 8.12.** Changing the text of a `DiagramBox` item

If the item is a `DiagramBox`, we pop up a `QInputDialog` to allow the user to change the text shown in the box. The `QInputDialog` class provides a label, a line editor, an OK button, and a Cancel button.

```
void DiagramView::bringToFront()
{
    if (activeItem) {
        ++maxZ;
        activeItem->setZ(maxZ);
        canvas()->update();
    }
}
```

The `bringToFront()` slot raises the currently active item to be on top of the other items in the canvas. This is accomplished by setting the item's $z$ coordinate to a value that is higher than any other value attributed to an item so far. When two items occupy the same $(x, y)$ position, the item that has the highest $z$ value is shown in front of the other item. (If the $z$ values are equal, QCanvas will break the tie by comparing the item pointers.)

```
void DiagramView::sendToBack()
{
    if (activeItem) {
        --minZ;
        activeItem->setZ(minZ);
        canvas()->update();
    }
}
```

The sendToBack() slot puts the currently active item behind all the other items in the canvas. This is done by setting the item's $z$ coordinate to a value that is lower than any other $z$ value attributed to an item so far.

```
void DiagramView::cut()
{
    copy();
    del();
}
```

The cut() slot is trivial.

```
void DiagramView::copy()
{
    if (activeItem) {
        QString str;
        if (activeItem->rtti() == DiagramBox::RTTI) {
            DiagramBox *box = (DiagramBox *)activeItem;
            str = QString("DiagramBox %1 %2 %3 %4 %5")
                    .arg(box->width())
                    .arg(box->height())
                    .arg(box->pen().color().name())
                    .arg(box->brush().color().name())
                    .arg(box->text());
        } else if (activeItem->rtti() == DiagramLine::RTTI) {
            DiagramLine *line = (DiagramLine *)activeItem;
            QPoint delta = line->endPoint() - line->startPoint();
            str = QString("DiagramLine %1 %2 %3")
                    .arg(delta.x())
                    .arg(delta.y())
                    .arg(line->pen().color().name());
        }
        QApplication::clipboard()->setText(str);
    }
}
```

The copy() slot converts the active item into a string and copies the string to the clipboard. The string contains all the information necessary to reconstruct the item. For example, a black-on-white 320 × 40 box containing "My Left Foot" would be represented by this string:

```
DiagramBox 320 40 #000000 #ffffff My Left Foot
```

We don't bother storing the position of the item on the canvas. When we paste the item, we simply put the duplicate near the canvas's top-left corner. Converting an object to a string is an easy way to add clipboard support, but it is also possible to put arbitrary binary data onto the clipboard, as we will see in Chapter 9 (Drag and Drop).

```cpp
void DiagramView::paste()
{
    QString str = QApplication::clipboard()->text();
    QTextIStream in(&str);
    QString tag;

    in >> tag;
    if (tag == "DiagramBox") {
        int width;
        int height;
        QString lineColor;
        QString fillColor;
        QString text;

        in >> width >> height >> lineColor >> fillColor;
        text = in.read();

        DiagramBox *box = new DiagramBox(canvas());
        box->move(20, 20);
        box->setSize(width, height);
        box->setText(text);
        box->setPen(QColor(lineColor));
        box->setBrush(QColor(fillColor));
        showNewItem(box);
    } else if (tag == "DiagramLine") {
        int deltaX;
        int deltaY;
        QString lineColor;

        in >> deltaX >> deltaY >> lineColor;

        DiagramLine *line = new DiagramLine(canvas());
        line->move(20, 20);
        line->setPoints(0, 0, deltaX, deltaY);
        line->setPen(QColor(lineColor));
        showNewItem(line);
    }
}
```

The `paste()` slot uses `QTextIStream` to parse the contents of the clipboard. `QTextIStream` works on whitespace-delimited fields in a similar way to `cin`. We extract each field using the `>>` operator, except the last field of the `DiagramBox` item, which might contain spaces. For this field, we use `QTextStream::read()`, which reads in the rest of the string.

```cpp
void DiagramView::del()
{
    if (activeItem) {
```

```
            QCanvasItem *item = activeItem;
            setActiveItem(0);
            delete item;
            canvas()->update();
        }
    }
```

The `del()` slot deletes the active item and calls `QCanvas::update()` to redraw the canvas.

```
    void DiagramView::properties()
    {
        if (activeItem) {
            PropertiesDialog dialog;
            dialog.exec(activeItem);
        }
    }
```

The `properties()` slot pops up a Properties dialog for the active item. The `PropertiesDialog` class is a "smart" dialog; we simply need to pass it a pointer to the item we want it to act on and it takes care of the rest.

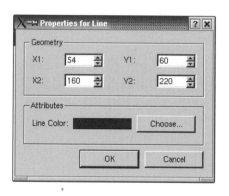
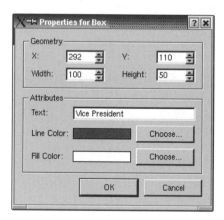

**Figure 8.13.** The Properties dialog's two appearances

The `.ui` and `.ui.h` files for the `PropertiesDialog` are on the CD that accompanies this book.

```
    void DiagramView::showNewItem(QCanvasItem *item)
    {
        setActiveItem(item);
        bringToFront();
        item->show();
        canvas()->update();
    }
```

The `showNewItem()` private function is called from a few places in the code to make a newly created canvas item visible and active.

```
    void DiagramView::setActiveItem(QCanvasItem *item)
    {
```

```
    if (item != activeItem) {
        if (activeItem)
            activeItem->setActive(false);
        activeItem = item;
        if (activeItem)
            activeItem->setActive(true);
        canvas()->update();
    }
}
```

Finally, the `setActiveItem()` private function clears the old active item's
"active" flag, sets the `activeItem` variable, and sets the new active item's flag.
The item's "active" flag is stored in `QCanvasItem`. Qt doesn't use the flag itself;
it is provided purely for the convenience of subclasses. We use the flag in the
`DiagramBox` and `DiagramLine` subclasses because we want them to paint themselves differently depending on whether they are active or not.

Let's now review the code for `DiagramBox` and `DiagramLine`.

```
const int Margin = 2;

void drawActiveHandle(QPainter &painter, const QPoint &center)
{
    painter.setPen(Qt::black);
    painter.setBrush(Qt::gray);
    painter.drawRect(center.x() - Margin, center.y() - Margin,
                     2 * Margin + 1, 2 * Margin + 1);
}
```

The `drawActiveHandle()` function is used by both `DiagramBox` and `DiagramLine` to
draw a tiny square indicating that an item is the active item.

```
DiagramBox::DiagramBox(QCanvas *canvas)
    : QCanvasRectangle(canvas)
{
    setSize(100, 60);
    setPen(black);
    setBrush(white);
    str = "Text";
}
```

In the `DiagramBox` constructor, we set the size of the rectangle to 100 × 60. We
also set the pen color to black and the brush color to white. The pen color is
used to draw the box outline and the text, while the brush color is used for the
background of the box.

```
DiagramBox::~DiagramBox()
{
    hide();
}
```

The `DiagramBox` destructor calls `hide()` on the item. This is necessary for all
classes that inherit from `QCanvasPolygonalItem` (`QCanvasRectangle`'s base class)
because of the way `QCanvasPolygonalItem` works.

```
void DiagramBox::setText(const QString &newText)
{
    str = newText;
    update();
}
```

The setText() function sets the text shown in the box and calls QCanvasItem::update() to mark this item as changed. The next time the canvas repaints itself, it will know that it must repaint this item.

```
void DiagramBox::drawShape(QPainter &painter)
{
    QCanvasRectangle::drawShape(painter);
    painter.drawText(rect(), AlignCenter, text());
    if (isActive()) {
        drawActiveHandle(painter, rect().topLeft());
        drawActiveHandle(painter, rect().topRight());
        drawActiveHandle(painter, rect().bottomLeft());
        drawActiveHandle(painter, rect().bottomRight());
    }
}
```

The drawShape() function is reimplemented from QCanvasPolygonalItem to draw the text, and if the item is active, the four handles. We use the base class to draw the rectangle itself.

```
QRect DiagramBox::boundingRect() const
{
    return QRect((int)x() - Margin, (int)y() - Margin,
                 width() + 2 * Margin, height() + 2 * Margin);
}
```

The boundingRect() function is reimplemented from QCanvasItem. It is used by QCanvas to perform collision-detection and to optimize painting. The rectangle it returns must be at least as large as the area painted in drawShape().

The default QCanvasRectangle implementation is not sufficient, because it does not take into account the handles that we paint at each corner of the rectangle if the item is active.

```
DiagramLine::DiagramLine(QCanvas *canvas)
    : QCanvasLine(canvas)
{
    setPoints(0, 0, 0, 99);
}
```

In the DiagramLine constructor, we set the two points that define the line to be (0, 0) and (0, 99). The result is a 100-pixel-long vertical line.

```
DiagramLine::~DiagramLine()
{
    hide();
}
```

Again, we must call hide() in the destructor.

```
void DiagramLine::drawShape(QPainter &painter)
{
    QCanvasLine::drawShape(painter);
    if (isActive()) {
        drawActiveHandle(painter, startPoint() + offset());
        drawActiveHandle(painter, endPoint() + offset());
    }
}
```

The `drawShape()` function is reimplemented from `QCanvasLine` to draw handles at both ends of the line if the item is active. We use the base class to draw the line itself. The `offset()` function was implemented in the `DiagramLine` class definition. It returns the position of the item on the canvas.

```
QPointArray DiagramLine::areaPoints() const
{
    const int Extra = Margin + 1;
    QPointArray points(6);
    QPoint pointA = startPoint() + offset();
    QPoint pointB = endPoint() + offset();

    if (pointA.x() > pointB.x())
        swap(pointA, pointB);

    points[0] = pointA + QPoint(-Extra, -Extra);
    points[1] = pointA + QPoint(-Extra, +Extra);
    points[3] = pointB + QPoint(+Extra, +Extra);
    points[4] = pointB + QPoint(+Extra, -Extra);
    if (pointA.y() > pointB.y()) {
        points[2] = pointA + QPoint(+Extra, +Extra);
        points[5] = pointB + QPoint(-Extra, -Extra);
    } else {
        points[2] = pointB + QPoint(-Extra, +Extra);
        points[5] = pointA + QPoint(+Extra, -Extra);
    }
    return points;
}
```

The `areaPoints()` function plays a similar role to the `boundingRect()` function in `DiagramBox`. For a diagonal line, and indeed for most polygons, a bounding rectangle is too crude an approximation. For these, we must reimplement `areaPoints()` and return the outline of the area painted by the item. The `QCanvasLine` implementation already returns a decent outline for a line, but it doesn't take the handles into account.

The first thing we do is to store the two points in `pointA` and `pointB` and to ensure that `pointA` is to the left of `pointB`, by swapping them if necessary using `swap()` (defined in `<algorithm>`). Then there are only two cases to consider: ascending and descending lines.

The bounding area of a line is always represented by six points, but these points vary depending on whether the line is ascending or descending. Nevertheless, four of the six points (numbered 0, 1, 3, and 4) are the same in both cases. For example, points 0 and 1 are always located at the top-left and bottomleft corners of handle A; in contrast, point 2 is located at the bottom-right corner of handle A for an ascending line and at the bottom-left corner of handle B for a descending line.

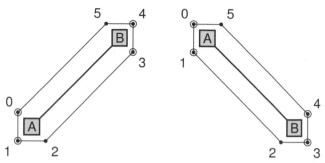

**Figure 8.14.** The bounding area of a `DiagramLine`

Considering how little code we have written, the `DiagramView` widget already provides considerable functionality, with support for selecting and moving items and for context menus.

One thing that is missing is that the handles shown when an item is active cannot be dragged to resize the item. If we wanted to change that, we would probably take a different approach to the one we have used here. Instead of drawing the handles in the items' `drawShape()` functions, we would probably make each handle a canvas item. If we wanted the cursor to change when hovering over a handle, we would call `setCursor()` in real time as it is moved. For this to work, we would need to call `setMouseTracking(true)` first, because normally Qt only sends mouse move events when a mouse button is pressed.

Another obvious improvement would be to support multiple selections and item grouping. The *Qt Quarterly* article "Canvas Item Groupies", available online at `http://doc.trolltech.com/qq/qq05-canvasitemgrouping.html`, presents one way to achieve this.

This section has provided a working example of `QCanvas` and `QCanvasView` use, but it has not covered all of `QCanvas`'s functionality. For example, canvas items can be set to move on the canvas at regular intervals by calling `setVelocity()`. See the documentation for `QCanvas` and its related classes for the details.

# Printing

Printing in Qt is similar to drawing on a widget or on a pixmap. It consists of the following steps:

1. Create a `QPrinter` to serve as the "paint device".

2. Call `QPrinter::setup()` to pop up a print dialog, allowing the user to choose a printer and to set a few options.

3. Create a `QPainter` to operate on the `QPrinter`.

4. Draw a page using the `QPainter`.

5. Call `QPrinter::newPage()` to advance to the next page.

6. Repeat steps 4 and 5 until all the pages are printed.

On Windows and Mac OS X, `QPrinter` uses the system's printer drivers. On Unix, it generates PostScript and sends it to `lp` or `lpr` (or to whatever program has been set using `QPrinter::setPrintProgram()`).

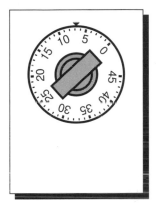 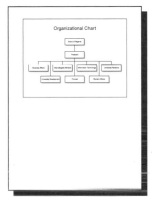 

**Figure 8.15.** Printing an `OvenTimer`, a `QCanvas`, and a `QImage`

Let's start with some simple examples that all print on a single page. The first example prints an `OvenTimer` widget:

```
void PrintWindow::printOvenTimer(OvenTimer *ovenTimer)
{
    if (printer.setup(this)) {
        QPainter painter(&printer);
        QRect rect = painter.viewport();
        int side = QMIN(rect.width(), rect.height());
        painter.setViewport(0, 0, side, side);
        painter.setWindow(-50, -50, 100, 100);
        ovenTimer->draw(&painter);
    }
}
```

We assume that the `PrintWindow` class has a member variable called `printer` of type `QPrinter`. We could simply have created the `QPrinter` on the stack in `printOvenTimer()`, but then it would not remember the user's settings from one print run to another.

We call `setup()` to pop up a print dialog. It returns `true` if the user clicked the OK button; otherwise, it returns `false`. After the call to `setup()`, the `QPrinter` object is ready to use.

We create a `QPainter` to draw on the `QPrinter`. Then we make the painter's viewport square and initialize the painter's window to (–50, –50, 100, 100), the rectangle expected by `OvenTimer`. We call `draw()` to do the painting. If we didn't bother making the viewport square, the OvenTimer would be vertically stretched to fill the entire page height.

By default, the QPainter's window is initialized so that the printer appears to have a similar resolution as the screen (usually somewhere between 72 and 100 dots per inch), making it easy to reuse widget-painting code for printing. Here, it didn't matter, because we set our own window to be (–50, –50, 100, 100).

Printing an OvenTimer isn't a very realistic example, because the widget is meant for on-screen user interaction. But for other widgets, such as the Plotter widget we developed in Chapter 5, it makes lots of sense to reuse the widget's painting code for printing.

A more practical example is printing a QCanvas. Applications that use it often need to be able to print what the user has drawn. This can be done in a generic way as follows:

```cpp
void PrintWindow::printCanvas(QCanvas *canvas)
{
    if (printer.setup(this)) {
        QPainter painter(&printer);
        QRect rect = painter.viewport();
        QSize size = canvas->size();
        size.scale(rect.size(), QSize::ScaleMin);
        painter.setViewport(rect.x(), rect.y(),
                            size.width(), size.height());
        painter.setWindow(canvas->rect());
        painter.drawRect(painter.window());
        painter.setClipRect(painter.viewport());

        QCanvasItemList items = canvas->collisions(canvas->rect());
        QCanvasItemList::const_iterator it = items.end();
        while (it != items.begin()) {
            --it;
            (*it)->draw(painter);
        }
    }
}
```

This time, we set the painter's window to the canvas's bounding rectangle, and we restrict the viewport to a rectangle with the same aspect ratio. To accomplish this, we use QSize::scale() with ScaleMin as its second argument. For example, if the canvas has a size of 640 × 480 and the painter's viewport has a size of 5000 × 5000, the resulting viewport size that we use is 5000 × 3750.

We call collisions() with the canvas's rectangle as argument to obtain the list of all visible canvas items sorted from highest to lowest $z$ value. We iterate over the list from the end to paint the items with a lower $z$ value before those with a higher $z$ value and call QCanvasItem::draw() on them. This ensures that the items that appear nearer the front are drawn on top of the items that are further back.

Our third example is to draw a QImage.

```
void PrintWindow::printImage(const QImage &image)
{
    if (printer.setup(this)) {
        QPainter painter(&printer);
        QRect rect = painter.viewport();
        QSize size = image.size();
        size.scale(rect.size(), QSize::ScaleMin);
        painter.setViewport(rect.x(), rect.y(),
                            size.width(), size.height());
        painter.setWindow(image.rect());
        painter.drawImage(0, 0, image);
    }
}
```

We set the window to the image's rectangle and the viewport to a rectangle with the same aspect ratio, and we draw the image at position (0, 0).

Printing items that take up no more than a single page is simple, as we have seen. But many applications need to print multiple pages. For those, we need to paint one page at a time and call newPage() to advance to the next page. This raises the problem of determining how much information we can print on each page.

There are two approaches to handling multi-page documents with Qt:

- We can convert the data we want to HTML and render it using QSimple-RichText, Qt's rich text engine.

- We can perform the drawing and the page breaking by hand.

We will review both approaches in turn.

As an example, we will print a flower guide: a list of flower names with a textual description. Each entry in the guide is stored as a string of the format *"name: description"*, for example:

```
Miltonopsis santanae: An most dangerous orchid species.
```

Since each flower's data is represented by a single string, we can represent all the flowers in the guide using one QStringList.

Here's the function that prints a flower guide using Qt's rich text engine:

```
void PrintWindow::printFlowerGuide(const QStringList &entries)
{
    QString str;
    QStringList::const_iterator it = entries.begin();
    while (it != entries.end()) {
        QStringList fields = QStringList::split(": ", *it);
        QString title = QStyleSheet::escape(fields[0]);
        QString body = QStyleSheet::escape(fields[1]);

        str += "<table width=\"100%\" border=1 cellspacing=0>\n"
               "<tr><td bgcolor=\"lightgray\"><font size=\"+1\">"
               "<b><i>" + title + "</i></b></font>\n<tr><td>"
               + body + "\n</table>\n<br>\n";
```

```
        ++it;
    }
    printRichText(str);
}
```

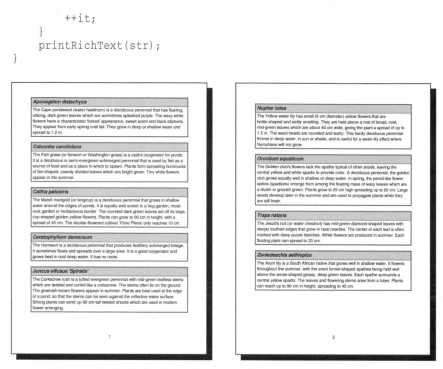

**Figure 8.16.** Printing a flower guide using `QSimpleRichText`

The first step is to convert the data into HTML. Each flower becomes an HTML table with two cells. We use `QStyleSheet::escape()` to replace the special characters '&', '<', '>' with the corresponding HTML entities ("&amp;", "&lt;", "&gt;"). Then we call `printRichText()` to print the text.

```
const int LargeGap = 48;

void PrintWindow::printRichText(const QString &str)
{
    if (printer.setup(this)) {
        QPainter painter(&printer);
        int pageHeight = painter.window().height() - 2 * LargeGap;
        QSimpleRichText richText(str, bodyFont, "", 0, 0,
                                 pageHeight);
        richText.setWidth(&painter, painter.window().width());
        int numPages = (int)ceil((double)richText.height()
                                  / pageHeight);
        int index;

        for (int i = 0; i < (int)printer.numCopies(); ++i) {
            for (int j = 0; j < numPages; ++j) {
                if (i > 0 || j > 0)
                    printer.newPage();

                if (printer.pageOrder()
                        == QPrinter::LastPageFirst) {
                    index = numPages - j - 1;
```

```
            } else {
                index = j;
            }
            printPage(&painter, richText, pageHeight, index);
        }
    }
}
}
```

The `printRichText()` function takes care of printing an HTML document. It can be reused "as is" in any Qt application to print arbitrary HTML.

We compute the height of one page based on the window size and the size of the gap we want to leave at the top and bottom of the page for a header and a footer. Then we create a `QSimpleRichText` object containing the HTML data. The last argument to the `QSimpleRichText` constructor is the page height; `QSimpleRichText` uses it to produce nice page breaks.

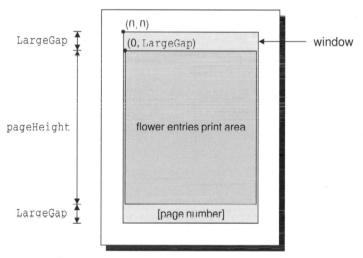

**Figure 8.17.** The flower guide's page layout

Then we print each page. The outer `for` loop iterates as many times as necessary to produce the number of copies requested by the user. Most printer drivers support multiple copies, so for those `QPrinter::numCopies()` always returns 1. If the printer driver doesn't support multiple copies, `numCopies()` returns the number of copies requested by the user, and the application is responsible for printing that amount. In the previous examples, we ignored `numCopies()` for the sake of simplicity.

The inner `for` loop iterates through the pages. If the page isn't the first page, we call `newPage()` to flush the old page and start painting on a fresh page. We call `printPage()` to paint each page.

The print dialog allows the user to print the pages in reverse order. It is our responsibility to honor that option.

We assume that `printer`, `bodyFont`, and `footerFont` are member variables of the
`PrintWindow` class.

```
void PrintWindow::printPage(QPainter *painter,
                            const QSimpleRichText &richText,
                            int pageHeight, int index)
{
    QRect rect(0, index * pageHeight + LargeGap,
               richText.width(), pageHeight);

    painter->saveWorldMatrix();
    painter->translate(0, -rect.y());
    richText.draw(painter, 0, LargeGap, rect, colorGroup());
    painter->restoreWorldMatrix();

    painter->setFont(footerFont);
    painter->drawText(painter->window(), AlignHCenter | AlignBottom,
                      QString::number(index + 1));
}
```

The `printPage()` function prints the (`index` + 1)-th page of the document. The
page consists of some HTML and of a page number in the footer area.

We translate the `QPainter` and call `draw()` with a position and rectangle specifying the portion of the rich text we want to draw. It might help to visualize
the rich text as a single very long page that must be cut into smaller portions,
each of height `pageHeight`.

Then we draw the page number centered at the bottom of the page. If we
wanted to have a header on each page, we would just use an extra `draw-
Text()` call.

The `LargeGap` constant is set to 48. Assuming a screen resolution of 96 dots
per inch, this is half an inch (12.7 mm). To obtain a precise length regardless
of screen resolution, we could have used the `QPaintDeviceMetrics` class as
follows:

```
QPaintDeviceMetrics metrics(&printer);
int LargeGap = metrics.logicalDpiY() / 2;
```

Here's one way we can initialize `bodyFont` and `footerFont` in the `PrintWindow`
constructor:

```
bodyFont = QFont("Helvetica", 14);
footerFont = bodyFont;
```

Let's now see how we can draw a flower guide using `QPainter`. Here's the new
`printFlowerGuide()` function:

```
void PrintWindow::printFlowerGuide(const QStringList &entries)
{
    if (printer.setup(this)) {
        QPainter painter(&printer);
        vector<QStringList> pages;
        int index;

        paginate(&painter, &pages, entries);
```

```
for (int i = 0; i < (int)printer.numCopies(); ++i) {
    for (int j = 0; j < (int)pages.size(); ++j) {
        if (i > 0 || j > 0)
            printer.newPage();

        if (printer.pageOrder() == QPrinter::LastPageFirst) {
            index = pages.size() - j - 1;
        } else {
            index = j;
        }
        printPage(&painter, pages, index);
    }
}
```

The first thing we do after setting up the printer and constructing the painter is to call the `paginate()` helper function to determine which entry should appear on which page. The result of this is a vector of `QStringLists`, with each `QStringList` holding the entries for one page.

For example, let's suppose that the flower guide contains 6 entries, which we will refer to as A, B, C, D, E, and F. Now let's suppose that there is room for A and B on the first page, C, D, and E on the second page, and F on the third page. The `pages` vector would then have the list [A, B] at index position 0, the list [C, D, E] at index position 1, and the list [F] at index position 2.

The rest of the function is nearly identical to what we did earlier in `printRichText()`. The `printPage()` function, however, is different, as we will see shortly.

```
void PrintWindow::paginate(QPainter *painter,
                           vector<QStringList> *pages,
                           const QStringList &entries)
{
    QStringList currentPage;
    int pageHeight = painter->window().height() - 2 * LargeGap;
    int y = 0;

    QStringList::const_iterator it = entries.begin();
    while (it != entries.end()) {
        int height = entryHeight(painter, *it);
        if (y + height > pageHeight && !currentPage.empty()) {
            pages->push_back(currentPage);
            currentPage.clear();
            y = 0;
        }
        currentPage.push_back(*it);
        y += height + MediumGap;
        ++it;
    }
    if (!currentPage.empty())
        pages->push_back(currentPage);
}
```

The `paginate()` function distributes the flower guide entries into pages. It relies on the `entryHeight()` function, which computes the height of one entry.

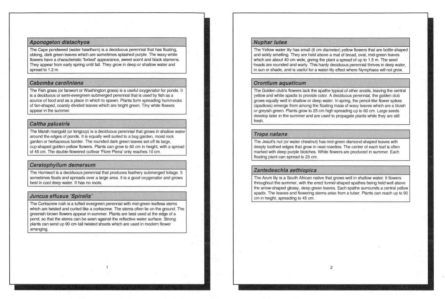

**Figure 8.18.** Printing a flower guide using `QPainter`

We iterate through the entries and append them to the current page until we come to an entry that doesn't fit; then we append the current page to the `pages` vector and start a new page.

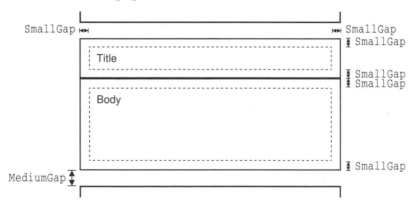

**Figure 8.19.** A flower entry's layout

```
int PrintWindow::entryHeight(QPainter *painter, const QString &entry)
{
    QStringList fields = QStringList::split(": ", entry);
    QString title = fields[0];
    QString body = fields[1];

    int textWidth = painter->window().width() - 2 * SmallGap;
    int maxHeight = painter->window().height();
```

```
    painter->setFont(titleFont);
    QRect titleRect = painter->boundingRect(0, 0,
                                            textWidth, maxHeight,
                                            WordBreak, title);
    painter->setFont(bodyFont);
    QRect bodyRect = painter->boundingRect(0, 0,
                                           textWidth, maxHeight,
                                           WordBreak, body);
    return titleRect.height() + bodyRect.height() + 4 * SmallGap;
}
```

The entryHeight() function uses QPainter::boundingRect() to compute the vertical space needed by one entry. Figure 8.19 shows the layout of a flower entry and the meaning of the SmallGap and MediumGap constants.

```
void PrintWindow::printPage(QPainter *painter,
                            const vector<QStringList> &pages,
                            int index)
{
    painter->saveWorldMatrix();
    painter->translate(0, LargeGap);
    QStringList::const_iterator it = pages[index].begin();
    while (it != pages[index].end()) {
        QStringList fields = QStringList::split(": ", *it);
        QString title = fields[0];
        QString body = fields[1];
        printBox(painter, titleFont, title, lightGray);
        printBox(painter, bodyFont, body, white);
        painter->translate(0, MediumGap);
        ++it;
    }
    painter->restoreWorldMatrix();

    painter->setFont(footerFont);
    painter->drawText(painter->window(), AlignHCenter | AlignBottom,
                      QString::number(index + 1));
}
```

The printPage() function iterates through all the flower guide entries and prints them using two calls to printBox(): one for the title (the flower's name) and one for the body (its description). It also draws the page number centered at the bottom of the page.

```
void PrintWindow::printBox(QPainter *painter, const QFont &font,
                           const QString &str, const QBrush &brush)
{
    painter->setFont(font);

    int boxWidth = painter->window().width();
    int textWidth = boxWidth - 2 * SmallGap;
    int maxHeight = painter->window().height();

    QRect textRect = painter->boundingRect(SmallGap, SmallGap,
                                           textWidth, maxHeight,
                                           WordBreak, str);
    int boxHeight = textRect.height() + 2 * SmallGap;
```

```
        painter->setPen(QPen(black, 2, SolidLine));
        painter->setBrush(brush);
        painter->drawRect(0, 0, boxWidth, boxHeight);
        painter->drawText(textRect, WordBreak, str);
        painter->translate(0, boxHeight);
    }
```

The `printBox()` function draws the outline of a box, then draws the text inside the box.

If the user prints a long document, or requests multiple copies of a short document, it is usually a good idea to pop up a `QProgressDialog` to give the user the opportunity of canceling the printing operation (by clicking Cancel). Here's a modified version of `printFlowerGuide()` that does this:

```
    void PrintWindow::printFlowerGuide(const QStringList &entries)
    {
        if (printer.setup(this)) {
            QPainter painter(&printer);
            vector<QStringList> pages;
            int index;

            paginate(&painter, &pages, entries);

            int numSteps = printer.numCopies() * pages.size();
            int step = 0;
            QProgressDialog progress(tr("Printing file..."),
                                     tr("Cancel"), numSteps, this);
            progress.setModal(true);

            for (int i = 0; i < (int)printer.numCopies(); ++i) {
                for (int j = 0; j < (int)pages.size(); ++j) {
                    progress.setProgress(step);
                    qApp->processEvents();
                    if (progress.wasCanceled()) {
                        printer.abort();
                        return;
                    }
                    ++step;

                    if (i > 0 || j > 0)
                        printer.newPage();

                    if (printer.pageOrder() == QPrinter::LastPageFirst) {
                        index = pages.size() - j - 1;
                    } else {
                        index = j;
                    }
                    printPage(&painter, pages, index);
                }
            }
        }
    }
```

When the user clicks Cancel, we call `QPrinter::abort()` to stop the printing operation.

# Graphics with OpenGL

OpenGL is a standard API for rendering 2D and 3D graphics. Qt applications can draw OpenGL graphics by using Qt's QGL module. This section assumes that you are familiar with OpenGL. If OpenGL is new to you, a good place to start learning it is http://www.opengl.org/.

Drawing graphics with OpenGL from a Qt application is straightforward: We must subclass QGLWidget, reimplement a few virtual functions, and link the application against the QGL and OpenGL libraries. Because QGLWidget inherits from QWidget, most of what we already know still applies. The main difference is that we use standard OpenGL functions to perform the drawing instead of QPainter.

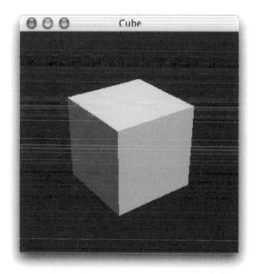

**Figure 8.20.** The Cube application

To show how this works, we will review the code of the Cube application shown in Figure 8.20. The application presents a 3D cube with faces of different colors. The user can rotate the cube by pressing a mouse button and dragging. The user can set the color of a face by double-clicking it and choosing a color from the QColorDialog that pops up.

```
class Cube : public QGLWidget
{
public:
    Cube(QWidget *parent = 0, const char *name = 0);

protected:
    void initializeGL();
    void resizeGL(int width, int height);
    void paintGL();
    void mousePressEvent(QMouseEvent *event);
    void mouseMoveEvent(QMouseEvent *event);
    void mouseDoubleClickEvent(QMouseEvent *event);
```

```
private:
    void draw();
    int faceAtPosition(const QPoint &pos);

    GLfloat rotationX;
    GLfloat rotationY;
    GLfloat rotationZ;
    QColor faceColors[6];
    QPoint lastPos;
};
```

Cube **inherits from** QGLWidget. **The** initializeGL(), resizeGL(), **and** paintGL() **functions are reimplemented from** QGLWidget. **The mouse event handlers are reimplemented from** QWidget **as usual.** QGLWidget **is defined in** <qgl.h>.

```
Cube::Cube(QWidget *parent, const char *name)
    : QGLWidget(parent, name)
{
    setFormat(QGLFormat(DoubleBuffer | DepthBuffer));
    rotationX = 0;
    rotationY = 0;
    rotationZ = 0;
    faceColors[0] = red;
    faceColors[1] = green;
    faceColors[2] = blue;
    faceColors[3] = cyan;
    faceColors[4] = yellow;
    faceColors[5] = magenta;
}
```

In the constructor, we call QGLWidget::setFormat() to specify the OpenGL display context, and we initialize the class's private variables.

```
void Cube::initializeGL()
{
    qglClearColor(black);
    glShadeModel(GL_FLAT);
    glEnable(GL_DEPTH_TEST);
    glEnable(GL_CULL_FACE);
}
```

The initializeGL() function is called once before paintGL() is called. This is the place where we can set up the OpenGL rendering context, define display lists, and perform other initializations.

All the code is standard OpenGL, except for the call to QGLWidget's qglClear-Color() function. If we wanted to stick to standard OpenGL, we would call gl-ClearColor() in RGBA mode and glClearIndex() in color index mode instead.

```
void Cube::resizeGL(int width, int height)
{
    glViewport(0, 0, width, height);
    glMatrixMode(GL_PROJECTION);
    glLoadIdentity();
    GLfloat x = (GLfloat)width / height;
    glFrustum(-x, x, -1.0, 1.0, 4.0, 15.0);
```

```
    glMatrixMode(GL_MODELVIEW);
}
```

The `resizeGL()` function is called once before `paintGL()` is called the first time, but after `initializeGL()` is called. This is the place where we can set up the OpenGL viewport, projection, and any other settings that depend on the widget's size.

```
void Cube::paintGL()
{
    glClear(GL_COLOR_BUFFER_BIT | GL_DEPTH_BUFFER_BIT);
    draw();
}
```

The `paintGL()` function is called whenever the widget needs to be repainted. This is similar to `QWidget::paintEvent()`, but instead of `QPainter` functions we use OpenGL functions. The actual drawing is performed by the private function `draw()`.

```
void Cube::draw()
{
    static const GLfloat coords[6][4][3] = {
        { { +1.0, -1.0, +1.0 }, { +1.0, -1.0, -1.0 },
          { +1.0, +1.0,  1.0 }, { +1.0, +1.0, +1.0 } },
        { { -1.0, -1.0, -1.0 }, { -1.0, -1.0, +1.0 },
          { -1.0, +1.0, +1.0 }, { -1.0, +1.0, -1.0 } },
        { { +1.0, -1.0, -1.0 }, { -1.0, -1.0, -1.0 },
          { -1.0, +1.0, -1.0 }, { +1.0, +1.0, -1.0 } },
        { { -1.0, -1.0, +1.0 }, { +1.0, -1.0, +1.0 },
          { +1.0, +1.0, +1.0 }, { -1.0, +1.0, +1.0 } },
        { { -1.0, -1.0, -1.0 }, { +1.0, -1.0, -1.0 },
          { +1.0, -1.0, +1.0 }, { -1.0, -1.0, +1.0 } },
        { { -1.0, +1.0, +1.0 }, { +1.0, +1.0, +1.0 },
          { +1.0, +1.0, -1.0 }, { -1.0, +1.0, -1.0 } }
    };

    glMatrixMode(GL_MODELVIEW);
    glLoadIdentity();
    glTranslatef(0.0, 0.0, -10.0);
    glRotatef(rotationX, 1.0, 0.0, 0.0);
    glRotatef(rotationY, 0.0, 1.0, 0.0);
    glRotatef(rotationZ, 0.0, 0.0, 1.0);

    for (int i = 0; i < 6; ++i) {
        glLoadName(i);
        glBegin(GL_QUADS);
        qglColor(faceColors[i]);
        for (int j = 0; j < 4; ++j) {
            glVertex3f(coords[i][j][0], coords[i][j][1],
                       coords[i][j][2]);
        }
        glEnd();
    }
}
```

In draw(), we draw the cube, taking into account the $x$, $y$, and $z$ rotations and the colors stored in the faceColors array. Everything is standard OpenGL, except for the qglColor() call. We could have used one of the OpenGL functions glColor3d() or glIndex(), depending on the mode.

```
void Cube::mousePressEvent(QMouseEvent *event)
{
    lastPos = event->pos();
}

void Cube::mouseMoveEvent(QMouseEvent *event)
{
    GLfloat dx = (GLfloat)(event->x() - lastPos.x()) / width();
    GLfloat dy = (GLfloat)(event->y() - lastPos.y()) / height();

    if (event->state() & LeftButton) {
        rotationX += 180 * dy;
        rotationY += 180 * dx;
        updateGL();
    } else if (event->state() & RightButton) {
        rotationX += 180 * dy;
        rotationZ += 180 * dx;
        updateGL();
    }
    lastPos = event->pos();
}
```

The mousePressEvent() and mouseMoveEvent() functions are reimplement from QWidget to allow the user to rotate the view by clicking and dragging. The left mouse button allows the user to rotate around the $x$ and $y$ axes, the right mouse button around the $x$ and $z$ axes.

After modifying the rotationX, rotationY, and/or rotationZ variables, we call updateGL() to redraw the scene.

```
void Cube::mouseDoubleClickEvent(QMouseEvent *event)
{
    int face = faceAtPosition(event->pos());
    if (face != -1) {
        QColor color = QColorDialog::getColor(faceColors[face],
                                              this);
        if (color.isValid()) {
            faceColors[face] = color;
            updateGL();
        }
    }
}
```

The mouseDoubleClickEvent() is reimplemented from QWidget to allow the user to set the color of a cube face by double-clicking it. We call the private function faceAtPosition() to determine which cube face, if any, is located under the cursor. If a face was double-clicked, we call QColorDialog::getColor() to obtain a new color for that face. Then we update the faceColors array with the new color, and we call updateGL() to redraw the scene.

```
int Cube::faceAtPosition(const QPoint &pos)
{
    const int MaxSize = 512;
    GLuint buffer[MaxSize];
    GLint viewport[4];

    glGetIntegerv(GL_VIEWPORT, viewport);
    glSelectBuffer(MaxSize, buffer);
    glRenderMode(GL_SELECT);

    glInitNames();
    glPushName(0);

    glMatrixMode(GL_PROJECTION);
    glPushMatrix();
    glLoadIdentity();
    gluPickMatrix((GLdouble)pos.x(),
                  (GLdouble)(viewport[3] - pos.y()),
                  5.0, 5.0, viewport);
    GLfloat x = (GLfloat)width() / height();
    glFrustum(-x, x, -1.0, 1.0, 4.0, 15.0);
    draw();
    glMatrixMode(GL_PROJECTION);
    glPopMatrix();

    if (!glRenderMode(GL_RENDER))
        return -1;
    return buffer[3];
}
```

The `faceAtPosition()` function returns the number of the face at a certain position on the widget, or –1 if there is no face at that position. The code for determining this in OpenGL is a bit complicated. Essentially, what we do is render the scene in `GL_SELECT` mode to take advantage of OpenGL's picking capabilities and then retrieve the face number (its "name") from the OpenGL hit record.

Here's `main.cpp`:

```
#include <qapplication.h>

#include "cube.h"

int main(int argc, char *argv[])
{
    QApplication app(argc, argv);
    if (!QGLFormat::hasOpenGL())
        qFatal("This system has no OpenGL support");

    Cube cube;
    cube.setCaption(QObject::tr("Cube"));
    cube.resize(300, 300);
    app.setMainWidget(&cube);

    cube.show();
    return app.exec();
}
```

If the user's system doesn't support OpenGL, we print an error message to the console and abort using Qt's `qFatal()` global function.

To link the application against the QGL and OpenGL libraries, the `.pro` file needs this entry:

```
CONFIG        += opengl
```

That completes the Cube application. For more information about the QGL module, see the reference documentation for `QGLWidget`, `QGLFormat`, `QGLContext`, and `QGLColormap`.

# Drag and Drop

Drag and drop is a modern and intuitive way of transferring information within an application or between different applications. It is often provided in addition to clipboard support for moving and copying data.

In this chapter, we will begin by showing how to add drag and drop support to a Qt application. Then we will reuse the drag and drop code to implement clipboard support. This code reuse is possible because both mechanisms rely on QMimeSource, an abstract base class that provides data in different formats.

## Enabling Drag and Drop

Drag and drop involves two distinct actions: dragging and dropping. Widgets can serve as drag sites, as drop sites, or as both.

Drag and drop is a powerful mechanism for transferring data between applications. But in some cases, it's possible to implement drag and drop without using Qt's drag and drop facilities. If all you want to do is to move data within one widget in one application, it is usually simpler to reimplement the widget's mouse event handlers. This is the approach we took in the DiagramView widget in Chapter 8 (p. 190).

Our first example shows how to make a Qt application accept a drag initiated by another application. The Qt application is a main window with a QTextEdit as its central widget. When the user drags a file from the desktop or from a file explorer and drops it onto the application, the application loads the file into the QTextEdit.

Here's the definition of the MainWindow class:

```
class MainWindow : public QMainWindow
{
```

```
    Q_OBJECT
public:
    MainWindow(QWidget *parent = 0, const char *name = 0);

protected:
    void dragEnterEvent(QDragEnterEvent *event);
    void dropEvent(QDropEvent *event);

private:
    bool readFile(const QString &fileName);
    QString strippedName(const QString &fullFileName);

    QTextEdit *textEdit;
};
```

The `MainWindow` class reimplements `dragEnterEvent()` and `dropEvent()` from `QWidget`. Since the purpose of the example is to show drag and drop, much of the functionality we would expect to be in a main window class has been omitted.

```
MainWindow::MainWindow(QWidget *parent, const char *name)
    : QMainWindow(parent, name)
{
    setCaption(tr("Drag File"));
    textEdit = new QTextEdit(this);
    setCentralWidget(textEdit);
    textEdit->viewport()->setAcceptDrops(false);
    setAcceptDrops(true);
}
```

In the constructor, we create a `QTextEdit` and set it as the central widget. We disable dropping on the `QTextEdit`'s viewport and enable dropping on the main window.

The reason we must disable dropping on the `QTextEdit` is that we want to take over drag and drop handling ourselves in our `MainWindow` subclass. By default, `QTextEdit` accepts textual drags from other applications, and if the user drops a file onto it, it will insert the file name into the text. Since we want to drop the entire contents of the file rather than the file's name, we cannot make use of `QTextEdit`'s drag and drop functionality and must implement our own.

Because drop events are propagated from child to parent, we get the drop events for the whole main window, including those for the `QTextEdit`, in `MainWindow`.

```
void MainWindow::dragEnterEvent(QDragEnterEvent *event)
{
    event->accept(QUriDrag::canDecode(event));
}
```

The `dragEnterEvent()` is called whenever the user drags an object onto a widget. If we call `accept(true)` on the event, we indicate that the user can drop the drag object on this widget; if we call `accept(false)`, we indicate that the widget can't accept the drag. Qt automatically changes the cursor to indicate to the user whether or not the widget is a legitimate drop site.

Here we want the user to be allowed to drag files, but nothing else. To do so, we ask `QUriDrag`, the Qt class that handles file drags, whether it can decode the dragged object. The class can more generally be used for any universal resource identifier (URI), such as HTTP and FTP paths; hence the name `QUriDrag`.

```
void MainWindow::dropEvent(QDropEvent *event)
{
    QStringList fileNames;
    if (QUriDrag::decodeLocalFiles(event, fileNames)) {
        if (readFile(fileNames[0]))
            setCaption(tr("%1 - Drag File")
                         .arg(strippedName(fileNames[0])));
    }
}
```

The `dropEvent()` is called when the user drops an object onto the widget. We call the static function `QUriDrag::decodeLocalFiles()` to get a list of file names dragged by the user and read in the first file in the list. (The second argument is passed as a non-const reference.) Typically, users only drag one file at a time, but it is possible for them to drag multiple files by dragging a selection.

`QWidget` also provides `dragMoveEvent()` and `dragLeaveEvent()`, but for most applications they don't need to be reimplemented.

The second example illustrates how to initiate a drag and accept a drop. We will create a `QListBox` subclass that supports drag and drop, and use it as a component in the Project Chooser application shown in Figure 9.1.

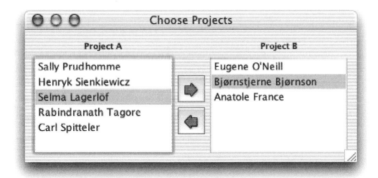

**Figure 9.1.** The Project Chooser application

The Project Chooser application presents the user with two list boxes, populated with names. Each list box represents a project. The user can drag and drop the names in the list boxes to move a person from one project to another.

The drag and drop code is all located in the `QListBox` subclass. Here's the class definition:

```
class ProjectView : public QListBox
{
    Q_OBJECT
```

```
public:
    ProjectView(QWidget *parent, const char *name = 0);

protected:
    void contentsMousePressEvent(QMouseEvent *event);
    void contentsMouseMoveEvent(QMouseEvent *event);
    void contentsDragEnterEvent(QDragEnterEvent *event);
    void contentsDropEvent(QDropEvent *event);

private:
    void startDrag();

    QPoint dragPos;
};
```

ProjectView reimplements four of the event handlers declared in QScrollView (QListBox's base class).

```
ProjectView::ProjectView(QWidget *parent, const char *name)
    : QListBox(parent, name)
{
    viewport()->setAcceptDrops(true);
}
```

In the constructor, we enable drops on the QScrollView viewport.

```
void ProjectView::contentsMousePressEvent(QMouseEvent *event)
{
    if (event->button() == LeftButton)
        dragPos = event->pos();
    QListBox::contentsMousePressEvent(event);
}
```

When the user presses the left mouse button, we store the mouse position in the dragPos private variable. We call QListBox's implementation of contents-MousePressEvent() to ensure that QListBox has the opportunity to process mouse press events as usual.

```
void ProjectView::contentsMouseMoveEvent(QMouseEvent *event)
{
    if (event->state() & LeftButton) {
        int distance = (event->pos() - dragPos).manhattanLength();
        if (distance > QApplication::startDragDistance())
            startDrag();
    }
    QListBox::contentsMouseMoveEvent(event);
}
```

When the user moves the mouse cursor while holding the left mouse button, we consider starting a drag. We compute the distance between the current mouse position and the position where the left mouse button was pressed.

If the distance is larger than QApplication's recommended drag start distance (normally 4 pixels), we call the private function startDrag() to start dragging. This avoids initiating a drag just because the user's hand shakes.

```
void ProjectView::startDrag()
{
    QString person = currentText();
    if (!person.isEmpty()) {
        QTextDrag *drag = new QTextDrag(person, this);
        drag->setSubtype("x-person");
        drag->setPixmap(QPixmap::fromMimeSource("person.png"));
        drag->drag();
    }
}
```

In startDrag(), we create an object of type QTextDrag with this as its parent. The QTextDrag class represents a drag and drop object for transferring text. It is one of several predefined types of drag objects that Qt provides; others include QImageDrag, QColorDrag, and QUriDrag. We also set a pixmap to represent the drag. The pixmap is a small icon that follows the cursor while the drag is taking place.

We call setSubtype() to set the subtype of the object's MIME type to x-person. This causes the object's full MIME type to be text/x-person. If we didn't call setSubtype(), the MIME type would be text/plain.

Standard MIME types are defined by the Internet Assigned Numbers Authority (IANA). They consist of a type and a subtype separated by a slash. When we create non-standard types, such as text/x-person, it is recommended that an x- is prepended to the subtype. MIME types are used by the clipboard and by the drag and drop system to identify different types of data.

The drag() call starts the dragging operation. After the call, the QTextDrag object will remain in existence until the drag operation is finished. Qt takes ownership of the drag object and will delete it when it is no longer required, even if it is never dropped.

```
void ProjectView::contentsDragEnterEvent(QDragEnterEvent *event)
{
    event->accept(event->provides("text/x-person"));
}
```

The ProjectView widget not only originates drags of type text/x-person, it also accepts such drags. When a drag enters the widget, we check whether it has the correct MIME type and reject it if it hasn't.

```
void ProjectView::contentsDropEvent(QDropEvent *event)
{
    QString person;

    if (QTextDrag::decode(event, person)) {
        QWidget *fromWidget = event->source();
        if (fromWidget && fromWidget != this
                && fromWidget->inherits("ProjectView")) {
            ProjectView *fromProject = (ProjectView *)fromWidget;
            QListBoxItem *item =
                    fromProject->findItem(person, ExactMatch);
            delete item;
```

```
                        insertItem(person);
            }
        }
    }
```

In `contentsDropEvent()`, we use the `QTextDrag::decode()` function to extract the text carried by the drag. The `QDropEvent::source()` function returns a pointer to the widget that initiated the drag, if that widget is part of the same application. If the source widget is different from the target widget and is a `ProjectView`, we remove the item from the source widget (by calling `delete`) and insert a new item into the target.

## Supporting Custom Drag Types

In the examples so far, we have relied on predefined Qt classes to hold the drag data. For example, we used `QUriDrag` for a file drag and `QTextDrag` for a text drag. Both of these classes inherit `QDragObject`, the base class for all drag objects. `QDragObject` itself inherits `QMimeSource`, an abstraction for providing MIME-typed data.

If we want to drag text, images, URIs, or colors, we can use Qt's `QTextDrag`, `QImageDrag`, `QUriDrag`, and `QColorDrag` classes. But if we want to drag custom data, none of these predefined classes is suitable, and so we must choose one of two alternatives:

- We can store the drag as binary data in a `QStoredDrag` object.

- We can create our own drag class by subclassing `QDragObject` and reimplementing a couple of virtual functions.

`QStoredDrag` allows us to store arbitrary binary data, so it can be used for any MIME type. For example, if we want to initiate a drag with the contents of a binary file that stores data in the (fictitious) ASDF format, we could use the following code:

```
void MyWidget::startDrag()
{
    QByteArray data = toAsdf();
    if (!data.isEmpty()) {
        QStoredDrag *drag = new QStoredDrag("octet-stream/x-asdf",
                                            this);
        drag->setEncodedData(data);
        drag->setPixmap(QPixmap::fromMimeSource("asdf.png"));
        drag->drag();
    }
}
```

One inconvenience of `QStoredDrag` is that it can only store a single MIME type. If we perform drag and drop within the same application or between multiple instances of the same application, this is seldom a problem. But if we want to interact nicely with other applications, one MIME type is rarely sufficient.

Another inconvenience is that we need to convert our data structure to a QByteArray even if the drag is not accepted in the end. If the data is large, this can slow down the application needlessly. It would be better to perform the data conversion only when the user actually drops the drag object.

A solution to both of these problems is to subclass QDragObject and reimplement format() and encodedData(), the two virtual functions used by Qt to obtain information about a drag. To show how this works, we will develop a Cell-Drag class that stores the contents of one or more cells in a rectangular QTable selection.

```cpp
class CellDrag : public QDragObject
{
public:
    CellDrag(const QString &text, QWidget *parent = 0,
             const char *name = 0);

    const char *format(int index) const;
    QByteArray encodedData(const char *format) const;

    static bool canDecode(const QMimeSource *source);
    static bool decode(const QMimeSource *source, QString &str);

private:
    QString toCsv() const;
    QString toHtml() const;

    QString plainText;
};
```

The CellDrag class inherits QDragObject. The two functions that really matter for dragging are format() and encodedData(). It is convenient, although not strictly necessary, to provide canDecode() and decode() static functions to extract the data on a drop.

```cpp
CellDrag::CellDrag(const QString &text, QWidget *parent,
                   const char *name)
    : QDragObject(parent, name)
{
    plainText = text;
}
```

The CellDrag constructor accepts a string that represents the contents of the cells that are being dragged. The string is in the "tabs and newlines" plain text format that we used in Chapter 4 when we added clipboard support to the Spreadsheet application (p. 80).

```cpp
const char *CellDrag::format(int index) const
{
    switch (index) {
    case 0:
        return "text/csv";
    case 1:
        return "text/html";
    case 2:
```

```
            return "text/plain";
        default:
            return 0;
        }
    }
```

The `format()` function is reimplemented from `QMimeSource` to return the different MIME types supported by the drag. We support three types: comma-separated values (CSV), HTML, and plain text.

When Qt needs to determine which MIME types are provided by the drag, it calls `format()` with an `index` parameter of 0, 1, 2, ..., up until `format()` returns a null pointer. The MIME types for CSV and HTML were obtained from the official list, available at `http://www.iana.org/assignments/media-types/`.

The precise order of the formats is usually irrelevant, but it's good practice to put the "best" formats first. Applications that support many formats will sometimes use the first one that matches.

```
    QByteArray CellDrag::encodedData(const char *format) const
    {
        QByteArray data;
        QTextOStream out(data);

        if (qstrcmp(format, "text/csv") == 0) {
            out << toCsv();
        } else if (qstrcmp(format, "text/html") == 0) {
            out << toHtml();
        } else if (qstrcmp(format, "text/plain") == 0) {
            out << plainText;
        }
        return data;
    }
```

The `encodedData()` function returns the data for a given MIME type. The value of the `format` parameter is normally one of the strings returned by `format()`, but we can't assume that, since not all applications check the MIME type against `format()` beforehand. In Qt applications, this check is usually done by calling `provides()` on a `QDragEnterEvent` or `QDragMoveEvent`, as we did earlier (p. 219).

To convert a `QString` into a `QByteArray`, the best approach is to use a `QTextStream`. If the string contains non-ASCII characters, `QTextStream` will assume that the encoding is the local 8-bit encoding. (For most European countries, this means ISO 8859-1 or ISO 8859-15; see Chapter 15 for details.) It can be instructed to use other encodings by calling `setEncoding()` or `setCodec()` on the stream, as explained in Chapter 15.

```
    QString CellDrag::toCsv() const
    {
        QString out = plainText;
        out.replace("\\", "\\\\");
        out.replace("\"", "\\\"");
        out.replace("\t", "\", \"");
```

```
    out.replace("\n", "\"\n\"");
    out.prepend("\"");
    out.append("\"");
    return out;
}

QString CellDrag::toHtml() const
{
    QString out = QStyleSheet::escape(plainText);
    out.replace("\t", "<td>");
    out.replace("\n", "\n<tr><td>");
    out.prepend("<table>\n<tr><td>");
    out.append("\n</table>");
    return out;
}
```

The `toCsv()` and `toHtml()` functions convert a "tabs and newlines" string into a CSV or an HTML string. For example, the data

```
Red     Green   Blue
Cyan    Yellow  Magenta
```

is converted to

```
"Red", "Green", "Blue"
"Cyan", "Yellow", "Magenta"
```

or to

```
<table>
<tr><td>Red<td>Green<td>Blue
<tr><td>Cyan<td>Yellow<td>Magenta
</table>
```

The conversion is performed in the simplest way possible, using `QString::replace()`. To escape HTML special characters, we use the `QStyleSheet::escape()` static convenience function.

```
    bool CellDrag::canDecode(const QMimeSource *source)
    {
        return source->provides("text/plain");
    }
```

The `canDecode()` function returns `true` if we can decode the given drag, `false` otherwise. For maximum flexibility, its argument is a `QMimeSource`. The `QMimeSource` class is a base class of `QDragObject`, `QDragEnterEvent`, `QDragMoveEvent`, and `QDropEvent`.

Although we provide the data in three different formats, we only accept plain text. The reason for this is that plain text is normally sufficient. If the user drags cells from a `QTable` to an HTML editor, we want the cells to be converted into an HTML table. But if the user drags arbitrary HTML into a `QTable`, we don't want to accept it.

```
    bool CellDrag::decode(const QMimeSource *source, QString &str)
    {
        QByteArray data = source->encodedData("text/plain");
```

```
        str = QString::fromLocal8Bit((const char *)data, data.size());
        return !str.isEmpty();
    }
```

Finally, the `decode()` function converts the `text/plain` data into a `QString`. Again, we assume the text is encoded using the local 8-bit encoding.

If we want to be certain of using the right encoding, we could use the `charset` parameter of the `text/plain` MIME type to specify an explicit encoding. Here are a few examples:

```
    text/plain;charset=US-ASCII
    text/plain;charset=ISO-8859-1
    text/plain;charset=Shift_JIS
```

When we use `QTextDrag`, it always exports UTF-8, UCS-2 (UTF-16), US-ASCII, and the local 8-bit encoding, and accepts drops from other encodings as well. Considering this, it might be smarter to implement `CellDrag::decode()` simply by calling `QTextDrag::decode()`. But even with this approach, it's still a good idea to provide a `CellDrag::decode()` separate from `QTextDrag::decode()`, in case we want to extend it later to decode another type of drag (for example, CSV drags) in addition to plain text.

Now we have our `CellDrag` class. To make it useful, we must integrate it with `QTable`. It turns out that `QTable` already does almost all of the work for us. All we need to do is to subclass it, call `setDragEnabled(true)` in our subclass's constructor, and reimplement `QTable::dragObject()` to return a `CellDrag`. Here's an example:

```
    QDragObject *MyTable::dragObject()
    {
        return new CellDrag(selectionAsString(), this);
    }
```

We have not shown the code for the `selectionAsString()`, because it is the same as the core of the `Spreadsheet::copy()` function (p. 80).

Adding drop support to a `QTable` would require us to reimplement `contents-DragEnterEvent()` and `contentsDropEvent()` in the same way as we did for the Project Chooser application.

## Advanced Clipboard Handling

Most applications make use of Qt's built-in clipboard handling in one way or another. For example, the `QTextEdit` class provides support for Ctrl+X, Ctrl+C, and Ctrl+V, along with `cut()`, `copy()`, and `paste()` slots, so little or no additional code is required.

When writing our own classes, we can access the clipboard through `QApplication::clipboard()`, which returns a pointer to the application's `QClipboard` object. Handling the system clipboard is easy: Call `setText()`, `setImage()`, or `setPixmap()` to put data on the clipboard, and `text()`, `image()`, or `pixmap()` to retrieve the data. We have already seen examples of clipboard use in the Spreadsheet application from Chapter 4 and in the Diagram application from Chapter 8.

For some applications, the built-in functionality might not be sufficient. For example, we might want to provide data that isn't just text or an image. Or we might want to provide data in many different formats, for maximum interoperability with other applications. The issue is very similar to what we encountered earlier with drag and drop, and the answer is also similar: We must subclass QMimeSource and reimplement format() and encodedData().

If our application supports drag and drop, we can simply reuse our custom QDragObject subclass and put it on the clipboard using the setData() function. Since QDragObject inherits QMimeSource and the clipboard understand QMime-Sources, this works seamlessly.

For example, here's how we could implement the copy() function of a QTable subclass:

```
void MyTable::copy()
{
    QApplication::clipboard()->setData(dragObject());
}
```

At the end of the previous section, we implemented dragObject() to return a CellDrag that stores the selected cells' contents.

To retrieve the data, we can call data() on the clipboard. Here's how we could implement the paste() function of a QTable subclass:

```
void MyTable::paste()
{
    QMimeSource *source = QApplication::clipboard()->data();
    if (CellDrag::canDecode(source)) {
        QString str;
        CellDrag::decode(source, str);
        performPaste(str);
    }
}
```

The performPaste() is essentially the same as the Spreadsheet::paste() function presented in Chapter 4 (p. 81).

This is all that is required, along with a custom QMimeSource, to add clipboard support for a custom type.

The X11 clipboard provides additional functionality not available on Windows or Mac OS X. On X11, it is usually possible to paste a selection by clicking the middle button of a three-button mouse. This is done using a separate "selection" clipboard. If you want your widgets to support this kind of clipboard as well as the standard one, you must pass QClipboard::Selection as an additional argument to the various clipboard calls. For example, here's how we would reimplement mouseReleaseEvent() in a text editor to support pasting using the middle mouse button:

```
void MyTextEditor::mouseReleaseEvent(QMouseEvent *event)
{
    QClipboard *clipboard = QApplication::clipboard();
    if (event->button() == MidButton
            && clipboard->supportsSelection()) {
        QString text = clipboard->text(QClipboard::Selection);
        pasteText(text);
    }
}
```

On X11, the supportsSelection() **function returns** true. **On other platforms, it returns** false.

# 10

# Input/Output

This chapter covers reading and writing files, traversing the file system, and interacting with external programs.

Qt's QDataStream and QTextStream classes make it simple to read and write files. These classes take care of issues such as byte ordering and text encodings, ensuring that Qt applications running on different platforms can read and write each other's files.

Many applications need to traverse directories or get information about a file. Qt's QDir and QFileInfo classes makes this possible.

In some situations, it is necessary to run external programs from within a GUI program. Qt's QProcess class allows us to execute external programs asynchronously, keeping the GUI responsive, with signals to tell us how the execution is progressing.

## Reading and Writing Binary Data

Reading and writing binary data using QDataStream is the simplest way to load and save custom data with Qt. QDataStream supports many Qt data types, including QByteArray, QFont, QImage, QMap<K, T>, QPixmap, QString, QValueList<T>, and QVariant. The data types that QDataStream understands and the formats it uses to store them are described online at http://doc.trolltech.com/3.2/datastreamformat.html.

To show how to handle binary data, we will use two example classes: Drawing and Gallery. The Drawing class holds some basic information about a drawing (the artist's name, the title, and the year it was created), and the Gallery class holds a list of Drawings.

We will start with the Gallery class.

```
class Gallery : public QObject
{
public:
    bool loadBinary(const QString &fileName);
    bool saveBinary(const QString &fileName);
    ...

private:
    enum { MagicNumber = 0x98c58f26 };

    void writeToStream(QDataStream &out);
    void readFromStream(QDataStream &in);
    void error(const QFile &file, const QString &message);
    void ioError(const QFile &file, const QString &message);

    QByteArray getData();
    void setData(const QByteArray &data);
    QString toString();

    std::list<Drawing> drawings;
};
```

The `Gallery` class contains public functions to save and load its data. The data
is a list of drawings held in the `drawings` data member. The private functions
will be reviewed as we make use of them.

Here is a simple function for saving a `Gallery`'s drawings as binary data:

```
bool Gallery::saveBinary(const QString &fileName)
{
    QFile file(fileName);
    if (!file.open(IO_WriteOnly)) {
        ioError(file, tr("Cannot open file %1 for writing"));
        return false;
    }

    QDataStream out(&file);
    out.setVersion(5);

    out << (Q_UINT32)MagicNumber;
    writeToStream(out);

    if (file.status() != IO_Ok) {
        ioError(file, tr("Error writing to file %1"));
        return false;
    }
    return true;
}
```

We open a file and make the file the target of a `QDataStream`. We set the `QData-`
`Stream`'s version to 5 (the most recent version in Qt 3.2). The version number
influences the way Qt data types are represented. Basic C++ data types are
always represented the same way.

We then output a number that identifies the Gallery file format (`MagicNumber`).
To ensure that the number is written as a 32-bit integer on all platforms, we
cast it to `Q_UINT32`, a data type that is guaranteed to be exactly 32 bits.

The file body is written by the writeToStream() private function. We don't need to explicitly close the file; this is done automatically when the QFile variable goes out of scope at the end of the function.

After the call to writeToStream(), we check the status of the QFile device. If there was an error, we call ioError() to present a message box to the user and return false.

```
void Gallery::ioError(const QFile &file, const QString &message)
{
    error(file, message + ": " + file.errorString());
}
```

The ioError() function relies on the more general error() function:

```
void Gallery::error(const QFile &file, const QString &message)
{
    QMessageBox::warning(0, tr("Gallery"), message.arg(file.name()));
}
```

Now let's review the writeToStream() function:

```
void Gallery::writeToStream(QDataStream &out)
{
    list<Drawing>::const_iterator it = drawings.begin();
    while (it != drawings.end()) {
        out << *it;
        ++it;
    }
}
```

The writeToStream() function iterates over all of the Gallery's drawings and outputs them to the stream it has been given, relying on the Drawing class's << operator. If we had used a QValueList<Drawing> to store the drawings instead of a list<Drawing>, we could have omitted the loop and simply written

```
out << drawings;
```

When a QValueList<T> is streamed, each item stored in the list is output using the item type's << operator.

```
QDataStream &operator<<(QDataStream &out, const Drawing &drawing)
{
    out << drawing.myTitle << drawing.myArtist << drawing.myYear;
    return out;
}
```

To output a Drawing, we simply output its three private member variables: myTitle, myArtist, and myYear. We need to declare operator<<() as a friend of Drawing for this to work. At the end of the function, we return the stream. This is a common C++ idiom that allows us to use a chain of << operators with an output stream. For example:

```
out << drawing1 << drawing2 << drawing3;
```

The definition of the Drawing class follows.

```
class Drawing
{
    friend QDataStream &operator<<(QDataStream &, const Drawing &);
    friend QDataStream &operator>>(QDataStream &, Drawing &);

public:
    Drawing() { myYear = 0; }
    Drawing(const QString &title, const QString &artist, int year)
    { myTitle = title; myArtist = artist; myYear = year; }

    QString title() const { return myTitle; }
    void setTitle(const QString &title) { myTitle = title; }
    QString artist() const { return myArtist; }
    void setArtist(const QString &artist) { myArtist = artist; }
    int year() const { return myYear; }
    void setYear(int year) { myYear = year; }

private:
    QString myTitle;
    QString myArtist;
    int myYear;
};
```

Now let's see how to read the data from a Gallery file:

```
bool Gallery::loadBinary(const QString &fileName)
{
    QFile file(fileName);
    if (!file.open(IO_ReadOnly)) {
        ioError(file, tr("Cannot open file %1 for reading"));
        return false;
    }

    QDataStream in(&file);
    in.setVersion(5);

    Q_UINT32 magic;
    in >> magic;
    if (magic != MagicNumber) {
        error(file, tr("File %1 is not a Gallery file"));
        return false;
    }

    readFromStream(in);

    if (file.status() != IO_Ok) {
        ioError(file, tr("Error reading from file %1"));
        return false;
    }
    return true;
}
```

We open the file for reading and create a QDataStream to extract the data from the file. We set the QDataStream's version to 5, because that's the version we used for writing. By using a fixed version number of 5, we guarantee that the application can always read and write the data, providing it is compiled with Qt 3.2 or later.

We start by reading back the magic number we wrote and compare it against MagicNumber. This ensures that we are really reading a Gallery file. We then read the data itself using the readFromStream() function.

```
void Gallery::readFromStream(QDataStream &in)
{
    drawings.clear();
    while (!in.atEnd()) {
        Drawing drawing;
        in >> drawing;
        drawings.push_back(drawing);
    }
}
```

In readFromStream(), we start by clearing any existing data. We then read in one drawing at a time, relying on the >> operator, and append each one to the Gallery's list of drawings. If we were using a QValueList<Drawing> to store the data instead of a list<Drawing>, we could read in all the drawings without looping:

```
in >> drawings;
```

QValueList<T> relies on the item type's >> operator to read in the items.

```
QDataStream &operator>>(QDataStream &in, Drawing &drawing)
{
    in >> drawing.myTitle >> drawing.myArtist >> drawing.myYear;
    return in;
}
```

The implementation of the >> operator mirrors that of the << operator. When we use QDataStream, we don't need to perform any kind of parsing.

If we want to read and write some raw binary data, we can use readRawBytes() and writeRawBytes() to read and write a block of bytes through a QDataStream. The raw bytes are *not* preceded by a block size.

We can read and write standard binary formats, such as DBF files and TEX DVI files, using the >> and << operators on basic types (like Q_UINT16 or float) or with readRawBytes() and writeRawBytes(). The default byte ordering used by QDataStream is big-endian. If we want to read and write data as little-endian, we must call

```
stream.setByteOrder(QDataStream::LittleEndian);
```

If the QDataStream is being used purely to read and write basic C++ data types, there is no need to use setVersion().

If we want to read or write a file in one go, we can avoid using QDataStream altogether and instead use QFile's writeBlock() and readAll() functions. For example:

```
file.writeBlock(getData());
```

Data written in this way is just a sequence of bytes. We are responsible for structuring the data when we write it and for parsing it when we read it back. We rely on Gallery's private getData() function to create the QByteArray and populate it with data. Reading it back is just as easy:

```
setData(file.readAll());
```

We use Gallery's setData() function to extract the information out of the QByteArray.

Having all the data in a QByteArray requires more memory, but it offers some advantages. For example, we can then use Qt's qCompress() function to compress the data (using zlib):

```
file.writeBlock(qCompress(getData()));
```

We can then use qUncompress() to uncompress the data:

```
setData(qUncompress(file.readAll()));
```

One way to implement getData() and setData() is to use a QDataStream on a QByteArray. Here's getData():

```
QByteArray Gallery::getData()
{
    QByteArray data;
    QDataStream out(data, IO_WriteOnly);
    writeToStream(out);
    return data;
}
```

We create a QDataStream that writes to a QByteArray rather than to a QFile, and we use the writeToStream() function we wrote earlier to fill the array with binary data.

Similarly, the setData() function can use the readFromStream() function we wrote earlier:

```
void Gallery::setData(const QByteArray &data)
{
    QDataStream in(data, IO_ReadOnly);
    readFromStream(in);
}
```

In the earlier examples, we loaded and saved the data with the stream's version hard-coded to 5. This approach is simple and safe, but it does have one small drawback: We cannot take advantage of new or updated formats. For example, if a later version of Qt added a new component to QFont (in addition to its point size, family, etc.), that component would not be saved or loaded.

One solution is to embed the QDataStream version number in the file:

```
QDataStream out(&file);
out << (Q_UINT32)MagicNumber;
out << (Q_UINT16)out.version();
writeToStream(out);
```

This ensures that we always write the data using the most recent version of
QDataStream, whatever that happens to be.

When we come to read the file, we read the magic number and the stream
version:

```
QDataStream in(&file);

Q_UINT32 magic;
Q_UINT16 streamVersion;
in >> magic >> streamVersion;

if (magic != MagicNumber) {
    error(file, tr("File %1 is not a Gallery file"));
    return false;
} else if ((int)streamVersion > in.version()) {
    error(file, tr("File %1 is from a more recent version of the "
                   "application"));
    return false;
}

in.setVersion(streamVersion);
readFromStream(in);
```

We can read the data as long as the stream version is less than or equal to the
version used by the application. Otherwise, we report an error.

If the file format contains a version number of its own, we can use that instead
of the stream version number. For example, let's suppose that the file format
is for version 1.3 of our application. We might then write the data as follows:

```
QDataStream out(&file);
out.setVersion(5);
out << (Q_UINT32)MagicNumber;
out << (Q_UINT16)0x0103;
writeToStream(out);
```

When we read it back, we determine which QDataStream version to use based
on the application's version number:

```
QDataStream in(&file);

Q_UINT32 magic;
Q_UINT16 appVersion;
in >> magic >> appVersion;

if (magic != MagicNumber) {
    error(file, tr("File %1 is not a Gallery file"));
    return false;
} else if (appVersion > 0x0103) {
    error(file, tr("File %1 is from a more recent version of the "
                   "application"));
    return false;
}

if (appVersion <= 0x0102) {
    in.setVersion(4);
```

```
    } else {
        in.setVersion(5);
    }
    readFromStream(in);
```

In this example, we say that any file saved with version 1.2 or earlier of the application uses data stream version 4, and that files saved with version 1.3 of the application use data stream version 5.

Once we have a policy for handling QDataStream versions, reading and writing binary data using Qt is simple and reliable.

## Reading and Writing Text

Qt provides the QTextStream class for reading and writing textual data. We can use QTextStream for reading and writing plain text files or files of other textual file formats, such as HTML, XML, and source files. It takes care of converting between Unicode and the system's local 8-bit encoding, and transparently handles the different line-ending conventions used by different operating systems.

QTextStream uses QChar as its fundamental unit of data. In addition to characters and strings, QTextStream supports C++'s basic numeric types, which it converts to and from strings.

To show how to use QTextStream, we will continue with the Gallery example from the previous section. Here's the code for a saveText() function that saves the drawings data from a Gallery:

```
    bool Gallery::saveText(const QString &fileName)
    {
        QFile file(fileName);
        if (!file.open(IO_WriteOnly | IO_Translate)) {
            ioError(file, tr("Cannot open file %1 for writing"));
            return false;
        }

        QTextStream out(&file);
        out.setEncoding(QTextStream::UnicodeUTF8);

        list<Drawing>::const_iterator it = drawings.begin();
        while (it != drawings.end()) {
            out << *it;
            ++it;
        }
        if (file.status() != IO_Ok) {
            ioError(file, tr("Error writing to file %1"));
            return false;
        }
        return true;
    }
```

We open the file with the IO_Translate flag to translate newline characters to the correct sequence for the target platform ("\r\n" on Windows, "\r" on

Mac OS X). Then we set the encoding to UTF-8, an ASCII-compatible encoding that can represent the entire Unicode character set. (For more information about Unicode, see Chapter 15.) To handle the output, we iterate over each drawing in the Gallery relying on the << operator:

```
QTextStream &operator<<(QTextStream &out, const Drawing &drawing)
{
    out << drawing.myTitle << ":" << drawing.myArtist << ":"
        << drawing.myYear << endl;
    return out;
}
```

When writing out a drawing, we use a colon to separate the drawing's title from the artist's name and another colon to separate the artist's name from the year, and we end the data with a newline. We assume that the title and the artist's name don't contain colons or newlines.

Here's an example file output by saveText():

```
The False Shepherds:Hans Bol:1576
Panoramic Landscape:Jan Brueghel the Younger:1619
Dune Landscape:Jan van Goyen:1630
River Delta:Jan van Goyen:1653
```

Now let's look at how we can read the data from the file:

```
bool Gallery::loadText(const QString &fileName)
{
    QFile file(fileName);
    if (!file.open(IO_ReadOnly | IO_Translate)) {
        ioError(file, tr("Cannot open file %1 for reading"));
        return false;
    }

    drawings.clear();
    QTextStream in(&file);
    in.setEncoding(QTextStream::UnicodeUTF8);

    while (!in.atEnd()) {
        Drawing drawing;
        in >> drawing;
        drawings.push_back(drawing);
    }

    if (file.status() != IO_Ok) {
        ioError(file, tr("Error reading from file %1"));
        return false;
    }
    return true;
}
```

The interesting part is the while loop. As long as there is more data available, we read it in using the >> operator.

Implementing the >> operator isn't trivial, because textual data is fundamentally ambiguous. Let's consider the following example:

```
out << "alpha" << "bravo";
```

If `out` is a `QTextStream`, the data that actually gets written is the string "alphabravo". We can't really expect this to work with a `QTextStream`:

```
in >> str1 >> str2;
```

In fact, what happens then is that `str1` gets the whole word "alphabravo", and `str2` gets nothing. `QDataStream` doesn't have that problem because it stores the length of each string in front of the character data.

If the text we write out consists of single words, we can put spaces between them and read the data back word by word. (The `DiagramView::copy()` and `DiagramView::paste()` functions of Chapter 8 use this approach.) We can't do this for the drawings because artist names and drawing titles usually contain more than one word. So we read each line in as a whole and then split it into fields using `QStringList::split()`:

```
QTextStream &operator>>(QTextStream &in, Drawing &drawing)
{
    QString str = in.readLine();
    QStringList fields = QStringList::split(":", str);
    if (fields.size() == 3) {
        drawing.myTitle = fields[0];
        drawing.myArtist = fields[1];
        drawing.myYear = fields[2].toInt();
    }
    return in;
}
```

We can read entire text files in one go using `QTextStream::read()`:

```
QString wholeFile = in.read();
```

In the resulting string, the end of each line is signified with a newline character ('\n') regardless of the line-ending convention used by the file being read.

Reading in an entire text file can be very convenient if we need to preprocess the data. For example:

```
wholeFile.replace("&", "&amp;");
wholeFile.replace("<", "&lt;");
wholeFile.replace(">", "&gt;");
```

For writing in one go, we could put all our data into a single string and simply output that.

```
QString Gallery::saveToString()
{
    QString result;
    QTextOStream out(&result);
    list<Drawing>::const_iterator it = drawings.begin();
    while (it != drawings.end()) {
        out << *it;
        ++it;
    }
```

```
        return result;
    }
```

It is just as easy to stream text into a string as it is to stream it to a file, again relying on the << operator.

```
    void Gallery::readFromString(const QString &data)
    {
        QString string = data;
        drawings.clear();
        QTextIStream in(&string);
        while (!in.atEnd()) {
            Drawing drawing;
            in >> drawing;
            drawings.push_back(drawing);
        }
    }
```

Extracting the data from a string using a QTextStream is straightforward. No parsing is necessary because we rely on the >> operator.

Writing text data isn't difficult, but reading text can be challenging. For complex formats, a full-blown parser might be required. Such a parser would typically work by reading the data character by character using >> on a QChar, or line by line using readLine() and iterating through the returned QString.

## Handling Files and Directories

Qt's QDir class provides a platform-independent means of traversing directories and retrieving information about files. To see how QDir is used, we will write a small console application that calculates the space consumed by all the images in a particular directory and all its subdirectories to any depth.

The heart of the application is the imageSpace() function, which computes the size of a given directory:

```
    int imageSpace(const QString &path)
    {
        QDir dir(path);
        QStringList::Iterator it;
        int size = 0;

        QStringList files = dir.entryList("*.png *.jpg *.jpeg",
                                          QDir::Files);
        it = files.begin();
        while (it != files.end()) {
            size += QFileInfo(path, *it).size();
            ++it;
        }

        QStringList dirs = dir.entryList(QDir::Dirs);
        it = dirs.begin();
        while (it != dirs.end()) {
            if (*it != "." && *it != "..")
                size += imageSpace(path + "/" + *it);
```

```
        ++it;
    }
    return size;
}
```

We begin by creating a QDir object using the given path. We pass the entry-List() function two arguments. The first is a space-separated list of file name filters. These can contain '*' and '?' wildcard characters. In this example, we are filtering to include only PNG and JPEG files. The second argument specifies what kind of entries we want (normal files, directories, drives, etc.).

We iterate over the list of files, accumulating their sizes. The QFileInfo class allows us to access a file's attributes, such as its size, permissions, owner, and timestamps.

The second entryList() call retrieves all the subdirectories in this directory. We iterate over them and recursively call imageSpace() to ascertain their accumulated image sizes.

To create each subdirectory's path, we combine the current directory's path with the subdirectory name (*it), separating them with a slash. QDir treats '/' as a directory separator on all platforms, in addition to '\' on Windows. When presenting paths to the user, we can call the static function QDir::convertSeparators() to convert slashes to the correct platform-specific separator.

Let's add a main() function to our small program:

```
int main(int argc, char *argv[])
{
    QString path = QDir::currentDirPath();
    if (argc > 1)
        path = argv[1];

    cerr << "Space used by images in " << endl
         << path.ascii() << endl
         << "and its subdirectories is "
         << (imageSpace(path) / 1024) << " KB" << endl;

    return 0;
}
```

For this example, we don't need a QApplication object, because we are only using Qt's tool classes. See http://doc.trolltech.com/3.2/tools.html for the list of these classes.

We use QDir::currentDirPath() to initialize the path to the current directory. Alternatively, we could have used QDir::homeDirPath() to initialize it to the user's home directory. If the user has specified a path on the command line, we use that instead. Finally, we call our imageSpace() function to calculate how much space is consumed by images.

The QDir class provides other file- and directory-related functions, including rename(), exists(), mkdir(), and rmdir(). The QFile class provides some static convenience functions, including remove() and exists().

# Inter-Process Communication

The QProcess class allows us to execute and interact with external programs. The class works asynchronously, doing its work in the background so that the user interface remains responsive. QProcess emits signals to notify us when the external process has data or has finished.

We will develop a small application that provides a user interface for an external image conversion program. For this example, we make use of the ImageMagick convert program, which is freely available for all major platforms.

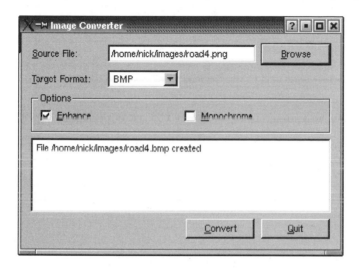

**Figure 10.1.** The Image Converter application

The Image Converter's user interface was created in *Qt Designer*. The .ui file is on the CD that accompanies this book. Here, we will focus on the .ui.h file that contains the code. Note that the process and fileFilters variables were declared in *Qt Designer*'s Members tab as follows:

```
QProcess *process;
QString fileFilters;
```

The uic tool includes these variables as part of the generated ConvertDialog class.

```
void ConvertDialog::init()
{
    process = 0;
    QStringList imageFormats = QImage::outputFormatList();
    targetFormatComboBox->insertStringList(imageFormats);
    fileFilters = tr("Images") + " (*."
                + imageFormats.join(" *.").lower() + ")";
}
```

A file filter consists of a descriptive text and one or more wildcard patterns (for example, "Text files (*.txt)"). The QImage::outputFormatList() function returns a list of the image output formats that are supported by **Qt**. This list can vary depending on the options that were selected when **Qt** was installed.

```
void ConvertDialog::browse()
{
    QString initialName = sourceFileEdit->text();
    if (initialName.isEmpty())
        initialName = QDir::homeDirPath();
    QString fileName =
            QFileDialog::getOpenFileName(initialName, fileFilters,
                                         this);
    fileName = QDir::convertSeparators(fileName);
    if (!fileName.isEmpty()) {
        sourceFileEdit->setText(fileName);
        convertButton->setEnabled(true);
    }
}
```

The dialog's Browse button is connected to the `browse()` slot. If the user has previously selected a file, we initialize the file dialog with that file's path; otherwise, we use the user's home directory.

```
void ConvertDialog::convert()
{
    QString sourceFile = sourceFileEdit->text();
    targetFile = QFileInfo(sourceFile).dirPath() + QDir::separator()
                 + QFileInfo(sourceFile).baseName();
    targetFile += ".";
    targetFile += targetFormatComboBox->currentText().lower();
    convertButton->setEnabled(false);
    outputTextEdit->clear();

    process = new QProcess(this);
    process->addArgument("convert");
    if (enhanceCheckBox->isChecked())
        process->addArgument("-enhance");
    if (monochromeCheckBox->isChecked())
        process->addArgument("-monochrome");
    process->addArgument(sourceFile);
    process->addArgument(targetFile);
    connect(process, SIGNAL(readyReadStderr()),
            this, SLOT(updateOutputTextEdit()));
    connect(process, SIGNAL(processExited()),
            this, SLOT(processExited()));
    process->start();
}
```

The dialog's Convert button is connected to the `convert()` slot. We copy the source file's name and change its suffix to match the target file format.

We then create a `QProcess` object. The first argument given to a `QProcess` object using `addArgument()` is the name of the external program to execute. Subsequent arguments become this program's arguments.

We connect the `QProcess`'s `readyReadStderr()` to the dialog's `updateOutputText-Edit()` slot to display error messages from the external program in the dialog's

QTextEdit as they are generated. We also connect the QProcess's processExited() signal to the dialog's slot of the same name.

```cpp
void ConvertDialog::updateOutputTextEdit()
{
    QByteArray data = process->readStderr();
    QString text = outputTextEdit->text() + QString(data);
    outputTextEdit->setText(text);
}
```

Whenever the external process writes to stderr, our updateOutputTextEdit() slot is called. We read the error text and append it to the QTextEdit.

```cpp
void ConvertDialog::processExited()
{
    if (process->normalExit()) {
        outputTextEdit->append(tr("File %1 created")
                                  .arg(targetFile));
    } else {
        outputTextEdit->append(tr("Conversion failed"));
    }
    delete process;
    process = 0;
    convertButton->setEnabled(true);
}
```

When the process has finished, we let the user know the outcome and then delete the process.

Wrapping a console application in this way can be useful because it allows us to make use of preexisting functionality rather than having to implement that functionality ourselves. Another use of QProcess is to launch other GUI applications, such as a web browser or an email client.

# 11

# Container Classes

Container classes are general purpose template classes that store items of a given type in memory. Standard C++ already includes many containers as part of the Standard Template Library (STL).

Qt provides its own container classes, so when we write Qt programs, we can use both the Qt and the STL containers. If you are already familiar with the STL containers and have STL available on your target platforms, there's no particular reason to use the Qt containers.

In this chapter, we review the most important STL and Qt containers. We also look at QString and QVariant, two classes that have many things in common with containers and that can be used as alternatives to containers in some contexts.

For more information about the STL classes and functions, a good place to start is SGI's STL web site: http://www.sgi.com/tech/stl/.

## Vectors

The STL and Qt classes for vectors, lists, and maps are template classes parameterized by the types of the objects we want to store in them. The values that can be stored in these classes can be basic types (like int and double), pointers, or classes that have a default constructor (a constructor that takes or needs no arguments), a copy constructor, and an assignment operator. Classes that qualify include QDateTime, QRegExp, QString, and QVariant. Qt classes that inherit from QObject don't qualify, because they don't implement a copy constructor and an assignment operator. This isn't usually a problem, since we can still store pointers to these types.

In this section, we will review the most common operations for vectors, and in the next two sections, we will review lists and maps. For most of the examples, we will use the `Film` class, which stores the title and duration of a film. (We will not call the class `Movie` because that looks too similar to Qt's `QMovie` class, which is used to show animated images.)

Here's the definition of `Film`:

```
class Film
{
public:
    Film(int id = 0, const QString &title = "", int duration = 0);

    int id() const { return myId; }
    void setId(int catalogId) { myId = catalogId; }
    QString title() const { return myTitle; }
    void setTitle(const QString &title) { myTitle = title; }
    int duration() const { return myDuration; }
    void setDuration(int minutes) { myDuration = minutes; }

private:
    int myId;
    QString myTitle;
    int myDuration;
};

int operator==(const Film &film1, const Film &film2);
int operator<(const Film &film1, const Film &film2);
```

We don't explicitly provide a copy constructor or an assignment operator because the ones automatically supplied by C++ suffice here. If the class had included pointers to memory allocated by the class, we would have to implement them ourselves.

In addition to the class, we provide an equality operator and a "less than" operator. The equality operator is used when we search a container to see if it contains a particular item. The "less than" operator is used for comparing items when sorting them. We don't need to implement the four other comparison operators (`!=`, `<=`, `>`, `>=`) since STL never uses them.

Here's the implementation of the three non-inline functions:

```
Film::Film(int id, const QString &title, int duration)
{
    myId = id;
    myTitle = title;
    myDuration = duration;
}

int operator==(const Film &film1, const Film &film2)
{
    return film1.id() == film2.id();
}

int operator<(const Film &film1, const Film &film2)
{
    return film1.id() < film2.id();
}
```

When comparing Film objects, we use IDs rather than titles because titles are not necessarily unique.

**Figure 11.1.** A vector of Films

A vector is a data structure that stores its items at adjacent positions in memory. What distinguishes a vector from a plain C++ array is that a vector knows its own size and can be resized. Appending extra elements to the end of a vector is fairly efficient, but inserting elements at the front or in the middle of a vector is expensive.

The STL's vector class is called std::vector<T> and is defined in <vector>. Here's an example:

```
vector<Film> films;
```

The Qt equivalent is called QValueVector<T>:

```
QValueVector<Film> films;
```

A vector created like this has size 0. If we know in advance how many elements we are going to need, we can give the vector an initial size when we define it and use the [] operator to assign a value to its elements; otherwise, we must either resize it later or append items.

A convenient way to populate a vector is to use push_back(). This function appends an element at the end, extending the vector by one:

```
films.push_back(Film(4812, "A Hard Day's Night", 85));
films.push_back(Film(5051, "Seven Days to Noon", 94));
films.push_back(Film(1301, "Day of Wrath", 105));
films.push_back(Film(9227, "A Special Day", 110));
films.push_back(Film(1817, "Day for Night", 116));
```

In general, Qt offers the same function names as the STL, although in some cases Qt has additional more Qt-like names. For example, if we are using the Qt classes, we can append items using either push_back() or append().

Another way to populate a vector is to give the vector an initial size and to initialize the elements individually:

```
vector<Film> films(5);
```

```
films[0] = Film(4812, "A Hard Day's Night", 85);
films[1] = Film(5051, "Seven Days to Noon", 94);
films[2] = Film(1301, "Day of Wrath", 105);
films[3] = Film(9227, "A Special Day", 110);
films[4] = Film(1817, "Day for Night", 116);
```

Vector entries that are created without being assigned an explicit value are initialized using the item class's default constructor. For basic and pointer types, the value is undefined, just as it is when we define variables of these types on the stack.

We can iterate over the vector's elements using the [] operator:

```
for (int i = 0; i < (int)films.size(); ++i)
    cerr << films[i].title().ascii() << endl;
```

Alternatively, we can use an iterator:

```
vector<Film>::const_iterator it = films.begin();
while (it != films.end()) {
    cerr << (*it).title().ascii() << endl;
    ++it;
}
```

Every container class has two iterator types: iterator and const_iterator. The difference between the two is that const_iterator doesn't allow us to modify the data.

A container's begin() function returns an iterator that refers to the first item in the container (for example, films[0]). A container's end() function returns an iterator that refers to the "one past the last" item (for example, films[5]). If a container is empty, begin() equals end(). This can be used to see if the container has any elements, although it is more convenient to call empty() for this purpose.

Iterators have an intuitive syntax that resembles the syntax of C++ pointers. We can use the ++ and -- operators to move to the next or previous item, and unary * to retrieve the item stored at the current iterator position. In fact, for vector<T>, the iterator and const_iterator types are merely typedefs for T * and const T *.

If we want to find an item in a vector using a linear search, we can use the STL find() function:

```
vector<Film>::iterator it = find(films.begin(), films.end(),
                                 Film(4812));
if (it != films.end())
    films.erase(it);
```

The find() function returns an iterator to the first item that compared equal (using operator==()) to the item passed as the last argument. It is defined in <algorithm>, along with many other template functions. These functions typically operate on iterators. Qt provides a few of these functions under different names (for example, qFind()). You can use them if you want to use Qt without the STL.

To sort the items in a vector, we can call `sort()`:

```
sort(films.begin(), films.end());
```

The `sort()` function uses the < operator to compare items, unless we pass a different comparison function.

Once sorted, we can use the `binary_search()` function to see if an item is present. On a sorted vector, `binary_search()` gives the same result as `find()` (assuming no two films have the same ID), but is much faster:

```
int id = 1817;
if (binary_search(films.begin(), films.end(), Film(id)))
    cerr << "Found " << id << endl;
```

Given a position indicated by an iterator, we can expensively insert a new item using `insert()` or remove an existing item using `erase()`:

```
films.erase(it);
```

The items that follow the erased item in the vector are then moved one position to the left to fill its position, and the vector's size is reduced by one.

## Lists

A list (or linked list) is a data structure that stores its items at non-adjacent locations in memory. Unlike vectors, lists have very poor random access performance; on the other hand, `insert()` and `erase()` are very fast.

Many algorithms that work on vectors don't work on lists, notably `sort()` and `binary_search()`. This is because lists don't provide fast random access. For sorting an STL list, we can use its `sort()` member function.

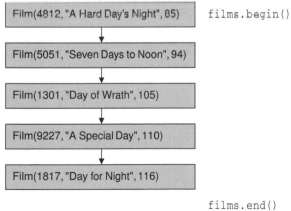

**Figure 11.2.** A list of `Films`

The STL's list class is called `std::list<T>` and is defined in `<list>`. Here's an example:

```
list<Film> films;
```

The **Qt** equivalent is called `QValueList<T>`:

```
QValueList<Film> films;
```

The `Film` class was presented in the previous section (p. 244).

New items can be added using `push_back()` or with `insert()`. Unlike vectors, inserting at the beginning or in the middle of a list is not expensive.

STL lists do not provide the `[]` operator, so iterators must be used to traverse their elements. (Qt lists support the `[]` operator, but it can be very slow on large lists.) The syntax and usage is exactly the same as for vectors, except that we write `list<T>` instead of `vector<T>` in front of the iterator type. For example:

```
list<Film>::const_iterator it = films.begin();
while (it != films.end()) {
    cerr << (*it).title().ascii() << endl;
    ++it;
}
```

Otherwise, lists mostly provide the same functions as vectors, including `empty()`, `size()`, `erase()`, and `clear()`. The `find()` algorithm can also be used on lists.

A few **Qt** functions return a `QValueList<T>`. If we want to iterate over the return value of a function, we must take a copy of the list and iterate over the copy. For example, the following code is the correct way to iterate over the `QValueList<int>` returned by `QSplitter::sizes()`:

```
QValueList<int> list = splitter->sizes();
QValueList<int>::const_iterator it = list.begin();
while (it != list.end()) {
    do_something(*it);
    ++it;
}
```

The following code is wrong:

```
// WRONG
QValueList<int>::const_iterator it = splitter->sizes().begin();
while (it != splitter->sizes().end()) {
    do_something(*it);
    ++it;
}
```

This is because `QSplitter::sizes()` returns a new `QValueList<int>` by value every time it is called. If we don't store the return value, C++ automatically destroys it before we have even started iterating, leaving us with a dangling iterator. To make matters worse, each time the loop is run, `QSplitter::sizes()` must generate a new copy of the list because of the `splitter->sizes().end()` call. In summary: Always iterate on a copy of a container returned by value.

Copying a container like this sounds expensive, but it isn't, because Qt uses an optimization called *implicit sharing*. This optimization means that we can program as if the data has been copied, even though behind the scenes no data copying has taken place.

The QStringList class, which is used in many places in Qt, is a subclass of QValueList<QString>. In addition to the functions it inherits from its base class, it provides some extra functions that make the class more powerful. These functions will be discussed in the last section of this chapter.

## Maps

A map holds an arbitrary number of items of the same type, indexed by a key. Maps store one unique value per key. Maps have good random access and insertion performance. If a new value is assigned to an existing key, the old value is replaced by the new value.

**Figure 11.3.** A map of Films

Since maps contain key–value pairs, it is common to design data structures that work with maps in a slightly different way from those that are designed for use with vectors and lists. Here's a version of the Film class that we will use to illustrate map usage:

```
class Film
{
public:
    Film(const QString &title = "", int duration = 0);

    QString title() const { return myTitle; }
    void setTitle(const QString &title) { myTitle = title; }
    int duration() const { return myDuration; }
    void setDuration(int minutes) { myDuration = minutes; }

private:
    QString myTitle;
    int myDuration;
};
```

```
Film::Film(const QString &title, int duration)
{
    myTitle = title;
    myDuration = duration;
}
```

We don't store the catalog ID in the `Film` class since we will use that as the key to the map. Nor do we need the comparison operators for `Film`. Maps are ordered by their keys, not by their values.

The STL's map class is called `std::map<K, T>` and is defined in `<map>`. Here's an example of a map whose keys are `int`s (catalog IDs) and whose values are `Film`s:

```
map<int, Film> films;
```

The Qt equivalent is `QMap<K, T>`:

```
QMap<int, Film> films;
```

The most natural way to insert items into a map is to assign a value to a given key:

```
films[4812] = Film("A Hard Day's Night", 85);
films[5051] = Film("Seven Days to Noon", 94);
films[1301] = Film("Day of Wrath", 105);
films[9227] = Film("A Special Day", 110);
films[1817] = Film("Day for Night", 116);
```

The map iterator provides a key–pair value. The key part is extracted using `(*it).first` and the value part using `(*it).second`:

```
map<int, Film>::const_iterator it = films.begin();
while (it != films.end()) {
    cerr << (*it).first << ": "
         << (*it).second.title().ascii() << endl;
    ++it;
}
```

Most compilers also allow us to write `it->first` and `it->second`, but it's more portable to write `(*it).first` and `(*it).second`.

The Qt map's iterator differs slightly from the STL one. In a Qt map, the key is retrieved from an iterator using `it.key()` and the value with `it.data()`:

```
QMap<int, Film>::const_iterator it = films.begin();
while (it != films.end()) {
    cerr << it.key() << ": " << it.data().title().ascii() << endl;
    ++it;
}
```

When iterating over a map, the items are always ordered by key.

The `[]` operator can be used for both insertion and retrieval, but if `[]` is used to retrieve a value for a non-existent key, a new item will be created with the given key and an empty value. To avoid accidentally creating empty values, use the `find()` member function to retrieve items:

```
map<int, Film>::const_iterator it = films.find(1817);
if (it != films.end())
    cerr << "Found " << (*it).second.title().ascii() << endl;
```

This function returns the `end()` iterator if the key is not in the map.

In the example we have used an integer key, but other types of keys are possible, one popular choice being a `QString` key. For example:

```
map<QString, QString> actorToNationality;
actorToNationality["Doris Day"] = "American";
actorToNationality["Greta Garbo"] = "Swedish";
```

If we need to store multiple values for the same key, we can use `multimap<K, T>`. If we only need to store keys, we can use `set<K>` or `multiset<K>`. Qt provides no equivalent for these classes.

Qt's `QMap<K, T>` class has a couple of additional convenience functions that are especially useful when dealing with small data sets. `QMap<K, T>::keys()` and `QMap<K, T>::values()` return `QValueLists` of a map's keys and values.

## Pointer-Based Containers

Along with the STL-like containers described in the previous sections, Qt also provides an additional set of container classes. These classes were developed in the early 1990s for Qt 1.0, before the STL became part of C++, and therefore have their own particular syntax. Because these classes operate on pointers to objects, they are often referred to as pointer-based containers, in contrast to Qt's and the STL's value-based containers. In Qt 4, the pointer-based containers will continue to be available for compatibility, but it is expected that their use will be deprecated in favor of the value-based containers.

The main reason for using the pointer-based classes in newly written Qt code is that a few important functions in Qt 3 rely on them. We have already seen one example of this in Chapter 3, where we iterated over an application's top-level widgets (p. 66), and another example in Chapter 6, where we iterated over an application's MDI windows (p. 156).

The main pointer-based containers are `QPtrVector<T>`, `QPtrList<T>`, `QDict<T>`, `QAsciiDict<T>`, `QIntDict<T>`, and `QPtrDict<T>`.

`QPtrVector<T>` stores a vector of pointers. Here's how we would populate a `QPtrVector<Film>` with five `Film` objects:

```
QPtrVector<Film> films(5);
films.setAutoDelete(true);
films.insert(0, new Film(4812, "A Hard Day's Night", 85));
films.insert(1, new Film(5051, "Seven Days to Noon", 94));
films.insert(2, new Film(1301, "Day of Wrath", 105));
films.insert(3, new Film(9227, "A Special Day", 110));
films.insert(4, new Film(1817, "Day for Night", 116));
```

`QPtrVector<T>` does not provide an `append()` function, so we must resize the vector ourselves and insert items at specific index positions. In this example, we are using the original `Film` class, which includes catalog IDs.

One nice feature of Qt's pointer-based containers is the "auto-delete" property. If auto-delete is enabled, Qt takes ownership of all the objects inserted into the container and deletes them when the container is deleted (or when `remove()` or `clear()` are used).

To remove an item from the vector, we can call `remove()` with an index:

```
films.remove(2);
```

The `remove()` operation does not change the size of the vector; instead, the item is set to a null pointer. If auto-delete is on, the item is automatically deleted.

To traverse a `QPtrVector<T>`, we can simply use indexes:

```
for (int i = 0; i < (int)films.count(); ++i) {
    if (films[i])
        cerr << films[i]->title().ascii() << endl;
}
```

We check that the pointer at the given index is not null before using it, in case it has been erased or has never had anything assigned to it.

The `QPtrList<T>` class stores a list of pointers. We can add new items to a `QPtrList<T>` by calling `append()`, `prepend()`, or `insert()`:

```
QPtrList<Film> films;
films.setAutoDelete(true);
films.append(new Film(4812, "A Hard Day's Night", 85));
films.append(new Film(5051, "Seven Days to Noon", 94));
```

Pointer lists have a "current" item, which is updated when we call traversal functions such as `first()`, `next()`, `prev()`, and `last()`. One way to iterate over a list is like this:

```
Film *film = films.first();
while (film) {
    cerr << film->title().ascii() << endl;
    film = films.next();
}
```

It's also possible to iterate over a list using `at()`:

```
for (int i = 0; i < (int)films.count(); ++i)
    cerr << films.at(i)->title().ascii() << endl;
```

A third option is to use `QPtrListIterator<T>`.

The `QDict<T>`, `QAsciiDict<T>`, `QIntDict<T>`, and `QPtrDict<T>` classes are the nearest pointer-based equivalents to `map<K, T>`. These classes also operate on key–value pairs. The key can be any one of four different types (`QString`, `const char *`, `int`, or `void *`), depending on which of the four classes is used. Since all four classes provide the same functions, we will just look at `QIntDict<T>`.

We will use this to store Films of the same type we used with map<K, T> earlier, using catalog IDs as keys.

```
QIntDict<Film> films(101);
films.setAutoDelete(true);
```

The QIntDict<T> constructor accepts a number. That number is used internally by the class to determine how many "buckets" it puts the data into. For good performance, that number should be a prime number a little larger than the number of items we expect to hold. A list of the prime numbers smaller than 10,000 is available at http://doc.trolltech.com/3.2/primes.html.

Inserting new items is done with insert(), which accepts a key and a value:

```
films.insert(4812, new Film("A Hard Day's Night", 85));
films.insert(5051, new Film("Seven Days to Noon", 94));
```

We can use find() or the [] operator to look up items, remove() to delete an item, and replace() to change the value associated with a given key.

If we call insert() multiple times with the same key, only the most recently inserted item will be accessible. If we call remove(), the items are removed in the reverse order in which they were inserted. To avoid multiple values under the same key, we can use replace() instead of insert().

The entire container can be traversed using an iterator:

```
QIntDictIterator<Film> it(films);
while (it.current()) {
    cerr << it.currentKey() << ": "
         << it.current()->title().ascii() << endl;
    ++it;
}
```

The iterator provides the current key with currentKey() and the current value with current(). The order in which the items appear is undefined.

Qt provides a special vector-like class, QMemArray<T>, for storing items of basic types like int and double or of structs of basic types. Few applications use it directly; however, its two subclasses QByteArray (QMemArray<char>) and QPointArray (QMemArray<QPoint>) are very common, and we have used them many times in earlier chapters.

For example, here's how to create a QByteArray:

```
QByteArray bytes(4);
bytes[0] = 'A';
bytes[1] = 'C';
bytes[2] = 'D';
bytes[3] = 'C';
```

When we create a QMemArray<T>, we can either pass it an initial size or call resize() later. We can then access array entries using the [] operator:

```
for (int i = 0; i < (int)bytes.size(); ++i)
    cerr << bytes[i] << endl;
```

We can search for an item using QMemArray<T>::find():

```
if (bytes.find('A') != -1)
    cerr << "Found" << endl;
```

A subtle pitfall with QMemArray<T> and its subclasses is that they are *explicitly shared*. This means that when we create a copy of an object (using the class's copy constructor or its assignment operator), both the original and the copy share the same data. When we modify one of them, the other one is also modified. Explicit sharing should not be confused with implicit sharing, which does not have this problem.

The defensive way to program using QMemArray<T> is to call copy() to force a deep copy of the container when copying it:

```
duplicate = bytes.copy();
```

This ensures that no two QMemArray<T> objects point to the same data.

To avoid the inherent problems of explicit sharing, the QMemArray<T> class will probably be deprecated in favor of QValueVector<T> in Qt 4. The QByteArray and QPointArray classes will then use QValueVector<T> as their base class.

## QString and QVariant

Strings are used by every GUI program, not only for the user interface, but often also as data structures.

C++ natively provides two kinds of strings: traditional C-style '\0'-terminated character arrays and the string class. Qt's QString class is more powerful than either of them. The QString class holds 16-bit Unicode values. Unicode contains ASCII and Latin-1 as a subset, with their usual numeric values. But since QString is 16-bit, it can represent thousands of other characters for writing most of the world's languages. See Chapter 15 for more information about Unicode.

QString provides a binary + operator to concatenate two strings and a += operator to append one string to another. Here's an example that combines both:

```
QString str = "User: ";
str += userName + "\n";
```

There is also a QString::append() function that does the same thing as the += operator:

```
str = "User: ";
str.append(userName);
str.append("\n");
```

A completely different way of combining strings is to use QString's sprintf() function:

```
str.sprintf("%s %.1f%%", "perfect competition", 100.0);
```

This function supports the same format specifiers as the C++ library's `sprintf()` function. In the example above, `str` is assigned "perfect competition 100.0%".

Yet another way of building a string from other strings or from numbers is to use `arg()`:

```
str = QString("%1 %2 (%3s-%4s)")
        .arg("permissive").arg("society").arg(1950).arg(1970);
```

In this example, "%1" is replaced by "permissive", "%2" is replaced by "society", "%3" is replaced by "1950", and "%4" is replaced by "1970". The result is "permissive society (1950s-1970s)". There are `arg()` overloads to handle various data types. Some overloads have extra parameters for controlling the field width, the numerical base, or the floating-point precision. In general, `arg()` is a much better solution than `sprintf()`, because it is type-safe, fully supports Unicode, and allows translators to change the order of the "%*n*" parameters.

`QString` can convert numbers into strings using the `QString::number()` static function:

```
str = QString::number(59.6);
```

Or using the `setNum()` function:

```
str.setNum(59.6);
```

The reverse conversion, from a string to a number, is achieved using `toInt()`, `toLongLong()`, `toDouble()`, and so on. For example:

```
bool ok;
double d = str.toDouble(&ok);
```

These functions also accept an optional pointer to a `bool` and set the `bool` to `true` or `false` depending on the success of the conversion. When the conversion fails, these functions always return 0.

Once we have a string, we often want to extract parts of it. The `mid()` function returns the substring starting at a given position and of a given length. For example, the following code prints "pays" to the console:

```
QString str = "polluter pays principle";
cerr << str.mid(9, 4).ascii() << endl;
```

If we omit the second argument (or pass –1), `mid()` returns the substring starting at a given position and ending at the end of the string. For example, the following code prints "pays principle" to the console:

```
QString str = "polluter pays principle";
cerr << str.mid(9).ascii() << endl;
```

There are also `left()` and `right()` functions that perform a similar job. Both accept a number of characters, *n*, and return the first or last *n* characters of the string. For example, the following code prints "polluter principle" to the console:

```
QString str = "polluter pays principle";
cerr << str.left(8).ascii() << " " << str.right(9).ascii()
     << endl;
```

If we want to check if a string starts or ends with something, we can use the startsWith() and endsWith() functions:

```
if (uri.startsWith("http:") && uri.endsWith(".png"))
    ...
```

This is both simpler and faster than this:

```
if (uri.left(5) == "http:" && uri.right(4) == ".png")
    ...
```

String comparison with the == operator is case sensitive. For case insensitive comparisons, we can use upper() or lower(). For example:

```
if (fileName.lower() == "readme.txt")
    ...
```

If we want to replace a certain part of a string by another string, we can use replace():

```
QString str = "a sunny day";
str.replace(2, 5, "cloudy");
```

The result is "a cloudy day". The code can be rewritten to use remove() and insert():

```
str.remove(2, 5);
str.insert(2, "cloudy");
```

First, we remove five characters starting at position 2, resulting in the string "a  day" (with two spaces), then we insert "cloudy" at position 2.

There are overloaded versions of replace() that replace all occurrences of their first argument with their second argument. For example, here's how to replace all occurrences of "&" with "&amp;" in a string:

```
str.replace("&", "&amp;");
```

One very frequent need is to strip the whitespace (such as spaces, tabs, and newlines) from a string. QString has a function that strips whitespace from both ends of a string:

```
QString str = "   BOB \t THE  \nDOG \n";
cerr << str.stripWhiteSpace().ascii() << endl;
```

String str can be depicted as

The string returned by stripWhiteSpace() is

When handling user input, we often also want to replace every sequence of one or more internal whitespace characters with single spaces, in addition to stripping whitespace from both ends. This is what the `simplifyWhiteSpace()` function does:

```
QString str = "  BOB \t THE  \nDOG \n";
cerr << str.simplifyWhiteSpace().ascii() << endl;
```

The string returned by `simplifyWhiteSpace()` is

```
BOB THE DOG
```

A string can be split into substrings using `QStringList::split()`:

```
QString str = "polluter pays principle";
QStringList words = QStringList::split(" ", str);
```

In the example above, we split the string "polluter pays principle" into three substrings: "polluter", "pays", and "principle". The `split()` function has an optional `bool` third argument that specifies whether empty substrings should be ignored (the default) or not.

The elements in a `QStringList` can be joined to form a single string using `join()`. The argument to `join()` is inserted between each pair of joined strings. For example, here's how to create a single string that is composed of all the strings contained in a `QStringList` sorted into alphabetical order and separated by newlines:

```
words.sort();
str = words.join("\n");
```

When dealing with strings, we often need to determine whether a string is empty or not. One way of testing this is to call `isEmpty()`; another way is to check whether `length()` is 0.

`QString` distinguishes between null strings and empty strings. This distinction has its roots in the C language, which differentiates between 0 (a null pointer) and "" (an empty string). To test whether a string is null, we can call `isNull()`. For most applications, what matters is whether or not a string contains any characters. The `isEmpty()` function provides this information, returning `true` if a string has no characters (is null or empty), and `false` otherwise.

The conversions between `const char *` strings and `QString` is automatic in most cases, for example:

```
str += " (1870)";
```

Here we add a `const char *` to a `QString` without formality.

In some situations, it is necessary to explicitly convert between `const char *` and `QString`. To convert a `QString` to a `const char *`, use `ascii()` or `latin1()`. To convert the other way, use a `QString` cast.

When we call `ascii()` or `latin1()` on a `QString`, or when we let the automatic conversion to `const char *` do its work, the returned string is owned by the `QString` object. This means that we don't need to worry about memory leaks; Qt will reclaim the memory for us. On the other hand, we must be careful not to use the pointer for too long. For example, if we modify the original `QString`, the pointer is not guaranteed to remain valid. If we need to store the `const char *` for any length of time, we can assign it to a variable of type `QByteArray` or `QCString`. These will hold a complete copy of the data.

`QString` is implicitly shared. This means that copying a `QString` is about as fast as copying a single pointer. Only if one of the copies is changed is data actually copied—and this is all handled automatically behind the scenes. For this reason, implicit sharing is sometimes referred to as "copy on write".

The beauty of implicit sharing is that it is an optimization that we don't have to think about; it simply works, without requiring any programmer intervention.

Qt uses implicit sharing for many other classes, including `QBrush`, `QFont`, `QPen`, `QPixmap`, `QMap<K, T>`, `QValueList<T>`, and `QValueVector<T>`. This makes these classes very efficient to pass by value, both as function parameters and as return values.

C++ is a strongly typed language, and this provides many benefits, including type safety and efficiency. However, in some situations, it is useful to be able to store data more generically, and one conventional way of doing so is to use strings. For example, a string could hold a textual value or a numeric value in string form. Qt provides a much cleaner way of handling variables that can hold different types: `QVariant`.

The `QVariant` class can hold values of many Qt types, including `QBrush`, `QColor`, `QCursor`, `QDateTime`, `QFont`, `QKeySequence`, `QPalette`, `QPen`, `QPixmap`, `QPoint`, `QRect`, `QRegion`, `QSize`, and `QString`. The `QVariant` class can also hold containers: `QMap<QString, QVariant>`, `QStringList`, and `QValueList<QVariant>`. We used a `QVariant` in the implementation of the Spreadsheet application in Chapter 4 to hold the value of a cell, which could be either a `QString`, a `double`, or an invalid value.

One common use of variants is in a map that uses strings as keys and variants as values. Configuration data is normally saved and retrieved using `QSettings`, but some applications may handle this data directly, perhaps storing it in a database. `QMap<QString, QVariant>` is ideal for such situations:

```
QMap<QString, QVariant> config;
config["Width"] = 890;
config["Height"] = 645;
config["ForegroundColor"] = black;
config["BackgroundColor"] = lightGray;
config["SavedDate"] = QDateTime::currentDateTime();
QStringList files;
files << "2003-05.dat" << "2003-06.dat" << "2003-07.dat";
config["RecentFiles"] = files;
```

## How Implicit Sharing Works

Implicit sharing works automatically behind the scenes, so when we use classes that are implicitly shared, we don't have to do anything in our code to make this optimization happen. But since it's nice to know how things work, we will study an example and see what happens under the hood.

```
QString str1 = "Humpty";
QString str2 = str1;
```

We set `str1` to "Humpty" and `str2` to be equal to `str1`. At this point, both `QString`s point to the same data structure in memory (of type `QStringData`). Along with the character data, the data structure holds a reference count that indicates how many `QString`s point to the same data structure. Since both `str1` and `str2` point to the same data, the reference count is 2.

```
str2[0] = 'D';
```

When we modify `str2`, it first makes a deep copy of the data, to ensure that `str1` and `str2` point to different data structures, and it then applies the change to its own copy of the data. The reference count of `str1`'s data ("Humpty") becomes 1, and the reference count of `str2`'s data ("Dumpty") is set to 1. A reference count of 1 means that the data isn't shared.

```
str2.truncate(4);
```

If we modify `str2` again, no copying takes place because the reference count of `str2`'s data is 1. The `truncate()` function operates directly on `str2`'s data, resulting in the string "Dump". The reference count stays at 1.

```
str1 = str2;
```

When we assign `str2` to `str1`, the reference count for `str1`'s data goes down to 0, which means that no `QString` is using the "Humpty" data anymore. The data is then freed from memory. Both `QString`s now point to "Dump", which now has a reference count of 2.

Writing implicitly shared classes isn't very difficult. The *Qt Quarterly* article "Data Sharing with Class", available online at `http://doc.trolltech.com/qq/qq02-data-sharing-with-class.html`, explains how to do it.

Iterating over a map that holds variant values can be slightly tricky if some of the values are containers. We need to use `type()` to check the type that a variant holds so that we can respond appropriately:

```
QMap<QString, QVariant>::const_iterator it = config.begin();
while (it != config.end()) {
    QString str;
    if (it.data().type() == QVariant::StringList)
        str = it.data().toStringList().join(", ");
    else
        str = it.data().toString();
    cerr << it.key().ascii() << ": " << str.ascii() << endl;
```

```
    ++it;
}
```

It is possible to create arbitrarily complex data structures using `QVariant` by holding values of container types:

```
QMap<QString, QVariant> price;
price["Orange"] = 2.10;
price["Pear"].asMap()["Standard"] = 1.95;
price["Pear"].asMap()["Organic"] = 2.25;
price["Pineapple"] = 3.85;
```

Here we have created a map with string keys (product names) and values that are either floating-point numbers (prices) or maps. The top level map contains three keys: "Orange", "Pear", and "Pineapple". The value associated with the "Pear" key is a map that contains two keys ("Standard" and "Organic").

Creating data structures like this can be very seductive since we can structure the data in any way we like. But the convenience of `QVariant` comes at a price. For the sake of readability, it is usually worth defining a proper C++ class to store our data. A custom class provides type safety and will also be more speed- and memory-efficient than using `QVariant`.

# 12

# Databases

Qt's SQL module provides a platform and database-independent interface for accessing SQL databases, and a set of classes for integrating databases into the user interface.

The chapter begins by showing how to open database connections and how to execute arbitrary SQL statements on a database. The second and third sections focus on providing the user with ways of viewing and modifying a database through the user interface, using QDataTable to present data in a table widget and using QSqlForm to present data as a form. These classes are designed to interact nicely with each other, making common database idioms such as master–detail views and drill-down easy to implement.

## Connecting and Querying

To execute SQL queries, we must first establish a connection with a database. Typically, database connections are set up in a separate function that we call at application startup. For example:

```
bool createConnection()
{
    QSqlDatabase *db = QSqlDatabase::addDatabase("QOCI8");
    db->setHostName("mozart.konkordia.edu");
    db->setDatabaseName("musicdb");
    db->setUserName("gbatstone");
    db->setPassword("T17aV44");
    if (!db->open()) {
        db->lastError().showMessage();
        return false;
    }
    return true;
}
```

First, we call `QSqlDatabase::addDatabase()` to create a `QSqlDatabase` object. The argument to `addDatabase()` specifies which database driver Qt must use to access the database. In this case, we use Oracle. The commercial version of Qt 3.2 includes the following drivers: `QODBC3` (ODBC), `QOCI8` (Oracle), `QTDS7` (Sybase Adaptive Server), `QPSQL7` (PostgreSQL), `QMYSQL3` (MySQL), and `QDB2` (IBM DB2). The free and non-commercial editions contain a subset of these.* See `http://doc.trolltech.com/3.2/sql-driver.html` for information on building the database drivers.

Next, we set the database host name, the database name, the user name, and the password, and we try to open the connection. If `open()` fails, we show an error message using `QSqlError::showMessage()`.

Typically, we would call `createConnection()` in `main()`:

```
int main(int argc, char *argv[])
{
    QApplication app(argc, argv);
    if (!createConnection())
        return 1;
    ...
    return app.exec();
}
```

Once a connection is established, we can use `QSqlQuery` to execute any SQL statement that the underlying database supports. For example, here's how to execute a SELECT statement:

```
QSqlQuery query;
query.exec("SELECT title, year FROM cd WHERE year >= 1998");
```

After the `exec()` call, we can navigate through the query's result set:

```
while (query.next()) {
    QString title = query.value(0).toString();
    int year = query.value(1).toInt();
    cerr << title.ascii() << ": " << year << endl;
}
```

We call `next()` once to position the `QSqlQuery` on the *first* record of the result set. Subsequent calls to `next()` advance the record pointer by one record each time, until the end is reached, at which point `next()` returns `false`. If the result set is empty, the first call to `next()` will return `false`.

The `value()` function returns the value of a field as a `QVariant`. The fields are numbered from 0 in the order given in the SELECT statement. The `QVariant` class can hold many C++ and Qt types, including `int` and `QString`. The different types of data that can be stored in a database are mapped into the corresponding C++ and Qt types and stored in `QVariant`s. For example, a VARCHAR is represented as a `QString` and a DATETIME as a `QDateTime`.

---

*The Qt packages on the accompanying CD include SQLite, a public domain in-process database, and `QSQLITEX`, an experimental driver. These are only intended for use with the examples on the CD.

`QSqlQuery` provides some other functions to navigate through the result set: `first()`, `last()`, `prev()`, `seek()`, and `at()`. These functions are convenient, but for some databases they can be slow and memory-hungry. For an easy optimization when operating on large data sets, we can call `QSqlQuery::setForwardOnly(true)` before calling `exec()`, and then only use `next()` for navigating the result set.

Earlier we specified the SQL query as an argument to `exec()`, but we can also pass it directly to the constructor, which executes it immediately:

```
QSqlQuery query("SELECT title, year FROM cd WHERE year >= 1998");
```

Here's how we would check for an error and pop up a `QMessageBox` if a problem occurred:

```
if (!query.isActive())
    query.lastError().showMessage();
```

Doing an INSERT is almost as easy as doing a SELECT:

```
QSqlQuery query("INSERT INTO cd (id, artistid, title, year) "
                "VALUES (203, 102, 'Living in America', 2002)");
```

After this, `QSqlQuery::numRowsAffected()` returns the number of rows that were affected by the SQL statement (or –1 if the database cannot provide that information).

If we need to insert a lot of records, or if we want to avoid converting values to strings (and escaping them correctly), we can use `prepare()` to specify a query that contains placeholders and then bind the values we want to insert. Qt supports both the Oracle-style and the ODBC-style syntax for placeholders for all databases, using native support where it is available and simulating it otherwise. Here's an example that uses the Oracle-style syntax with named placeholders:

```
QSqlQuery query(db);
query.prepare("INSERT INTO cd (id, artistid, title, year) "
              "VALUES (:id, :artistid, :title, :year)");
query.bindValue(":id", 203);
query.bindValue(":artistid", 102);
query.bindValue(":title", QString("Living in America"));
query.bindValue(":year", 2002);
query.exec();
```

Here's the same example using ODBC-style positional placeholders:

```
QSqlQuery query(db);
query.prepare("INSERT INTO cd (id, artistid, title, year) "
              "VALUES (?, ?, ?, ?)");
query.addBindValue(203);
query.addBindValue(102);
query.addBindValue(QString("Living in America"));
query.addBindValue(2002);
query.exec();
```

After the call to prepare(), we can call bindValue() or addBindValue() to bind new values, then call exec() again to execute the query with the new values.

Placeholders are often used to specify binary data or strings that contain non-ASCII or non-Latin-1 characters. Behind the scenes, Qt uses Unicode with those databases that support Unicode, and for those that don't, Qt transparently converts strings to the appropriate encoding.

Qt supports SQL transactions on databases where they are available. To start a transaction, we call transaction() on the QSqlDatabase object that represents the database connection. To terminate the transaction, we call either commit() or rollback(). For example, here's how we would look up a foreign key and execute an INSERT statement inside a transaction:

```
QSqlDatabase::database()->transaction();
QSqlQuery query;
query.exec("SELECT id FROM artist WHERE name = 'Gluecifer'");
if (query.next()) {
    int artistId = query.value(0).toInt();
    query.exec("INSERT INTO cd (id, artistid, title, year) "
               "VALUES (201, " + QString::number(artistId)
               + ", 'Riding the Tiger', 1997)");
}
QSqlDatabase::database()->commit();
```

The QSqlDatabase::database() function returns a pointer to the QSqlDatabase object we created in createConnection(). If a transaction cannot be started, QSqlDatabase::transaction() returns false.

Some databases don't support transactions. For those, the transaction(), commit(), and rollback() functions do nothing. We can test whether a database supports transactions using hasFeature() on the QSqlDriver associated with the database:

```
QSqlDriver *driver = QSqlDatabase::database()->driver();
if (driver->hasFeature(QSqlDriver::Transactions))
    ...
```

In the examples so far, we have assumed that the application is using a single database connection. If we want to use multiple connections, we can pass a name as second argument to addDatabase(). For example:

```
QSqlDatabase *db = QSqlDatabase::addDatabase("QPSQL7", "OTHER");
db->setHostName("saturn.mcmanamy.edu");
db->setDatabaseName("starsdb");
db->setUserName("gilbert");
db->setPassword("ixtapa6");
```

We can then retrieve a pointer to the QSqlDatabase object by passing the name to QSqlDatabase::database():

```
QSqlDatabase *db = QSqlDatabase::database("OTHER");
```

To execute queries using the other connection, we pass the QSqlDatabase object to the QSqlQuery constructor:

```
QSqlQuery query(db);
query.exec("SELECT id FROM artist WHERE name = 'Mando Diao'");
```

Multiple connections are useful if we want to perform more than one transaction at a time, since each connection can only handle a single active transaction. When we use multiple database connections, we can still have one nameless connection, and QSqlQuery will use that connection if none is specified.

In addition to QSqlQuery, Qt provides the QSqlCursor class, a higher-level class that inherits QSqlQuery and extends it with convenience functions so that we can avoid typing raw SQL for performing the most common SQL operations: SELECT, INSERT, UPDATE, and DELETE. QSqlCursor is also the class that ties a QDataTable to a database. We will cover QSqlCursor here, and in the next section we will see how to use QDataTable, a database-aware QTable subclass.

Here's an example that uses QSqlCursor to perform a SELECT:

```
QSqlCursor cursor("cd");
cursor.select("year >= 1998");
```

An equivalent QSqlQuery would be

```
QSqlQuery query("SELECT id, artistid, title, year FROM cd "
                "WHERE year >= 1998");
```

Navigating through the result set is the same as for QSqlQuery, except that we can pass field names to value() instead of field numbers:

```
while (cursor.next()) {
    QString title = cursor.value("title").toString();
    int year = cursor.value("year").toInt();
    cerr << title.ascii() << ": " << year << endl;
}
```

To insert a record into a table, we must first call primeInsert(), which returns a pointer to a new QSqlRecord. Then we call setValue() for each of the fields in the QSqlRecord that we want to set, and we call insert() to insert the QSqlRecord's data into the database. For example:

```
QSqlCursor cursor("cd");
QSqlRecord *buffer = cursor.primeInsert();
buffer->setValue("id", 113);
buffer->setValue("artistid", 224);
buffer->setValue("title", "Shanghai My Heart");
buffer->setValue("year", 2003);
cursor.insert();
```

To update a record, we must first position the QSqlCursor on the record we want to modify (for example, using select() and next()). Then we call primeUpdate() to get a pointer to a QSqlRecord that contains a copy of the record's data. We can then use setValue() to set the fields we want to change, and call update() to write these changes back to the database. For example:

```
QSqlCursor cursor("cd");
cursor.select("id = 125");
```

```
if (cursor.next()) {
    QSqlRecord *buffer = cursor.primeUpdate();
    buffer->setValue("title", "Melody A.M.");
    buffer->setValue("year", buffer->value("year").toInt() + 1);
    cursor.update();
}
```

Deleting a record is similar to updating, but easier:

```
QSqlCursor cursor("cd");
cursor.select("id = 128");
if (cursor.next()) {
    cursor.primeDelete();
    cursor.del();
}
```

The QSqlQuery and QSqlCursor classes provide an interface between Qt and a SQL database. In the next two sections, we will see how to use them from within a GUI application to allow the user to view and interact with the data stored in a database.

## Presenting Data in Tabular Form

The QDataTable class is a database-aware QTable widget that supports browsing and editing. It interacts with a database through a QSqlCursor. Here, we will review two dialogs that use QDataTable. Together with the QSqlForm-based dialog presented in the next section, these forms constitute the CD Collection application.

The application uses three tables, defined as follows:

```
CREATE TABLE artist (
    id INTEGER PRIMARY KEY,
    name VARCHAR(40) NOT NULL,
    country VARCHAR(40));

CREATE TABLE cd (
    id INTEGER PRIMARY KEY,
    artistid INTEGER NOT NULL,
    title VARCHAR(40) NOT NULL,
    year INTEGER NOT NULL,
    FOREIGN KEY (artistid) REFERENCES artist);

CREATE TABLE track (
    id INTEGER PRIMARY KEY,
    cdid INTEGER NOT NULL,
    number INTEGER NOT NULL,
    title VARCHAR(40) NOT NULL,
    duration INTEGER NOT NULL,
    FOREIGN KEY (cdid) REFERENCES cd);
```

Some databases don't support foreign keys. For those, we must remove the FOREIGN KEY clauses. The example will still work, but the database will not enforce referential integrity.

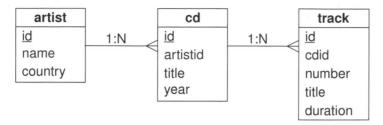

**Figure 12.1.** The CD Collection application's tables

The first class that we will write is a dialog that allows the user to edit a list of artists. The user can insert, update, or delete artists using the QDataTable's context menu. The changes are applied to the database when the user clicks Update.

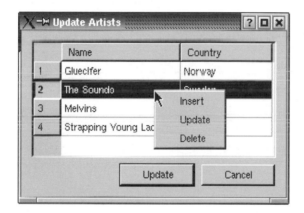

**Figure 12.2.** The ArtistForm dialog

Here's the class definition for the dialog:

```cpp
class ArtistForm : public QDialog
{
    Q_OBJECT
public:
    ArtistForm(QWidget *parent = 0, const char *name = 0);

protected slots:
    void accept();
    void reject();

private slots:
    void primeInsertArtist(QSqlRecord *buffer);
    void beforeInsertArtist(QSqlRecord *buffer);
    void beforeDeleteArtist(QSqlRecord *buffer);

private:
    QSqlDatabase *db;
    QDataTable *artistTable;
    QPushButton *updateButton;
```

```
        QPushButton *cancelButton;
    };
```

The `accept()` and `reject()` slots are reimplemented from `QDialog`.

```
    ArtistForm::ArtistForm(QWidget *parent, const char *name)
        : QDialog(parent, name)
    {
        setCaption(tr("Update Artists"));

        db = QSqlDatabase::database("ARTIST");
        db->transaction();

        QSqlCursor *artistCursor = new QSqlCursor("artist", true, db);
        artistTable = new QDataTable(artistCursor, false, this);
        artistTable->addColumn("name", tr("Name"));
        artistTable->addColumn("country", tr("Country"));
        artistTable->setAutoDelete(true);
        artistTable->setConfirmDelete(true);
        artistTable->setSorting(true);
        artistTable->refresh();

        updateButton = new QPushButton(tr("Update"), this);
        updateButton->setDefault(true);
        cancelButton = new QPushButton(tr("Cancel"), this);
```

In the `ArtistForm` constructor, we start a transaction using the "ARTIST" database connection. Then we create a `QSqlCursor` on the database's `artist` table, and a `QDataTable` to display it.

The second argument to the `QSqlCursor` constructor is an "auto-populate" flag. By passing `true`, we tell `QSqlCursor` to load information about every field in the table and to operate on all the fields.

The `QDataTable` constructor's second argument is also an auto-populate flag. If `true`, the `QDataTable` automatically creates columns for each field in the `QSqlCursor`'s result set. We pass `false` and call `addColumn()` to provide two columns corresponding to the result set's `name` and `country` fields.

We pass ownership of the `QSqlCursor` to the `QDataTable` by calling `setAutoDelete()`, so we don't need to delete it ourselves. We call `setConfirmDelete()` to make the `QDataTable` pop up a message box asking the user to confirm deletions. We call `setSorting(true)` to allow the user to click on the column headers to sort the table according to a certain column. Finally, we call `refresh()` to populate the `QDataTable` with data from the database.

We also create an Update and a Cancel button.

```
        connect(artistTable, SIGNAL(beforeDelete(QSqlRecord *)),
                this, SLOT(beforeDeleteArtist(QSqlRecord *)));
        connect(artistTable, SIGNAL(primeInsert(QSqlRecord *)),
                this, SLOT(primeInsertArtist(QSqlRecord *)));
        connect(artistTable, SIGNAL(beforeInsert(QSqlRecord *)),
                this, SLOT(beforeInsertArtist(QSqlRecord *)));
        connect(updateButton, SIGNAL(clicked()),
                this, SLOT(accept()));
```

```
connect(cancelButton, SIGNAL(clicked()),
        this, SLOT(reject())));
```

We connect three of the QDataTable's signals to three private slots. We connect the Update button to accept() and the Cancel button to reject().

```
QHBoxLayout *buttonLayout = new QHBoxLayout;
buttonLayout->addStretch(1);
buttonLayout->addWidget(updateButton);
buttonLayout->addWidget(cancelButton);

QVBoxLayout *mainLayout - new QVBoxLayout(this);
mainLayout->setMargin(11);
mainLayout->setSpacing(6);
mainLayout->addWidget(artistTable);
mainLayout->addLayout(buttonLayout);
}
```

Finally, we put the QPushButtons into a horizontal layout, and we put the QDataTable and the horizontal layout into a vertical layout.

```
void ArtistForm::accept()
{
    db->commit();
    QDialog::accept();
}
```

If the user clicks Update, we commit the transaction and call the base class's accept() function.

```
void ArtistForm::reject()
{
    db->rollback();
    QDialog::reject();
}
```

If the user clicks Cancel, we roll back the transaction and call the base class's reject() function.

```
void ArtistForm::beforeDeleteArtist(QSqlRecord *buffer)
{
    QSqlQuery query(db);
    query.exec("DELETE FROM track WHERE track.id IN "
               "(SELECT track.id FROM track, cd "
               "WHERE track.cdid = cd.id AND cd.artistid = "
               + buffer->value("id").toString() + ")");
    query.exec("DELETE FROM cd WHERE artistid = "
               + buffer->value("id").toString());
}
```

The beforeDeleteArtist() slot is connected to the QDataTable's beforeDelete() signal, which is emitted just before a record is deleted. Here, we perform a cascading delete by executing two queries: one to delete all the tracks from CDs by the artist and one to delete all the CDs by the artist. Performing these deletions does not risk relational integrity, because they are all done within the context of the transaction that began in the form's constructor.

Another approach would have been to prevent the user from deleting artists that are referred to by the cd table. To achieve this, we would have to reimplement QDataTable::contextMenuEvent() so that we could handle the deletion ourselves. A crude alternative that will work if the database has been set up to enforce relational integrity is to simply attempt the deletion and leave it to the database to prevent it.

```
void ArtistForm::primeInsertArtist(QSqlRecord *buffer)
{
    buffer->setValue("country", "USA");
}
```

The primeInsertArtist() slot is connected to the QDataTable's primeInsert() signal, which is emitted just before the user starts editing a new record. We use it to set the default value of the new record's country field to "USA", the ideal default for a U.S.-centric application.

This is one way of setting default values for fields. Another way is to subclass QSqlCursor and reimplement primeInsert(), which makes sense if we will use the same QSqlCursor many times in the same application and want to ensure consistent behavior. A third way is to do it at the database level, using DEFAULT clauses in the CREATE TABLE statements.

```
void ArtistForm::beforeInsertArtist(QSqlRecord *buffer)
{
    buffer->setValue("id", generateId("artist", db));
}
```

The beforeInsertArtist() slot is connected to the QDataTable's beforeInsert() signal, which is emitted when the user has finished editing a new record and presses Enter to save it. We set the value of the id field to a generated value. We rely on a function called generateId() to produce a unique primary key.

Since we will need generateId() a few times, we define it inline in a header file and include it each time we need it. Here's a quick (and inefficient) way of implementing it:

```
inline int generateId(const QString &table, QSqlDatabase *db)
{
    QSqlQuery query(db);
    query.exec("SELECT max(id) FROM " + table);
    query.next();
    return query.value(0).toInt() + 1;
}
```

The generateId() function can only be guaranteed to work correctly if it is executed within the context of the same transaction as the corresponding INSERT statement.

Some databases support auto-generated fields. For these, we simply need to tell the database to auto-generate the id field and call setGenerated("id", false) on the QSqlCursor to tell it *not* to generate the value of the id field.

We will now review another dialog that uses QDataTable. For this dialog, we will implement a master–detail view. The master view is a list of CDs. The detail view is a list of tracks for the current CD. This dialog is the main window of the CD Collection application.

This time, we provide Add, Edit, and Delete buttons to allow the user to modify the CD list, rather than relying on a context menu. When the user clicks Add or Edit, a CdForm dialog pops up. (CdForm is covered in the next section.)

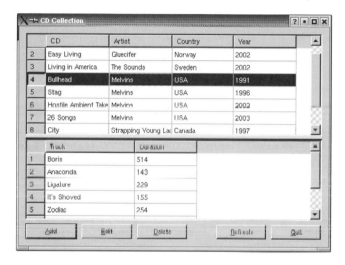

**Figure 12.3.** The MainForm dialog

Another difference between this example and the previous one is that we must resolve a foreign key, so we can show the artist's name and country rather than the artist's ID. To accomplish this, we must use QSqlSelectCursor, a subclass of QSqlCursor that supports arbitrary SELECT statements, in this case a join.

First, the class definition:

```
class MainForm : public QDialog
{
    Q_OBJECT
public:
    MainForm(QWidget *parent = 0, const char *name = 0);

private slots:
    void addCd();
    void editCd();
    void deleteCd();
    void currentCdChanged(QSqlRecord *record);

private:
    QSplitter *splitter;
    QDataTable *cdTable;
    QDataTable *trackTable;
    QPushButton *addButton;
    ...
```

```
        QPushButton *quitButton;
};
```

The `MainForm` class inherits from `QDialog`.

```
MainForm::MainForm(QWidget *parent, const char *name)
    : QDialog(parent, name)
{
    setCaption(tr("CD Collection"));

    splitter = new QSplitter(Vertical, this);

    QSqlSelectCursor *cdCursor = new QSqlSelectCursor(
                    "SELECT cd.id, title, name, country, year "
                    "FROM cd, artist WHERE cd.artistid = artist.id");
    if (!cdCursor->isActive()) {
        QMessageBox::critical(this, tr("CD Collection"),
                tr("The database has not been created.\n"
                "Run the cdtables example to create a sample "
                "database, then copy cdcollection.dat into "
                "this directory and restart this application."));
        qApp->quit();
    }

    cdTable = new QDataTable(cdCursor, false, splitter);
    cdTable->addColumn("title", tr("CD"));
    cdTable->addColumn("name", tr("Artist"));
    cdTable->addColumn("country", tr("Country"));
    cdTable->addColumn("year", tr("Year"));
    cdTable->setAutoDelete(true);
    cdTable->refresh();
```

In the constructor, we create a read-only `QDataTable` for the `cd` table and its associated cursor. The cursor is based on a query that joins the `cd` and the `artist` tables. The `QDataTable` is read-only because it operates on a `QSqlSelectCursor`. Read-only tables don't provide a context menu.

If the cursor query fails, we pop up a message box indicating that something is wrong and terminate the application.

```
        QSqlCursor *trackCursor = new QSqlCursor("track");
        trackCursor->setMode(QSqlCursor::ReadOnly);
        trackTable = new QDataTable(trackCursor, false, splitter);
        trackTable->setSort(trackCursor->index("number"));
        trackTable->addColumn("title", tr("Track"));
        trackTable->addColumn("duration", tr("Duration"));
```

We create the second `QDataTable` and its cursor. We make the table read-only by calling `setMode(QSqlCursor::ReadOnly)` on the cursor, and call `setSort()` to sort the tracks by track number.

```
        addButton = new QPushButton(tr("&Add"), this);
        editButton = new QPushButton(tr("&Edit"), this);
        deleteButton = new QPushButton(tr("&Delete"), this);
        refreshButton = new QPushButton(tr("&Refresh"), this);
        quitButton = new QPushButton(tr("&Quit"), this);
```

```
        connect(addButton, SIGNAL(clicked()),
                this, SLOT(addCd()));
        ...
        connect(quitButton, SIGNAL(clicked()),
                this, SLOT(close()));
        connect(cdTable, SIGNAL(currentChanged(QSqlRecord *)),
                this, SLOT(currentCdChanged(QSqlRecord *)));
        connect(cdTable,
                SIGNAL(doubleClicked(int, int, int, const QPoint &)),
                this, SLOT(editCd()));
        ...
    }
```

We set up the rest of the user interface and create the signal–slot connections necessary to produce the desired behavior.

```
    void MainForm::addCd()
    {
        CdForm form(this);
        if (form.exec()) {
            cdTable->refresh();
            trackTable->refresh();
        }
    }
```

When the user clicks Add, we pop up a modal `CdForm` dialog, and if the user clicks Update on it, we refresh the QDataTables.

```
    void MainForm::editCd()
    {
        QSqlRecord *record = cdTable->currentRecord();
        if (record) {
            CdForm form(record->value("id").toInt(), this);
            if (form.exec()) {
                cdTable->refresh();
                trackTable->refresh();
            }
        }
    }
```

When the user clicks Edit, we pop up a modal `CdForm` dialog, with the current CD's ID as argument to the `CdForm` constructor. This will cause the dialog to start up with its fields populated with the current CD's data.

When we parameterize a form with an ID as we have done here, it is possible that the ID will not be valid by the time the form appears. For example, the user could click Edit a fraction of a second before another user deletes the CD. What we could have done in `CdForm` is to execute a SELECT on the ID that is passed in immediately after the `transaction()` call and only proceed if the ID still exists. Here, we simply rely on the database to report an error if an attempt to use an invalid ID is made.

```
    void MainForm::deleteCd()
    {
        QSqlRecord *record = cdTable->currentRecord();
```

```
        if (record) {
            QSqlQuery query;
            query.exec("DELETE FROM track WHERE cdid = "
                       + record->value("id").toString());
            query.exec("DELETE FROM cd WHERE id = "
                       + record->value("id").toString());
            cdTable->refresh();
            trackTable->refresh();
        }
    }
```

When the user clicks Delete, we remove all the tracks for the current CD from the `track` table and then the current CD from the `cd` table. Then we update both tables.

```
    void MainForm::currentCdChanged(QSqlRecord *record)
    {
        trackTable->setFilter("cdid = "
                              + record->value("id").toString());
        trackTable->refresh();
    }
```

The `currentCdChanged()` slot is connected to the `cdTable`'s `currentChanged()` signal, which is emitted when the user modifies the current CD or when the user makes another CD current. Whenever the current CD changes, we call `setFilter()` on the `track` table and refresh it to make it display the tracks related to the current CD, and we call `refresh()` to force the table to repopulate itself with the relevant data.

This is all the code that is needed to implement `MainForm`. One possible improvement would be to show the duration of each track split into minutes and seconds (for example, "02:35") rather than just as seconds ("155"). We could accomplish this by subclassing `QSqlCursor` and reimplementing the `calculate-Field()` function to transform the `duration` field into a `QString` with the desired format:

```
    QVariant TrackSqlCursor::calculateField(const QString &name)
    {
        if (name == "duration") {
            int duration = value("duration").toInt();
            return QString("%1:%2").arg(duration / 60, 2)
                                   .arg(duration % 60, 2);
        }
        return QVariant();
    }
```

We would also need to call `setCalculated("duration", true)` on the cursor to tell `QDataTable` to use the value returned by `calculateField()` for the `duration` field, instead of simply using `value()`.

# Creating Data-Aware Forms

Qt takes an innovative approach to database interaction with forms. Instead of having a separate database-enabled version of every built-in widget, Qt is able to make any widget data-aware, using `QSqlForm` and `QSqlPropertyMap` to relate database fields to widgets. Any built-in or custom widget can be made data-aware using these classes.

`QSqlForm` is a `QObject` subclass that makes it easy to create forms to browse or edit individual records in a database. The common pattern of usage is this:

1. Create the editor widgets (`QLineEdits`, `QComboBoxes`, `QSpinBoxes`, etc.) for the record's fields.
2. Create a `QSqlCursor` and move it to the record to edit.
3. Create a `QSqlForm` object.
4. Tell the `QSqlForm` which editor widget is bound to which database field.
5. Call the `QSqlForm::readFields()` function to populate the editor widgets with the data from the current record.
6. Show the dialog.
7. Call the `QSqlForm::writeFields()` function to copy the updated values back into the database.

To illustrate this, we will look at the code for the `CdForm` dialog. This dialog allows the user to create or edit a CD record. The user can specify the CD's title, artist, and release year, and the title and duration of each track.

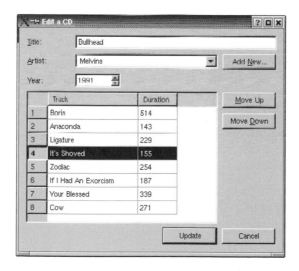

**Figure 12.4.** The `CdForm` dialog

Let's start with the class definition:

```
class CdForm : public QDialog
{
```

```
    Q_OBJECT
public:
    CdForm(QWidget *parent = 0, const char *name = 0);
    CdForm(int id, QWidget *parent = 0, const char *name = 0);
    ~CdForm();

protected slots:
    void accept();
    void reject();

private slots:
    void addNewArtist();
    void moveTrackUp();
    void moveTrackDown();
    void beforeInsertTrack(QSqlRecord *buffer);
    void beforeDeleteTrack(QSqlRecord *buffer);

private:
    void init();
    void createNewRecord();
    void swapTracks(int trackA, int trackB);

    QLabel *titleLabel;
    QLabel *artistLabel;
    ...
    QDataTable *trackTable;
    QSqlForm *sqlForm;
    QSqlCursor *cdCursor;
    QSqlCursor *trackCursor;
    int cdId;
    bool newCd;
};
```

We have declared two constructors: one for inserting a new CD into the
database, the other for updating an existing CD. The `accept()` and `reject()`
slots are reimplemented from `QDialog`.

```
CdForm::CdForm(QWidget *parent, const char *name)
    : QDialog(parent, name)
{
    setCaption(tr("Add a CD"));
    cdId = -1;
    init();
}
```

The first constructor sets the dialog's caption to "Add a CD" and calls the
private `init()` function to do the rest.

```
CdForm::CdForm(int id, QWidget *parent, const char *name)
    : QDialog(parent, name)
{
    setCaption(tr("Edit a CD"));
    cdId = id;
    init();
}
```

The second constructor sets the caption to "Edit a CD" and also calls `init()`.

```
void CdForm::init()
{
    db = QSqlDatabase::database("CD");
    db->transaction();
    if (cdId == -1)
        createNewRecord();
```

In `init()`, we start a transaction using the "CD" database connection. We need to use different connections in `CdForm` and `ArtistForm`, because we can have both forms open at the same time, and we don't want one form to roll back the transaction initiated by the other form.

If we have no CD to operate on, we call the private function `createNewRecord()` to insert a blank one into the database. This will allow us to use the CD ID as a foreign key in the tracks' `QDataTable`. If the user clicks Cancel, we roll back the transaction and the blank record will disappear.

For this dialog, we use a different connection to the database than in the `ArtistForm`. This is because we can only have one active transaction per connection, and we can end up in a situation where we need two, for example, if the user clicks Add New to pop up the `ArtistForm`.

```
    titleLabel = new QLabel(tr("&Title:"), this);
    artistLabel = new QLabel(tr("&Artist:"), this);
    yearLabel = new QLabel(tr("&Year:"), this);
    titleLineEdit = new QLineEdit(this);
    yearSpinBox = new QSpinBox(this);
    yearSpinBox->setRange(1900, 2100);
    yearSpinBox->setValue(QDate::currentDate().year());
    artistComboBox = new ArtistComboBox(db, this);
    artistButton = new QPushButton(tr("Add &New..."), this);
    ...
    cancelButton = new QPushButton(tr("Cancel"), this);
```

We create the labels, the line edit, the spin box, the combobox, and the buttons that form the user interface. The combobox is of type `ArtistComboBox`, which we will cover later on.

```
    trackCursor = new QSqlCursor("track", true, db);
    trackTable = new QDataTable(trackCursor, false, this);
    trackTable->setFilter("cdid = " + QString::number(cdId));
    trackTable->setSort(trackCursor->index("number"));
    trackTable->addColumn("title", tr("Track"));
    trackTable->addColumn("duration", tr("Duration"));
    trackTable->refresh();
```

We set up the `QDataTable` that allows the user to browse and edit the tracks on the current CD. This is very similar to what we did in the previous section with the `ArtistForm` class.

```
    cdCursor = new QSqlCursor("cd", true, db);
    cdCursor->select("id = " + QString::number(cdId));
    cdCursor->next();
```

We set up the `QSqlCursor` associated with the `QSqlForm` and make it point to the record with the correct ID.

```
QSqlPropertyMap *propertyMap = new QSqlPropertyMap;
propertyMap->insert("ArtistComboBox", "artistId");
sqlForm = new QSqlForm(this);
sqlForm->installPropertyMap(propertyMap);
sqlForm->setRecord(cdCursor->primeUpdate());
sqlForm->insert(titleLineEdit, "title");
sqlForm->insert(artistComboBox, "artistid");
sqlForm->insert(yearSpinBox, "year");
sqlForm->readFields();
```

We create a QSqlPropertyMap. The QSqlPropertyMap class tells QSqlForm which
Qt property holds the value of a certain type of editor widget. By default,
QSqlForm already knows that a QLineEdit stores its value in the text property
and that a QSpinBox stores its value in the value property. But it doesn't know
anything about custom widgets such as ArtistComboBox. By inserting the pair
("ArtistComboBox", "artistId") in the property map and by calling install-
PropertyMap() on the QSqlForm, we tell QSqlForm to use the artistId property for
widgets of type ArtistComboBox.

The QSqlForm object also needs a buffer to operate on, which we obtain by
calling primeUpdate() on the QSqlCursor, and it needs to know which editor
widget corresponds to which database field. At the end, we call readFields()
to read the data from the database into the editor widgets.

```
    connect(artistButton, SIGNAL(clicked()),
            this, SLOT(addNewArtist()));
    connect(moveUpButton, SIGNAL(clicked()),
            this, SLOT(moveTrackUp()));
    connect(moveDownButton, SIGNAL(clicked()),
            this, SLOT(moveTrackDown()));
    connect(updateButton, SIGNAL(clicked()),
            this, SLOT(accept()));
    connect(cancelButton, SIGNAL(clicked()),
            this, SLOT(reject()));
    connect(trackTable, SIGNAL(beforeInsert(QSqlRecord *)),
            this, SLOT(beforeInsertTrack(QSqlRecord *)));
    ...
}
```

We connect the buttons' clicked() signals and the QDataTable's beforeInsert()
signal to the private slots that are described next.

```
void CdForm::accept()
{
    sqlForm->writeFields();
    cdCursor->update();
    db->commit();
    QDialog::accept();
}
```

If the user clicks Update, we write the data into the QSqlCursor's edit buffer,
we call update() to perform an UPDATE on the database, we call commit() to
really write the record into the database, and we call the base class's accept()
implementation to close the form.

```
void CdForm::reject()
{
    db->rollback();
    QDialog::reject();
}
```

If the user clicks Cancel, we roll back, leaving the database unchanged, and close the form.

```
void CdForm::addNewArtist()
{
    ArtistForm form(this);
    if (form.exec()) {
        artistComboBox->refresh();
        updateButton->setEnabled(artistComboBox->count() > 0);
    }
}
```

If the user clicks Add New, we pop up a modal ArtistForm dialog. The dialog allows the user to add new artists, and also to edit and delete existing artists. If the user clicks Update, we call ArtistComboBox::refresh() to ensure that its list of artists is up to date.

We enable or disable the Update button depending on whether there are any artists, since we don't want to allow a new CD to be created without an artist name.

```
void CdForm::beforeInsertTrack(QSqlRecord *buffer)
{
    buffer->setValue("id", generateId("track", db));
    buffer->setValue("number", trackCursor->size() + 1);
    buffer->setValue("cdid", cdId);
}
```

The beforeInsertTrack() slot is connected to the QDataTable's beforeInsert() signal. We set the record's id, number, and cdid fields.

```
void CdForm::beforeDeleteTrack(QSqlRecord *buffer)
{
    QSqlQuery query(db);
    query.exec("UPDATE track SET number = number - 1 "
               "WHERE track.number > "
               + buffer->value("number").toString());
}
```

The beforeDeleteTrack() slot is connected to the QDataTable's beforeDelete() signal. We renumber all the tracks that have a number higher than the track we delete to ensure that the track numbers remain consecutive. For example, if the CD contains six tracks and the user deletes track 4, then track 5 becomes track 4 and track 6 becomes track 5.

There are four functions that we have not covered: moveTrackUp(), moveTrackDown(), swapTracks(), and createNewRecord(). These are necessary to make the application usable, but their implementations do not show any new techniques, so we will not review them here. Their source code is on the CD.

Now that we have seen all the forms in the CD Collection application, we are ready to review the custom `ArtistComboBox`. As usual, we start with the class definition:

```
class ArtistComboBox : public QComboBox
{
    Q_OBJECT
    Q_PROPERTY(int artistId READ artistId WRITE setArtistId)
public:
    ArtistComboBox(QSqlDatabase *database, QWidget *parent = 0,
                   const char *name = 0);

    void refresh();
    int artistId() const;
    void setArtistId(int id);

private:
    void populate();

    QSqlDatabase *db;
    QMap<int, int> idFromIndex;
    QMap<int, int> indexFromId;
};
```

The `ArtistComboBox` class inherits `QComboBox` and adds an `artistId` property and a few functions.

In the private section, we declare a `QMap<int, int>` that associates artist IDs with combobox indexes and a `QMap<int, int>` that associates combobox indexes with artist IDs.

```
ArtistComboBox::ArtistComboBox(QSqlDatabase *database,
                                QWidget *parent, const char *name)
    : QComboBox(parent, name)
{
    db = database;
    populate();
}
```

In the constructor, we call the private function `populate()` to fill the combobox with the names and IDs in the `artist` table.

```
void ArtistComboBox::refresh()
{
    int oldArtistId = artistId();
    clear();
    idFromIndex.clear();
    indexFromId.clear();
    populate();
    setArtistId(oldArtistId);
}
```

In the `refresh()` function, we repopulate the combobox with the latest data from the database. We are also careful to ensure that the artist who was selected before the refresh is still selected afterward, unless that artist has have been deleted from the database.

```
void ArtistComboBox::populate()
{
    QSqlCursor cursor("artist", true, db);
    cursor.select(cursor.index("name"));

    int index = 0;
    while (cursor.next()) {
        int id = cursor.value("id").toInt();
        insertItem(cursor.value("name").toString(), index);
        idFromIndex[index] = id;
        indexFromId[id] = index;
        ++index;
    }
}
```

In the private function populate(), we iterate through all the artists and call
QComboBox::insertItem() to add them to the combobox. We also update the
idFromIndex and the indexFromId maps.

```
int ArtistComboBox::artistId() const
{
    return idFromIndex[currentItem()];
}
```

The artistId() function returns the ID for the current artist.

```
void ArtistComboBox::setArtistId(int id)
{
    if (indexFromId.contains(id))
        setCurrentItem(indexFromId[id]);
}
```

The setArtistId() function sets the current artist based on an artist ID.

In applications that often need comboboxes that show foreign keys, it would
probably be worthwhile creating a generic DatabaseComboBox class whose
constructor would allow us to specify the table name, the field to display, and
the field to use for IDs.

Let's finish the CD Collection application by implementing its createConnec-
tions() and main() functions.

```
inline bool createOneConnection(const QString &name)
{
    QSqlDatabase *db;
    if (name.isEmpty())
        db = QSqlDatabase::addDatabase("QSQLITEX");
    else
        db = QSqlDatabase::addDatabase("QSQLITEX", name);
    db->setDatabaseName("cdcollection.dat");
    if (!db->open()) {
        db->lastError().showMessage();
        return false;
    }
    return true;
}
```

```
inline bool createConnections()
{
    return createOneConnection("")
           && createOneConnection("ARTIST")
           && createOneConnection("CD");
}
```

In `createConnections()`, we create three identical connections to the CD database. We don't give any name to the first one; it is used by default when we don't specify a database. The other ones are called "ARTIST" and "CD"; they are used by `ArtistForm` and `CdForm`.

```
int main(int argc, char *argv[])
{
    QApplication app(argc, argv);
    if (!createConnections())
        return 1;

    MainForm mainForm;
    app.setMainWidget(&mainForm);
    mainForm.resize(480, 320);
    mainForm.show();
    return app.exec();
}
```

The `main()` function is the same as most other Qt `main()` functions, except for the addition of a `createConnections()` call.

As we mentioned at the end of the previous section, one possible improvement would be to display the duration of each track as minutes and seconds rather than just seconds. Besides reimplementing `QSqlCursor::calculateField()`, this would also involve subclassing `QSqlEditorFactory` to provide a custom editor (which we could base on `QTimeEdit`) and using a `QSqlPropertyMap` to tell `QDataTable` how to get the value back from the editor. See the documentation for `QDataTable`'s `installEditorFactory()` and `installPropertyMap()` functions for more information.

Another improvement would be to store an image of each CD's cover in the database and to show it in the `CdForm`. To implement this, we could store the image data as a `BLOB` in the database, retrieve it as a `QByteArray`, and pass the `QByteArray` to the `QImage` constructor.

# 13

# Networking

Qt provides the QFtp and QHttp classes for working with FTP and HTTP. These protocols are easy to use for downloading and uploading files and, in the case of HTTP, for sending requests to web servers and retrieving the results.

Qt's QFtp and QHttp classes are built on the lower-level QSocket class, which provides a TCP socket. TCP operates in terms of data streams transmitted between network nodes. QSocket is in turn implemented on top of QSocketDevice, a thin wrapper around the platform-specific network APIs. The QSocketDevice class supports both TCP and UDP.

In this chapter, we will learn how to use the four classes mentioned above and other closely related classes, like QServerSocket and QSocketNotifier. We will also cover uploading and downloading files and how to use a web form programmatically. We will use TCP in a server application and in a corresponding client application. Similarly, we will use UDP in a sender application and in a corresponding receiver application. The coverage of QFtp and QHttp should be accessible to anyone, but the coverage of QSocket and especially QSocketDevice does assume some networking experience.

## Using QFtp

The QFtp class implements the client side of the FTP protocol in Qt. It provides various functions to perform the most common FTP operations, including get(), put(), remove(), and mkdir(), and provides a means of executing arbitrary FTP commands.

The QFtp class works asynchronously. When we call a function like get() or put(), it returns immediately and the data transfer occurs when control passes back to Qt's event loop. This ensures that the user interface remains responsive while FTP commands are executed.

We will start with an example that shows how to retrieve a single file using get(). The example assumes that the application's MainWindow class needs to retrieve a price list from an FTP site.

```cpp
class MainWindow : public QMainWindow
{
    Q_OBJECT
public:
    MainWindow(QWidget *parent = 0, const char *name = 0);

    void getPriceList();
    ...

private slots:
    void ftpDone(bool error);

private:
    QFtp ftp;
    QFile file;
    ...
};
```

The class has a public function, getPriceList(), that retrieves the price list file, and a private slot, ftpDone(bool), that is called when the file transfer is completed. The class also has two private variables: The ftp variable, of type QFtp, encapsulates the connection to an FTP server; the file variable is used for writing the downloaded file to disk.

```cpp
MainWindow::MainWindow(QWidget *parent, const char *name)
    : QMainWindow(parent, name)
{
    ...
    connect(&ftp, SIGNAL(done(bool)), this, SLOT(ftpDone(bool)));
}
```

In the constructor, we connect the QFtp object's done(bool) signal to our ftp-Done(bool) private slot. QFtp emits the done(bool) signal when it has finished processing all requests. The bool parameter indicates whether an error occurred or not.

```cpp
void MainWindow::getPriceList()
{
    file.setName("price-list.csv");
    if (!file.open(IO_WriteOnly)) {
        QMessageBox::warning(this, tr("Sales Pro"),
                             tr("Cannot write file %1\n%2.")
                             .arg(file.name())
                             .arg(file.errorString()));
        return;
    }

    ftp.connectToHost("ftp.trolltech.com");
    ftp.login();
    ftp.cd("/topsecret/csv");
    ftp.get("price-list.csv", &file);
    ftp.close();
}
```

The `getPriceList()` function downloads the `ftp://ftp.trolltech.com/top-secret/csv/price-list.csv` file and saves it as `price-list.csv` in the current directory.

We start by opening the `QFile` for writing. Then we execute a sequence of five FTP commands using our `QFtp` object. The second argument to `get()` specifies the output I/O device.

The FTP commands are queued and executed in Qt's event loop. The completion of the commands is indicated by `QFtp`'s `done(bool)` signal, which we connected to `ftpDone(bool)` in the constructor.

```
void MainWindow::ftpDone(bool error)
{
    if (error)
        QMessageBox::warning(this, tr("Sales Pro"),
                             tr("Error while retrieving file with "
                                "FTP: %1.")
                             .arg(ftp.errorString()));
    file.close();
}
```

Once the FTP commands are executed, we close the file. If an error occurred, we display it in a `QMessageBox`.

`QFtp` provides these operations: `connectToHost()`, `login()`, `close()`, `list()`, `cd()`, `get()`, `put()`, `remove()`, `mkdir()`, `rmdir()`, and `rename()`. All of these functions schedule an FTP command and return an ID number that identifies the command. Arbitrary FTP commands can be executed using `rawCommand()`. For example, here's how to execute a SITE CHMOD command:

```
ftp.rawCommand("SITE CHMOD 755 fortune");
```

`QFtp` emits the `commandStarted(int)` signal when it starts executing a command, and it emits the `commandFinished(int, bool)` signal when the command is finished. The `int` parameter is the ID number that identifies a command. If we are interested in the fate of individual commands, we can store the ID numbers when we schedule the commands. Keeping track of the ID numbers allows us to provide detailed feedback to the user. For example:

```
void MainWindow::getPriceList()
{
    ...
    connectId = ftp.connectToHost("ftp.trolltech.com");
    loginId = ftp.login();
    cdId = ftp.cd("/topsecret/csv");
    getId = ftp.get("price-list.csv", &file);
    closeId = ftp.close();
}

void MainWindow::commandStarted(int id)
{
    if (id == connectId) {
        statusBar()->message(tr("Connecting..."));
```

```
        } else if (id == loginId) {
            statusBar()->message(tr("Logging in..."));
        ...
    }
```

Another way of providing feedback is to connect to QFtp's stateChanged()
signal.

In most applications, we are only interested in the fate of the whole sequence
of commands. We can then simply connect to the done(bool) signal, which is
emitted whenever the command queue becomes empty.

When an error occurs, QFtp automatically clears the command queue. This
means that if the connection or the login fails, the commands that follow in the
queue are never executed. But if we schedule new commands after the error
has occurred using the same QFtp object, these commands will be queued and
executed as if nothing had happened.

We will now review a more advanced example:

```
class Downloader : public QObject
{
    Q_OBJECT
public:
    Downloader(const QUrl &url);

signals:
    void finished();

private slots:
    void ftpDone(bool error);
    void listInfo(const QUrlInfo &urlInfo);

private:
    QFtp ftp;
    std::vector<QFile *> openedFiles;
};
```

The Downloader class downloads all the files located in an FTP directory. The
directory is specified as a QUrl passed to the class's constructor. The QUrl class
is a Qt class that provides a high-level interface for extracting the different
parts of a URL, such as the file name, path, protocol, and port.

```
Downloader::Downloader(const QUrl &url)
{
    if (url.protocol() != "ftp") {
        QMessageBox::warning(0, tr("Downloader"),
                             tr("Protocol must be 'ftp'."));
        emit finished();
        return;
    }

    int port = 21;
    if (url.hasPort())
        port = url.port();
```

```
            connect(&ftp, SIGNAL(done(bool)),
                    this, SLOT(ftpDone(bool)));
            connect(&ftp, SIGNAL(listInfo(const QUrlInfo &)),
                    this, SLOT(listInfo(const QUrlInfo &)));

            ftp.connectToHost(url.host(), port);
            ftp.login(url.user(), url.password());
            ftp.cd(url.path());
            ftp.list();
        }
```

In the constructor, we first check that the URL starts with "ftp:". Then we extract a port number. If no port is specified, we use port 21, the default port for FTP.

Next, we establish two signal–slot connections, and we schedule four FTP commands. The last FTP command, list(), retrieves the name of every file in the directory and emits a listInfo(const QUrlInfo &) signal for each name that it retrieves. This signal is connected to a slot also called listInfo(), which downloads the file associated with the URL it is given

```
        void Downloader::listInfo(const QUrlInfo &urlInfo)
        {
            if (urlInfo.isFile() && urlInfo.isReadable()) {
                QFile *file = new QFile(urlInfo.name());
                if (!file->open(IO_WriteOnly)) {
                    QMessageBox::warning(0, tr("Downloader"),
                                         tr("Error: Cannot open file "
                                            "%1:\n%2.")
                                         .arg(file->name())
                                         .arg(file->errorString()));
                    emit finished();
                    return;
                }

                ftp.get(urlInfo.name(), file);
                openedFiles.push_back(file);
            }
        }
```

The listInfo() slot's QUrlInfo parameter provides detailed information about a remote file. If the file is a normal file (not a directory) and is readable, we call get() to download it. The QFile object used for downloading is allocated using new and a pointer to it is stored in the openedFiles vector.

```
        void Downloader::ftpDone(bool error)
        {
            if (error)
                QMessageBox::warning(0, tr("Downloader"),
                                     tr("Error: %1.")
                                     .arg(ftp.errorString()));

            for (int i = 0; i < (int)openedFiles.size(); ++i)
                delete openedFiles[i];
            emit finished();
        }
```

The `ftpDone()` slot is called when all the FTP commands have finished, or if an error occurred. We delete the `QFile` objects to prevent memory leaks, and also to close each file. (The `QFile` destructor automatically closes the file if it's open.)

If there are no errors, the sequence of FTP commands and signals is as follows:

```
connectToHost(host)
login()
cd(path)
list()
    emit listInfo(file_1)
        get(file_1)
    emit listInfo(file_2)
        get(file_2)
    ...
    emit listInfo(file_N)
        get(file_N)
emit done()
```

If a network error occurs while downloading the fifth of, say, twenty files to download, the remaining files will not be downloaded. If we wanted to download as many files as possible, one solution would be to schedule the GET operations one at a time and to wait for the `done(bool)` signal before scheduling a new GET operation. In `listInfo()`, we would simply append the file name to a `QStringList`, instead of calling `get()` right away, and in `done(bool)` we would call `get()` on the next file to download in the `QStringList`. The sequence of execution would then look like this:

```
connectToHost(host)
login()
cd(path)
list()
    emit listInfo(file_1)
    emit listInfo(file_2)
    ...
    emit listInfo(file_N)
emit done()

get(file_1)
emit done()

get(file_2)
emit done()
...
get(file_N)
emit done()
```

Another solution would be to use one `QFtp` object per file. This would enable us to download the files in parallel, through separate FTP connections.

```
int main(int argc, char *argv[])
{
    QApplication app(argc, argv);
```

```
    QUrl url("ftp://ftp.example.com/");
    if (argc >= 2)
        url = argv[1];
    Downloader downloader(url);
    QObject::connect(&downloader, SIGNAL(finished()),
                     &app, SLOT(quit()));
    return app.exec();
}
```

The `main()` function completes the program. If the user specifies a URL on the command line, we use it; otherwise, we fall back on `ftp://ftp.example.com/`.

In both examples, the data retrieved using `get()` was written to a `QFile`. This doesn't have to be the case. If we wanted the data in memory, we could use a `QBuffer`, the `QIODevice` subclass that wraps a `QByteArray`. For example:

```
    QBuffer *buffer = new QBuffer(byteArray);
    buffer->open(IO_WriteOnly);
    ftp.get(urlInfo.name(), buffer);
```

We could also omit the I/O device argument to `get()`, or pass a null pointer. The `QFtp` class then emits a `readyRead()` signal every time new data is available, and the data can be read using `readBlock()` or `readAll()`.

If we want to provide the user with feedback while the data is being downloaded, we can connect `QFtp`'s `dataTransferProgress(int, int)` signal to the `setProgress(int, int)` slot in a `QProgressBar` or in a `QProgressDialog`. We would then also connect the `QProgressBar` or `QProgressDialog`'s `canceled()` signal to `QFtp`'s `abort()` slot.

## Using QHttp

The `QHttp` class implements the client side of the HTTP protocol in Qt. It provides various functions to perform the most common HTTP operations, including `get()` and `post()`, and provides a means of sending arbitrary HTTP requests. If you have read the previous section about `QFtp`, you will find that there are many similarities between `QFtp` and `QHttp`.

The `QHttp` class works asynchronously. When we call a function like `get()` or `post()`, the function returns immediately, and the data transfer occurs later, when control returns to Qt's event loop. This ensures that the application's user interface remains responsive while HTTP requests are being processed.

We will review an example that shows how to download an HTML file from Trolltech's web site from a Qt application's `MainWindow` class. We will omit the header file because it is very similar to the one we used in the previous section (p. 284), with a private slot (`httpDone(bool)`) and private variables (`http` of type `QHttp` and `file` of type `QFile`).

```
    MainWindow::MainWindow(QWidget *parent, const char *name)
        : QMainWindow(parent, name)
    {
        ...
```

```
        connect(&http, SIGNAL(done(bool)), this, SLOT(httpDone(bool)));
    }
```

In the constructor, we connect the `QHttp` object's `done(bool)` signal to the `MainWindow`'s `httpDone(bool)` slot.

```
    void MainWindow::getFile()
    {
        file.setName("aboutqt.html");
        if (!file.open(IO_WriteOnly)) {
            QMessageBox::warning(this, tr("HTTP Get"),
                                 tr("Cannot write file %1\n%2.")
                                 .arg(file.name())
                                 .arg(file.errorString()));
            return;
        }

        http.setHost("doc.trolltech.com");
        http.get("/3.2/aboutqt.html", &file);
        http.closeConnection();
    }
```

The `getFile()` function downloads the `http://doc.trolltech.com/3.2/aboutqt.html` file and saves it as `aboutqt.html` in the current directory.

We open the `QFile` for writing and schedule a sequence of three HTTP requests using our `QHttp` object. The second argument to `get()` specifies the output I/O device.

The HTTP requests are queued and executed in Qt's event loop. The completion of the commands is indicated by `QHttp`'s `done(bool)` signal, which we connected to `httpDone(bool)` in the constructor.

```
    void MainWindow::httpDone(bool error)
    {
        if (error)
            QMessageBox::warning(this, tr("HTTP Get"),
                                 tr("Error while fetching file with "
                                    "HTTP: %1.")
                                 .arg(http.errorString()));
        file.close();
    }
```

Once the HTTP requests are finished, we close the file. If an error occurred, we display the error message in a `QMessageBox`.

`QHttp` provides the following operations: `setHost()`, `get()`, `post()`, and `head()`. For example, here's how we would use `post()` to send a list of *"name = value"* pairs to a CGI script:

```
    http.setHost("www.example.com");
    http.post("/cgi/somescript.py", QCString("x=200&y=320"), &file);
```

For more control, we can use the `request()` function, which accepts an arbitrary HTTP header and data. For example:

```
QHttpRequestHeader header("POST", "/search.html");
header.setValue("Host", "www.trolltech.com");
header.setContentType("application/x-www-form-urlencoded");
http.setHost("www.trolltech.com");
http.request(header, QCString("qt-interest=on&search=opengl"));
```

`QHttp` emits the `requestStarted(int)` signal when it starts executing a request, and it emits the `requestFinished(int, bool)` signal when the request has finished. The `int` parameter is an ID number that identifies a request. If we are interested in the fate of individual requests, we can store the ID numbers when we schedule the requests. Keeping track of the ID numbers allows us to provide detailed feedback to the user.

In most applications, we only want to know whether the entire sequence of requests completed successfully or not. This is easily achieved by connecting to the `done(bool)` signal, which is emitted when the request queue becomes empty.

When an error occurs, the request queue is automatically cleared. But if we schedule new requests after the error has occurred using the same `QHttp` object, these requests will be queued and sent as usual.

Like `QFtp`, `QHttp` provides a `readyRead()` signal as well as the `readBlock()` and `readAll()` functions that we can use instead of specifying an I/O device. It also provides a `dataTransferProgress(int, int)` signal that can be connected to a `QProgressBar` or to a `QProgressDialog`'s `setProgress(int, int)` slot.

## TCP Networking with QSocket

The `QSocket` class can be used to implement TCP clients and servers. TCP is a transport protocol that forms the basis of many application-level Internet protocols, including FTP and HTTP, and that can also be used for custom protocols.

TCP is a stream-oriented protocol. For applications, the data appears to be a long stream, rather like a large flat file. The high-level protocols built on top of TCP are typically either line-oriented or block-oriented:

* Line-oriented protocols transfer data as lines of text, each terminated by a newline.
* Block-oriented protocols transfer data as binary data blocks. Each block consists of a size field followed by *size* bytes of data.

`QSocket` inherits from `QIODevice`, so it can be read from and written to using a `QDataStream` or a `QTextStream`. One notable difference when reading data from a network compared with reading from a file is that we must make sure that we have received enough data from the peer before we use the `>>` operator. Failing to do so may result in undefined behavior.

In this section, we will review the code of a client and a server that use a custom block-oriented protocol. The client is called Trip Planner and allows users to plan their next train trip. The server is called Trip Server and provides the trip information to the client. We will start by writing the Trip Planner application.

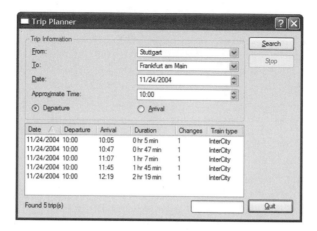

**Figure 13.1.** The Trip Planner application

The Trip Planner provides a From field, a To field, a Date field, an Approximate Time field, and two radio buttons to select whether the approximate time is that of departure or arrival. When the user clicks Search, the application sends a request to the server, which responds with a list of train trips that match the user's criteria. The list is shown in a QListView in the Trip Planner window. The very bottom of the window is occupied by a QLabel that shows the status of the last operation and a QProgressBar.

The Trip Planner's user interface was created using *Qt Designer*. Here, we will focus on the source code in the corresponding .ui.h file. Note that the following four variables were declared in *Qt Designer*'s Members tab:

```
QSocket socket;
QTimer connectionTimer;
QTimer progressBarTimer;
Q_UINT16 blockSize;
```

The socket variable of type QSocket encapsulates the TCP connection. The connectionTimer variable is used to time out a connection that lasts too long. The progressBarTimer variable is used to refresh the progress bar periodically when the application is busy. Finally, the blockSize variable is used when parsing the blocks received from the server.

```
void TripPlanner::init()
{
    connect(&socket, SIGNAL(connected()),
            this, SLOT(sendRequest()));
    connect(&socket, SIGNAL(connectionClosed()),
            this, SLOT(connectionClosedByServer()));
    connect(&socket, SIGNAL(readyRead()),
            this, SLOT(updateListView()));
```

```
    connect(&socket, SIGNAL(error(int)),
            this, SLOT(error(int)));

    connect(&connectionTimer, SIGNAL(timeout()),
            this, SLOT(connectionTimeout()));
    connect(&progressBarTimer, SIGNAL(timeout()),
            this, SLOT(advanceProgressBar()));

    QDateTime dateTime = QDateTime::currentDateTime();
    dateEdit->setDate(dateTime.date());
    timeEdit->setTime(QTime(dateTime.time().hour(), 0));
}
```

In `init()`, we connect the `QSocket`'s `connected()`, `connectionClosed()`, `ready-Read()`, and `error(int)` signals, and the two timers' `timeout()` signals, to our own slots. We also fill the Date and Approximate Time fields with default values based on the current date and time.

```
void TripPlanner::advanceProgressBar()
{
    progressBar->setProgress(progressBar->progress() + 2);
}
```

The `advanceProgressBar()` slot is connected to the `progressBarTimer`'s `timeout()` signal. We advance the progress bar by two units. In *Qt Designer*, the progress bar's `totalSteps` property was set to 0, a special value meaning that the bar should behave as a busy indicator.

```
void TripPlanner::connectToServer()
{
    listView->clear();

    socket.connectToHost("tripserver.zugbahn.de", 6178);

    searchButton->setEnabled(false);
    stopButton->setEnabled(true);
    statusLabel->setText(tr("Connecting to server..."));

    connectionTimer.start(30 * 1000, true);
    progressBarTimer.start(200, false);

    blockSize = 0;
}
```

The `connectToServer()` slot is executed when the user clicks Search to start a search. We call `connectToHost()` on the `QSocket` object to connect to the server, which we assume is accessible at port 6178 on the fictitious host `tripserver.zugbahn.de`. (If you want to try the example on your own machine, replace the host name with `localhost`.) The `connectToHost()` call is asynchronous; it always returns immediately. The connection is typically established later. The `QSocket` object emits the `connected()` signal when the connection is up and running, or `error(int)` (with an error code) if the connection failed.

Next, we update the user interface and start the two timers. The first timer, `connectionTimer`, is a single-shot timer that gets triggered when the connection has been idle for 30 seconds. The second timer, `progressBarTimer`, times out every 200 milliseconds to update the application's progress bar, giving a visual cue to the user that the application is working.

Finally, we set the `blockSize` variable to 0. The `blockSize` variable stores the length of the next block received from the server. We have chosen to use the value of 0 to mean that we don't yet know the size of the next block.

```
void TripPlanner::sendRequest()
{
    QByteArray block;
    QDataStream out(block, IO_WriteOnly);
    out.setVersion(5);
    out << (Q_UINT16)0 << (Q_UINT8)'S'
        << fromComboBox->currentText()
        << toComboBox->currentText() << dateEdit->date()
        << timeEdit->time();
    if (departureRadioButton->isOn())
        out << (Q_UINT8)'D';
    else
        out << (Q_UINT8)'A';
    out.device()->at(0);
    out << (Q_UINT16)(block.size() - sizeof(Q_UINT16));
    socket.writeBlock(block.data(), block.size());

    statusLabel->setText(tr("Sending request..."));
}
```

The `sendRequest()` slot is executed when the `QSocket` object emits the `connected()` signal, indicating that a connection has been established. The slot's task is to generate a request to the server, with all the information entered by the user.

The request is a binary block with the following format:

| Q_UINT16 | Block size in bytes (excluding this field) |
|----------|--------------------------------------------|
| Q_UINT8  | Request type (always 'S')                  |
| QString  | Departure city                             |
| QString  | Arrival city                               |
| QDate    | Date of travel                             |
| QTime    | Approximate time of travel                 |
| Q_UINT8  | Time is for departure ('D') or arrival ('A') |

We first write the data to a `QByteArray` called `block`. We can't write the data directly to the `QSocket` because we don't know the size of the block, which must be sent first, until after we have put all the data into the block.

We initially write 0 as the block size, followed by the rest of the data. Then we call `at(0)` on the I/O device (a `QBuffer` created by `QDataStream` behind the scenes) to move back to the beginning of the byte array, and overwrite the initial 0 with the size of the block's data. The size is calculated by taking the block's size and subtracting `sizeof(Q_UINT16)` (that is, 2) to exclude the size field from the byte count. After that, we call `writeBlock()` on the `QSocket` to send the block to the server.

```
void TripPlanner::updateListView()
{
    connectionTimer.start(30 * 1000, true);

    QDataStream in(&socket);
    in.setVersion(5);

    for (;;) {
        if (blockSize == 0) {
            if (socket.bytesAvailable() < sizeof(Q_UINT16))
                break;
            in >> blockSize;
        }

        if (blockSize == 0xFFFF) {
            closeConnection();
            statusLabel->setText(tr("Found %1 trip(s)")
                                 .arg(listView->childCount()));
            break;
        }

        if (socket.bytesAvailable() < blockSize)
            break;

        QDate date;
        QTime departureTime;
        QTime arrivalTime;
        Q_UINT16 duration;
        Q_UINT8 changes;
        QString trainType;

        in >> date >> departureTime >> duration >> changes
            >> trainType;
        arrivalTime = departureTime.addSecs(duration * 60);

        new QListViewItem(listView,
                          date.toString(LocalDate),
                          departureTime.toString(tr("hh:mm")),
                          arrivalTime.toString(tr("hh:mm")),
                          tr("%1 hr %2 min").arg(duration / 60)
                                           .arg(duration % 60),
                          QString::number(changes),
                          trainType);
        blockSize = 0;
    }
}
```

The `updateListView()` slot is connected to the `QSocket`'s `readyRead()` signal, which is emitted whenever the `QSocket` has received new data from the server. The first thing we do is to restart the single-shot connection timer. Whenever we receive some data from the server, we know that the connection is alive, so we set the timer running for another 30 seconds.

The server sends us a list of possible train trips that match the user's criteria. Each matching trip is sent as a single block, and each block starts with a size. What complicates the code in the `for` loop is that we don't necessarily get one block of data from the server at a time. We might have received an entire block, or just part of a block, or one and a half blocks, or even all of the blocks at once.

**Figure 13.2.** The Trip Server's blocks

So how does the `for` loop work? If the `blockSize` variable is 0, this means that we have not read the size of the next block. We try to read it (assuming there are at least 2 bytes available for reading). The server uses a size value of 0xFFFF to signify that there is no more data to receive, so if we read this value, we know that we have reached the end.

If the block size is not 0xFFFF, we try to read in the next block. First, we check to see if there are block size bytes available to read. If there are not, we stop there for now. The `readyRead()` signal will be emitted again when more data is available, and we will try again then.

Once we are sure that an entire block has arrived, we can safely use the `>>` operator on the `QDataStream` we set up on the `QSocket` to extract the information related to a trip, and we create a `QListViewItem` with that information. A block received from the server has the following format:

| Q_UINT16 | Block size in bytes (excluding this field) |
|----------|--------------------------------------------|
| QDate    | Departure date                             |
| QTime    | Departure time                             |
| Q_UINT16 | Duration (in minutes)                      |
| Q_UINT8  | Number of changes                          |
| QString  | Train type                                 |

At the end, we reset the `blockSize` variable to 0 to indicate that the next block's size is unknown and needs to be read.

```
void TripPlanner::closeConnection()
{
    socket.close();
    searchButton->setEnabled(true);
    stopButton->setEnabled(false);
    connectionTimer.stop();
    progressBarTimer.stop();
    progressBar->setProgress(0);
}
```

The `closeConnection()` private function closes the connection to the TCP server, updates the user interface, and stops the timers. It is called from `updateListView()` when the 0xFFFF is read and from several other slots that we will cover shortly.

```
void TripPlanner::stopSearch()
{
    statusLabel->setText(tr("Search stopped"));
    closeConnection();
}
```

The `stopSearch()` slot is connected to the Stop button's `clicked()` signal. Essentially it just calls `closeConnection()`.

```
void TripPlanner::connectionTimeout()
{
    statusLabel->setText(tr("Error: Connection timed out"));
    closeConnection();
}
```

The `connectionTimeout()` slot is connected to the `connectionTimer`'s `timeout()` signal.

```
void TripPlanner::connectionClosedByServer()
{
    if (blockSize != 0xFFFF)
        statusLabel->setText(tr("Error: Connection closed by "
                                "server"));
    closeConnection();
}
```

The `connectionClosedByServer()` slot is connected to `socket`'s `connectionClosed()` signal. If the server closes the connection and we have not yet received the 0xFFFF end-of-stream marker, we tell the user that an error occurred. We call `closeConnection()` as usual to update the user interface and to stop the timers.

```
void TripPlanner::error(int code)
{
    QString message;

    switch (code) {
    case QSocket::ErrConnectionRefused:
        message = tr("Error: Connection refused");
        break;
    case QSocket::ErrHostNotFound:
        message = tr("Error: Server not found");
        break;
    case QSocket::ErrSocketRead:
    default:
        message = tr("Error: Data transfer failed");
    }
    statusLabel->setText(message);
    closeConnection();
}
```

The error(int) slot is connected to socket's error(int) signal. We produce an error message based on the error code.

The main() function for the Trip Planner application looks just as we would expect:

```
int main(int argc, char *argv[])
{
    QApplication app(argc, argv);
    TripPlanner tripPlanner;
    app.setMainWidget(&tripPlanner);
    tripPlanner.show();
    return app.exec();
}
```

Now let's implement the server. The server consists of two classes: TripServer and ClientSocket. The TripServer class inherits QServerSocket, a class that allows us to accept incoming TCP connections. ClientSocket reimplements QSocket and handles a single connection. At any one time, there are as many ClientSocket objects in memory as there are clients being served.

```
class TripServer : public QServerSocket
{
public:
    TripServer(QObject *parent = 0, const char *name = 0);

    void newConnection(int socket);
};
```

The TripServer class reimplements the newConnection() function from QServerSocket. This function is called whenever a client attempts to connect to the port the server is listening to.

```
TripServer::TripServer(QObject *parent, const char *name)
    : QServerSocket(6178, 1, parent, name)
{
}
```

In the TripServer constructor, we pass the port number (6178) to the base class constructor. The second argument, 1, is the number of pending connections we want to allow.

```
void TripServer::newConnection(int socketId)
{
    ClientSocket *socket = new ClientSocket(this);
    socket->setSocket(socketId);
}
```

In newConnection(), we create a ClientSocket object as a child of the TripServer object, and we set its socket ID to the number provided to us.

```
class ClientSocket : public QSocket
{
    Q_OBJECT
public:
    ClientSocket(QObject *parent = 0, const char *name = 0);
```

```
private slots:
    void readClient();

private:
    void generateRandomTrip(const QString &from, const QString &to,
                            const QDate &date, const QTime &time);

    Q_UINT16 blockSize;
};
```

The `ClientSocket` class inherits from `QSocket` and encapsulates the state of a single client.

```
ClientSocket::ClientSocket(QObject *parent, const char *name)
    : QSocket(parent, name)
{
    connect(this, SIGNAL(readyRead()),
            this, SLOT(readClient()));
    connect(this, SIGNAL(connectionClosed()),
            this, SLOT(deleteLater()));
    connect(this, SIGNAL(delayedCloseFinished()),
            this, SLOT(deleteLater()));

    blockSize = 0;
}
```

In the constructor, we establish the necessary signal–slot connections, and we set the `blockSize` variable to 0, indicating that we do not yet know the size of the block sent by the client.

The `connectionClosed()` and `delayedCloseFinished()` signals are connected to `deleteLater()`, a `QObject`-inherited function that deletes the object when control returns to Qt's event loop. This ensures that the `ClientSocket` object is deleted when the connection is closed by the peer or when a delayed close is finished. We will see what that means in a moment.

```
void ClientSocket::readClient()
{
    QDataStream in(this);
    in.setVersion(5);

    if (blockSize == 0) {
        if (bytesAvailable() < sizeof(Q_UINT16))
            return;
        in >> blockSize;
    }
    if (bytesAvailable() < blockSize)
        return;

    Q_UINT8 requestType;
    QString from;
    QString to;
    QDate date;
    QTime time;
    Q_UINT8 flag;

    in >> requestType;
```

```
        if (requestType == 'S') {
            in >> from >> to >> date >> time >> flag;

            srand(time.hour() * 60 + time.minute());
            int numTrips = rand() % 8;
            for (int i = 0; i < numTrips; ++i)
                generateRandomTrip(from, to, date, time);

            QDataStream out(this);
            out << (Q_UINT16)0xFFFF;
        }
        close();
        if (state() == Idle)
            deleteLater();
    }
```

The readClient() slot is connected to QSocket's readyRead() signal. If blockSize is 0, we start by reading the blockSize; otherwise, we have already read it, and instead we check to see if a whole block has arrived. Once an entire block is ready for reading, we read it. We use the QDataStream directly on the QSocket (the this object) and read the fields using the >> operator.

Once we have read the client's request, we are ready to generate a reply. If this were a real application, we would look up the information in a train schedule database and try to find matching train trips. But here we will be content with a function called generateRandomTrip() that will generate a random trip. We call the function a random number of times, and we send 0xFFFF to signify the end of the data.

Finally, we close the connection. If the socket's output buffer is empty, the connection is terminated immediately and we call deleteLater() to delete this object when control returns to Qt's event loop. (This is safer than delete this.) Otherwise, QSocket will complete sending out all the data, and will then close the connection and emit the delayedCloseFinished() signal.

```
    void ClientSocket::generateRandomTrip(const QString &,
            const QString &, const QDate &date, const QTime &time)
    {
        QByteArray block;
        QDataStream out(block, IO_WriteOnly);
        out.setVersion(5);
        Q_UINT16 duration = rand() % 200;
        out << (Q_UINT16)0 << date << time << duration
            << (Q_UINT8)1 << QString("InterCity");
        out.device()->at(0);
        out << (Q_UINT16)(block.size() - sizeof(Q_UINT16));

        writeBlock(block.data(), block.size());
    }
```

The generateRandomTrip() function shows how to send a block of data over a TCP connection. This is very similar to what we did in the client in the sendRequest() function (p. 294). Once again, we write the block to a QByteArray so that we can determine its size before we send it using writeBlock().

```
int main(int argc, char *argv[])
{
    QApplication app(argc, argv);
    TripServer server;
    if (!server.ok()) {
        qWarning("Failed to bind to port");
        return 1;
    }
    QPushButton quitButton(QObject::tr("&Quit"), 0);
    quitButton.setCaption(QObject::tr("Trip Server"));
    app.setMainWidget(&quitButton);
    QObject::connect(&quitButton, SIGNAL(clicked()),
                     &app, SLOT(quit()));
    quitButton.show();
    return app.exec();
}
```

In `main()`, we create a `TripServer` object and a `QPushButton` that enables the user to stop the server.

This completes our client–server example. In this case, we used a block-oriented protocol that allows us to use `QDataStream` for reading and writing. If we wanted to use a line-oriented protocol, the simplest approach would be to use `QSocket`'s `canReadLine()` and `readLine()` functions in a slot connected to the `readyRead()` signal:

```
QStringList lines;
while (socket.canReadLine())
    lines.append(socket.readLine());
```

We would then process each line that has been read. As for sending data, that can be done using a `QTextStream` on the `QSocket`.

The server implementation that we have used doesn't scale very well when there are lots of connections. The problem is that while we are processing a request, we don't handle the other connections. A more scalable approach would be to start a new thread for each connection. But `QSocket` can only be used in the thread that contains the event loop (the call to `QApplication::exec()`), for reasons that are explained in Chapter 17 (Multithreading). The solution is to use the low-level `QSocketDevice` class directly, which doesn't rely on the event loop.

# UDP Networking with QSocketDevice

The `QSocketDevice` class provides a low-level interface that can be used for TCP and for UDP. For most TCP applications, the higher-level `QSocket` class is all we need, but if we want to use UDP, we must use `QSocketDevice` directly.

UDP is an unreliable, datagram-oriented protocol. Some application-level protocols use UDP because it is more lightweight than TCP. With UDP, data is sent as packets (datagrams) from one host to another. There is no concept of connection, and if a UDP packet doesn't get delivered successfully, no error is reported to the system.

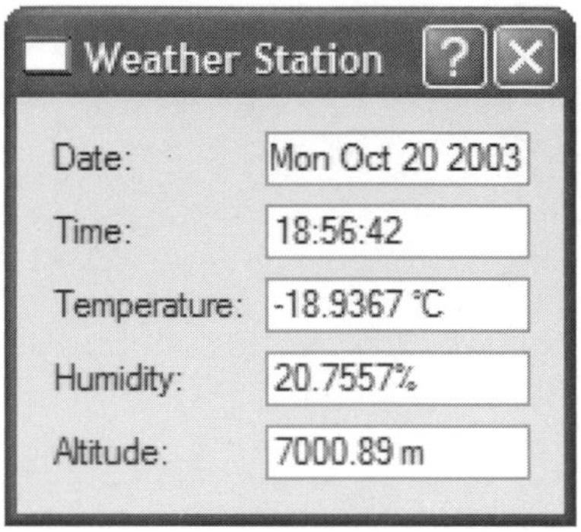

**Figure 13.3.** The Weather Station application

We will see how to use UDP from a Qt application through the Weather Balloon and Weather Station example. The Weather Balloon application is a non-GUI application that sends a UDP datagram containing the current atmospheric conditions every 5 seconds. The Weather Station application receives these datagrams and displays them on screen. We will start by reviewing the code for the Weather Balloon.

```
class WeatherBalloon : public QPushButton
{
    Q_OBJECT
public:
    WeatherBalloon(QWidget *parent = 0, const char *name = 0);

    double temperature() const;
    double humidity() const;
    double altitude() const;

protected:
    void timerEvent(QTimerEvent *event);

private:
    QSocketDevice socketDevice;
    int myTimerId;
};
```

The `WeatherBalloon` class inherits from `QPushButton`. It uses its `QSocketDevice` private variable for communicating with the Weather Station.

```
WeatherBalloon::WeatherBalloon(QWidget *parent, const char *name)
    : QPushButton(tr("Quit"), parent, name),
      socketDevice(QSocketDevice::Datagram)
{
    socketDevice.setBlocking(false);
    myTimerId = startTimer(5 * 1000);
}
```

In the constructor's initialization list, we pass QSocketDevice::Datagram to the QSocketDevice constructor to create a UDP socket device. In the constructor body, we call setBlocking(false) to make the QSocketDevice asynchronous. (By default, QSocketDevice is synchronous.)

We call startTimer() to generate a timer event every 5 seconds.

```
void WeatherBalloon::timerEvent(QTimerEvent *event)
{
    if (event->timerId() == myTimerId) {
        QByteArray datagram;
        QDataStream out(datagram, IO_WriteOnly);
        out.setVersion(5);
        out << QDateTime::currentDateTime() << temperature()
            << humidity() << altitude();
        socketDevice.writeBlock(datagram, datagram.size(),
                                0x7F000001, 5824);
    } else {
        QPushButton::timerEvent(event);
    }
}
```

In the timer event handler, we generate a datagram containing the current date, time, temperature, humidity, and altitude:

| QDateTime | Date and time of measurement |
|-----------|------------------------------|
| double    | Temperature (in °C)          |
| double    | Humidity (in %)              |
| double    | Altitude (in meters)         |

The datagram is sent using writeBlock(). The third and fourth arguments to writeBlock() are the IP address and the port number of the peer (the Weather Station). For this example, we assume that the Weather Station is running on the same machine as the Weather Balloon, so we use an IP address of 127.0.0.1 (0x7F000001), a special address that designates the local host. Unlike QSocket, QSocketDevice does not accept host names, only host numbers. If we wanted to resolve a host name to its IP address here, we would need to use the QDns class.

As usual, we need a main() function:

```
int main(int argc, char *argv[])
{
    QApplication app(argc, argv);
    WeatherBalloon balloon;
    balloon.setCaption(QObject::tr("Weather Balloon"));
    app.setMainWidget(&balloon);
    QObject::connect(&balloon, SIGNAL(clicked()),
                     &app, SLOT(quit()));
    balloon.show();
    return app.exec();
}
```

The `main()` function simply creates a `WeatherBalloon` object, which serves both as a UDP peer and as a `QPushButton` on screen. By clicking the `QPushButton`, the user can quit the application.

Now let's review the source code for the Weather Station.

```
class WeatherStation : public QDialog
{
    Q_OBJECT
public:
    WeatherStation(QWidget *parent = 0, const char *name = 0);

private slots:
    void dataReceived();

private:
    QSocketDevice socketDevice;
    QSocketNotifier *socketNotifier;

    QLabel *dateLabel;
    QLabel *timeLabel;
    ...
    QLineEdit *altitudeLineEdit;
};
```

The `WeatherStation` class inherits from `QDialog`. It listens to a certain UDP port, parses any incoming datagrams (from the Weather Balloon), and displays their contents in five read-only `QLineEdit`s.

The class has two private variables of interest here: `socketDevice` and `socket-Notifier`. The `socketDevice` variable, of type `QSocketDevice`, is used for reading datagrams. The `socketNotifier` variable, of type `QSocketNotifier`, is used to make the application aware of incoming datagrams.

```
WeatherStation::WeatherStation(QWidget *parent, const char *name)
    : QDialog(parent, name),
      socketDevice(QSocketDevice::Datagram)
{
    socketDevice.setBlocking(false);
    socketDevice.bind(QHostAddress(), 5824);

    socketNotifier = new QSocketNotifier(socketDevice.socket(),
                                         QSocketNotifier::Read,
                                         this);
    connect(socketNotifier, SIGNAL(activated(int)),
            this, SLOT(dataReceived()));
    ...
}
```

In the constructor's initialization list, we pass `QSocketDevice::Datagram` to the `QSocketDevice` constructor to create a UDP socket device. In the constructor body, we call `setBlocking(false)` to make the socket asynchronous and we call `bind()` to assign a port number to the socket. The first argument is the IP address of the Weather Station. By passing `QHostAddress()`, we indicate that we will accept datagrams to any IP address that belongs to the machine the Weather Station is running on. The second argument is the port number.

Then we create a `QSocketNotifier` object to monitor the socket. The `QSocket-Notifier` will emit an `activated(int)` signal whenever the socket receives a datagram. We connect that signal to our `dataReceived()` slot.

```
void WeatherStation::dataReceived()
{
    QDateTime dateTime;
    double temperature;
    double humidity;
    double altitude;

    QByteArray datagram(socketDevice.bytesAvailable());
    socketDevice.readBlock(datagram.data(), datagram.size());

    QDataStream in(datagram, IO_ReadOnly);
    in.setVersion(5);
    in >> dateTime >> temperature >> humidity >> altitude;

    dateLineEdit->setText(dateTime.date().toString());
    timeLineEdit->setText(dateTime.time().toString());
    temperatureLineEdit->setText(tr("%1 °C").arg(temperature));
    humidityLineEdit->setText(tr("%1%").arg(humidity));
    altitudeLineEdit->setText(tr("%1 m").arg(altitude));
}
```

In `dataReceived()`, we call `readBlock()` on the `QSocketDevice` to read in the datagram. `QByteArray::data()` returns a pointer to the `QByteArray`'s data, which `readBlock()` populates. Then, we extract the different fields using a `QData-Stream`, and we update the user interface to show the information we received. From the application's point of view, datagrams are always sent and received as a single unit of data. This means that if any bytes are available, then exactly one datagram has arrived and can be read.

```
int main(int argc, char *argv[])
{
    QApplication app(argc, argv);
    WeatherStation station;
    app.setMainWidget(&station);
    station.show();
    return app.exec();
}
```

Finally, in `main()`, we create a `WeatherStation` and make it the application's main widget.

We have now finished our UDP sender and receiver. The applications are as simple as possible, with the Weather Balloon sending datagrams and the Weather Station receiving them. In most real-world applications, both applications would need to both read and write on their socket. The `QSocketDevice` class has a `peerAddress()` and a `peerPort()` function that can be used by the server to determine what address and port to reply to.

# 14

# XML

XML (Extensible Markup Language) is a text file format that is popular for data interchange and for data storage.

Qt provides two distinct APIs for processing XML documents:

- SAX (Simple API for XML) reports parsing events directly to the application through virtual functions.

- DOM (Document Object Model) converts an XML document into a tree structure, which the application can then navigate.

There are many factors to take into account when choosing between DOM and SAX for a particular application. SAX is more low-level and usually faster, which makes it especially appropriate both for simple tasks (like finding all occurrences of a given tag in an XML document) and for reading very large files that may not fit in memory. But for many applications, the convenience offered by DOM outweighs the potential speed and memory benefits of SAX.

In this chapter, we will see how to read XML files using both APIs, and we will show how to write XML files. This chapter assumes a basic knowledge of XML.

## Reading XML with SAX

SAX is a public domain de-facto standard Java API for reading XML documents. Qt's SAX classes are modeled after the SAX2 Java implementation, with some differences in naming to match the Qt conventions. For more information about SAX, see http://www.saxproject.org/.

Qt provides a SAX-based non-validating XML parser called QXmlSimpleReader. This parser recognizes well-formed XML and supports XML namespaces. When the parser goes through the document, it calls virtual functions in registered handler classes to indicate parsing events. (These "parsing events" are unrelated to Qt events, such as key and mouse events.) For example, let's assume the parser is analyzing the following XML document:

```
<doc>
    <quote>Errare humanum est</quote>
</doc>
```

The parser would call the following parsing event handlers:

```
startDocument()
startElement("doc")
startElement("quote")
characters("Errare humanum est")
endElement("quote")
endElement("doc")
endDocument()
```

The above functions are all declared in QXmlContentHandler. For simplicity, we omitted some of the arguments of startElement() and endElement().

QXmlContentHandler is just one of many handler classes that can be used in conjunction with QXmlSimpleReader. The others are QXmlEntityResolver, QXml-DTDHandler, QXmlErrorHandler, QXmlDeclHandler, and QXmlLexicalHandler. These classes only declare pure virtual functions and give information about different kinds of parsing events. For most applications, QXmlContentHandler and QXmlErrorHandler are the only two that are needed.

For convenience, Qt also provides QXmlDefaultHandler, a class that inherits (through multiple inheritance) from all the handler classes and that provides trivial implementations for all the functions. This design, with many abstract handler classes and one trivial subclass, is rather unusual for Qt; it was adopted to closely follow the model Java implementation.

We will now review an example that shows how to use QXmlSimpleReader and QXmlDefaultHandler to parse an ad-hoc XML file format and render its contents in a QListView. The QXmlDefaultHandler subclass is called SaxHandler, and the format it handles is that of a book index, with index entries and subentries.

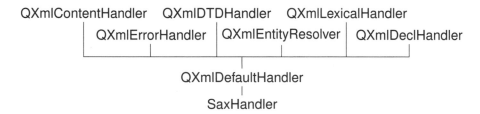

**Figure 14.1.** Inheritance tree for SaxHandler

Here's the book index file that is displayed in the QListView in Figure 14.2:

```
<?xml version="1.0"?>
<bookindex>
```

```
<entry term="sidebearings">
    <page>10</page>
    <page>34-35</page>
    <page>307-308</page>
</entry>
<entry term="subtraction">
    <entry term="of pictures">
        <page>115</page>
        <page>244</page>
    </entry>
    <entry term="of vectors">
        <page>9</page>
    </entry>
</entry>
</bookindex>
```

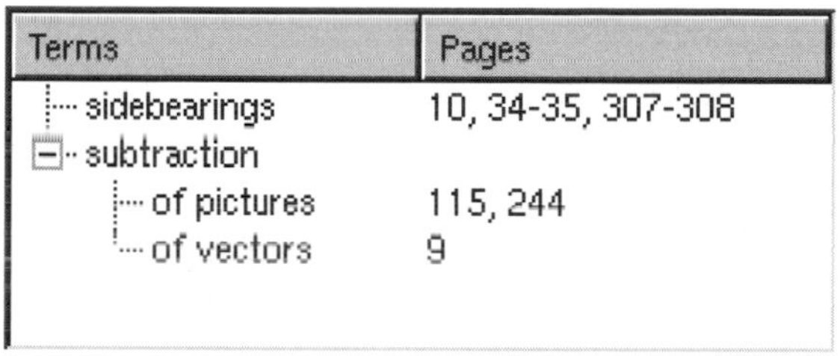

| Terms | Pages |
|-------|-------|
| ┄ sidebearings | 10, 34-35, 307-308 |
| ⊟┄ subtraction | |
| ┄ of pictures | 115, 244 |
| ┄ of vectors | 9 |

**Figure 14.2.** A book index file loaded in a `QListView`

The first step to implement the parser is to subclass `QXmlDefaultHandler`:

```
class SaxHandler : public QXmlDefaultHandler
{
public:
    SaxHandler(QListView *view);

    bool startElement(const QString &namespaceURI,
                      const QString &localName,
                      const QString &qName,
                      const QXmlAttributes &attribs);
    bool endElement(const QString &namespaceURI,
                    const QString &localName,
                    const QString &qName);
    bool characters(const QString &str);
    bool fatalError(const QXmlParseException &exception);

private:
    QListView *listView;
    QListViewItem *currentItem;
    QString currentText;
};
```

The `SaxHandler` class inherits `QXmlDefaultHandler` and reimplements four functions: `startElement()`, `endElement()`, `characters()`, and `fatalError()`. The first three functions are declared in `QXmlContentHandler`; the last function is declared in `QXmlErrorHandler`.

```
SaxHandler::SaxHandler(QListView *view)
{
    listView = view;
    currentItem = 0;
}
```

The `SaxHandler` **constructor accepts the** `QListView` **we want to fill with the information stored in the XML file.**

```
bool SaxHandler::startElement(const QString &, const QString &,
                              const QString &qName,
                              const QXmlAttributes &attribs)
{
    if (qName == "entry") {
        if (currentItem) {
            currentItem = new QListViewItem(currentItem);
        } else {
            currentItem = new QListViewItem(listView);
        }
        currentItem->setOpen(true);
        currentItem->setText(0, attribs.value("term"));
    } else if (qName == "page") {
        currentText = "";
    }
    return true;
}
```

The `startElement()` function is called when the reader encounters a new opening tag. The third parameter is the tag's name (or more precisely, its "qualified name"). The fourth parameter is the list of attributes. In this example, we ignore the first and second parameters. They are useful for XML files that use XML's namespace mechanism, a subject that is discussed in detail in the reference documentation.

If the tag is <entry>, we create a new `QListView` item. If the tag is nested within another <entry> tag, the new tag defines a subentry in the index, and the new `QListViewItem` is created as a child of the `QListViewItem` that represents the encompassing entry. Otherwise, we create the `QListViewItem` with `listView` as its parent, making it a top-level item. We call `setOpen(true)` on the item to show its children, and we call `setText()` to set the text shown in column 0 to the value of the <entry> tag's `term` attribute.

If the tag is <page>, we set the `currentText` to be an empty string. The `currentText` serves as an accumulator for the text located between the <page> and </page> tags.

At the end, we return `true` to tell SAX to continue parsing the file. If we wanted to report unknown tags as errors, we would return `false` in those cases. We would then also reimplement `errorString()` from `QXmlDefaultHandler` to return an appropriate error message.

```
bool SaxHandler::characters(const QString &str)
{
    currentText += str;
```

```
        return true;
    }
```

The `characters()` function is called to report character data in the XML document. We simply append the characters to the `currentText` variable.

```
    bool SaxHandler::endElement(const QString &, const QString &,
                                const QString &qName)
    {
        if (qName == "entry") {
            currentItem = currentItem->parent();
        } else if (qName == "page") {
            if (currentItem) {
                QString allPages = currentItem->text(1);
                if (!allPages.isEmpty())
                    allPages += ", ";
                allPages += currentText;
                currentItem->setText(1, allPages);
            }
        }
        return true;
    }
```

The `endElement()` function is called when the reader encounters a closing tag. Just as with `startElement()`, the third parameter is the name of the tag.

If the tag is `</entry>`, we update the `currentItem` private variable to point to the current `QListViewItem`'s parent. This ensures that the `currentItem` variable is restored to the value it held before the corresponding `<entry>` tag was read.

If the tag is `</page>`, we add the specified page number or page range to the comma-separated list in the current item's text in column 1.

```
    bool SaxHandler::fatalError(const QXmlParseException &exception)
    {
        qWarning("Line %d, column %d: %s", exception.lineNumber(),
                 exception.columnNumber(), exception.message().ascii());
        return false;
    }
```

The `fatalError()` function is called when the reader fails to parse the XML file. If this occurs, we simply output a warning, giving the line number, the column number, and the parser's error text.

This completes the implementation of the `SaxHandler` class. Now let's see how we can make use of the class:

```
    bool parseFile(const QString &fileName)
    {
        QListView *listView = new QListView(0);
        listView->setCaption(QObject::tr("SAX Handler"));
        listView->setRootIsDecorated(true);
        listView->setResizeMode(QListView::AllColumns);
        listView->addColumn(QObject::tr("Terms"));
        listView->addColumn(QObject::tr("Pages"));
```

```
        listView->show();

        QFile file(fileName);
        QXmlSimpleReader reader;

        SaxHandler handler(listView);
        reader.setContentHandler(&handler);
        reader.setErrorHandler(&handler);
        return reader.parse(&file);
    }
```

We set up a `QListView` with two columns. Then we create a `QFile` object for the file that is to be read and a `QXmlSimpleReader` to parse the file. We don't need to open the `QFile` ourselves; Qt does that automatically.

Finally, we create a `SaxHandler` object, we install it on the reader both as a content handler and as an error handler, and we call `parse()` on the reader to perform the parsing.

In `SaxHandler`, we only reimplemented functions from the `QXmlContentHandler` and `QXmlErrorHandler` classes. If we had implemented functions from other handler classes, we would also have needed to call their corresponding setter functions on the reader.

## Reading XML with DOM

DOM is a standard API for parsing XML developed by the World Wide Web Consortium (W3C). Qt provides a non-validating DOM Level 2 implementation for reading, manipulating, and writing XML documents.

DOM represents an XML file as a tree in memory. We can navigate through the DOM tree as much as we want, and we can modify the tree and save it back to disk as an XML file.

Let's consider the following XML document:

```
<doc>
    <quote>Errare humanum est</quote>
    <translation>To err is human</translation>
</doc>
```

It corresponds to the following DOM tree:

```
Document
    └─Element (doc)
            ├─Element (quote)
            │      └─Text ("Errare humanum est")
            └─Element (translation)
                    └─Text ("To err is human")
```

The DOM tree contains nodes of different types. For example, an `Element` node corresponds to an opening tag and its matching closing tag. The material that falls between the tags appears as child nodes of the `Element` node.

In Qt, the node types (like all other DOM-related classes) have a `QDom` prefix. Thus, `QDomElement` represents an `Element` node, and `QDomText` represents a `Text` node.

Different types of nodes can have different kinds of child nodes. For example, an `Element` node can contain other `Element` nodes, and also `EntityReference`, `Text`, `CDATASection`, `ProcessingInstruction`, and `Comment` nodes. Figure 14.3 specifies which nodes can have which kinds of child nodes. The nodes shown in gray cannot have any child nodes of their own.

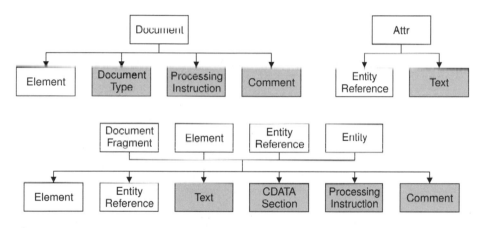

**Figure 14.3.** Parent–child relationships between DOM nodes

To illustrate how to use DOM for reading XML files, we will write a parser for the book index file format described in the previous section (p. 308).

```
class DomParser
{
public:
    DomParser(QIODevice *device, QListView *view);

private:
    void parseEntry(const QDomElement &element,
                    QListViewItem *parent);

    QListView *listView;
};
```

We define a class called `DomParser` that will parse a book index XML document and display the result in a `QListView`. The class does not inherit from any other class.

```
DomParser::DomParser(QIODevice *device, QListView *view)
{
    listView = view;
```

```
        QString errorStr;
        int errorLine;
        int errorColumn;
        QDomDocument doc;
        if (!doc.setContent(device, true, &errorStr, &errorLine,
                            &errorColumn)) {
            qWarning("Line %d, column %d: %s", errorLine, errorColumn,
                     errorStr.ascii());
            return;
        }

        QDomElement root = doc.documentElement();
        if (root.tagName() != "bookindex") {
            qWarning("The file is not a bookindex file");
            return;
        }

        QDomNode node = root.firstChild();
        while (!node.isNull()) {
            if (node.toElement().tagName() == "entry")
                parseEntry(node.toElement(), 0);
            node = node.nextSibling();
        }
    }
```

In the constructor, we create a QDomDocument object and call setContent() on it to have it read the XML document provided by the QIODevice. The setContent() function automatically opens the device if it isn't already open. Then we call documentElement() on the QDomDocument to obtain its single QDomElement child, and we check that it is a <bookindex> element. Then we iterate over all the child nodes, and if the node is an <entry> element, we call parseEntry() to parse it.

The QDomNode class can store any type of node. If we want to process a node further, we must first convert it to the right data type. In this example, we only care about Element nodes, so we call toElement() on the QDomNode to convert it to a QDomElement and then call tagName() to retrieve the element's tag name. If the node is not of type Element, the toElement() function returns a null QDomElement object, with an empty tag name.

```
    void DomParser::parseEntry(const QDomElement &element,
                               QListViewItem *parent)
    {
        QListViewItem *item;
        if (parent) {
            item = new QListViewItem(parent);
        } else {
            item = new QListViewItem(listView);
        }
        item->setOpen(true);
        item->setText(0, element.attribute("term"));

        QDomNode node = element.firstChild();
        while (!node.isNull()) {
            if (node.toElement().tagName() == "entry") {
```

```
                    parseEntry(node.toElement(), item);
          } else if (node.toElement().tagName() == "page") {
              QDomNode childNode = node.firstChild();
              while (!childNode.isNull()) {
                  if (childNode.nodeType() == QDomNode::TextNode) {
                      QString page = childNode.toText().data();
                      QString allPages = item->text(1);
                      if (!allPages.isEmpty())
                          allPages += ", ";
                      allPages += page;
                      item->setText(1, allPages);
                      break;
                  }
                  childNode = childNode.nextSibling();
              }
          }
      }
      node = node.nextSibling();
  }
}
```

In `parseEntry()`, we create a `QListView` item. If the tag is nested within another `<entry>` tag, the new tag defines a subentry in the index, and we create the `QListViewItem` as a child of the `QListViewItem` that represents the encompassing entry. Otherwise, we create the `QListViewItem` with `listView` as its parent, making it a top-level item. We call `setOpen(true)` on the item to ensure that any subentries will be visible, and call `setText()` to set the text shown in column 0 to the value of the `<entry>` tag's `term` attribute.

Once we have initialized the `QListViewItem`, we iterate over the child nodes of the `QDomElement` node corresponding to the current `<entry>` tag.

If the element is `<entry>`, we call `parseEntry()` with the current item as the second argument. The new entry's `QListViewItem` will then be created with the encompassing entry's `QListViewItem` as its parent.

If the element is `<page>`, we navigate through the element's child list to find a Text node. Once we have found it, we call `toText()` to convert it to a `QDomText` object, and `data()` to extract the text as a `QString`. Then we add the text to the comma-separated list of page numbers in column 1 of the `QListViewItem`.

Let's now see how we can use the `DomParser` class to parse a file:

```
void parseFile(const QString &fileName)
{
    QListView *listView = new QListView(0);
    listView->setCaption(QObject::tr("DOM Parser"));
    listView->setRootIsDecorated(true);
    listView->setResizeMode(QListView::AllColumns);
    listView->addColumn(QObject::tr("Terms"));
    listView->addColumn(QObject::tr("Pages"));
    listView->show();

    QFile file(fileName);
    DomParser(&file, listView);
}
```

We start by setting up a `QListView`. Then we create a `QFile` and a `DomParser`. When the `DomParser` is constructed, it parses the file and populates the list view.

As the example illustrates, navigating through a DOM tree can be cumbersome. Simply extracting the text between `<page>` and `</page>` required us to iterate through a list of `QDomNode`s using `firstChild()` and `nextSibling()`. Programmers who use DOM a lot often write their own higher level wrapper functions to simplify commonly needed operations, such as extracting the text between tags.

# Writing XML

There are basically two approaches for generating XML files from Qt applications:

- We can build a DOM tree and call `save()` on it.
- We can generate XML by hand.

The choice between these approaches is often independent of whether we use SAX or DOM for reading XML documents.

Here's a code snippet that illustrates how we can create a DOM tree and write it using a `QTextStream`:

```
const int Indent = 4;

QDomDocument doc;
QDomElement root = doc.createElement("doc");
QDomElement quote = doc.createElement("quote");
QDomElement translation = doc.createElement("translation");
QDomText quoteText = doc.createTextNode("Errare humanum est");
QDomText translationText = doc.createTextNode("To err is human");

doc.appendChild(root);
root.appendChild(quote);
root.appendChild(translation);
quote.appendChild(quoteText);
translation.appendChild(translationText);

QTextStream out(&file);
doc.save(out, Indent);
```

The second argument to `save()` is the indentation size to use. A non-zero value makes the file easier for humans to read. Here's the XML file output:

```
<doc>
    <quote>Errare humanum est</quote>
    <translation>To err is human</translation>
</doc>
```

Another scenario occurs in applications that use the DOM tree as their primary data structure. These applications would normally read in XML documents using DOM, then modify the DOM tree in memory, and finally call `save()` to convert the tree back to XML.

In the example above, we used UTF-8 as the encoding. We can use another encoding by prepending

```
<?xml version="1.0" encoding="ISO-8859-1"?>
```

to the DOM tree. The following code snippet shows how to do this:

```
QTextStream out(&file);
QDomNode xmlNode = doc.createProcessingInstruction("xml",
                        "version=\"1.0\" encoding=\"ISO-8859-1\"");
doc.insertBefore(xmlNode, doc.firstChild());
doc.save(out, Indent);
```

Generating XML files by hand isn't much harder than using DOM. We can use `QTextStream` and write the strings as we would do with any text file. The most tricky part is to escape special characters in text and attribute values. We can do this in a separate function:

```
QString escapeXml(const QString &str)
{
    QString xml = str;
    xml.replace("&", "&amp;");
    xml.replace("<", "&lt;");
    xml.replace(">", "&gt;");
    xml.replace("'", "&apos;");
    xml.replace("\"", "&quot;");
    return xml;
}
```

Here's an example that makes use of it:

```
QTextStream out(&file);
out.setEncoding(QTextStream::UnicodeUTF8);
out << "<doc>\n"
    << "    <quote>" << escapeXml(quoteText) << "</quote>\n"
    << "    <translation>" << escapeXml(translationText)
    << "</translation>\n"
    << "</doc>\n";
```

The *Qt Quarterly* article "Generating XML", available online at `http://doc.trolltech.com/qq/qq05-generating-xml.html`, presents a very simple class that makes it easy to generate XML files. The class takes care of the details such as special characters, indentation, and encoding issues, leaving us free to concentrate on the XML we want to generate.

# 15

# Internationalization

In this chapter, we will cover how to write Qt applications in languages other than English and how to translate an existing Qt application to other languages.

The first section discusses Unicode, Qt's native character encoding. The information contained in this section is useful to all Qt developers, since even an application with an English user interface could one day be run on a Greek or Japanese user's machine.

The second section shows how to make applications translation-ready. This process is so easy that it's worth doing even if you don't have plans to offer translated versions of your software. It then leaves you in a good position to hire a translator and create a new market for your applications at a later date.

The third section is aimed at truly international applications and shows how to make an application change language on the fly.

The last section describes the translation process as a whole. It also shows how programmers and translators can work together using *Qt Linguist* and Qt's other translation tools.

## Working with Unicode

Unicode is a character encoding standard that supports most of the world's writing systems. The original idea behind Unicode is that by using 16 bits for storing characters instead of 8 bits, it would be possible to encode around 65,000 characters instead of only 256. Unicode contains ASCII and ISO 8859-1 (Latin-1) as subsets at the same code positions. For example, the character 'A' has value 0x41 in ASCII, Latin-1, and Unicode, and the character 'ß' has value 0xDF in both Latin-1 and Unicode.

Qt's `QString` class stores strings as Unicode. Each character in a `QString` is a 16-bit `QChar` rather than an 8-bit `char`. Here are two ways of setting the first character of a string to 'A':

```
str[0] = 'A';
str[0] = QChar(0x41);
```

If the source file is encoded in Latin-1, specifying Latin-1 characters is just as easy:

```
str[0] = 'ß';
```

And if the source file has another encoding, the numeric value works:

```
str[0] = QChar(0xDF);
```

We can specify any Unicode character by its numeric value. For example, here's how to specify the Greek capital letter sigma ('Σ') and the euro currency symbol ('€'):

```
str[0] = QChar(0x3A3);
str[0] = QChar(0x20AC);
```

The numeric values of all the characters supported by Unicode are listed at `http://www.unicode.org/unicode/standard/standard.html`. If you rarely need non-Latin-1 Unicode characters, looking up characters online is sufficient; but Qt provides more convenient ways of entering Unicode strings in a Qt program, as we will see later in this section.

Qt 3.2's text engine supports the following writing systems on all platforms: Arabic, Chinese, Cyrillic, Greek, Hebrew, Japanese, Korean, Lao, Latin, Thai, and Vietnamese. It also supports all the Unicode 3.2 scripts that don't require any special processing. In addition, the following writing systems are supported on X11 with Xft and on NT-based versions of Windows: Bengali, Devanagari, Gujarati, Gurmukhi, Kannada, Khmer, Syriac, Tamil, Telugu, and Thaana. Finally, Malayalam and Tibetan are supported on X11, and Divehi is supported on Windows XP. Assuming that the proper fonts are installed on the system, Qt can render text using any of these writing systems. And assuming that the proper input methods are installed, users will be able to enter text that uses these writing systems in their Qt applications.

Programming with `QChar` is slightly different from programming with `char`. To obtain the numeric value of a `QChar`, call `unicode()` on it. To obtain the ASCII or Latin-1 value of a `QChar` (as a `char`), call `latin1()`. For non-Latin-1 characters, `latin1()` returns 0.

If we know that all the strings in a program are ASCII or Latin-1, we can use standard `<cctype>` functions like `isalpha()`, `isdigit()`, and `isspace()`. These work because `QChar`s automatically convert into `char`s (as Latin-1) given the right context, just as `QString`s automatically convert into `const char *`. However, it is generally better to use `QChar`'s member functions for performing these operations, since they will work for any Unicode character. The functions

QChar **provides include** isPrint(), isPunct(), isSpace(), isMark(), isLetter(), isNumber(), isLetterOrNumber(), isDigit(), isSymbol(), lower(), **and** upper(). For example, here's one way to test that a character is a digit or an upper-case letter:

```
if (ch.isDigit() || ch != ch.lower())
    ...
```

The lower() function returns the lower-case version of the character. If the lower-case version of the character is different from the character itself, then the character must be upper-case (or title-case). The code snippet works for any alphabet that distinguishes between upper- and lower-case, including Latin, Greek, and Cyrillic.

Once we have a Unicode string, we can use it anywhere in Qt's API where a QString is expected. It is then Qt's responsibility to display it properly and to convert it to other encodings when talking to the operating system.

Special care is needed when we read and write text files. Text files can use a variety of encodings, and it's often impossible to guess a text file's encoding from its contents. By default, QTextStream uses the system's local 8-bit encoding (available as QTextCodec::codecForLocale()) for both reading and writing. For American and West European locales, this usually means Latin-1.

If we design our own file format and want to be able to read and write arbitrary Unicode characters, we can save the data as Unicode by calling setEncoding(QTextStream::Unicode) before we start writing to the QTextStream. The data will then be saved in UTF-16, a format that requires two bytes per character. The UTF-16 format is very close to the memory representation of a QString, so reading and writing Unicode strings in UTF-16 can be very fast. However, there is an inherent overhead when saving pure ASCII data in UTF-16 format, since it stores two bytes for every character instead of just one.

When reading back the text, QTextStream normally detects Unicode automatically, but for absolute certainty it is best to call setEncoding(QTextStream::Unicode) before reading.

Another encoding that supports the whole of Unicode is UTF-8. Its main advantage over UTF-16 is that it is a superset of ASCII. Any character in the range 0x00 to 0x7F is represented as a single byte. Other characters, including Latin-1 characters above 0x7F, are represented by multi-byte sequences. For text that is mostly ASCII, UTF-8 takes up about half the space consumed by UTF-16. To use UTF-8 with QTextStream, call setEncoding(QTextStream::UnicodeUTF8) before reading and writing.

If we always want to read and write Latin-1 regardless of the user's locale, we can call setEncoding(QTextStream::Latin1) on the QTextStream.

Other encodings can be specified by calling setCodec() with an appropriate QTextCodec. A QTextCodec is an object that converts between Unicode and a given encoding. QTextCodecs are used in a variety of contexts by Qt. Internally, they are used to support fonts, input methods, the clipboard, drag and drop, and file names. But they are also available to us when we write Qt applications.

For example, if we want to read in a file with the EUC-KR encoding, we can write this:

```
QTextStream in(&file);
QTextCodec *koreanCodec = QTextCodec::codecForName("EUC-KR");
if (koreanCodec)
    in.setCodec(koreanCodec);
```

Some file formats specify their encoding in their header. The header is typically plain ASCII to ensure that it is read correctly no matter what encoding is used (assuming that it is a superset of ASCII). The XML file format is an interesting example of this. XML files are normally encoded as UTF-8 or UTF-16. The proper way to read them in is to call setEncoding(QTextStream::UnicodeUTF8). If the format is UTF-16, QTextStream will automatically detect this and adjust itself. The <?xml?> header of an XML file sometimes contains an encoding argument, for example:

```
<?xml version="1.0" encoding="EUC-KR"?>
```

Since QTextStream doesn't allow us to change the encoding once it has started reading, the right way to respect an explicit encoding is to start reading the file anew, using the correct codec (obtained from QTextCodec::codecForName()).

In the case of XML, we can avoid having to handle the encoding ourselves by using Qt's XML classes, described in Chapter 14.

Another use of QTextCodecs is to specify the encoding of strings that occur in the source code. Let's consider the example of a team of Japanese programmers who are writing an application targeted primarily at Japan's home market. These programmers are likely to write their source code in a text editor that uses an encoding such as EUC-JP or Shift-JIS. Such an editor allows them to type in Japanese characters seamlessly, so that they can write code like this:

```
QPushButton *button = new QPushButton(tr("日諾"), 0);
```

By default, Qt interprets arguments to tr() as Latin-1. To change this, call the QTextCodec::setCodecForTr() static function. For example:

```
QTextCodec *japaneseCodec = QTextCodec::codecForName("EUC-JP");
QTextCodec::setCodecForTr(japaneseCodec);
```

This must be done before the first call to tr(). Typically, we would do this in main(), right after the QApplication object is created.

Other strings specified in the program will still be interpreted as Latin-1 strings. If the programmers want to enter Japanese characters in those as well, they can explicitly convert them to Unicode using a QTextCodec:

```
QString text = japaneseCodec->toUnicode("海鮮料理");
```

Alternatively, they can tell Qt to use a specific codec when converting between `const char *` and `QString` by calling `QTextCodec::setCodecForCStrings()`:

```
QTextCodec::setCodecForCStrings(japaneseCodec);
```

Because Qt's internals sometimes convert ASCII strings to `QString`, the encoding must be a superset of ASCII.

The techniques described above can be applied to any non-Latin-1 language, including Chinese, Greek, Korean, and Russian.

Here's a list of the encodings supported by Qt 3.2:

- Apple Roman
- Big5-HKSCS
- CP874
- CP1250
- CP1251
- CP1252
- CP1253
- CP1254
- CP1255
- CP1256
- CP1257

- CP1258
- EUC-JP
- EUC-KR
- GB2312
- GB18030
- GBK
- IBM-850
- IBM-866
- ISO 8859-1
- ISO 8859-2
- ISO 8859-3

- ISO 8859-4
- ISO 8859-5
- ISO 8859-6
- ISO 8859-7
- ISO 8859-8
- ISO 8859-8-I
- ISO 8859-9
- ISO 8859-10
- ISO 8859-11
- ISO 8859-13
- ISO 8859-14

- ISO 8859-15
- ISO 10646 UCS-2
- JIS7
- KOI8-R
- KOI8-U
- Shift-JIS
- TIS-620
- TSCII
- UTF-8

For all of these, `QTextCodec::codecForName()` will always return a valid pointer. Other encodings can be supported either by subclassing `QTextCodec` or by creating a charmap file and using `QTextCodec::loadCharmapFile()`. See the `QTextCodec` reference documentation for details.

## Making Applications Translation-Aware

If we want to make our applications available in multiple languages, we must do two things:

- Make sure that every user-visible string goes through `tr()`.
- Load a translation (`.qm`) file at startup.

Neither of these is necessary for applications that will never be translated. However, using `tr()` requires almost no effort and leaves the door open for doing translations at a later date.

The `tr()` function is a static function defined in `QObject` and overridden in every subclass defined with the `Q_OBJECT` macro. When writing code inside a `QObject` subclass, we can call `tr()` without formality. A call to `tr()` returns a translation if one is available; otherwise, the original text is returned.

To prepare translation files, we must run Qt's `lupdate` tool. This tool extracts all the string literals that appear in `tr()` calls and produces translation files that contain all of these strings ready to be translated. The files can then be sent to a translator to have the translations added. This process is explained in the "Translating Applications" section later in this chapter.

A `tr()` call has the following general syntax:

*Context*`::tr(`*sourceText, comment*`)`

The *Context* part is the name of a `QObject` subclass defined with the `Q_OBJECT` macro. We don't need to specify it if we call `tr()` from a member function of the class in question. The *sourceText* part is the string literal that needs to be translated. The *comment* part is optional; it can be used to provide additional information to the translator.

Here are a few examples:

```
BlueWidget::BlueWidget(QWidget *parent, const char *name)
    : QWidget(parent, name)
{
    QString str1 = tr("Legal");
    QString str2 = BlueWidget::tr("Legal");
    QString str3 = YellowDialog::tr("Legal");
    QString str4 = YellowDialog::tr("Legal", "US paper size");
}
```

The first two calls to `tr()` have "BlueWidget" as context, and the last two calls have "YellowDialog". All four have "Legal" as source text. The last call also has a comment to help the translator understand the meaning of the source text.

Strings in different contexts (classes) are translated independently of each other. Translators normally work on one context at a time, often with the application running and showing the widget or dialog being translated.

When we call `tr()` from a global function, we must specify the context explicitly. Any `QObject` subclass in the application can be used as the context. If none is appropriate, we can always use `QObject` itself. For example:

```
int main(int argc, char *argv[])
{
    QApplication app(argc, argv);
    ...
    QPushButton button(QObject::tr("Hello Qt!"), 0);
    app.setMainWidget(&button);
    button.show();
    return app.exec();
}
```

This idiom is useful for translating the name of the application. Instead of typing it multiple times and leaving the translator to translate it for each class it appears in, it is usually more convenient to define an `APPNAME` macro that expands to the translated application name and to put the macro in a header file included by all the application's files:

```
#define APPNAME MainWindow::tr("OpenDrawer 2D")
```

In every example so far, the context has been a class name. This is convenient, because we can almost always omit it, but this doesn't have to be the case. The most general way of translating a string in Qt is to use the QApplication:: translate() function, which accepts up to three arguments: the context, the source text, and the optional comment. For example, here's another way to define APPNAME:

```
#define APPNAME qApp->translate("Global Stuff", "OpenDrawer 2D")
```

This time, we put the text in the "Global Stuff" context.

The tr() and translate() functions serve a dual purpose: They are markers that lupdate uses to find user-visible strings, and at the same time they are C++ functions that translate text. This has an impact on how we write code. For example, the following will not work:

```
// WRONG
const char *appName = "OpenDrawer 2D";
QString translated = tr(appName);
```

The problem here is that lupdate will not be able to extract the "OpenDrawer 2D" string literal, as it doesn't appear inside a tr() call. This means that the translator will not have the opportunity to translate the string. This issue often arises in conjunction with dynamic strings:

```
// WRONG
statusBar()->message(tr("Host " + hostName + " found"));
```

Here, the string we pass to tr() varies depending on the value of hostName, so we can't reasonably expect tr() to translate it correctly.

The solution is to use QString::arg():

```
statusBar()->message(tr("Host %1 found").arg(hostName));
```

Notice how it works: The string literal "Host %1 found" is passed to tr(). Assuming a French translation file is loaded, tr() would return something like "Hôte %1 trouvé". Then the "%1" parameter is replaced with the contents of the hostName variable.

Although it is generally inadvisable to call tr() on a variable, it can be made to work. We must use the QT_TR_NOOP() macro to mark the string literals for translation before we assign them to a variable. This is mostly useful for static arrays of strings. For example:

```
void OrderForm::init()
{
    static const char * const flowers[] = {
        QT_TR_NOOP("Medium Stem Pink Roses"),
        QT_TR_NOOP("One Dozen Boxed Roses"),
        QT_TR_NOOP("Calypso Orchid"),
        QT_TR_NOOP("Dried Red Rose Bouquet"),
        QT_TR_NOOP("Mixed Peonies Bouquet"),
        0
    };
```

```
        int i = 0;
        while (flowers[i]) {
            comboBox->insertItem(tr(flowers[i]));
            ++i;
        }
    }
```

The QT_TR_NOOP() simply returns its argument. But lupdate will extract all the strings wrapped in QT_TR_NOOP(), so that they can be translated. When using the variable later on, we call tr() to perform the translation as usual. Even though we have passed tr() a variable, the translation will still work.

There is also a QT_TRANSLATE_NOOP() macro, which works like QT_TR_NOOP() but also takes a context. This macro is useful when initializing variables outside of a class:

```
static const char * const flowers[] = {
    QT_TRANSLATE_NOOP("OrderForm", "Medium Stem Pink Roses"),
    QT_TRANSLATE_NOOP("OrderForm", "One Dozen Boxed Roses"),
    QT_TRANSLATE_NOOP("OrderForm", "Calypso Orchid"),
    QT_TRANSLATE_NOOP("OrderForm", "Dried Red Rose Bouquet"),
    QT_TRANSLATE_NOOP("OrderForm", "Mixed Peonies Bouquet"),
    0
};
```

The context argument must be the same as the context given to tr() or translate() later on.

When we start using tr() in an application, it's easy to forget to surround some user-visible strings with a tr() call, especially when we first start doing it. These missing tr() calls are eventually discovered by the translator or, worse, by users of the translated application, when some strings appear in the original language. To avoid this problem, we can tell Qt to forbid implicit conversions from const char * to QString. We do this by defining the QT_NO_CAST_ASCII preprocessor symbol before including <qstring.h>. The easiest way to ensure this symbol is set is to add the following line to the application's .pro file:

```
DEFINES       += QT_NO_CAST_ASCII
```

This will force every string literal to need to be wrapped by tr() or QString::fromAscii(), depending on whether it should be translated or not. Strings that are not suitably wrapped will produce a compile-time error, thereby compelling us to add the missing tr() or QString::fromAscii() call.

Once we have wrapped every user-visible string by a tr() call, the only thing left to do to enable translation is to load a translation file. Typically, we would do this in the application's main() function. For example, here's how we would try to load a translation file depending on the user's locale:

```
int main(int argc, char *argv[])
{
    QApplication app(argc, argv);
```

```
        QTranslator appTranslator;
        appTranslator.load(QString("app_") + QTextCodec::locale(),
                           qApp->applicationDirPath());
        app.installTranslator(&appTranslator);
        ...
        return app.exec();
}
```

The `QTextCodec::locale()` function returns a string that specifies the user's locale. Locales can be more or less precise; for example, `fr` specifies a French-language locale, `fr_CA` specifies a French Canadian locale, and `fr_CA.ISO8859-15` specifies a French Canadian locale with ISO 8859-15 encoding (an encoding that supports '€', 'Œ', 'œ', and 'Ÿ').

Assuming that the locale is `fr_CA.ISO8859-15`, `load()` first attempts to load the file `app_fr_CA.ISO8859-15.qm`. If this file does not exist, `load()` next tries `app_fr_CA.qm`, then `app_fr.qm`, and finally `app.qm` before giving up. Normally, we would only provide `app_fr.qm`, containing a standard French translation, but if we need a different file for French-speaking Canada, we can also provide `app_fr_CA.qm` and it will be used for `fr_CA` locales.

The second argument to `load()` is the directory where we want `load()` to look for the translation file. In this case, we assume that the translation files are located in the same directory as the executable.

The Qt library itself contains a few strings that need to be translated. Trolltech provides French and German translations in Qt's `translations` directory. (A few other languages are provided as well, but these are contributed by Qt users and are not officially supported.) The Qt library's translation file should also be loaded:

```
        QTranslator qtTranslator;
        qtTranslator.load(QString("qt_") + QTextCodec::locale(),
                          qApp->applicationDirPath());
        app.installTranslator(&qtTranslator);
```

A `QTranslator` object can only hold one translation file at a time, so we use a separate `QTranslator` for Qt's translation. Having just one file per translator is not a problem since we can install as many translators as we need. `QApplication` will use all of them when searching for a translation.

Some languages, such as Arabic and Hebrew, are written right-to-left instead of left-to-right. In those languages, the whole layout of the application must be reversed, which is done by calling `QApplication::setReverseLayout(true)`. The translation files for the Qt library contain a special marker called "LTR" that tells Qt whether the language is left-to-right or right-to-left, so we normally don't need to worry about it.

It may prove more convenient for our users if we supply our applications with the translation files embedded into the executable. Not only does this reduce the number of files distributed as part of the product, but it also avoids the risk of translation files getting lost or deleted by accident. Qt provides the qembed tool (located in Qt's tools directory), which can convert .qm files to a C++ array that can be passed to QTranslator::load().

We have now covered all that is required to make an application able to operate using translations into other languages. But language and the direction of the writing system are not the only things that vary between countries and cultures. An internationalized program must also take into account the local date and time formats, monetary formats, numeric formats, and string collation order. Qt 3.2 provides no specific functions for accessing these, but we can use the standard C++ setlocale() and localeconv() functions to query the program's current locale.★

Some Qt classes and functions adapt their behavior to the locale:

- QString::localeAwareCompare() compares two strings in a locale-dependent manner. It is used by classes like QIconView and QListView for sorting items.

- The toString() function provided by QDate, QTime, and QDateTime returns a string in a local format when called with Qt::LocalDate as argument.

- By default, QDateEdit, QTimeEdit, and QDateTimeEdit present dates in the local format.

Finally, a translated application may need to use different icons in certain situations rather than the original icons. For example, the left and right arrows on a web browser's Back and Forward buttons should be swapped when dealing with a right-to-left language. We can do this as follows:

```
if (QApplication::reverseLayout()) {
    backAct->setIconSet(forwardIcon);
    forwardAct->setIconSet(backIcon);
} else {
    backAct->setIconSet(backIcon);
    forwardAct->setIconSet(forwardIcon);
}
```

Icons that contain alphabetic characters very commonly need to be translated. For example, the letter 'I' on a toolbar button associated with a word processor's Italic option should be replaced by a 'C' in Spanish (Cursivo) and by a 'K' in Danish, Dutch, German, Norwegian, and Swedish (Kursiv). Here's a quick way to do it:

```
if (tr("Italic")[0] == 'C') {
    italicAct->setIconSet(iconC);
} else if (tr("Italic")[0] == 'K') {
    italicAct->setIconSet(iconK);
} else {
    italicAct->setIconSet(iconI);
}
```

★Qt 3.3 will probably include a QLocale class that will provide localized numeric formats.

# Dynamic Language Switching

For most applications, detecting the user's preferred language in main() and loading the appropriate .qm files there is perfectly satisfactory. But there are some situations where users might need the ability to switch language dynamically. An application that is used continuously by different people in shifts may need to change language without having to be restarted. For example, applications used by call center operators, by simultaneous translators, and by computerized cash register operators often require this capability.

Making an application able to switch language dynamically requires a little more work than loading a single translation at startup, but it is not difficult. Here's what must be done:

- Provide a means by which the user can switch language.

- For every widget or dialog, set all of its translatable strings in a separate function (often called retranslateStrings()) and call this function when the language changes.

Let's review the relevant parts of a Call Center application's source code. The application provides a Language menu to allow the user to set the language at run-time. The default language is English.

**Figure 15.1.** The Call Center application's Language menu

Since we don't know which language the user will want to use when the application is started, we no longer load translations in the main() function. Instead we will load them dynamically when they are needed, so all the code that we need to handle translations must go in the main window and dialog classes.

Let's have a look at the Call Center application's QMainWindow subclass:

```
MainWindow::MainWindow(QWidget *parent, const char *name)
    : QMainWindow(parent, name)
{
    journalView = new JournalView(this);
    setCentralWidget(journalView);

    qmPath = qApp->applicationDirPath() + "/translations";
```

```
    appTranslator = new QTranslator(this);
    qtTranslator = new QTranslator(this);
    qApp->installTranslator(appTranslator);
    qApp->installTranslator(qtTranslator);

    createActions();
    createMenus();

    retranslateStrings();
}
```

In the constructor, we set the central widget to be a `JournalView`, a `QListView` subclass. Then we set up a few private member variables related to translation:

- The `qmPath` variable is a `QString` that specifies the path of the directory that contains the application's translation files.

- The `appTranslator` variable is a pointer to the `QTranslator` object used for storing the current application translation.

- The `qtTranslator` variable is a pointer to the `QTranslator` object used for storing Qt's translation.

At the end, we call the `createActions()` and `createMenus()` private functions to create the menu system, and we call `retranslateStrings()`, also a private function, to set the user-visible strings for the first time.

```
    void MainWindow::createActions()
    {
        newAct = new QAction(this);
        connect(newAct, SIGNAL(activated()), this, SLOT(newFile()));
        ...
        aboutQtAct = new QAction(this);
        connect(aboutQtAct, SIGNAL(activated()), qApp, SLOT(aboutQt()));
    }
```

The `createActions()` function creates the `QAction` objects as usual, but without setting any of the texts or accelerator keys. These will be done in `retranslateStrings()`.

```
    void MainWindow::createMenus()
    {
        fileMenu = new QPopupMenu(this);
        newAct->addTo(fileMenu);
        openAct->addTo(fileMenu);
        saveAct->addTo(fileMenu);
        exitAct->addTo(fileMenu);
        ...
        createLanguageMenu();
    }
```

The `createMenus()` function creates menus, but does not insert these menus into the menu bar. Again, this will be done in `retranslateStrings()`.

At the end of the function, we call `createLanguageMenu()` to fill the Language menu with the list of supported languages. We will review its source code in a moment. First, let's look at `retranslateStrings()`:

```
void MainWindow::retranslateStrings()
{
    setCaption(tr("Call Center"));

    newAct->setMenuText(tr("&New"));
    newAct->setAccel(tr("Ctrl+N"));
    newAct->setStatusTip(tr("Create a new journal"));
    ...
    aboutQtAct->setMenuText(tr("About &Qt"));
    aboutQtAct->setStatusTip(tr("Show the Qt library's About box"));

    menuBar()->clear();
    menuBar()->insertItem(tr("&File"), fileMenu);
    menuBar()->insertItem(tr("&Edit"), editMenu);
    menuBar()->insertItem(tr("&Reports"), reportsMenu);
    menuBar()->insertItem(tr("&Language"), languageMenu);
    menuBar()->insertItem(tr("&Help"), helpMenu);
}
```

The `retranslateStrings()` function is where all the `tr()` calls for the `MainWindow` class occur. It is called at the end of the `MainWindow` constructor and also every time a user changes the application's language using the Language menu.

We set each `QAction`'s menu text, accelerator, and status tip. We also insert the menus into the menu bar, with their translated names. (The call to `clear()` is necessary when `retranslateStrings()` is called more than once.)

The `createMenus()` function referred to earlier called `createLanguageMenu()` to populate the Language menu with a list of languages:

```
void MainWindow::createLanguageMenu()
{
    QDir dir(qmPath);
    QStringList fileNames = dir.entryList("callcenter_*.qm");

    for (int i = 0; i < (int)fileNames.size(); ++i) {
        QTranslator translator;
        translator.load(fileNames[i], qmPath);

        QTranslatorMessage message =
                translator.findMessage("MainWindow", "English");
        QString language = message.translation();

        int id = languageMenu->insertItem(
                        tr("&%1 %2").arg(i + 1).arg(language),
                        this, SLOT(switchToLanguage(int)));
        languageMenu->setItemParameter(id, i);
        if (language == "English")
            languageMenu->setItemChecked(id, true);

        QString locale = fileNames[i];
        locale = locale.mid(locale.find('_') + 1);
        locale.truncate(locale.find('.'));
```

```
        locales.push_back(locale);
    }
}
```

Instead of hard-coding the languages supported by the application, we create one menu entry for each .qm file located in the application's `translations` directory. For simplicity, we assume that English also has a .qm file. An alternative would have been to call `clear()` on the `QTranslator` objects when the user chooses English.

One particular difficulty is to present a nice name for the language provided by each .qm file. Just showing "en" for "English" or "de" for "Deutsch", based on the name of the .qm file, looks crude and will confuse some users. The solution used in `createLanguageMenu()` is to check the translation of the string "English" in the "MainWindow" context. That string should be translated to "Deutsch" in a German translation, to "Français" in a French translation, and to "日本語" in a Japanese translation.

We create menu items using `QPopupMenu::insertItem()`. They are all connected to the main window's `switchToLanguage(int)` slot, which we will review next. The parameter to the `switchToLanguage(int)` slot is the value set using `set-ItemParameter()`. This is very similar to what we did in Chapter 3 when we implemented the Spreadsheet application's recently opened files list (p. 54).

At the end, we append the locale in a `QStringList` called `locales`, which we will use for implementing `switchToLanguage()`.

```
void MainWindow::switchToLanguage(int param)
{
    appTranslator->load("callcenter_" + locales[param], qmPath);
    qtTranslator->load("qt_" + locales[param], qmPath);

    for (int i = 0; i < (int)languageMenu->count(); ++i)
        languageMenu->setItemChecked(languageMenu->idAt(i),
                                     i == param);
    retranslateStrings();
}
```

The `switchToLanguage()` slot is called when the user chooses a language from the Language menu. We start by loading the translation files for the application and for Qt. Then we update the check marks next to the Language menu entries so that the language in use is ticked, and we call `retranslateStrings()` to retranslate all the strings for the main window.

On Microsoft Windows, an alternative to providing a Language menu is to respond to `LocaleChange` events, a type of event emitted by Qt when it detects a change in the environment's locale. The event type exists on all platforms supported by Qt, but is only actually generated on Windows, when the user changes the system's locale settings (in the Regional and Language Options from the Control Panel). To handle `LocaleChange` events, we can reimplement `QObject::event()` as follows:

```
bool MainWindow::event(QEvent *event)
{
    if (event->type() == QEvent::LocaleChange) {
        appTranslator->load(QString("callcenter_")
                                    + QTextCodec::locale(),
                                qmPath);
        qtTranslator->load(QString("qt_") + QTextCodec::locale(),
                                qmPath);
        retranslateStrings();
    }
    return QMainWindow::event(event);
}
```

If the user switches locale while the application is being run, we attempt to load the correct translation files for the new locale and call retranslate-Strings() to update the user interface.

In all cases, we pass the event on to the base class's event() function, since one of our base classes may also be interested in LocaleChange events.

We have now finished our review of the MainWindow code. We will now review the code for one of the application's widget classes, the JournalView class, to see what changes are needed to make it support dynamic translation.

```
JournalView::JournalView(QWidget *parent, const char *name)
    : QListView(parent, name)
{
    ...
    retranslateStrings();
}
```

The JournalView class is a QListView subclass. At the end of the constructor, we call the private function retranslateStrings() to set the widget's strings. This is similar to what we did for MainWindow.

```
bool JournalView::event(QEvent *event)
{
    if (event->type() == QEvent::LanguageChange)
        retranslateStrings();
    return QListView::event(event);
}
```

We reimplement the event() function to call retranslateStrings() on LanguageChange events.

Qt generates a LanguageChange event when the contents of a QTranslator currently installed on QApplication changes. In the Call Center application, this occurs when we call load() on appTranslator or qtTranslator, either from MainWindow::switchToLanguage() or from MainWindow::event().

LanguageChange events are not the same as LocaleChange events. A LocaleChange event tells the application, "Maybe you should load a new translation." In contrast, a LanguageChange event tells the application's widgets, "Maybe you should retranslate all your strings."

When we implemented `MainWindow`, we didn't need to respond to `Language-Change`. Instead, we simply called `retranslateStrings()` whenever we called `load()` on a `QTranslator`.

```
void JournalView::retranslateStrings()
{
    for (int i = columns() - 1; i >= 0; --i)
        removeColumn(i);
    addColumn(tr("Time"));
    addColumn(tr("Priority"));
    addColumn(tr("Phone Number"));
    addColumn(tr("Subject"));
}
```

The `retranslateStrings()` function recreates the `QListView` column headers with newly translated texts. We do this by removing all column headings and then adding new column headings. This operation only affects the `QListView` header, not the data stored in the `QListView`.

This completes the translation-related code of a hand-written widget. For widgets and dialogs developed with *Qt Designer*, the `uic` tool automatically generates a function similar to our `retranslateStrings()` function that is automatically called in response to `LanguageChange` events. All we need to do is to load a translation file when the user switches language.

## Translating Applications

Translating a Qt application that contains `tr()` calls is a three-step process:

1. Run `lupdate` to extract all the user-visible strings from the application's source code.
2. Translate the application using *Qt Linguist*.
3. Run `lrelease` to generate binary `.qm` files that the application can load using `QTranslator`.

Steps 1 and 3 are performed by application developers. Step 2 is handled by translators. This cycle can be repeated as often as necessary during the application's development and lifetime.

As an example, we will show how to translate the Spreadsheet application of Chapter 3. The application already contains `tr()` calls around every user-visible string.

First, we must modify the application's `.pro` file slightly to specify which languages we want to support. For example, if we want to support German and French in addition to English, we would add the following TRANSLATIONS entry to `spreadsheet.pro`:

```
TRANSLATIONS  = spreadsheet_de.ts \
                spreadsheet_fr.ts
```

Here, we specify two translation files: one for German and one for French. These files will be created the first time we run `lupdate`, and are updated every time we subsequently run `lupdate`.

These files normally have a `.ts` extension. They are in a straightforward XML format and are not as compact as the binary `.qm` files understood by `QTranslator`. It is `lrelease`'s job to convert human-readable `.ts` files into machine-efficient `.qm` files. For the curious, `.ts` stands for "translation source" and `.qm` for "Qt message" file.

Assuming that we are located in the directory that contains the Spreadsheet application's source code, we can run `lupdate` on `spreadsheet.pro` from the command line as follows:

```
lupdate -verbose spreadsheet.pro
```

The `-verbose` argument is optional. It tells `lupdate` to provide more feedback than usual. Here's the expected output:

```
Updating 'spreadsheet_de.ts'...
  0 known, 101 new and 0 obsoleted messages
Updating 'spreadsheet_fr.ts'...
  0 known, 101 new and 0 obsoleted messages
```

Every string that appears within a `tr()` call in the application's source code is stored in the `.ts` files, along with an empty translation. Strings that appear in the application's `.ui` files are also included.

The `lupdate` tool assumes by default that the arguments to `tr()` are Latin-1 strings. If this isn't the case, we must add a `CODEC` entry to the `.pro` file. For example:

```
CODEC          = EUC-JP
```

This must be done in addition to calling `QTextCodec::setCodecForTr()` from the application's `main()` function.

Translations then need to be added to the `spreadsheet_de.ts` and `spreadsheet_fr.ts` files using *Qt Linguist*, a GUI tool for translating Qt applications.

To launch *Qt Linguist*, click Qt 3.2.x|Qt Linguist in the Start menu on Windows, type `linguist` on the command line on Unix, or double-click `linguist` in the Mac OS X Finder. To start adding translations to a `.ts` file, click File|Open and choose the file.

The left-hand side of *Qt Linguist*'s main window shows the list of contexts for the application being translated. For the Spreadsheet application, the contexts are "FindDialog", "GoToCellDialog", "MainWindow", "SortDialog", and "Spreadsheet". The top-right area is the list of source texts for the current context. Each source text is shown along with with a translation and a Done flag. The middle-right area is where we can enter a translation for the current source item. The bottom-right area is a list of suggestions automatically provided by *Qt Linguist*.

Once we have a translated .ts file, we need to convert it to a binary .qm file for it to be understandable by QTranslator. To do this from within *Qt Linguist*, click File|Release. Typically, we would start by translating only a few strings and run the application with the .qm file to make sure that everything works.

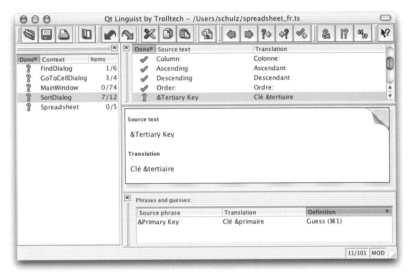

**Figure 15.2.** *Qt Linguist* in action

If we want to regenerate the .qm files for all .ts files, we can use the lrelease command-line tool as follows:

```
lrelease -verbose spreadsheet.pro
```

Assuming that we translated 19 strings to French and clicked the Done flag for 17 of them, lrelease produces the following output:

```
Updating 'spreadsheet_de.qm'...
 0 finished, 0 unfinished and 101 untranslated messages
Updating 'spreadsheet_fr.qm'...
 17 finished, 2 unfinished and 82 untranslated messages
```

Untranslated strings are shown in the original languages when running the application. The Done flag isn't used by lrelease; it can be used by translators to identify which translations are finished and which ones must be revisited.

When we modify the source code of the application, the translation files may become out of date. The solution is to run lupdate again, provide translations for the new strings, and regenerate the .qm files. Some development teams find it useful to run lupdate frequently, while others prefer to wait until just before a final product release.

The lupdate and *Qt Linguist* tools are quite smart. Translations that are no longer used are kept in the .ts files in case they are needed in later releases. When updating .ts files, lupdate uses an intelligent merging algorithm that can save translators considerable time with text that is the same or similar in different contexts.

For more information about *Qt Linguist*, `lupdate`, and `lrelease`, refer to the *Qt Linguist* manual at `http://doc.trolltech.com/3.2/linguist-manual.html`. The manual contains a full explanation of *Qt Linguist*'s user interface and a step-by-step tutorial for programmers.

# 16

# Providing Online Help

Most applications provide their users with online help. Some help is short, such as tooltips, status tips, and "What's This?" help. Qt supports all of these. Other help can be much more extensive, involving many pages of text. For this kind of help, you can use QTextBrowser as a simple online help browser, or you can invoke *Qt Assistant* or another HTML browser from your application.

## Tooltips, Status Tips, and "What's This?" Help

A tooltip is a small piece of text that appears when the mouse hovers over a widget for a certain period of time. Tooltips are presented with black text on a yellow background. Their primary use is to provide textual descriptions of toolbar buttons.

We can add tooltips to arbitrary widgets in code using QToolTip::add(). For example:

```
QToolTip::add(findButton, tr("Find next"));
```

To set the tooltip of a toolbar button that corresponds to a QAction, we can simply call setToolTip() on the action. For example:

```
newAct = new QAction(tr("&New"), tr("Ctrl+N"), this);
newAct->setToolTip(tr("New file"));
```

If we don't explicitly set a tooltip, QAction will automatically derive one from the action text and the accelerator key (for example, "New (Ctrl+N)").

A status tip is also a short piece of descriptive text, usually a little longer than a tooltip. When the mouse hovers over a toolbar button or a menu option, a status tip appears in the status bar. Call setStatusTip() to add a status tip to an action:

```
newAct->setStatusTip(tr("Create a new file"));
```

In the absence of a status tip, `QAction` will use the tooltip text instead.

If we don't use `QActions`, we need to pass a `QToolTipGroup` object and a status tip as the third and fourth arguments to `QToolTip::add()`:

```
QToolTip::add(findButton, tr("Find next"), toolTipGroup,
              tr("Find the next occurrence of the search text"));
```

The application can be made to show the longer text in the status bar by connecting the `QToolTipGroup`'s `showTip()` and `removeTip()` signals to the status bar's `message()` and `clear()` slots. The `QToolTipGroup` object is responsible for maintaining contact between tooltips and a widget that can show the longer help text.

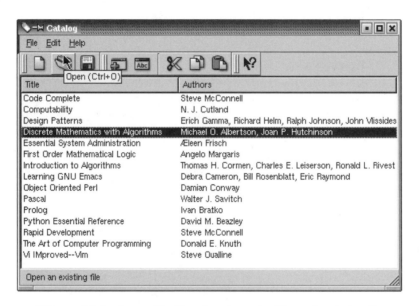

**Figure 16.1.** An application showing a tooltip and a status tip

In *Qt Designer*, tooltips and status tips are accessible through the `toolTip` and `statusTip` properties of a widget or action.

In some situations, it is desirable to provide more information about a widget than can be given by tooltips or status tips. For example, we might want to provide a complex dialog with explanatory text about each field without forcing the user to invoke a separate help window. "What's This?" mode is an ideal solution for this. When a window is in "What's This?" mode, the cursor changes to ⓀⓇ? and the user can click on any user interface component to obtain its help text. To enter "What's This?" mode, the user can either click the ? button in the dialog's title bar (on Windows and KDE) or press Shift+F1.

The help text can be set by calling `QWhatsThis::add()`. Here's an example:

```
QWhatsThis::add(sourceLineEdit,
    tr("<img src=\"icon.png\">"
       " The meaning of the Source field depends on the "
       "Type field:"
       "<ul>"
       "<li><b>Books</b> have a Publisher</li>"
       "<li><b>Articles</b> have a Journal name with volume and "
       "issue number</li>"
       "<li><b>Thesis</b> have an Institution name and a "
       "department name</li>"
       "</ul>"));
```

As with many other Qt widgets, we can use HTML-style tags to format the text of a tooltip. In the example, we include an image (which is listed in the application's `.pro` file `IMAGE` entry), a bulleted list, and some text in bold. The tags that Qt supports are specified in the `QStyleSheet` documentation.

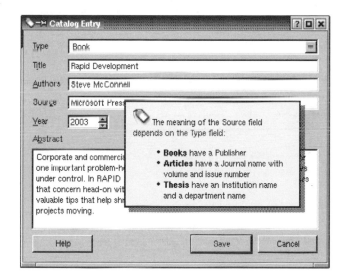

**Figure 16.2.** A dialog showing a "What's This?" help text

We can also set a "What's This?" text on an action:

```
openAct->setWhatsThis(tr("<img src=open.png> "
                         "Click this option to open an "
                         "existing file."));
```

The text will be shown when the user clicks the menu item or toolbar button or presses the accelerator key while in "What's This?" mode. In *Qt Designer*, the "What's This?" text for a widget or action is available through the `whatsThis` property.

When the user interface components of an application's main window provide "What's This?" text, it is customary to provide a What's This? option in the Help menu as well as a What's This? toolbar button. This can be done by creating a What's This? action and connecting its `activated()` signal to the `QMainWindow`'s `whatsThis()` slot, which enters "What's This?" mode when executed.

# Using QTextBrowser as a Simple Help Engine

Large and sophisticated applications may require more online help than tooltips, status tips, and "What's This?" help can provide. A simple solution to this is to provide a help browser. Applications that provide a help browser typically have a Help entry in the main window's Help menu and a Help button in every dialog.

In this section, we present the simple help browser shown in Figure 16.3 and explain how it can be used within an application. The window uses a QTextBrowser to display help pages that are marked up with an HTML-based syntax. QTextBrowser can handle a lot of simple HTML tags, so it is ideal for this purpose.

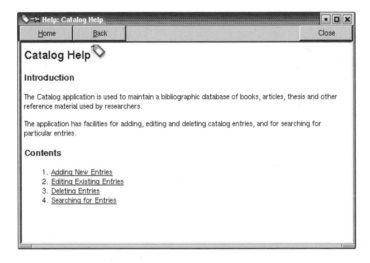

**Figure 16.3.** The HelpBrowser widget

We begin with the header file:

```
#include <qwidget.h>

class QPushButton;
class QTextBrowser;

class HelpBrowser : public QWidget
{
    Q_OBJECT
public:
    HelpBrowser(const QString &path, const QString &page,
                QWidget *parent = 0, const char *name = 0);

    static void showPage(const QString &page);

private slots:
    void updateCaption();

private:
```

```
            QTextBrowser *textBrowser;
            QPushButton *homeButton;
            QPushButton *backButton;
            QPushButton *closeButton;
        };
```

The `HelpBrowser` provides a static function that can be called from anywhere in the application. This function creates a `HelpBrowser` window and shows the given page.

Here's the beginning of the implementation:

```
        #include <qapplication.h>
        #include <qlayout.h>
        #include <qpushbutton.h>
        #include <qtextbrowser.h>

        #include "helpbrowser.h"

        HelpBrowser::HelpBrowser(const QString &path, const QString &page,
                                 QWidget *parent, const char *name)
            : QWidget(parent, name, WGroupLeader | WDestructiveClose)
        {
            textBrowser = new QTextBrowser(this);
            homeButton = new QPushButton(tr("&Home"), this);
            backButton = new QPushButton(tr("&Back"), this);
            closeButton = new QPushButton(tr("Close"), this);
            closeButton->setAccel(tr("Esc"));

            QVBoxLayout *mainLayout = new QVBoxLayout(this);
            QHBoxLayout *buttonLayout = new QHBoxLayout(mainLayout);
            buttonLayout->addWidget(homeButton);
            buttonLayout->addWidget(backButton);
            buttonLayout->addStretch(1);
            buttonLayout->addWidget(closeButton);
            mainLayout->addWidget(textBrowser);

            connect(homeButton, SIGNAL(clicked()),
                    textBrowser, SLOT(home()));
            connect(backButton, SIGNAL(clicked()),
                    textBrowser, SLOT(backward()));
            connect(closeButton, SIGNAL(clicked()),
                    this, SLOT(close()));
            connect(textBrowser, SIGNAL(sourceChanged(const QString &)),
                    this, SLOT(updateCaption()));

            textBrowser->mimeSourceFactory()->addFilePath(path);
            textBrowser->setSource(page);
        }
```

The layout is simply a row of buttons above a `QTextBrowser`. The `path` parameter is a path in the file system that contains the application's documentation. The `page` parameter is the name of the documentation file, with an optional HTML anchor.

We use the `WGroupLeader` flag because we want to pop up `HelpBrowser` windows from modal dialogs in addition to the main window. Modal dialogs normally prevent the user from interacting with any other window in the application. However, after requesting help, the user must obviously be allowed to interact with both the modal dialog and the help browser. Using the WGroupLeader flag makes this interaction possible.

```
void HelpBrowser::updateCaption()
{
    setCaption(tr("Help: %1").arg(textBrowser->documentTitle()));
}
```

Whenever the source page changes, the updateCaption() slot is executed. The documentTitle() function returns the text specified in the page's <title> tag.

```
void HelpBrowser::showPage(const QString &page)
{
    QString path = qApp->applicationDirPath() + "/doc";
    HelpBrowser *browser = new HelpBrowser(path, page);
    browser->resize(500, 400);
    browser->show();
}
```

In the showPage() static function, we create the HelpBrowser window and then show it. The window will be destroyed automatically when the user closes it, since we set the WDestructiveClose flag in the constructor.

For this example, we assume that the documentation is located in the doc subdirectory of the directory containing the application's executable. All the pages passed to the showPage() function will be taken from this doc subdirectory.

Now we are ready to invoke the help browser from the application. In the application's main window, we would create a Help action and connect it to a help() slot that could look like this:

```
void MainWindow::help()
{
    HelpBrowser::showPage("index.html");
}
```

This assumes that the main help file is called index.html. For dialogs, we would connect the Help button to a help() slot that could look like this:

```
void EntryDialog::help()
{
    HelpBrowser::showPage("dialogs.html#entrydialog");
}
```

Here we look in a different help file, dialogs.html, and scroll the QTextBrowser to the entrydialog anchor.

One other place from which we might want to invoke help is a "What's This?" text. We can link the "What's This?" text to the documentation by using HTML <a href="..."> tags.

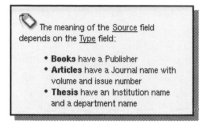

The meaning of the <u>Source</u> field
depends on the <u>Type</u> field:

- **Books** have a Publisher
- **Articles** have a Journal name with
  volume and issue number
- **Thesis** have an Institution name
  and a department name

**Figure 16.4.** A "What's This?" text with links

To make hypertext links work from "What's This?" text, we must use a QWhats-This that is aware of the help browser. This is accomplished by subclassing QWhatsThis and reimplementing its clicked() function to call HelpBrowser::showPage(). Here's the class definition:

```
class MyWhatsThis : public QWhatsThis
{
public:
    MyWhatsThis(QWidget *widget, const QString &text);

    QString text(const QPoint &point);
    bool clicked(const QString &page);

private:
    QString myText;
};
```

The text() and clicked() functions are reimplemented from QWhatsThis.

```
MyWhatsThis::MyWhatsThis(QWidget *widget, const QString &text)
    : QWhatsThis(widget)
{
    myText = text;
}
```

The constructor accepts a widget and a "What's This?" text for that widget. We pass on the widget to the base class and store the text in a private variable.

```
QString MyWhatsThis::text(const QPoint &)
{
    return myText;
}
```

The text() function returns the "What's This?" text for a widget given a certain mouse cursor position. For some widgets, it might make sense to return a different text depending on where the user clicked on it, but here we always return the same text.

```
bool MyWhatsThis::clicked(const QString &page)
{
    if (page.isEmpty()) {
        return true;
    } else {
        HelpBrowser::showPage(page);
```

```
            return false;
        }
    }
```

The `clicked()` function is called by `QWhatsThis` when the user clicks on the "What's This?" window. If the user clicked on an HTML link, `QWhatsThis` passes the target page to the `clicked()` function. (If anything else is clicked, an empty string is passed.) We invoke the help browser with the given page.

The return value of `clicked()` is used by `QWhatsThis` to determine whether it should hide the "What's This?" text (indicated by `true`) or continue to show it. When the user clicks a link, we want the "What's This?" to stay visible along with the help window, so we return `false`. If the user clicked elsewhere in the "What's This?" window, we return `true` to hide the "What's This?" window.

Here's how the `MyWhatsThis` class can be used:

```
new MyWhatsThis(sourceLineEdit,
    tr("<img src=\"icon.png\">"
       " The meaning of the "
       "<a href=\"fields.html#source\">Source</a> field depends on "
       "the <a href=\"fields.html#type\">Type</a> field:"
       "<ul>"
       "<li><b>Books</b> have a Publisher</li>"
       "<li><b>Articles</b> have a Journal name with volume and "
       "issue number</li>"
       "<li><b>Thesis</b> have an Institution name and a department "
       "name</li>"
       "</ul>"));
```

Instead of calling `QWhatsThis::add()`, we create a `MyWhatsThis` object with the widget and its associated text. But this time, if the user clicks a link, the help browser is invoked.

It may look strange that we allocate an object with `new` and don't assign the value to a variable. This is not a problem here because Qt keeps track of all `QWhatsThis` objects and deletes them when they are no longer needed.

## Using Qt Assistant for Powerful Online Help

*Qt Assistant* is a redistributable online help application supplied by Trolltech. Its main virtues are that it supports indexing and full text search and that it can handle multiple documentation sets for multiple applications.

To make use of *Qt Assistant*, we must incorporate the necessary code in our application, and we must make *Qt Assistant* aware of our documentation.

Communication between a Qt application and *Qt Assistant* is handled by the `QAssistantClient` located in a separate library. To link this library with an application, we must add the following line to the application's `.pro` file:

```
LIBS          += -lqassistantclient
```

We will now review the code of a new `HelpBrowser` class that uses *Qt Assistant*.

```
#ifndef HELPBROWSER_H
#define HELPBROWSER_H

class QAssistantClient;

class HelpBrowser
{
public:
    static void showPage(const QString &page);

private:
    static QAssistantClient *assistant;
};

#endif
```

Here's the new `helpbrowser.cpp`:

```
#include <qassistantclient.h>

#include "helpbrowser.h"

QAssistantClient *HelpBrowser::assistant = 0;

void HelpBrowser::showPage(const QString &page)
{
    if (!assistant)
        assistant = new QAssistantClient("");
    assistant->showPage(page);
}
```

The `QAssistantClient` constructor accepts a path string as its first argument, which it uses to locate the *Qt Assistant* executable. By passing an empty path, we signify that `QAssistantClient` should look for the executable in the `PATH` environment variable. `QAssistantClient` has its own `showPage()` function that accepts a page name with an optional HTML anchor, just like the earlier `QTextBrowser` subclass's `showPage()` function.

The next step is to tell *Qt Assistant* where the documentation is located. This is done by creating a *Qt Assistant* profile and creating a `.dcf` file that provides information about the documentation. All this is explained in *Qt Assistant*'s online documentation, so we will not duplicate that information here.

An alternative to using `QTextBrowser` or *Qt Assistant* is to use platform-specific approaches to providing online help. For Windows applications, it might be desirable to create Windows HTML Help files and to provide access to them using Microsoft Internet Explorer. You could use Qt's `QProcess` class or the ActiveQt framework for this. For Unix and Mac OS X applications, a suitable approach might be to provide HTML files and launch a web browser.

# 17

# Multithreading

Conventional GUI applications have one thread of execution and perform one operation at a time. If the user invokes a time-consuming operation from the user interface in a single-threaded application, the interface typically freezes while the operation is in progress. Chapter 7 (Event Processing) provides some solutions to this problem. Multithreading is another solution.

In a multithreaded Qt application, the GUI runs in its own thread and the processing takes place in one or more other threads. This results in applications that have responsive GUIs even during intensive processing. Another benefit of multithreading is that on multiprocessor machines different threads may be executed simultaneously on different processors, resulting in better performance.

In this chapter, we will start by showing how to subclass QThread and how to use QMutex, QSemaphore, and QWaitCondition to synchronize threads. Then we will see how to communicate with the GUI thread from non-GUI threads while the event loop is running, and round off with a review of which Qt classes can be used in non-GUI threads and which cannot.

Multithreading is a large topic with many books devoted exclusively to the subject. Here, it is assumed that you already understand the fundamentals of multithreaded programming; the focus is on explaining how to develop multithreaded Qt applications rather than on the subject of threading itself.

## Working with Threads

Providing multiple threads in a Qt application is straightforward: We just subclass QThread and reimplement its run() function. To show how this works, we will start by reviewing the code for a very simple QThread subclass that repeatedly prints the same text on a console.

349

```
class Thread : public QThread
{
public:
    Thread();

    void setMessage(const QString &message);
    void run();
    void stop();

private:
    QString messageStr;
    volatile bool stopped;
};
```

The `Thread` class inherits from `QThread` and reimplements the `run()` function. It provides two additional functions: `setMessage()` and `stop()`.

The `stopped` variable is declared volatile because it is accessed from different threads and we want to be sure that it is freshly read every time it is needed. If we omitted the `volatile` keyword, the compiler might optimize access to the variable, possibly leading to incorrect results.

```
Thread::Thread()
{
    stopped = false;
}
```

We set `stopped` to `false` in the constructor.

```
void Thread::run()
{
    while (!stopped)
        cerr << messageStr.ascii();
    stopped = false;
    cerr << endl;
}
```

The `run()` function is called to start executing the thread. As long as the `stopped` variable is `false`, the function keeps printing the given message to the console. The thread terminates when control leaves the `run()` function.

```
void Thread::stop()
{
    stopped = true;
}
```

The `stop()` function sets the `stopped` variable to `true`, thereby telling `run()` to stop printing text to the console. This function can be called from any thread at any time. For the purposes of this example, we assume that assignment to a `bool` is an atomic operation. This is a reasonable assumption, considering that a `bool` is either `true` or `false`. We will see later in this section how to use `QMutex` to guarantee that assigning to a variable is an atomic operation.

`QThread` provides a `terminate()` function that terminates the execution of a thread while it is still running. Using `terminate()` is not recommended, since it can stop the thread at any point and does not give the thread any chance to clean up after itself. It is always safer to use a `stopped` variable and a `stop()` function, as we did here.

**Figure 17.1.** The Threads application

We will now see how to use the `Thread` class in a small Qt application that uses two threads, A and B, in addition to the initial thread.

```cpp
class ThreadForm : public QDialog
{
    Q_OBJECT
public:
    ThreadForm(QWidget *parent = 0, const char *name = 0);

protected:
    void closeEvent(QCloseEvent *event);

private slots:
    void startOrStopThreadA();
    void startOrStopThreadB();

private:
    Thread threadA;
    Thread threadB;
    QPushButton *threadAButton;
    QPushButton *threadBButton;
    QPushButton *quitButton;
};
```

The `ThreadForm` class declares two variables of type `Thread` and some buttons to provide a basic user interface.

```cpp
ThreadForm::ThreadForm(QWidget *parent, const char *name)
    : QDialog(parent, name)
{
    setCaption(tr("Threads"));

    threadA.setMessage("A");
    threadB.setMessage("B");

    threadAButton = new QPushButton(tr("Start A"), this);
    threadBButton = new QPushButton(tr("Start B"), this);
    quitButton = new QPushButton(tr("Quit"), this);
    quitButton->setDefault(true);

    connect(threadAButton, SIGNAL(clicked()),
            this, SLOT(startOrStopThreadA()));
    connect(threadBButton, SIGNAL(clicked()),
            this, SLOT(startOrStopThreadB()));
```

```
connect(quitButton, SIGNAL(clicked()),
        this, SLOT(close()));
...
}
```

In the constructor, we call `setMessage()` to make the first thread repeatedly print "A" and the second thread "B".

```
void ThreadForm::startOrStopThreadA()
{
    if (threadA.running()) {
        threadA.stop();
        threadAButton->setText(tr("Start A"));
    } else {
        threadA.start();
        threadAButton->setText(tr("Stop A"));
    }
}
```

When the user clicks the button for thread A, `startOrStopThreadA()` stops the thread if it was running and starts it otherwise. It also updates the button's text.

```
void ThreadForm::startOrStopThreadB()
{
    if (threadB.running()) {
        threadB.stop();
        threadBButton->setText(tr("Start B"));
    } else {
        threadB.start();
        threadBButton->setText(tr("Stop B"));
    }
}
```

The code for `startOrStopThreadB()` is very similar.

```
void ThreadForm::closeEvent(QCloseEvent *event)
{
    threadA.stop();
    threadB.stop();
    threadA.wait();
    threadB.wait();
    event->accept();
}
```

If the user clicks Quit or closes the window, we stop any running threads and wait for them to finish (using `QThread::wait()`) before we call `QCloseEvent::accept()`. This ensures that the application exits in a clean state, although it doesn't really matter in this example.

To compile the application, we must add this line to the `.pro` file:

```
CONFIG      += thread
```

This tells `qmake` to use the threaded version of the Qt library. To build a threaded Qt library, pass the `-thread` command-line option to the `configure` script on

Unix and Mac OS X. On Windows, the Qt library is threaded by default. For this particular example, we also need the `console` option since we want the program's output to appear in the console on Windows:

```
win32:CONFIG += console
```

If you run the application and click Start A, the console will be filled with 'A's. If you click Start B, it will now fill with alternating sequences of 'A's and 'B's. Click Stop A, and now it will only print 'B's.

A common requirement for multithreaded applications is that of synchronizing several threads. Qt provides the following classes to do this: `QMutex`, `QMutexLocker`, `QSemaphore`, and `QWaitCondition`.

The `QMutex` class provides a means of protecting a variable or a piece of code so that only one thread can access it at a time. The class provides a `lock()` function that locks the mutex. If the mutex is unlocked, the current thread seizes it immediately and locks it; otherwise, the current thread is blocked until the thread that holds the mutex unlocks it. Either way, when the call to `lock()` returns, the current thread holds the mutex until it calls `unlock()`. `QMutex` also provides a `tryLock()` function that returns immediately if the mutex is already locked.

For example, let's suppose that we wanted to protect the `stopped` variable of the `Thread` class with a `QMutex`. We would then add the following data member to `Thread`:

```
QMutex mutex;
```

The `run()` function would change to this:

```
void Thread::run()
{
    for (;;) {
        mutex.lock();
        if (stopped) {
            stopped = false;
            mutex.unlock();
            break;
        }
        mutex.unlock();

        cerr << messageStr.ascii();
    }
    cerr << endl;
}
```

The `stop()` function would become this:

```
void Thread::stop()
{
    mutex.lock();
    stopped = true;
    mutex.unlock();
}
```

Locking and unlocking a mutex in complex functions, especially functions that use C++ exceptions, can be error-prone. Qt provides the `QMutexLocker` convenience class to simplify mutex handling. `QMutexLocker`'s constructor accepts a `QMutex` as argument and locks it. `QMutexLocker`'s destructor unlocks the mutex. For example, we could rewrite the `stop()` function above as follows:

```
void Thread::stop()
{
    QMutexLocker locker(&mutex);
    stopped = true;
}
```

`QSemaphore` provides semaphores in Qt. A semaphore is a generalization of mutexes that can be used to guard a certain number of identical resources.

The following two code snippets show the correspondence between `QSemaphore` and `QMutex`:

```
QSemaphore semaphore(1);        QMutex mutex;
semaphore++;                    mutex.lock();
semaphore--;                    mutex.unlock();
```

The postfix ++ and -- operators acquire and release one resource protected by the semaphore. By passing 1 to the constructor, we tell the semaphore that it controls a single resource. The advantage of using a semaphore is that we can pass numbers other than 1 to the constructor and then call ++ multiple times to acquire many resources.

A typical application of semaphores is when transfering a certain amount of data (`DataSize`) between two threads using a shared circular buffer of a certain size (`BufferSize`):

```
const int DataSize = 100000;
const int BufferSize = 4096;
char buffer[BufferSize];
```

The producer thread writes data to the buffer until it reaches the end, and then restarts from the beginning, overwriting existing data. The consumer thread reads the data as it is generated. Figure 17.2 illustrates this, assuming a tiny 16-byte buffer.

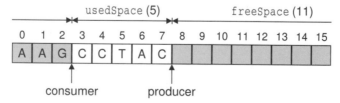

**Figure 17.2.** The producer–consumer model

The need for synchronization in the producer–consumer example is twofold: If the producer generates the data too fast, it will overwrite data that the consumer hasn't yet read; if the consumer reads the data too fast, it will pass the producer and read garbage.

A crude way to solve this problem is to have the producer fill the buffer, then wait until the consumer has read the *entire* buffer, and so on. However, on multiprocessor machines, this isn't as fast as letting the producer and consumer threads operate on different parts of the buffer at the same time.

One way to efficiently solve the problem is to use two semaphores:

```
QSemaphore freeSpace(BufferSize);
QSemaphore usedSpace(BufferSize);
```

The `freeSpace` semaphore governs the part of the buffer that the producer can fill with data. The `usedSpace` semaphore governs the area that the consumer can read. These two areas are complementary. Both are initialized with `BufferSize` (4096), meaning that they can administer up to that many resources.

For this example, each byte counts as one resource. In a real-world application, we would probably operate on larger units (for example, 64 or 256 bytes at a time) to reduce the overhead associated with using semaphores.

```
void acquire(QSemaphore &semaphore)
{
    semaphore++;
}
```

The `acquire()` function attempts to acquire one resource (one byte in the buffer). QSemaphore uses the postfix `++` operator for this, but in our particular example it is more intuitive to use a function called `acquire()`.

```
void release(QSemaphore &semaphore)
{
    semaphore--;
}
```

Similarly, we implement the `release()` function as a synonym for the postfix `--` operator.

```
void Producer::run()
{
    for (int i = 0; i < DataSize; ++i) {
        acquire(freeSpace);
        buffer[i % BufferSize] = "ACGT"[(uint)rand() % 4];
        release(usedSpace);
    }
}
```

In the producer, we start by acquiring one "free" byte. If the buffer is full of data that the consumer hasn't read yet, the call to `acquire()` will block until the consumer has started to consume the data. Once we have acquired the byte, we fill it with some random data ('A', 'C', 'G', or 'T') and release the byte as "used", so that it can be read by the consumer thread.

```
void Consumer::run()
{
    for (int i = 0; i < DataSize; ++i) {
```

```
            acquire(usedSpace);
            cerr << buffer[i % BufferSize];
            release(freeSpace);
        }
        cerr << endl;
    }
```

In the consumer, we start by acquiring one "used" byte. If the buffer contains no data to read, the call to `acquire()` will block until the producer has produced some. Once we have acquired the byte, we print it and release the byte as "free", making it possible for the producer to fill it with data again.

```
    int main()
    {
        usedSpace += BufferSize;

        Producer producer;
        Consumer consumer;
        producer.start();
        consumer.start();
        producer.wait();
        consumer.wait();
        return 0;
    }
```

Finally, in `main()`, we start by acquiring all the "used" space (using `QSemaphore`'s counterintuitive += operator) to ensure that the consumer will not acquire it and read garbage. Then we start the producer and consumer threads. What happens then is that the producer converts some "free" space into "used" space, and the consumer can then convert it back to "free" space.

When we run the program, it writes a random sequence of 100,000 'A's, 'C's, 'G's, and 'T's to the console and then terminates. To really understand what is going on, we can disable writing the output and instead write 'P' each time the producer generates a byte and 'c' each time the consumer reads a byte. And to make things as simple to follow as possible, we can use much smaller values for `DataSize` and `BufferSize`.

For example, here's a possible run with a `DataSize` of 10 and a `BufferSize` of 4: "PcPcPcPcPcPcPcPcPcPc". In this case, the consumer reads the bytes as soon as they are generated by the producer; the two threads are executing at the same speed. Another possibility is that the producer fills the whole buffer before the consumer even starts reading it: "PPPPccccPPPPccccPPcc". There are many other possibilities. Semaphores give a lot of latitude to the system-specific thread scheduler, which can study the threads' behavior and choose an optimal scheduling policy.

A different approach to the problem of synchronizing a producer and a consumer is to use `QWaitCondition` and `QMutex`. A `QWaitCondition` allows a thread to wake up other threads when some condition has been met. This allows for more precise control than is possible with mutexes alone. To show how it works, we will redo the producer–consumer example using wait conditions.

```
const int DataSize = 100000;
const int BufferSize = 4096;
char buffer[BufferSize];

QWaitCondition bufferIsNotFull;
QWaitCondition bufferIsNotEmpty;
QMutex mutex;
int usedSpace = 0;
```

In addition to the buffer, we declare two QWaitConditions, one QMutex, and one variable that stores how many bytes in the buffer are "used" bytes.

```
void Producer::run()
{
    for (int i = 0; i < DataSize; ++i) {
        mutex.lock();
        while (usedSpace == BufferSize)
            bufferIsNotFull.wait(&mutex);
        buffer[i % BufferSize] = "ACGT"[(uint)rand() % 4];
        ++usedSpace;
        bufferIsNotEmpty.wakeAll();
        mutex.unlock();
    }
}
```

In the producer, we start by checking whether the buffer is full. If it is, we wait on the "buffer is not full" condition. When that condition is met, we write one byte to the buffer, increment usedSpace, and wake any thread waiting for the "buffer is not empty" condition to turn true.

We use a mutex to protect all accesses to the usedSpace variable. The QWaitCondition::wait() function can take a locked mutex as its first argument, which it unlocks before blocking the current thread and then locks before returning.

For this example, we could have replaced the while loop

```
while (usedSpace == BufferSize)
    bufferIsNotFull.wait(&mutex);
```

with this if statement:

```
if (usedSpace == BufferSize) {
    mutex.unlock();
    bufferIsNotFull.wait();
    mutex.lock();
}
```

However, this would break as soon as we allow more than one producer thread, since another producer could seize the mutex immediately after the wait() call and make the "buffer is not full" condition false again.

```
void Consumer::run()
{
    for (int i = 0; i < DataSize; ++i) {
        mutex.lock();
        while (usedSpace == 0)
            bufferIsNotEmpty.wait(&mutex);
```

```
            cerr << buffer[i % BufferSize];
            --usedSpace;
            bufferIsNotFull.wakeAll();
            mutex.unlock();
        }
        cerr << endl;
    }
```

The consumer does the opposite of the producer: It waits for the "buffer is not empty" condition and wakes up any thread waiting for the "buffer is not full" condition.

In all the examples so far, our threads have accessed the same global variables. But some threaded applications need to have a global variable hold different values in different threads. This is often called thread-local storage (TLS) or thread-specific data (TSD). We can fake it using a map keyed on thread IDs (returned by `QThread::currentThread()`), but a nicer approach is to use the `QThreadStorage<T>` class.

A common use of `QThreadStorage<T>` is for caches. By having a separate cache in different threads, we avoid the overhead of locking, unlocking, and possibly waiting for a mutex. For example:

```
QThreadStorage<QMap<int, double> *> cache;

void insertIntoCache(int id, double value)
{
    if (!cache.hasLocalData())
        cache.setLocalData(new QMap<int, double>);
    cache.localData()->insert(id, value);
}

void removeFromCache(int id)
{
    if (cache.hasLocalData())
        cache.localData()->remove(id);
}
```

The `cache` variable holds one pointer to a `QMap<int, double>` per thread. (Because of problems with some compilers, the template type in `QThreadStorage<T>` must be a pointer type.) The first time we use the cache in a particular thread, `hasLocalData()` returns `false` and we create the `QMap<int, double>` object.

In addition to caching, `QThreadStorage<T>` can be used for global error-state variables (similar to `errno`), to ensure that modifications in one thread don't affect other threads.

# Communicating with the GUI Thread

When a Qt application starts, only one thread is running—the initial thread. This is the only thread that is allowed to create the `QApplication` object and call `exec()` on it. For this reason, we normally refer to this thread as the GUI thread. After the call to `exec()`, this thread is either waiting for an event or processing an event.

The GUI thread can start new threads by creating objects of a `QThread` subclass, as we did in the previous section. If these new threads need to communicate among themselves, they can use shared variables together with mutexes, semaphores, or wait conditions. But none of these techniques can be used to communicate with the GUI thread, since they would lock the event loop and freeze the user interface.

The solution for communicating from a non-GUI thread to the GUI thread is to use custom events. Qt's event mechanism allows us to define custom event types in addition to the built-in types, and allows us to post events of those types using `QApplication::postEvent()`. Furthermore, since `postEvent()` is thread-safe, we can use it from any thread to post events to the GUI thread.

**Figure 17.3.** The Image Pro application

To illustrate how this works, we will review the code of the Image Pro application, a basic image processing application that allows the user to rotate, resize, and change the color depth of an image. The application uses one non-GUI thread to perform operations on images without locking the event loop. This makes a significant difference when processing large images. The non-GUI

thread has a list of tasks, or "transactions", to accomplish, and sends events to
the main window to report progress.

```
ImageWindow::ImageWindow(QWidget *parent, const char *name)
    : QMainWindow(parent, name)
{
    thread.setTargetWidget(this);
    ...
}
```

In the `ImageWindow` constructor, we set the "target widget" of the non-GUI
thread to be the `ImageWindow`. The thread will post progress events to that
widget. The `thread` variable is of type `TransactionThread`, which we will cover
in a moment.

```
void ImageWindow::flipHorizontally()
{
    addTransaction(new FlipTransaction(Horizontal));
}
```

The `flipHorizontally()` slot creates a "flip" transaction and registers it using
the private function `addTransaction()`. The `flipVertical()`, `resizeImage()`,
`convertTo32Bit()`, `convertTo8Bit()`, and `convertTo1Bit()` functions are similar.

```
void ImageWindow::addTransaction(Transaction *transact)
{
    thread.addTransaction(transact);
    openAct->setEnabled(false);
    saveAct->setEnabled(false);
    saveAsAct->setEnabled(false);
}
```

The `addTransaction()` function adds a transaction to the non-GUI thread's
transaction queue and disables the Open, Save, and Save As actions while
transactions are being processed.

```
void ImageWindow::customEvent(QCustomEvent *event)
{
    if ((int)event->type() == TransactionStart) {
        TransactionStartEvent *startEvent =
                (TransactionStartEvent *)event;
        infoLabel->setText(startEvent->message);
    } else if ((int)event->type() == AllTransactionsDone) {
        openAct->setEnabled(true);
        saveAct->setEnabled(true);
        saveAsAct->setEnabled(true);
        imageLabel->setPixmap(QPixmap(thread.image()));
        infoLabel->setText(tr("Ready"));
        modLabel->setText(tr("MOD"));
        modified = true;
        statusBar()->message(tr("Done"), 2000);
    } else {
        QMainWindow::customEvent(event);
    }
}
```

The customEvent() function is reimplemented from QObject to handle custom events. The TransactionStart and AllTransactionsDone constants are defined in transactionthread.h as

```
enum { TransactionStart = 1001, AllTransactionsDone = 1002 };
```

Qt's built-in events have values below 1000. Higher values can be used for custom events.

The data type for custom events is QCustomEvent, a QEvent subclass that stores a void pointer in addition to the event type. For TransactionStart events, we use a QCustomEvent subclass that stores an additional data member:

```
class TransactionStartEvent : public QCustomEvent
{
public:
    TransactionStartEvent();

    QString message;
};

TransactionStartEvent::TransactionStartEvent()
    : QCustomEvent(TransactionStart)
{
}
```

In the constructor, we pass the TransactionStart constant to the base class constructor.

Now, let's turn to the TransactionThread class:

```
class TransactionThread : public QThread
{
public:
    void run();
    void setTargetWidget(QWidget *widget);
    void addTransaction(Transaction *transact);
    void setImage(const QImage &image);
    QImage image();

private:
    QWidget *targetWidget;
    QMutex mutex;
    QImage currentImage;
    std::list<Transaction *> transactions;
};
```

The TransactionThread class maintains a list of transactions to process and executes them one after the other in the background.

```
void TransactionThread::addTransaction(Transaction *transact)
{
    QMutexLocker locker(&mutex);
    transactions.push_back(transact);
    if (!running())
        start();
}
```

The addTransaction() function adds a transaction to the transaction queue and starts the transaction thread if it isn't already running.

```cpp
void TransactionThread::run()
{
    Transaction *transact;

    for (;;) {
        mutex.lock();
        if (transactions.empty()) {
            mutex.unlock();
            break;
        }
        QImage oldImage = currentImage;
        transact = *transactions.begin();
        transactions.pop_front();
        mutex.unlock();

        TransactionStartEvent *event = new TransactionStartEvent;
        event->message = transact->messageStr();
        QApplication::postEvent(targetWidget, event);

        QImage newImage = transact->apply(oldImage);
        delete transact;

        mutex.lock();
        currentImage = newImage;
        mutex.unlock();
    }
    QApplication::postEvent(targetWidget,
                            new QCustomEvent(AllTransactionsDone));
}
```

The run() function goes through the transaction queue and executes each transaction in turn (by calling apply() on them). All accesses to the transactions and currentImage member variables are protected with a mutex.

When a transaction is started, we post a TransactionStart event to the target widget (the ImageWindow). When all the transactions have finished processing, we post an AllTransactionsDone event.

```cpp
class Transaction
{
public:
    virtual QImage apply(const QImage &image) = 0;
    virtual QString messageStr() = 0;
};
```

The Transaction class is an abstract base class for operations that the user can perform on an image. It has three concrete subclasses: FlipTransaction, ResizeTransaction, and ConvertDepthTransaction. We will only review FlipTransaction; the other two classes are similar.

```cpp
class FlipTransaction : public Transaction
{
public:
```

```
        FlipTransaction(Qt::Orientation orient);

        QImage apply(const QImage &image);
        QString messageStr();

    private:
        Qt::Orientation orientation;
    };
```

The `FlipTransaction` constructor takes one parameter that specifies the orientation of the flip (`Horizontal` or `Vertical`).

```
    QImage FlipTransaction::apply(const QImage &image)
    {
        return image.mirror(orientation == Qt::Horizontal,
                            orientation == Qt::Vertical);
    }
```

The `apply()` function calls `QImage::mirror()` on the `QImage` it receives as parameter and returns the resulting `QImage`.

```
    QString FlipTransaction::messageStr()
    {
        if (orientation == Qt::Horizontal)
            return QObject::tr("Flipping image horizontally...");
        else
            return QObject::tr("Flipping image vertically...");
    }
```

The `messageStr()` returns the message to display in the status bar while the operation is in progress. This function is called in `ImageWindow::customEvent()`, in the GUI thread.

For long-running operations, it might be desirable to report fine-grained progress. We can achieve this by creating an additional custom event and posting it when a certain percentage of the processing is completed.

## Using Qt's Classes in Non-GUI Threads

A function is said to be *thread-safe* when it can safely be called from different threads simultaneously. If two thread-safe functions are called from different threads on the same shared data, the result is always defined. By extension, a class is said to be thread-safe when all of its functions can be called from different threads simultaneously without interfering with each other, even when operating on the same object.

Qt's thread-safe classes are `QThread`, `QMutex`, `QMutexLocker`, `QSemaphore`, `QThread-Storage<T>`, and `QWaitCondition`. In addition, the following functions are thread-safe: `QApplication::postEvent()`, `QApplication::removePostedEvent()`, `QApplication::removePostedEvents()`, and `QEventLoop::wakeUp()`.

Most of Qt's non-GUI classes meet a less stringent requirement: They are *reentrant*. A class is reentrant if different instances of the class can be used simultaneously in different threads. However, accessing the same reentrant object in multiple threads simultaneously is not safe, and such accesses should be protected with a mutex. Reentrant classes are marked as such in the Qt reference documentation. Typically, any C++ class that doesn't reference global or otherwise shared data is reentrant.

QObject is reentrant, but none of Qt's QObject subclasses are reentrant. One consequence of this is that we cannot directly call functions on a widget from a non-GUI thread. If we want to, say, change the text of a QLabel from a non-GUI thread, we must post a custom event to the GUI thread, asking it to change the text for us.

Deleting a QObject with delete is not reentrant. To delete a QObject from a non-GUI thread, we can call QObject::deleteLater(), which posts a "deferred delete" event.

QObject's signals and slots mechanism can be used in any thread. When a signal is emitted in one thread, the slots that are connected to it are called immediately, and the execution takes place in the same thread—not in the thread where the receiver object was created. This means that we can't use signals and slots to communicate with the GUI thread from other threads.

The QTimer class and the networking classes QFtp, QHttp, QSocket, and QSocketNotifier all depend on the event loop, so we cannot use them in non-GUI threads. The only networking class available is QSocketDevice, the low-level wrapper for the platform-specific networking APIs. A common technique is to use a synchronous QSocketDevice in a non-GUI thread. Some programmers find that it leads to simpler code than using QSocket (which works asynchronously), and by working in a non-GUI thread, they don't block the event loop.

Qt's SQL and OpenGL modules can also be used in multithreaded applications, but have their own restrictions, which vary from system to system. For details, see http://doc.trolltech.com/3.2/sql-driver.html as well as the *Qt Quarterly* article "Glimpsing the Third Dimension", available online at http://doc.trolltech.com/qq/qq06-glimpsing.html.

Many of Qt's non-GUI classes, including QImage, QString, and the container classes, use implicit or explicit sharing as an optimization technique. These classes are reentrant except for their copy constructors and assignment operators. When a copy of an instance of these classes is taken, only a pointer to the internal data is copied. This is dangerous if multiple threads attempt to modify the data simultaneously. In such cases, a solution is to use the QDeepCopy<T> class when performing an assignment to an instance of an implicitly or explicitly shared class. For example:

```
QString password;
QMutex mutex;

void setPassword(const QString &str)
{
    mutex.lock();
    password = QDeepCopy<QString>(str);
```

```
        mutex.unlock();
}
```

Qt 4 will probably provide enhanced threading support. Among other things, it is expected that the signal–slot mechanism will be extended to support connections across threads, eliminating the need to use custom events for communicating with the GUI thread. It is also expected that non-GUI classes like `QSocket` and `QTimer` will be available in non-GUI threads, and that `QDeepCopy<T>` will no longer be necessary when copying instances of implicitly and explicitly shared classes across threads.

# Platform-Specific Features

In this chapter, we will look at some of the platform specific options available to Qt programmers. We begin by looking at how to access native APIs such as the Win32 API on Windows, Core Graphics on Mac OS X, and Xlib on X11. We then move on to explore Qt's ActiveQt extension, showing how to use ActiveX controls within Qt/Windows applications and how to create applications that act as ActiveX servers. And in the last section, we explain how to make Qt applications cooperate with the session manager under X11.

In addition to the features presented here, the Enterprise Edition of Qt includes the Qt/Motif extension to ease the migration of Motif and Xt applications to Qt. A similar extension for Tcl/Tk applications is provided by froglogic, and a Microsoft Windows resource converter is available from Klarälvdalens Datakonsult. And for embedded development, Trolltech provides the Qtopia application framework. See the following web pages for details:

- http://doc.trolltech.com/3.2/motif-extension.html
- http://www.froglogic.com/tq/
- http://www.klaralvdalens-datakonsult.se/?page=products&sub=knut
- http://www.trolltech.com/products/qtopia/

## Interfacing with Native APIs

Qt provides a comprehensive API that caters for most needs on all platforms. But in some circumstances, we may want to use the underlying, platform-specific APIs. In this section, we will show how to use the native APIs for the different platforms supported by Qt to accomplish particular tasks.

On every platform, QWidget provides a winId() function that returns the window ID (the HWND on Windows). QWidget also provides a static function called find() that returns the QWidget with a particular window ID. We can pass this ID to native API functions to achieve platform-specific effects. For example, the following code uses `winId()` to make a `QLabel` semi-transparent on Mac OS X using native Core Graphics functions:*

```
#include <qapplication.h>
#include <qlabel.h>
#include <qt_mac.h>

int main(int argc, char *argv[])
{
    QApplication app(argc, argv);
    QLabel *label = new QLabel("Hello Qt!", 0);
    app.setMainWidget(label);

    CGSWindowRef winRef =
        GetNativeWindowFromWindowRef((WindowRef)label->winId());
    CGSSetWindowAlpha(_CGSDefaultConnection(), winRef, 0.5);

    label->show();
    return app.exec();
}
```

Here's how to achieve the same effect on Windows, using the Win32 API:

```
#define _WIN32_WINNT 0x0501

#include <qapplication.h>
#include <qt_windows.h>

int main(int argc, char *argv[])
{
    QApplication app(argc, argv);
    QLabel *label = new QLabel("Hello Qt!", 0);
    app.setMainWidget(label);

    int exstyle = GetWindowLong(label->winId(), GWL_EXSTYLE);
    exstyle |= WS_EX_LAYERED;
    SetWindowLong(label->winId(), GWL_EXSTYLE, exstyle);
    SetLayeredWindowAttributes(label->winId(), 0, 128,
                               LWA_ALPHA);

    label->show();
    return app.exec();
}
```

This code assumes that the platform is Windows 2000 or XP. If we wanted the application to compile and run on older versions of Windows that don't support semi-transparency, we could use `QLibrary` to resolve the `SetLayeredWindowAttributes` symbol at run-time instead of at link-time:

```
typedef BOOL (__stdcall *PSetLayeredWindowAttributes)
        (HWND, COLORREF, BYTE, DWORD);
PSetLayeredWindowAttributes pSetLayeredWindowAttributes =
        (PSetLayeredWindowAttributes) QLibrary::resolve("user32",
                "SetLayeredWindowAttributes");
```

---

*Qt 3.3 will probably provide a function to achieve this without resorting to native API calls.

```
if (pSetLayeredWindowAttributes) {
    int exstyle = GetWindowLong(label->winId(), GWL_EXSTYLE);
    exstyle |= WS_EX_LAYERED;
    SetWindowLong(label->winId(), GWL_EXSTYLE, exstyle);
    pSetLayeredWindowAttributes(label->winId(), 0, 128,
                                LWA_ALPHA);
}
```

Qt/Windows uses this technique internally to ensure that Qt applications take advantage of advanced features such as native Unicode support and font transformations where they are available, while still being able to run on old Windows versions.

On X11, there is no standard way to achieve transparency. However, here's how we would modify an X11 window property:

```
Atom atom = XInternAtom(win->x11Display(), "MY_PROPERTY", False);
long data = 1;
XChangeProperty(win->x11Display(), win->winId(), atom, atom,
                32, PropModeReplace, (unsigned char *)&data, 1);
```

Qt/Embedded differs from the other Qt versions in that it is implemented directly on top of the Linux frame buffer, with no native API in between. It also provides its own window system, QWS, which can be configured by subclassing Qt/Embedded-specific classes like `QWSDecoration` and `QWSInputMethod`. Another difference of Qt/Embedded is that its size can be reduced by compiling out unused classes and features. For more information about Qt/Embedded, see `http://www.trolltech.com/products/embedded/` and `http://doc.trolltech.com/3.2/winsystem.html`.

If we want to use platform-specific code in an otherwise portable Qt application, we can surround the native code with `#if` and `#endif`. For example:

```
#if defined(Q_WS_MAC)
    CGSWindowRef winRef =
        GetNativeWindowFromWindowRef((WindowRef)label->winId());
    CGSSetWindowAlpha(_CGSDefaultConnection(), winRef, 0.5);
#endif
```

Qt defines one of the following four window system symbols: `Q_WS_WIN`, `Q_WS_X11`, `Q_WS_MAC`, and `Q_WS_QWS`. We must make sure to include at least one Qt header before we use them in applications. Qt also provides preprocessor symbols to identify the operating system:

- `Q_OS_WIN32`
- `Q_OS_DGUX`
- `Q_OS_LINUX`
- `Q_OS_QNX6`
- `Q_OS_WIN64`
- `Q_OS_DYNIX`
- `Q_OS_LYNX`
- `Q_OS_RELIANT`
- `Q_OS_CYGWIN`
- `Q_OS_FREEBSD`
- `Q_OS_NETBSD`
- `Q_OS_SCO`
- `Q_OS_MAC`
- `Q_OS_HPUX`
- `Q_OS_OPENBSD`
- `Q_OS_SOLARIS`
- `Q_OS_AIX`
- `Q_OS_HURD`
- `Q_OS_OSF`
- `Q_OS_ULTRIX`
- `Q_OS_BSDI`
- `Q_OS_IRIX`
- `Q_OS_QNX`
- `Q_OS_UNIXWARE`

We can assume that at most one of these will be defined. For convenience, Qt defines `Q_OS_WIN` when either Win32 or Win64 is detected, and `Q_OS_UNIX` when any Unix-based operating system (including Mac OS X) is detected. At run-time, we can call `QApplication::winVersion()` or `QApplication::macVersion()` to distinguish between different versions of Windows (95, 98, etc.) or Mac OS X (10.0, 10.1, etc.).

Several of Qt's GUI-related classes provide a platform-specific `handle()` function that returns a low-level handle to the object. Figure 18.1 lists the return type of `handle()` on different platforms.

| | Windows | X11 | Mac OS X | Embedded |
|---|---|---|---|---|
| QCursor | HCURSOR | Cursor | int | int |
| QFont | HFONT | Font | FMFontFamily | FontID |
| QPaintDevice | HDC | Drawable | GWorldPtr | N/A |
| QPainter | HDC | Drawable | GWorldPtr | N/A |
| QRegion | HRGN | Region | RgnHandle | void * |
| QSessionManager | N/A | SmcConn | N/A | N/A |

**Figure 18.1.** Platform-specific handle types

The `QWidget`, `QPixmap`, `QPrinter`, and `QPicture` classes all inherit from `QPaintDevice`. On X11 and Mac OS X, `handle()` means the same thing as `winId()` on a `QWidget`. On Windows, `handle()` returns the device context, whereas `winId()` returns the window handle. Similarly, `QPixmap` provides a `hbm()` function that returns a bitmap handle (`HBITMAP`) on Windows.

On X11, `QPaintDevice` provides many functions that return various pointers or handles, including `x11Display()` and `x11Screen()`. We can use these to set up an X11 graphics context on a `QWidget` or `QPixmap`, for example.

Qt applications that need to interface with other toolkits or libraries frequently need to access the low-level events (`XEvent`s on X11, `MSG`s on Windows and Mac OS X, `QWSEvent`s on Qt/Embedded) before they are converted into `QEvent`s. We can do this by subclassing `QApplication` and reimplementing the relevant platform-specific event filter, one of `winEventFilter()`, `x11EventFilter()`, `macEventFilter()`, and `qwsEventFilter()`.

We can access the platform-specific events that are sent to a given `QWidget` by reimplementing one of `winEvent()`, `x11Event()`, `macEvent()`, and `qwsEvent()`. This can be useful for handling certain types of events that Qt normally ignores, such as joystick events.

For more information about platform-specific issues, including how to get started with Qt/Embedded and how to deploy Qt applications on different platforms, see `http://doc.trolltech.com/3.2/winsystem.html`.

# Using ActiveX

Microsoft's ActiveX technology allows applications to incorporate user interface components provided by other applications or libraries. It is built on Microsoft COM and defines one set of interfaces for applications that use components and another set of interfaces for applications and libraries that provide components.

Qt/Windows Enterprise Edition provides the ActiveQt framework to seamlessly combine ActiveX and Qt. ActiveQt consists of two modules:

- The *QAxContainer* module allows us to use COM objects and to embed ActiveX controls in Qt applications.

- The *QAxServer* module allows us to export custom COM objects and ActiveX controls written using Qt.

Our first example will embed the Windows Media Player in a Qt application using *QAxContainer*. The Qt application adds an Open button, a Play/Pause button, a Stop button, and a slider to the Windows Media Player ActiveX control.

**Figure 18.2.** The Media Player application

The application's main window is of type `PlayerWindow`:

```
class PlayerWindow : public QWidget
{
    Q_OBJECT
    Q_ENUMS(ReadyStateConstants)
public:
    enum PlayStateConstants { Stopped = 0, Paused = 1, Playing = 2 };
    enum ReadyStateConstants { Uninitialized = 0, Loading = 1,
                               Interactive = 3, Complete = 4 };

    PlayerWindow(QWidget *parent = 0, const char *name = 0);

protected:
    void timerEvent(QTimerEvent *event);
```

```
    private slots:
        void onPlayStateChange(int oldState, int newState);
        void onReadyStateChange(ReadyStateConstants readyState);
        void onPositionChange(double oldPos, double newPos);
        void sliderValueChanged(int newValue);
        void openFile();
```

The `PlayerWindow` class inherits from `QWidget`. The `Q_ENUMS()` macro is necessary to tell `moc` that the `ReadyStateConstants` type used in the `onReadyStateChange()` slot is an enum type.

```
    private:
        QAxWidget *wmp;
        QToolButton *openButton;
        QToolButton *playPauseButton;
        QToolButton *stopButton;
        QSlider *seekSlider;
        QString fileFilters;
        int updateTimer;
    };
```

In the private section, we declare a `QAxWidget *` data member.

```
    PlayerWindow::PlayerWindow(QWidget *parent, const char *name)
        : QWidget(parent, name)
    {
        ...
        wmp = new QAxWidget(this);
        wmp->setControl("{22D6F312-B0F6-11D0-94AB-0080C74C7E95}");
```

In the constructor, we create a `QAxWidget` object to encapsulate the Windows Media Player ActiveX control. The *QAxContainer* module consists of three classes: `QAxObject` encapsulates a COM object, `QAxWidget` encapsulates an ActiveX control, and `QAxBase` implements the core COM functionality for `QAxObject` and `QAxWidget`.

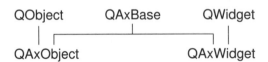

**Figure 18.3.** Inheritance tree for the *QAxContainer* module

We call `setControl()` on the `QAxWidget` with the class ID of the Windows Media Player 6.4 control. This will create an instance of the required component. From then on, all the properties, events, and methods of the ActiveX control are available as Qt properties, signals, and slots through the `QAxWidget` object.

The COM data types are automatically converted into the corresponding Qt types, as summarized in Figure 18.4. For example, an in-parameter of type `VARIANT_BOOL` becomes a `bool`, and an out-parameter of type `VARIANT_BOOL` becomes a `bool &`. If the resulting type is a Qt class (`QString`, `QDateTime`, etc.), the in-parameter is a const reference (for example, `const QString &`).

| COM types | Qt type |
|---|---|
| `VARIANT_BOOL` | `bool` |
| `char, short, int, long` | `int` |
| `unsigned char, unsigned short,`<br>`unsigned int, unsigned long` | `uint` |
| `float, double` | `double` |
| `CY` | `Q_LLONG` |
| `BSTR` | `QString` |
| `DATE` | `QDateTime` |
| `OLE_COLOR` | `QColor` |
| `SAFEARRAY(VARIANT)` | `QValueList<QVariant>` |
| `SAFEARRAY(BYTE)` | `QByteArray` |
| `VARIANT` | `QVariant` |
| `IFontDisp *` | `QFont` |
| `IPictureDisp *` | `QPixmap` |

**Figure 18.4.** Relationship between COM types and Qt types

To obtain the list of all the properties, signals, and slots available in a `QAxObject` or `QAxWidget` with their Qt data types, call `generateDocumentation()` or use Qt's `dumpdoc` command-line tool, located in Qt's `extensions\activeqt\example` directory.

```
wmp->setProperty("ShowControls", QVariant(false, 0));
wmp->setSizePolicy(QSizePolicy::Expanding,
                   QSizePolicy::Expanding);
connect(wmp, SIGNAL(PlayStateChange(int, int)),
        this, SLOT(onPlayStateChange(int, int)));
connect(wmp, SIGNAL(ReadyStateChange(ReadyStateConstants)),
        this, SLOT(onReadyStateChange(ReadyStateConstants)));
connect(wmp, SIGNAL(PositionChange(double, double)),
        this, SLOT(onPositionChange(double, double)));
```

After calling `setControl()` in the `PlayerWindow` constructor, we call `setProperty()` to set the `ShowControls` property of the Windows Media Player to `false`, since we provide our own buttons to manipulate the component. The `setProperty()` function is defined in `QObject` and can be used both for COM properties and for normal Qt properties. Its second parameter is of type `QVariant`. Because some C++ compilers don't support the `bool` type properly yet, the `QVariant` constructor that takes a `bool` also has a dummy `int` parameter. For types other than `bool`, the conversion to `QVariant` is automatic.

Next, we call `setSizePolicy()` to make the ActiveX control take all the available space in the layout, and we connect three ActiveX events from the COM component to three slots.

The rest of the `PlayerWindow` constructor follows the usual pattern, except that we connect some Qt signals to slots provided by the COM object (`Play()`, `Pause()`, and `Stop()`).

Let's leave the constructor and look at the `timerEvent()` function:

```
void PlayerWindow::timerEvent(QTimerEvent *event)
{
    if (event->timerId() == updateTimer) {
        double curPos = wmp->property("CurrentPosition").toDouble();
        onPositionChange(-1, curPos);
    } else {
        QWidget::timerEvent(event);
    }
}
```

The `timerEvent()` function is called at regular intervals while a media clip is playing. We use it to advance the slider. This is done by calling `property()` on the ActiveX control to obtain the value of the `CurrentPosition` property as a `QVariant` and calling `toDouble()` to convert it to a `double`. We then call `onPositionChange()` to perform the update.

We will not review the rest of the code because most of it isn't directly relevant to ActiveX and doesn't show anything that we haven't covered already. The code is included on the CD.

In the `.pro` file, we need this entry to link with the *QAxContainer* module:

```
LIBS          += -lqaxcontainer
```

One frequent need when dealing with COM objects is to be able to call a COM method directly (as opposed to connecting it to a Qt signal). The easiest way to do this is to call `dynamicCall()` with the name and signature of the method as first parameter and the arguments to the method as additional parameters. For example:

```
wmp->dynamicCall("TitlePlay(uint)", 6);
```

The `dynamicCall()` function takes up to eight parameters of type `QVariant` and returns a `QVariant`. If we need to pass an `IDispatch *` or an `IUnknown *` this way, we can encapsulate the component in a `QAxObject` and call `asVariant()` on it to convert it to a `QVariant`. If we need to call a COM method that returns an `IDispatch *` or an `IUnknown *`, or if we need to access a COM property of one of those types, we must use `querySubObject()` instead:

```
QAxObject *session = outlook.querySubObject("Session");
QAxObject *defaultContacts =
        session->querySubObject("GetDefaultFolder(OlDefaultFolders)",
                                "olFolderContacts");
```

If we want to call functions that have unsupported data types in their parameter list, we can use `QAxBase::queryInterface()` to retrieve the COM interface and call the function directly. We must call `Release()` when we have finished using the interface.

If we often need to call such functions, we can subclass `QAxObject` or `QAxWidget` and provide member functions that encapsulate the COM interface calls. However, be aware that `QAxObject` and `QAxWidget` subclasses cannot define their own properties, signals, and slots.

We will now review the *QAxServer* module. This module enables us to turn a standard Qt program into an ActiveX server. The server can either be a shared library or a stand-alone application. Servers built as shared libraries are often called in-process servers, and stand-alone applications are called out-of-process servers.

Our first *QAxServer* example is an in-process server that provides a widget that shows a ball bouncing left and right. We will also see how to embed the widget in Internet Explorer.

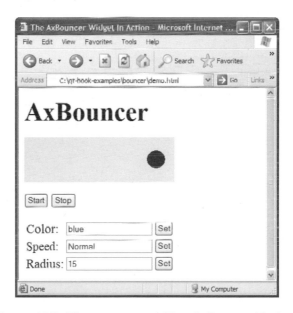

**Figure 18.5.** The `AxBouncer` widget in Internet Explorer

Here's the beginning of the class definition of the `AxBouncer` widget:

```
class AxBouncer : public QWidget, public QAxBindable
{
    Q_OBJECT
    Q_ENUMS(Speed)
    Q_PROPERTY(QColor color READ color WRITE setColor)
    Q_PROPERTY(Speed speed READ speed WRITE setSpeed)
    Q_PROPERTY(int radius READ radius WRITE setRadius)
    Q_PROPERTY(bool running READ isRunning)
```

AxBouncer **inherits from both** QWidget **and** QAxBindable. **The** QAxBindable **class provides an interface between the widget and an ActiveX client. Any** QWidget **can be exported as an ActiveX control, but by subclassing** QAxBindable **we can notify the client when a property's value changes, and we can implement COM interfaces to supplement those already implemented by** *QAxServer*.

**When doing multiple inheritance involving a** QObject-**derived class, we must always put the** QObject-**derived class first so that** moc **can pick it up.**

**We declare three read-write properties and one read-only property. The** Q_ ENUMS() **macro is necessary to tell** moc **that the** Speed **type is an enum type. The** Speed **enum is declared in the public section of the class.**

```cpp
public:
    enum Speed { Slow, Normal, Fast };

    AxBouncer(QWidget *parent = 0, const char *name = 0);

    void setSpeed(Speed newSpeed);
    Speed speed() const { return ballSpeed; }
    void setRadius(int newRadius);
    int radius() const { return ballRadius; }
    void setColor(const QColor &newColor);
    QColor color() const { return ballColor; }
    bool isRunning() const { return myTimerId != 0; }
    QSize sizeHint() const;
    QAxAggregated *createAggregate();

public slots:
    void start();
    void stop();

signals:
    void bouncing();
```

**The** AxBouncer **constructor is a standard constructor for a widget, with a** parent **and a** name **parameter. The** QAXFACTORY_DEFAULT() **macro, which we will use to export the component, expects a constructor with this signature.**

**The** createAggregate() **function is reimplemented from** QAxBindable. **We will explain it in a moment.**

```cpp
protected:
    void paintEvent(QPaintEvent *event);
    void timerEvent(QTimerEvent *event);

private:
    int intervalInMilliseconds() const;

    QColor ballColor;
    Speed ballSpeed;
    int ballRadius;
    int myTimerId;
    int x;
    int delta;
};
```

The protected and private sections of the class are the same as what we would have in a standard Qt widget.

```
AxBouncer::AxBouncer(QWidget *parent, const char *name)
    : QWidget(parent, name, WNoAutoErase)
{
    ballColor = blue;
    ballSpeed = Normal;
    ballRadius = 15;
    myTimerId = 0;
    x = 20;
    delta = 2;
}
```

The `AxBouncer` constructor initializes the class's private variables.

```
void AxBouncer::setColor(const QColor &newColor)
{
    if (newColor != ballColor && requestPropertyChange("color")) {
        ballColor = newColor;
        update();
        propertyChanged("color");
    }
}
```

The `setColor()` function sets the value of the `color` property. It calls `update()` to repaint the widget.

The unusual part is the `requestPropertyChange()` and `propertyChanged()` calls. These functions are inherited from `QAxBindable` and should ideally be called whenever we change a property. The `requestPropertyChange()` asks the client's permission to change a property, and returns `true` if the client allows the change. The `propertyChanged()` function notifies the client that the property has been changed.

The `setSpeed()` and `setRadius()` property setters also follow this pattern, and so do the `start()` and `stop()` slots, since they change the value of the `running` property.

There is one interesting `AxBouncer` member function left:

```
QAxAggregated *AxBouncer::createAggregate()
{
    return new ObjectSafetyImpl;
}
```

The `createAggregate()` function is reimplemented from `QAxBindable`. It allows us to implement COM interfaces that the *QAxServer* module doesn't already implement or to bypass *QAxServer*'s default COM interfaces. Here, we do it to provide the `IObjectSafety` interface, which is used by Internet Explorer to access a component's safety options. This is the standard trick to get rid of Internet Explorer's infamous "Object not safe for scripting" error message.

Here's the definition of the class that implements the `IObjectSafety` interface:

```
class ObjectSafetyImpl : public QAxAggregated, public IObjectSafety
{
public:
    long queryInterface(const QUuid &iid, void **iface);

    QAXAGG_IUNKNOWN

    HRESULT WINAPI GetInterfaceSafetyOptions(REFIID riid,
            DWORD *pdwSupportedOptions, DWORD *pdwEnabledOptions);
    HRESULT WINAPI SetInterfaceSafetyOptions(REFIID riid,
            DWORD pdwSupportedOptions, DWORD pdwEnabledOptions);
};
```

The `ObjectSafetyImpl` class inherits both `QAxAggregated` and `IObjectSafety`. The `QAxAggregated` class is an abstract base class for implementations of additional COM interfaces. The COM object that the `QAxAggregated` extends is accessible through `controllingUnknown()`. This COM object is created behind the scenes by the *QAxServer* module.

The `QAXAGG_IUNKNOWN` macro provides standard implementations of `QueryInterface()`, `AddRef()`, and `Release()`. These implementations simply call the same functions on the controlling COM object.

```
long ObjectSafetyImpl::queryInterface(const QUuid &iid, void **iface)
{
    *iface = 0;
    if (iid == IID_IObjectSafety)
        *iface = (IObjectSafety *)this;
    else
        return E_NOINTERFACE;

    AddRef();
    return S_OK;
}
```

The `queryInterface()` function is a pure virtual function of `QAxAggregated`. It is called by the controlling COM object to give access to the interfaces provided by the `QAxAggregated` subclass. We must return `E_NOINTERFACE` for interfaces that we don't implement and for `IUnknown`.

```
HRESULT WINAPI ObjectSafetyImpl::GetInterfaceSafetyOptions(
            REFIID riid, DWORD *pdwSupportedOptions,
            DWORD *pdwEnabledOptions)
{
    *pdwSupportedOptions = INTERFACESAFE_FOR_UNTRUSTED_DATA
                            | INTERFACESAFE_FOR_UNTRUSTED_CALLER;
    *pdwEnabledOptions = *pdwSupportedOptions;
    return S_OK;
}

HRESULT WINAPI ObjectSafetyImpl::SetInterfaceSafetyOptions(REFIID,
            DWORD, DWORD)
{
    return S_OK;
}
```

The `GetInterfaceSafetyOptions()` and `SetInterfaceSafetyOptions()` functions are declared in `IObjectSafety`. We implement them to tell the world that our object is safe for scripting.

Let's now review `main.cpp`:

```cpp
#include <qaxfactory.h>

#include "axbouncer.h"

QAXFACTORY_DEFAULT(AxBouncer,
                   "{5e2461aa-a3e8-4f7a-8b04-307459a4c08c}",
                   "{533af11f-4899-43de-8b7f-2ddf588d1015}",
                   "{772c14a5-a840-4023-b79d-19549ece0cd9}",
                   "{dbce1e56-70dd-4f74-85e0-95c65d86254d}",
                   "{3f3db5e0-78ff-4e35-8a5d-3d3b96c83e09}")

int main()
{
    return 0;
}
```

The `QAXFACTORY_DEFAULT()` macro exports an ActiveX control. We can use it for ActiveX servers that export only one control. Otherwise, we must subclass `QAxFactory` and use a macro called `QAXFACTORY_EXPORT()`. The next example in this section shows how to do it.

The first argument to `QAXFACTORY_DEFAULT()` is the name of the Qt class to export. This is also the name under which the control is exported. The other five arguments are the class ID, the interface ID, the event interface ID, the type library ID, and the application ID. We can use standard tools like `guidgen` or `uuidgen` to generate these identifiers.

Because the server is a library, we don't need a real `main()` function. We must still provide a fake implementation to pacify the linker.

Here's the `.pro` file for our in-process ActiveX server:

```
TEMPLATE      = lib
CONFIG       += activeqt dll
HEADERS       = axbouncer.h \
                objectsafetyimpl.h
SOURCES       = axbouncer.cpp \
                main.cpp \
                objectsafetyimpl.cpp
RC_FILE       = qaxserver.rc
DEF_FILE      = qaxserver.def
```

The `qaxserver.rc` and `qaxserver.def` files referred to in the `.pro` file are standard files that can be copied from Qt's `extensions\activeqt\control` directory.

The makefile or Visual C++ project file generated by `qmake` contains rules to register the server in the Windows registry. To register the server on end user machines, we can use the `regsvr32` tool available on all Windows systems.

We can then include the Bouncer component in an HTML page using the
`<object>` tag:

```
<object id="AxBouncer"
        classid="clsid:5e2461aa-a3e8-4f7a-8b04-307459a4c08c">
<b>The ActiveX control is not available. Make sure you have built and
registered the component server.</b>
</object>
```

We can create buttons that invoke slots:

```
<input type="button" value="Start" onClick="AxBouncer.start()">
<input type="button" value="Stop" onClick="AxBouncer.stop()">
```

And we can manipulate the widget using JavaScript or VBScript just like any
other ActiveX control. See the `demo.html` file on the CD for a rudimentary page
that uses the ActiveX server.

Our last example is a scriptable Address Book application. The application
can serve as a standard Qt/Windows application or an out-of-process ActiveX
server. The latter possibility allows us to script the application using, say,
Visual Basic.

```
class AddressBook : public QMainWindow
{
    Q_OBJECT
    Q_PROPERTY(int count READ count)
public:
    AddressBook(QWidget *parent = 0, const char *name = 0);
    ~AddressBook();

    int count() const;

public slots:
    ABItem *createEntry(const QString &contact);
    ABItem *findEntry(const QString &contact) const;
    ABItem *entryAt(int index) const;
    ...
};
```

The `AddressBook` widget is the application's main window. The property and
the slots it provides will be available for scripting.

```
class ABItem : public QObject, public QListViewItem
{
    Q_OBJECT
    Q_PROPERTY(QString contact READ contact WRITE setContact)
    Q_PROPERTY(QString address READ address WRITE setAddress)
    Q_PROPERTY(QString phoneNumber READ phoneNumber
                WRITE setPhoneNumber)
public:
    ABItem(QListView *listView);

    void setContact(const QString &contact);
    QString contact() const { return text(0); }
    void setAddress(const QString &address);
    QString address() const { return text(1); }
```

```
    void setPhoneNumber(const QString &number);
    QString phoneNumber() const { return text(2); }

public slots:
    void remove();
};
```

The `ABItem` class represents one entry in the address book. It inherits from `QListViewItem` so that it can be shown in a `QListView` and from `QObject` so that it can be exported as a COM object.

```
int main(int argc, char *argv[])
{
    QApplication app(argc, argv);
    if (!QAxFactory::isServer()) {
        AddressBook addressBook;
        app.setMainWidget(&addressBook);
        addressBook.show();
        return app.exec();
    }
    return app.exec();
}
```

In `main()`, we check whether the application is being run stand-alone or as a server. The `-activex` command-line option makes it run as a server. If the application isn't run as a server, we create the main widget and show it as we would normally do in any stand-alone Qt application.

In addition to `-activex`, ActiveX servers understand the following command-line options:

- `-regserver` registers the server in the system registry.

- `-unregserver` unregisters the server from the system registry.

- `-dumpidl` *file* writes the server's IDL to the specified file.

For the case where the application is run as a server, we need to export the `AddressBook` and `ABItem` classes as COM components:

```
QAXFACTORY_EXPORT(ABFactory,
                  "{2b2b6f3e-86cf-4c49-9df5-80483b47f17b}",
                  "{8e827b25-148b-4307-ba7d-23f275244818}")
```

The `QAXFACTORY_EXPORT()` macro exports a factory for creating COM objects. Since we want to export two types of COM objects, we cannot simply use `QAXFACTORY_DEFAULT()` as we did in the previous example.

The first argument to `QAXFACTORY_EXPORT()` is the name of the `QAxFactory` class that provides the application's COM objects. The other two arguments are the type library ID and the application ID.

```
class ABFactory : public QAxFactory
{
public:
    ABFactory(const QUuid &lib, const QUuid &app);
    QStringList featureList() const;
```

```
        QWidget *create(const QString &key, QWidget *parent,
                        const char *name);
        QUuid classID(const QString &key) const;
        QUuid interfaceID(const QString &key) const;
        QUuid eventsID(const QString &key) const;
        QString exposeToSuperClass(const QString &key) const;
    };
```

The `ABFactory` **class inherits** `QAxFactory` **and reimplements virtual functions to export the** `AddressBook` **class as an ActiveX control and the** `ABItem` **class as a COM component.**

```
ABFactory::ABFactory(const QUuid &lib, const QUuid &app)
    : QAxFactory(lib, app)
{
}
```

The `ABFactory` **constructor simply forwards its two parameters to the base class constructor.**

```
QStringList ABFactory::featureList() const
{
    return QStringList() << "AddressBook" << "ABItem";
}
```

The `featureList()` **function returns a list of the COM components provided by the factory.**

```
QWidget *ABFactory::create(const QString &key, QWidget *parent,
                           const char *name)
{
    if (key == "AddressBook")
        return new AddressBook(parent, name);
    else
        return 0;
}
```

The `create()` **function creates an instance of an ActiveX control. We return a null pointer for** `ABItem` **because we don't want users to create** `ABItem` **objects. Furthermore, the return type of** `create()` **is** `QWidget *`**, which prevents it from returning COM objects that aren't ActiveX controls.**

```
QUuid ABFactory::classID(const QString &key) const
{
    if (key == "AddressBook")
        return QUuid("{588141ef-110d-4beb-95ab-ee6a478b576d}");
    else if (key == "ABItem")
        return QUuid("{bc82730e-5f39-4e5c-96be-461c2cd0d282}");
    else
        return QUuid();
}
```

The `classId()` **function returns the class ID for all the classes exported by the factory.**

```
QUuid ABFactory::interfaceID(const QString &key) const
{
    if (key == "AddressBook")
        return QUuid("{718780ec-b30c-4d88-83b3-79b3d9e78502}");
    else if (key == "ABItem")
        return QUuid("{c8bc1656-870e-48a9-9937-fbe1ceff8b2e}");
    else
        return QUuid();
}
```

The `interfaceId()` function returns the interface ID for the classes exported by the factory.

```
QUuid ABFactory::eventsID(const QString &key) const
{
    if (key -- "AddressBook")
        return QUuid("{0a06546f-9f02-4f14-a269-d6d56ffeb861}");
    else if (key == "ABItem")
        return QUuid("{105c6b0a-3fc7-460b-ac59-746d9d4b1724}");
    else
        return QUuid();
}
```

The `eventsId()` function returns the event interface ID for the classes exported by the factory.

```
QString ABFactory::exposeToSuperClass(const QString &key) const
{
    return key;
}
```

By default, ActiveX controls expose not only their own properties, signals, and slots to clients, but also those of their superclasses up to `QWidget`. We can reimplement the `exposeToSuperClass()` function to return the highest superclass (in the inheritance tree) that we want to expose.

Here, we return the class name of the component ("AddressBook" or "ABItem") as the highest superclass to export, meaning that properties, signals, and slots defined in `AddressBook`'s and `ABItem`'s superclasses will not be exported.

This is the `.pro` file for our out-of-process ActiveX server:

```
CONFIG      += activeqt
HEADERS     = abfactory.h \
              abitem.h \
              addressbook.h \
              editdialog.h
SOURCES     = abfactory.cpp \
              abitem.cpp \
              addressbook.cpp \
              editdialog.cpp \
              main.cpp
RC_FILE     = qaxserver.rc
```

The `qaxserver.rc` file referred to in the `.pro` file is a standard file that can be copied from Qt's `extensions\activeqt\control` directory.

Look in the example's vb directory for a Visual Basic project that uses the Address Book server.

This completes our overview of the ActiveQt framework. The Qt distribution includes additional examples, and the documentation contains information about how to build the *QAxContainer* and *QAxServer* modules and how to solve common interoperability issues.

## Session Management

When we log out on X11, some window managers ask us whether we want to save the session. If we say yes, the applications that were running are automatically restarted the next time we log in, with the same screen positions and, ideally, with the same state as they had when we logged out.

The X11-specific component that takes care of saving and restoring the session is called the *session manager*. To make a Qt application aware of the session manager, we must reimplement QApplication::saveState() and save the application's state there.

**Figure 18.6.** Logging out on KDE

Windows 2000 and XP (and some Unix systems) offer a different mechanism, called hibernation. When the user puts the computer into hibernation, the operating system simply dumps the computer's memory onto disk and reloads it on startup. Applications do not need to do anything or even be aware that this happens.

When the user initiates a shutdown, we can take control just before the shutdown occurs by reimplementing QApplication::commitData(). This allows us to save any unsaved data and to interact with the user if required. This works the same way on both X11 and Windows.

We will explore session management by going through the code of a session-aware Tic-Tac-Toe application. First, let's look at the main() function:

```
int main(int argc, char *argv[])
{
    Application app(argc, argv);
    TicTacToe tic(0, "tic");
    app.setTicTacToe(&tic);
    tic.show();
    return app.exec();
}
```

We create an `Application` object. The `Application` class inherits from `QApplication` and reimplements both `commitData()` and `saveState()` to support session management.

Next, we create a `TicTacToe` widget, make the `Application` object aware of it, and show it. We have called the `TicTacToe` widget "tic". We must give unique names to top-level widgets if we want the session manager to restore the windows' sizes and positions.

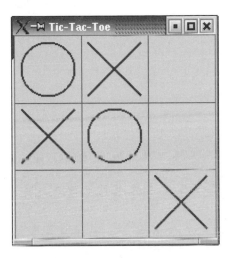

**Figure 18.7.** The Tic-Tac-Toe application

Here's the definition of the `Application` class:

```
class Application : public QApplication
{
    Q_OBJECT
public:
    Application(int &argc, char *argv[]);

    void setTicTacToe(TicTacToe *tic);
    void commitData(QSessionManager &sessionManager);
    void saveState(QSessionManager &sessionManager);

private:
    TicTacToe *ticTacToe;
};
```

The `Application` class keeps a pointer to the `TicTacToe` widget as a private variable.

```
void Application::saveState(QSessionManager &sessionManager)
{
    QString fileName = ticTacToe->saveState();

    QStringList discardCommand;
    discardCommand << "rm" << fileName;
    sessionManager.setDiscardCommand(discardCommand);
}
```

On X11, the `saveState()` function is called when the session manager wants the application to save its state. The function is available on other platforms as well, but it is never called. The `QSessionManager` parameter allows us to communicate with the session manager.

We start by asking the `TicTacToe` widget to save its state to a file. Then we set the session manager's discard command. A *discard command* is a command that the session manager must execute to delete any stored information regarding the current state. For this example, we set it to

```
rm file
```

where *file* is the name of the file that contains the saved state for the session, and `rm` is the standard Unix command to remove files.

The session manager also has a *restart command*. This is the command that the session manager must execute to restart the application. By default, Qt provides the following restart command:

```
appname -session id_key
```

The first part, *appname*, is derived from `argv[0]`. The *id* part is the session ID provided by the session manager; it is guaranteed to be unique among different applications and among different runs of the same application. The *key* part comes in addition to uniquely identify the time at which the state was saved. For various reasons, the session manager can call `saveState()` multiple times during the same session, and the different states must be distinguished.

Because of limitations in existing session managers, we need to make sure that the application's directory is in the PATH environment variable if we want the application to restart correctly. In particular, if you want to try out the Tic-Tac-Toe example for yourself, you must install it in, say, /usr/bin and invoke it as `tictactoe`.

For simple applications, including Tic-Tac-Toe, we could save the state as an additional command-line argument to the restart command. For example:

```
tictactoe -state OX-XO-X-O
```

This would save us from storing the data in a file and providing a discard command to remove the file.

```cpp
void Application::commitData(QSessionManager &sessionManager)
{
    if (ticTacToe->gameInProgress()
            && sessionManager.allowsInteraction()) {
        int ret = QMessageBox::warning(ticTacToe, tr("Tic-Tac-Toe"),
                    tr("The game hasn't finished.\n"
                       "Do you really want to quit?"),
                    QMessageBox::Yes | QMessageBox::Default,
                    QMessageBox::No | QMessageBox::Escape);
        if (ret == QMessageBox::Yes)
            sessionManager.release();
```

```
            else
                sessionManager.cancel();
        }
    }
```

The `commitData()` function is called when the user logs out. We can reimplement it to pop up a message box warning the user about potential data loss. The default implementation closes all top-level widgets, which results in the same behavior as when the user closes the windows one after another by clicking the X button in their title bars. In Chapter 3, we saw how to reimplement `closeEvent()` to catch this and pop up a message box.

For the purposes of this example, we reimplement `commitData()` and pop up a message box asking the user to confirm the log out if a game is in progress and if the session manager allows us to interact with the user. If the user clicks Yes, we call `release()` to tell the session manager to continue logging out; if the user clicks No, we call `cancel()` to cancel the log out.

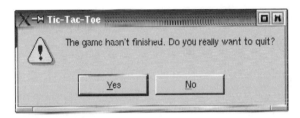

**Figure 18.8.** "Do you really want to quit?"

Now let's look at the `TicTacToe` class:

```
class TicTacToe : public QWidget
{
    Q_OBJECT
public:
    TicTacToe(QWidget *parent = 0, const char *name = 0);

    QSize sizeHint() const;
    bool gameInProgress() const;
    QString saveState() const;

protected:
    void paintEvent(QPaintEvent *event);
    void mousePressEvent(QMouseEvent *event);

private:
    enum { Empty = '-', Cross = 'X', Nought = 'O' };

    void clearBoard();
    void restoreState();
    QString sessionFileName() const;
    QRect cellRect(int row, int col) const;
    int cellWidth() const { return width() / 3; }
    int cellHeight() const { return height() / 3; }

    char board[3][3];
```

```
        int turnNumber;
};
```

The `TicTacToe` class inherits from `QWidget` and reimplements `sizeHint()`, `paintEvent()`, and `mousePressEvent()`. It also provides the `gameInProgress()` and `saveState()` functions that we used in `Application`.

```
TicTacToe::TicTacToe(QWidget *parent, const char *name)
    : QWidget(parent, name)
{
    setCaption(tr("Tic-Tac-Toe"));
    clearBoard();
    if (qApp->isSessionRestored())
        restoreState();
}
```

In the constructor, we clear the board, and if the application was invoked with the `-session` option, we call the private function `restoreState()` to reload the old session.

```
void TicTacToe::clearBoard()
{
    for (int row = 0; row < 3; ++row) {
        for (int col = 0; col < 3; ++col) {
            board[row][col] = Empty;
        }
    }
    turnNumber = 0;
}
```

In `clearBoard()`, we clear all the cells and set `turnNumber` to 0.

```
QString TicTacToe::saveState() const
{
    QFile file(sessionFileName());
    if (file.open(IO_WriteOnly)) {
        QTextStream out(&file);
        for (int row = 0; row < 3; ++row) {
            for (int col = 0; col < 3; ++col) {
                out << board[row][col];
            }
        }
    }
    return file.name();
}
```

In `saveState()`, we write the state of the board to disk. The format is straightforward, with 'X' for crosses, 'O' for noughts, and '-' for empty cells.

```
QString TicTacToe::sessionFileName() const
{
    return QDir::homeDirPath() + "/.tictactoe_"
            + qApp->sessionId() + "_" + qApp->sessionKey();
}
```

The `sessionFileName()` private function returns the file name for the current session ID and session key. This function is used for both `saveState()` and `restoreState()`. The file name is derived from the session ID and session key.

```
void TicTacToe::restoreState()
{
    QFile file(sessionFileName());
    if (file.open(IO_ReadOnly)) {
        QTextStream in(&file);
        for (int row = 0; row < 3; ++row) {
            for (int col = 0; col < 3; ++col) {
                in >> board[row][col];
                if (board[row][col] != Empty)
                    ++turnNumber;
            }
        }
    }
    repaint();
}
```

In `restoreState()`, we load the file that corresponds to the restored session and fill the board with that information. We deduce the value of `turnNumber` from the number of X's and O's on the board.

In the `TicTacToe` constructor, we called `restoreState()` if `QApplication::isSessionRestored()` returned true. In that case, `sessionId()` and `sessionKey()` return the same values as when the application's state was saved, and so `sessionFileName()` returns the file name for that session.

Testing and debugging session management can be frustrating, because we need to log in and out all the time. One way to avoid this is to use the standard xsm utility provided with X11. The first time we invoke xsm, it pops up a session manager window and a terminal. The applications we start from that terminal will all use xsm as their session manager instead of the usual, system-wide session manager. We can then use xsm's window to end, restart, or discard a session, and see if our application behaves as it should. For details about how to do this, see http://doc.trolltech.com/3.2/session.html.

# Appendices

# Installing Qt

This appendix explains how to install Qt from the CD onto your system. The CD has editions of Qt 3.2.1 for Windows, Mac OS X, and X11 (for Linux and most versions of Unix). They all include SQLite, a public domain in-process database, together with an experimental driver. The editions of Qt on the CD are provided for your convenience. For serious software development, it is best to download the latest version of Qt from http://www.trolltech.com/download/ or to buy a commercial version.

Trolltech also provides Qt/Embedded for building applications for Linux-based embedded devices such as PDAs and mobile phones. If you are interested in creating embedded applications, you can obtain Qt/Embedded from Trolltech's download web page.

The example applications used in the book are on the CD in the examples directory. In addition, Qt provides many small example applications located in the examples, tools\designer\examples, and extensions\activeqt\examples subdirectories.

## A Note on Licensing

Qt is produced in three forms: free, non-commercial, and commercial. The free and non-commercial editions are available free of charge; the commercial editions must be paid for.

The software on the CD is suitable for creating applications for your own educational and personal use.

If you want to distribute the applications that you create with a free or non-commercial edition of Qt, you must comply with the specific terms and conditions laid down in the licenses for the software you use to create the applications. For free editions, the terms and conditions include the requirement to use an open license—for example, the GNU General Public License (GPL). Open licenses like the GPL give the applications' users certain rights, including the right to view and modify the source and to distribute the applications (on the same terms). The non-commercial license has similar provisions. If you want to distribute your applications without source code (to keep your code private) or if you want to apply your own commercial license conditions to your applications, you must buy commercial editions of the software you use to create the applications. The commercial editions of the software allow you to sell and distribute your applications on your own terms.

The CD contains a non-commercial version of Qt/Windows, a free edition of Qt/Mac, and a free edition of Qt/X11. It also contains some other non-commercial software, including Borland C++ Builder 5 and a trial version of Borland C++ Builder 6. Each product on the CD has its own specific license conditions; for example, the non-commercial Qt/Windows edition may not be redistributed, and its license isn't compatible with the GPL. The full legal texts of the licenses are included with the packages on the CD, along with information on how to obtain commercial versions.

## Installing Qt/Windows

When you insert the CD on a Windows machine, a setup program should start automatically. If this doesn't occur, run `setup.exe` located in the CD's root directory.

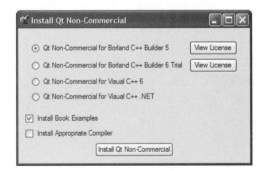

**Figure A.1.** Qt/Windows Non-Commercial installer

The setup program will ask you which compiler you want to use for Qt development. If you have chosen a Borland compiler, check the Install Appropriate Compiler option if you also want to install the compiler. If you check the Install Book Examples option, the example applications shown in this book will be installed in `C:\Qt\3.2.1\book` (assuming `C:\Qt\3.2.1` is the location where you installed Qt).

If you choose to install a Borland compiler, note that there may be a delay between the completion of the Borland installation and the start of the Qt installation.

In the Qt installer, check the Set QTDIR option. If you are using Microsoft Visual C++, you must specify Visual Studio's path so that Qt can integrate itself with the development environment.

If you are installing on a Windows 95, 98, or ME system, the compilation step is skipped due to technical limitations in the operating system. The setup program writes the steps needed to build Qt into a batch file and puts a shortcut to the batch file in the Start menu. To build Qt, simply click this shortcut.

Some Windows versions may require a reboot to set the environment variables. If you installed Borland C++ Builder 5, you must update your PATH environment variable to include the Borland executable directory (for example, C:\Borland\Bcc55\bin). You must also create two configuration files in the Borland executable directory. The first file must be called bcc32.cfg and contain the lines

```
-I"C:\Borland\Bcc55\include"
-L"C:\Borland\Bcc55\lib"
```

The second file must be called ilink32.cfg and contain the line

```
-L"C:\Borland\Bcc55\lib"
```

If you installed the Borland compiler in a non-default location, you must replace C:\Borland\Bcc55 with the appropriate path.

## Installing Qt/Mac

The Mac OS X installation is done from a terminal. To launch a terminal, look in Applications/Utilities with Finder.

If your system does not have a C++ compiler installed, you must install one yourself before installing Qt. An easy option is to install GCC from Apple's Developer Tools CD.

1. Unpack the archive file from the CD:

   ```
   cd /Developer
   tar zxf /Volumes/Qt\ 3\ Programming/mac/qt-mac-free-3.2.1.tar.gz
   ```

   The archive is unpacked into /Developer/qt-mac-free-3.2.1.

2. Create a symlink from this directory to /Developer/qt:

   ```
   ln -sf qt-mac-free-3.2.1 qt
   ```

3. Set up certain environment variables for Qt.

   The variables are set differently depending on which shell you are using. For example, if your user name is kelly, you can find out which shell you are using with the finger command:

   ```
   finger kelly
   ```

If your shell is bash, ksh, zsh, or sh, add the following lines to the .profile file in your home directory:

```
QTDIR=/Developer/qt
PATH=$QTDIR/bin:$PATH
MANPATH=$QTDIR/doc/man:$MANPATH
DYLD_LIBRARY_PATH=$QTDIR/lib:$DYLD_LIBRARY_PATH
export QTDIR PATH MANPATH DYLD_LIBRARY_PATH
```

If your shell is csh or tcsh, add the following lines to your .login file:

```
setenv QTDIR /Developer/qt
setenv PATH $QTDIR/bin:$PATH
setenv MANPATH $QTDIR/doc/man:$MANPATH
setenv DYLD_LIBRARY_PATH $QTDIR/lib:$DYLD_LIBRARY_PATH
```

If you encounter "undefined variable" problems, change the last two lines above to these:

```
setenv MANPATH $QTDIR/doc/man
setenv DYLD_LIBRARY_PATH $QTDIR/lib
```

After you have done this, the settings must be activated. The easiest way to do this is to close the terminal window and then open a new terminal window.

4. Execute the configure tool in the new terminal with your preferred options to build the Qt library and the tools supplied with it:

```
cd $QTDIR
./configure
```

You can run ./configure -help to get a list of configuration options. For example, you can use the -thread option to create a threaded version of the library.

5. Type make.

6. Make your applications launchable from Finder.

If you built Qt using the -static option, your executables will contain the Qt library and can be run from Finder automatically. Otherwise, your executables will need to use the Qt library on your system. This is achieved by creating two symlinks:

```
ln -sf $QTDIR/lib/libqt.3.dylib /usr/lib
ln -sf $QTDIR/lib/libqui.1.dylib /usr/lib
```

If you built a multithreaded version of Qt, replace libqt.3.dylib with libqt-mt.3.dylib in the first ln command above.

Creating these links may require administrator access; if this is the case, run the commands preceded by sudo:

```
sudo ln -sf $QTDIR/lib/libqt.3.dylib /usr/lib
```

```
sudo ln -sf $QTDIR/lib/libqui.1.dylib /usr/lib
```

If you don't have administrator access or just want to install Qt locally, use these links instead:

```
ln -sf $QTDIR/lib/libqt.3.dylib $HOME/lib
ln -sf $QTDIR/lib/libqui.1.dylib $HOME/lib
```

As mentioned above, if you built a multithreaded version of Qt, replace `libqt.3.dylib` with `libqt-mt.3.dylib`.

If you want to customize how you install Qt or if you encounter problems with installing Qt, refer to the INSTALL file in $QTDIR for more information.

## Installing Qt/X11

To install Qt on X11, you may need to be root, depending on the permissions of the directory where you choose to install Qt.

1. Change directory to where you want to install Qt. For example:

```
cd /usr/local
```

2. Unpack the archive file from the CD:

```
cp /cdrom/x11/qt-x11-free3.2.1.tar.gz .
gunzip qt-x11-free-3.2.1.tar.gz
tar xf qt-x11-free-3.2.1.tar
```

This will create the directory `qt-x11-free-3.2.1`, assuming that your CD-ROM is mounted at /cdrom.

3. Set up certain environment variables for Qt.

The variables are set differently depending on which shell you are using. For example, if your user name is `gregory`, you can find out which shell you are using with the `finger` command:

```
finger gregory
```

If your shell is bash, ksh, zsh, or sh, add the following lines to the .profile file in your home directory:

```
QTDIR=/usr/local/qt-x11-free-3.2.1
PATH=$QTDIR/bin:$PATH
MANPATH=$QTDIR/doc/man:$MANPATH
LD_LIBRARY_PATH=$QTDIR/lib:$LD_LIBRARY_PATH
export QTDIR PATH MANPATH LD_LIBRARY_PATH
```

If your shell is csh or tcsh, add the following lines to your .login file:

```
setenv QTDIR /usr/local/qt-x11-free-3.2.1
setenv PATH $QTDIR/bin:$PATH
setenv MANPATH $QTDIR/doc/man:$MANPATH
setenv LD_LIBRARY_PATH $QTDIR/lib:$LD_LIBRARY_PATH
```

If you encounter "undefined variable" problems, change the last two lines above to these:

```
setenv MANPATH $QTDIR/doc/man
setenv LD_LIBRARY_PATH $QTDIR/lib
```

Irrespective of which shell you use, if you install Qt on AIX, replace all occurrences of `LD_LIBRARY_PATH` with `LIBPATH`. And if you install Qt on HP-UX, replace `LD_LIBRARY_PATH` with `SHLIB_PATH`.

After you have done this, you must either login again or re-source the `.profile` or `.login` file before continuing.

4. Execute the `configure` tool with your preferred options to build the Qt library and the tools supplied with it:

```
cd $QTDIR
./configure
```

You can run `./configure -help` to get a list of configuration options. For example, you can use the `-thread` option to create a threaded version of the library.

5. Type `make`.

If you want to customize how you install Qt or if you encounter problems with installing Qt, refer to the `INSTALL` file in `$QTDIR` for more information.

# B

## Qt's Class Hierarchy

Qt 3.2 provides more than 400 public classes. The class hierarchy depicted on the following pages presents the majority of them, but omits those that are more specialized and those that are infrequently used.

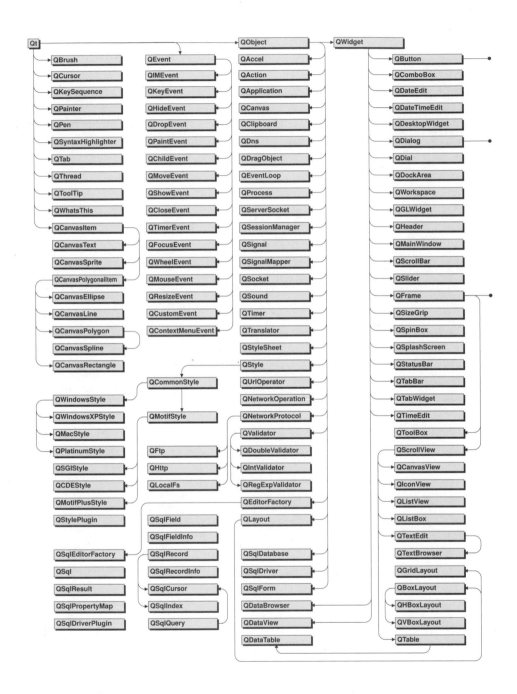

| | | | |
|---|---|---|---|
| | QWidgetFactory | QAccessible | QMemArray |
| QCheckBox | QWidgetPlugin | QAsciiCache | QMenuData | QByteArray |
| QToolButton | | QAsyncIO | QMetaObject | QPointArray |
| QPushButton | QXmlAttributes | QChar | QMetaProperty | QBitArray |
| QRadioButton | QXmlContentHandler | QColor | QMovie | QCString |
| | QXmlDeclHandler | QColorGroup | QMimeSource | QMimeSourceFactory |
| QWizard | QXmlDTDHandler | QDataStream | QMutex | QMutexLocker |
| QTabDialog | QXmlEntityResolver | QDate | QPaintDevice | |
| QFileDialog | QXmlLexicalHandler | QDateTime | QPaintDeviceMetrics | QPrinter |
| QFontDialog | QXmlLocator | QDeepCopy | QPair | QPicture |
| QInputDialog | QXmlNamespaceSupport | QDir | QPalette | QPixmap |
| QColorDialog | QXmlReader | QDomNode | QPixmapCache | QBitmap |
| QMessageBox | | QFileInfo | QPoint | |
| QErrorMessage | QDomAttr | QFont | QPtrCollection | |
| QProgressDialog | QDomEntity | QFontDatabase | QPtrQueue | QDict |
| | QDomElement | QFontInfo | QPtrStack | QCache |
| QGrid | QDomDocument | QFontManager | QRangeControl | QPtrList |
| QLabel | QDomCharacterData | QFontMetrics | QRect | QIntDict |
| QHBox | | QGL | QRegExp | QPtrDict |
| QVBox | QGLFormat | QGLColormap | QRegion | QAsciiDict |
| QSplitter | QGLContext | QGuardedPtr | QSemaphore | QPtrVector |
| QLineEdit | | QHostAddress | QSettings | QObjectList |
| QMenuBar | | QIconSet | QSimpleRichText | QSortedList |
| QGroupBox | | QImage | QSize | QValueList |
| QPopupMenu | QFile | QImageFormatPlugin | QSizePolicy | QStringList |
| QProgressBar | QBuffer | QImageIO | QString | QValueStack |
| QLCDNumber | QSocketDevice | QIntCache | QConstString | QValueVector |
| QWidgetStack | | QIODevice | QTextCodec | QUrl |
| QDockWindow | QStyleSheetItem | QLibrary | QTextCodecPlugin | QUrlInfo |
| QToolBar | QCustomMenuItem | QMap | QTextStream | QVariant |
| QIconViewItem | QListBoxItem | | QTime | QWMatrix |
| QListViewItem | QListBoxText | QAsciiCacheIterator | QPtrDictIterator | QHButtonGroup |
| QCheckListItem | QListBoxPixmap | QCacheIterator | QMapIterator | QVButtonGroup |
| QTableItem | QLayoutItem | QIntCacheIterator | QValueListIterator | QButtonGroup |
| QCheckTableItem | QSpacerItem | QAsciiDictIterator | QPtrListIterator | QHGroupBox |
| QComboTableItem | QWidgetItem | QDictIterator | QIntDictIterator | QVGroupBox |

# Index

# N

# informIT

## YOUR GUIDE TO IT REFERENCE

### Articles

Keep your edge with thousands of free articles, in-depth features, interviews, and IT reference recommendations – all written by experts you know and trust.

### Online Books

Answers in an instant from **InformIT Online Book's** 600+ fully searchable on line books. Sign up now and get your first 14 days **free**.

POWERED BY

**Safari**

### Catalog

Review online sample chapters, author biographies and customer rankings and choose exactly the right book from a selection of over 5,000 titles.

## THE LINUX DEVELOPMENT PLATFORM

BY RAFEEQ UR REHMAN AND CHRISTOPHER PAUL
• ©2003, paper with CD ROM, 512 pages, 0-13-009115-4

This is an all-in-one resource for setting up, maintaining, and using Linux as an enterprise-level deployment environment. It provides information for all the latest versions of the tools needed for development on Linux systems, with examples about how to build, install, and use these tools.

## EMBEDDED SOFTWARE DEVELOPMENT WITH eCOS

BY ANTHONY I. MASSA • ©2003, paper with CD-ROM, 432 pages, 0-13-035473-2

This book shows developers and managers the advantages of using eCos — the Embedded Configurable Operating System — over proprietary or commercial embedded operating systems.

## RAPID APPLICATION DEVELOPMENT WITH MOZILLA

BY NIGEL MCFARLANE • ©2004, paper, 800 pages, 0-13-142343-6

In *Rapid Application Development with Mozilla*, Web, XML, and Open Standards expert Nigel McFarlane explores Mozilla's revolutionary XML User interface Language (XUL) and its library of well over 1,000 pre-built objects.

### COMING EARLY 2004

## UNDERSTANDING THE LINUX VIRTUAL MEMORY MANAGER

BY MEL GORMAN • ©2004, paper with CD-ROM, 832 pages, 0-13-145348-3

Your expert guide to the 2.6 Linux Kernel's most important component: The Virtual Memory Manager. Plus, the amazing CD-ROM is a virtual VM "learning lab" with tools developed specifically for VM study PLUS all of the 2.6 kernel source code.

### COMING SOON

## SAMBA-3 BY EXAMPLE
### Practical Exercises to Successful Deployment

JOHN H. TERPSTRA • ©2004, paper with CD-ROM, 256 pages, 0-13-147221-6

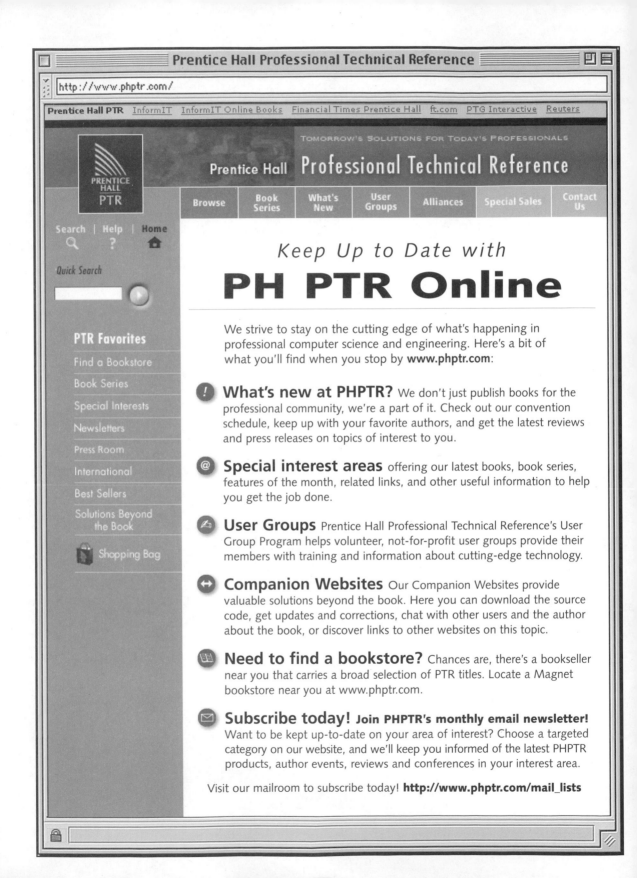

# About the Authors

## Jasmin Blanchette

Jasmin graduated in computer science in 2001 from the University of Sherbrooke, Quebec, and was awarded the Fernand Seguin medal of excellence. He did a work term at Trolltech in the summer of 2000 as a software engineer and has been working there continuously since early 2001. Now a senior software engineer, he is the driving force behind the *Qt Linguist* translation tool and provides *Qt Quarterly*, Trolltech's technical newsletter, with much of its content. In his spare time, he is writing a novel in Norwegian and Swedish. He lives in Oslo with his girlfriend Anne-Lene.

## Mark Summerfield

Mark graduated in computer science in 1993 from the University of Wales Swansea. He followed this with a year's postgraduate research before going into industry. He spent many years working as a software engineer for a variety of firms before joining Trolltech. For the past few years, he has been Trolltech's documentation manager, responsible for maintaining over 1500 pages of online Qt documentation and for editing *Qt Quarterly*. In his free time, he writes open source software. He lives in the Swansea Valley in South Wales, UK, with his wife Andrea.

---

# Production

The authors wrote the text using NEdit and Vim. They typeset and indexed the text themselves, marking it up with a modified Lout syntax that they converted to pure Lout using a custom preprocessor written in Python. They produced all the diagrams in Lout and used ImageMagick to convert screenshots to PostScript. The monospaced font used for code is derived from Courier and was created using PfaEdit. The cover was provided by the publisher; the photograph is of the fall of the Berlin Wall, November 1989. The marked-up text was converted to PostScript by Lout, then to PDF by Ghostscript. The authors did all the editing and processing on Debian GNU/Linux systems under KDE. The example programs were tested on Windows, Linux, and Mac OS X.

# About the CD-ROM

The CD-ROM included with *C++ GUI Programming with Qt 3* contains all the software and source code needed to create and run applications on Windows, Mac OS X, and Unix/Linux with X11. The CD-ROM includes the following:

- Qt 3.2.1 Non-Commercial Edition for Windows (MSVC and Borland)
- Qt 3.2.1 Free Edition for Mac OS X
- Qt 3.2.1 Free Edition for Unix/Linux with X11
- Borland C++ Builder 5 Non-Commercial Edition
- Borland C++ Builder 6 Trial Edition
- Source code for the book's examples

All versions of Qt come with the Qt library and a set of tools including the qmake build tool, *Qt Designer* for visual dialog design, *Qt Linguist* for internationalization support, and *Qt Assistant* for presenting documentation.

The CD-ROM can be used on Microsoft Windows 95, 98, NT 4, ME, 2000, XP, Mac OS X, Linux, and most versions of Unix.

## License Agreement

Each of the software packages on the CD-ROM has its own license agreement. The full legal texts of the licenses are included with the packages on the CD-ROM.

## Technical Support

Neither Prentice Hall nor Trolltech offers any technical support for any of the software on the CD-ROM. (Fully supported commercial editions of Qt are available from Trolltech; fully supported commercial editions of Borland C++ Builder are available from Inprise.) If the CD-ROM is damaged, you can obtain a replacement copy by sending an email that describes the problem to disc_exchange@prenhall.com.